PERFECTING
FRIENDSHIP

PERFECTING FRIENDSHIP

Politics and
Affiliation in
Early American
Literature

IVY SCHWEITZER

The University of
North Carolina Press
Chapel Hill

Designed by Jacquline Johnson
Set in Bulmer by Keystone Typesetting, Inc.

The paper in this book meets the guidelines for
permanence and durability of the Committee on
Production Guidelines for Book Longevity of the
Council on Library Resources.

Chapter 2 originally appeared in *Early American
Literature* 4.3 (2005): 441–69, and chapter 3 origi-
nally appeared in *Arizona Quarterly* 61.2 (Summer
2005): 1–32. Parts of chapter 4 are forthcoming as
"Cooper's Blood Brothers: Romancing National
Identity," in *After American Exceptionalism*, edited
by Don Pease (Durham, N.C.: Duke University
Press).

Library of Congress Cataloging-in-Publication Data
Schweitzer, Ivy.
Perfecting friendship : politics and affiliation in early
American literature / Ivy Schweitzer.
p. cm.
Includes bibliographical references and index.
ISBN-13: 978-0-8078-3069-7 (alk. paper)
ISBN-10: 0-8078-3069-0 (alk. paper)
ISBN-13: 978-0-8078-5778-6 (pbk.: alk. paper)
ISBN-10: 0-8078-5778-5 (pbk.: alk. paper)
1. American literature—History and criticism.
2. Friendship in literature. 3. Winthrop, John, 1588–
1649. 4. Cooper, James Fenimore, 1789–1851—
Criticism and interpretation. 5. Sedgwick, Catharine
Maria, 1789–1867. Hope Leslie. 6. Foster, Hannah
Webster, 1759–1840. Coquette. 7. Politics and
literature—United States—History. 8. National
characteristics, American, in literature.
9. Friendship—Sociological aspects. 10. Political
culture—United States—History. I. Title.
PS169.F69S39   2006
810.9'353—dc22   2006018318

cloth   10 09 08 07 06   5 4 3 2 1
paper   10 09 08 07 06   5 4 3 2 1

CONTENTS

ILLUSTRATIONS

ACKNOWLEDGMENTS

After many years of pondering the meanings and strange slippage of liking and likeness, I have developed an even greater respect, if that were possible, for friendship and for the people and things that sustain me. This project has gone through many transformations. It began in the early 1990s when a prescient undergraduate student named Sharry Fisher, despondent over the state of interracial relations on the Dartmouth campus, urged me to teach courses on the historical and literary representations of women's interracial relations. I discovered a large and growing body of works on the topic—remarkable stories like Grace Paley's "The Long Distance Runner," Toni Morrison's "Recitatif," and Tillie Olsen's "O Yes." I was particularly gripped by an early dialogue co-authored by philosophers María Lugones and Elizabeth Spelman, who conclude that, because friendship creates "a non-coerced space," it is the "only appropriate and understandable motive" for doing feminist theory across racial and ethnic differences (23). But after several attempts to write a book focused on representations of women's interracial relations, I realized that I did not know what friendship meant. Of course, I understood it in a personal and commonsensical way, but not as a cultural or historical discourse. Going back to the foundational texts about friendship in the Western tradition allowed me to see friendship as part of a very long philosophical discourse and as the preeminent affiliative and democratic mode it was and could be again.

Teaching and learning have been crucial to this study. Over the years I have worked with other remarkable students on related projects that have inspired me: Lisa DiIorio, Jean Young, Michelle Seldin, Tiffany West, Amanda Gilliam, Kinohi Nishikawa, Swati Rana, Mosopefoluwa A. Ogunyemi, Diana Bellonby, Matthew Duques, Paloma Wu, and Lauren Leblanc, among others. Several of my undergraduate research assistants at Dartmouth have been particularly helpful to this project and deserve thanks: Matthew Fujisawa, Liz Bertko, Tim Stanne, Miranda Johnson, Stacey Sherriff, Sue Kim, and Rebecca Slisz.

I have also benefited immensely from an active, courageous, and supportive feminist community of scholars, especially the faculty in the Women's and Gender

Studies program at Dartmouth College and our ongoing Feminist Inquiry Seminar. Members of the English department have enriched my scholarship through conversation and collegiality, especially Colleen Boggs, Bill Cook, Jonathan Crewe, George Edmondson, Marty Favor, Mishuana Goeman, Lou Renza, Brenda Silver, Barbara Will, and Melissa Zeiger. The gifted Rachel Bagby offered tough love in the beginning, and her amazing story, "See Color," still resonates in my mind. Likewise, Grace Paley's writings, her unstoppable activist spirit, and her iridescent presence in our community and as a visitor in my classes have been a constant joy. Fellow Americanists Mary Kelley and Annelise Orleck and compañera Silvia Spitta shared books, sources, meals, and an unshakable belief in the healing balm of friendship. Colin Calloway never failed to answer my questions about Indian history and culture, Jim Tatum was generous with my queries about ancient texts, and Amy Allen and Susan Brison amiably talked philosophy with me. Laura Braunstein, Dartmouth's humanities librarian and literary sleuth extraordinaire, has answered all my requests and more. Jay Satterfield in Special Collections has enriched my knowledge of early modern material culture, and Josh Shaw has provided scanning services. I would also like to thank Peter Travis, chair of the English department, who has been a wonderful scholar and leader, and Dartmouth College for a senior faculty fellowship during the course of my research that allowed me to follow my nose and rewrite my first draft into a much more ambitious and intellectually profound study.

There is also a large group of scholars nationally and internationally who have provided rich conversation and collegiality in the difficult and often lonely work we do. For the last several years, many have descended upon the Hanover plain in mid-June for the annual American Studies Institute organized by Don Pease. I was fortunate to be one of the original members of the first summer institute in 1997 and a seminar leader in several subsequent years, drawing energy from these intellectual fests. I want to thank scholars who have been working on subjects related to my own and with whom I have shared work, especially Chris Castiglia, Priscilla Wald, John Stauffer, and Matt Cohen. The early American studies crowd has been a constant source of support and fun: Ralph Bauer, Renée Bergland, Michelle Burnham, Russ Castronovo, Jim Egan, Phil Gould, Lisa Gordis, Michael Householder, David Shields, and Ezra Tawil. Many thanks go to Dana Nelson and Elizabeth Dillon, whose amazing work and friendship I prize dearly. Len Tennenhouse and Nancy Armstrong have been unfailingly supportive. I owe Len big time for a walk in the Tucson desert where he enacted the most difficult office of friendship—speaking frankly. Andrew Hook has been an honorary family member, and Susan Castillo, at our home-away-from-home at the University of

Glasgow, Scotland, is the best collaborator, colleague, and crony. A very special thanks goes to Greg Jackson, who offered brilliant readerly support at crucial moments that I really appreciate.

Finally, I cannot begin to express my thanks to Marianne Hirsch and Leo Spitzer, role models and colleagues. Marianne, you truly know what friendship is. My parents, Sue and Harold, have been always encouraging and generous. My extraordinary children, Rebekah Rosa and Isaac Jesse—best and always friends— and my spouse, Tom Luxon, who was also studying marriage and friendship during the years of my research, help me know myself. This book is dedicated to all these mirrors of my best self.

Over the carnage rose prophetic a voice,
Be not dishearten'd, affection
shall solve the problems of freedom yet,
Those who love each other
shall become invincible,
They shall make Columbia victorious.
—Walt Whitman,
"Over the Carnage Rose
Prophetic a Voice,"
Leaves of Grass

I would suggest, as a corrective
to Freud, that it might be more
useful, and more accurate, to
think of politics as originating
not in proximity but in distance,
not in similitude but in difference,
or in the difference that makes a
fantasy of similitude possible. To
be "like" the other is to be different
from the other, to be precisely *not*
the same. . . . Politics thus emerges
not out of sameness but out of the
noncoincidence between self and
other that gives rise to a desire
for an illusory sameness.
—Diana Fuss, *Identification Papers*

The Renascence of Friendship

A Story of American
Social and Political Life

In 1862, a black servant named Addie Brown who worked in households in Connecticut and New York wrote to her friend Rebecca Primus, the daughter of a prominent black family from Hartford, rapturously recommending a novel she had just read (Griffin 59). The book was *Woman's Friendship; A Story of Domestic Life*, published posthumously in 1848 by the Anglo-Jewish writer Grace Aguilar, which first appeared in New York in 1850. Eager to impress her well-educated correspondent (after the war, Rebecca was one of many black Northerners who went south to teach in schools for freed slaves), Addie quotes breathlessly, running the sentences together without punctuation. In the scene she cites from the novel's opening pages, Mrs. Leslie, the matron of an impoverished though genteel family living in Devonshire, England, gently chides her "irrepressible" daughter Florence not to count on the future of an attachment she has begun with an older woman named Lady Ida, whose family winters in the seaside town of Torquay. "Because," Mrs. Leslie explains, "friendship, even more than love, demands equality of station. Friends cannot be to each other what they ought to be, if the rank of one party be among the nobles of the land, that of the other lowly as your own" (9).

Addie stops quoting there, but Mrs. Leslie, an invalid doomed to die shortly, continues at length, hoping to provide her daughter with practical wisdom in the face of impending maternal absence. She tells Florence:

> "I have longed for you to find a friend of your own sex, and nearly of your own age. . . . [T]he young require more than their natural relatives whom to respect and love. . . . [T]hey need an interchange of sentiment and pursuit, and all their innocent recreations and graver duties acquire a double zest from being shared by another. Sympathy is the magic charm of life; and a friend will both give it, and feel it, and never shrink from speaking truth, however painful, kindly indeed, but faithfully, and will infuse and receive strength by the mutual confidence of high and religious principle. . . . Your respective stations cannot permit the confidence of perfect friendship, and my Florence has too much of her mother's pride to seek to be a *humble* friend." (9–12; her emphasis)

For an English novelist at midcentury to make friendship, rather than romance, the focus of her tale is not particularly notable.[1] But the specific understanding of friendship Aguilar expresses through Mrs. Leslie deserves our attention. Under the banner of "high" religiosity, it combines what recent studies of eighteenth-century culture and the history of emotion describe as an Enlightenment vision of sympathetic attachments with the less familiar classical ideal of dyadic, same-sex friendship based on a near equality of status and virtue. More striking still is the transatlantic effect of Mrs. Leslie's vision of affiliation on an African American servant struggling to improve her literacy and social position. Conduct books, moral tracts, and didactic literature recommending a similar synthesis of friendship discourses appeared in the early republican and antebellum periods. In chapter 1, for example, I examine in detail an essay from *The Lady's Magazine and Musical Repository* of November 1801 that begins, "Friendship is an affectionate union of two persons, nearly of the same age, the same situation in life, the same dispositions and sentiments, and, as some writers will have it, of the same sex" (245). I open with Addie's powerful response more than half a century later to illustrate the longevity and popularity of the concerns raised by this study: the character and significance of friendship in early American culture, specifically, how friendly "affection," as Walt Whitman declared in a poem from *Leaves of*

Grass, "shall solve the problems of freedom yet" (*Complete Poetry* 449). I am especially interested in how gender, class, and race renovate traditional models of affiliation and the democratic politics they have conventionally implied.

In her role as maternal advisor, the wise Mrs. Leslie, who has undoubtedly read Shakespeare and Milton but did not have a classical education, enumerates many of the central elements of classical friendship doctrine: equality in social rank as well as age and sex as a requirement for what she calls "perfect friendship." In fact, Aristotle uses the same term, *teleia*, "complete" or "perfected," to describe what he considered friendship's highest ideal—"the friendship of good people alike in virtue" (*NE* 8:3, 4).[2] In her emphasis on equality and virtue, Mrs. Leslie echoes Aristotle's famous formulation from the *Nicomachean Ethics* that in friendship's highest form, the friend is "another" or "second" self (*NE* 9:4, 29). As she observes, this "perfection" produces a disinterest allowing for freedom and frankness of speech that friends exercise as a necessary corrective for one another. The increase of virtue resulting from ideal friendship was, for thinkers like Aristotle, necessary for the very constitution and stability of the polis, a Greek conception of the dominant politico-social structure that excluded most women, who, except for the rare female aristocrat, were consigned to the domestic sphere.

As if to quell fears of women trespassing on public turf, Aguilar gives her novel a subtitle that explicitly identifies Mrs. Leslie's Victorian account of friendship as a "story of domestic life." Furthermore, Mrs. Leslie adeptly sidesteps the exclusivity of the androcentric classical ideal by qualifying it with phrases that echo the moral philosophy of Scottish Enlightenment thinker Adam Smith, who strongly recommended "the healing consolation of sympathy" and asserted "that to feel much for others . . . and to indulge our benevolent affections, constitutes the perfection of human nature; and can alone produce among mankind that harmony of sentiments and passions" (15, 25). Mrs. Leslie's conflation of ideas from these sources not only freely adapts a masculine ideal for women but calls attention to the history of regarding friendship as an important form of social and public affiliation. Although scholars have recently begun to pay more attention to friendship as a sociological trend, they generally consider it a private relation outside of formal social regulation, difficult to quantify and, thus, beyond the ken of critical analysis.[3]

Addie's impassioned response to Aguilar's tale tells a different story, one that delineates friendship as a historically situated, politically inflected cultural practice. In this story, which I argue is deeply "American"—perhaps our quintessential story—the second self is not an exact mirror image of the self but an undeniable possibility of personhood created through relation and affinity. These selves can be asymmetrical, as Addie and Rebecca are in terms of class status. In representations of interracial friendships, as we will see, the second self can even be a potential enemy, so that friendship becomes the process of passing through or bridging over various scenarios of enmity. Recently, a resurgence of interest in the political ideas of German philosopher Carl Schmitt has focused attention on enmity, in particular Schmitt's understanding that politics can be reduced to the distinction between friend and enemy (26).[4] I bracket a consideration of that argument in order first to recover and then to explore the classical and early modern sources of friendship.

In this American story, friendship requires freedom and vice versa. For, as Whitman's "voice prophetic" optimistically proclaims over the literal and spiritual "carnage" of the Civil War, America's "problems of freedom" will "yet" be solved by the "affection" of friendship (*Complete Poetry* 449). This story discloses how friends need to be free *not* to be equals and suggests the proximate nature of democratic equality and similitude: that we can only ever approach but not inhabit these elusive qualities. It tells how difference produces the possibility of freedom within friendship so that we can understand the American democratic project as the necessary and ongoing work of "perfecting friendship." Friendship, thus, continually negotiates and mediates between liberty and equality, making the tension between the two possible to sustain.

Despite the novel's anatomy of English Victorian society, Addie recognized in Florence's friendship dilemma the disparity in social status between herself and Rebecca, two African American women living through the American Civil War in New England. Though she made no further commentary on the novel, Addie was probably delighted with its dramatic revelation that Florence was, in fact, of noble birth and had been adopted into the middle-class Leslie family. This familiar nineteenth-century romantic trope allows for readings of the "affinity" between Florence and Lady Ida that contemporary readers would have recognized as "elective." Popularized by Johann Wolfgang von Goethe as the title of his darkly romantic fictional portrait of the landed gentry, the phrase "elective affinity" was coined by a Swedish scientist to describe chemical processes and implied a natural or organic—and, thus, ineluctable—basis for love and passion.[5]

Florence and Ida's irresistible attraction appears at first like a democratic sub-version of England's rigid class system and its exclusions based on birth. From the outset, Ida dismisses the differences of age and rank between the two women as barriers to their intimacy, which causes the uninhibited Florence to gush, "I loved her from that moment" (9). But when Florence's noble lineage is revealed, it is possible to understand the women's connection as grounded in the inescapable draw of like to like—what Victorians would have understood as the notion that blood tells. Thus, Aguilar's narrative preserves competing and contradictory notions of equality in friendship: as a temperamental (spiritual and psychological) affinity that transcends differences (a democratizing idea that devalues inherited status) *and* as a product of a genealogical inheritance preserved through endogamous allegiances (an older notion of clan or tribal affiliation).

Both of these readings would have appealed to the indomitable Addie, who wanted to minimize class differences in her pursuit of Rebecca and also harbored fantasies of being revealed as socially superior to her servant status. We have no record of Rebecca's response to Addie's recommendation that she read Aguilar's novel except the knowledge that their lively correspondence, with its evidence of an evolving and sustaining friendship, continued for nine years from 1859 to 1868.[6] Given the extensive scholarship on American women's relations during this century by historians like Carroll Smith-Rosenberg, Paula Giddings, and Nancy Cott, the existence and intensity of such a friendship is not surprising. What is notable is the revelation that a young working-class, self-educated black woman at midcentury considered same-sex friendship an affiliation that not only connected her to a wide network of female relations but also was vital to her sense of self and her agency in the world. Friendship was important to Addie Brown not just as a private expression of affection or individual predilection but as a public social structure of affiliation, self-improvement, and gender/racial identification. On a practical level, friendship with the educated, socially privileged Rebecca, like Florence's upwardly mobile intimacy with Lady Ida, rendered the hard-working Addie worthy of notice from a social superior and downplayed their class differences. It expressed what Diana Fuss aptly identifies as the "fantasy of similitude" and the "desire for illusory sameness" from which she speculates politics emerge (19).

Addie's recognition of her own situation in the fictional plot of Aguilar's tale, despite its alien setting among the English gentry in Devonshire, suggests the portability of representations of friendship. It is noteworthy that she recommended reading a novel about women's friendship as a way of enlightening her friend. Literary representations of friendship serve as a mode of transmitting the cultural and political meanings of same-sex affiliation in various historical moments and, as we see with Addie Brown, among surprisingly diverse populations. But if such representations provide a window into the existence of same-sex affiliations, it is a view frequently obscured from the gaze of critics by supposedly racier narratives of heterosexual romance, miscegenation, and reproduction. In this study, I argue that the prevailing understandings of early American culture and politics have been so dominated by the affiliative modes of romance, marriage, and fraternity that we have not sufficiently recognized a crucial alternative strain of thought and practice involving friendship. Even the major groundbreaking studies of "interraciality" appearing in the 1990s, like Werner Sollors's *Neither Black nor White yet Both* (1997), operate in heterosexual and biological terms, excluding same-sex relations, friendships, and alliances from consideration.

Indeed, the lens of modern heteronormativity has such force that critics have typically construed same-sex friendships in early American texts as "homosocial" in a sense that inevitably implies homoeroticism.[7] This conflation is the result of a larger cultural trend, initiated in the early modern period, of applying the terminology of classical friendship to heterosexual marriage in order to redefine and recenter marriage as a form of spiritual companionship. In *The Doctrine and Discipline of Divorce*, for example, John Milton argues for the necessity of divorce by distinguishing the "rationall burning" of the soul for which, in his view, Paul recommended marriage as the remedy from "that other burning, which is but as it were the venom of a lusty and over-abounding concoction . . . the meer motion of carnall lust" (book 1:4). Adam experienced this "rational burning" even "before the fall, when man was much more perfect in himselfe." Rooted in what Milton calls "conversation," such "burning" resembles the rational desire of classical friendship. Emphasizing marriage's spiritual connection, Milton declares: "[T]his pure and more inbred desire of joining to it selfe in conjugall fellowship a fit conversing soul (which desire is properly called love) is stronger then death" (book 1:4).[8]

Without denying the erotic and sexual potential of friendship, I think it is crucial to reject the binarism of heterosexuality and homosexuality. By drawing attention to friendship and especially by recovering its classical sources, I will demonstrate that a very different logic guided its understandings in this period, a logic of elective affiliation or rational desire that encouraged and enabled an array of social and political relations that critics have frequently overlooked.[9] From Aguilar's detailed focus on women's bonds and the dilemma of equality they pose, we can infer that intermingled strands of friendship discourses were in transatlantic circulation in the nineteenth century and—judging from Addie's impassioned response to their depiction—afforded women and people of color from a wide social spectrum the opportunity to consider and ameliorate their personal, social, and, as I will argue below, political status.

Historicizing Affiliation

Early feminist scholarship of the 1970s and 1980s on women's friendships brought these extraordinarily rich and important relationships out of the shadow of masculinist literary and social history. These scholars were responding, at least in part, to accounts of early American literature and culture promulgated most famously by D. H. Lawrence, R. W. B. Lewis, Leslie Fiedler, and Richard Slotkin that depict male friendship of the purportedly unsentimental ("rugged") kind as the grounds for a political ideal or social compact that excluded women and demonized sentimentality and domesticity while it appropriated men of color and valorized violence and heroic individualism. Mainly concerned with excavating what had been buried or deemed trivial and historically inconsequential, feminist historians considered women's friendships in the early period sui generis, categorically different from male friendship with its long history in Western philosophical thought. Smith-Rosenberg suggests how strange these friendships and same-sex friendship in general appeared to modern readers when she characterizes them as "an intriguing and almost alien form of human relationship" (*Disorderly Conduct* 55). Passionate, erotic, enduring, but not clearly sexual and usually compatible with heterosexual marriage, this form of affiliation constituted a subculture with elaborate rituals, specific locations, and characteristic discourses. In contrast to sites dominated by masculinity—the bitterly contentious political sphere or the competitive marketplace of the early Republic—female affiliation established alternative, egalitarian traditions of its own: "separate spheres," maternal genealogies, romantic friendships, and the contested "sisterhoods" of the first and second waves of feminism. But the idealization of separate spheres and feminist sisterhoods promulgated by this scholarship and by second-wave feminist activists came under sharp attack, especially by women of color who objected to the appropriation of minority interests.[10]

In the 1990s, the next generation of scholars brought renewed critical attention to the cultural and political importance of sentiment in early American literature, throwing female friendship, interracial relations, and an emerging interdisciplinary history of emotions into high relief.[11] In her 1999 study, *Cato's Tears and the Making of Anglo-American Emotion*, however, Julie Ellison counters the almost exclusive focus on female sentimentality by exploring the masculine and transatlantic character of the early American culture of affiliation. She argues that "the dominant discourse of sensibility has never been decisively identified as a masculine political invention, nor have the consequences of this fact been explored" (9). In fact, she concludes, "the strategies of female authors only make sense in the context of the early cultural prestige of masculine tenderheartedness" (9). Ellison focuses on "the dilemmas of Whig masculinity," a heady brew of "civic prestige and mutual friendship practiced by men of equally high social status" laced with conspiratorial anxieties about liberty, empire, gender, and racial inequality and personified by the stoic and sentimental characters of Joseph Addison's 1713 "Roman play" *Cato* (9, 17). Where before critics saw only male stoicism, now an emotionalized Roman republicanism filtered through Adam Smith's *The Theory of Moral Sentiments* infuses the model Ellison elucidates for Anglo-American affiliation. She captures its essence in this pithy observation about John Dennis's 1704 drama *Liberty Asserted* that set its "Roman" story in the North American wilds: "Because friendship is only possible in the pure absence of coercion, liberty and manly affection signify each other" (79).

Several other studies take up the subject of male affiliation, its vexed genealogy, and its literary and political implications. In *American Sympathy: Men, Friend-ship, and Literature in the New Nation*, for example, Caleb Crain gives copious evidence of the existence of "romantic" male friendships based on sympathy in both its light and dark guises in the late eighteenth and early nineteenth centuries. These affiliations, he observes, were inextricably linked with a republican ethos of egalitarian attachment and helped create the major literature of the age by writers like Charles Brockden Brown, Ralph Waldo Emerson, and Herman Melville (4–5). Despite this masculine literary trajectory, Crain acknowledges that the subculture of women's friendships first detailed by Smith-Rosenberg was an important source for male writers who borrowed extensively from the feminine discourse of sentimentality (13). But in light of Ellison's argument, we should ask, what was the source, rather than the effect, of feminine sentimentality?

The gendered interchanges highlighted by Ellison and Crain point, through their divergent teleologies, to the necessity of studying the history of affiliation across genders and, as I argue, in terms of other intersecting conditions like race and class. Intending to write entirely about male friendships, Crain discovered that their narratives are "unintelligible" without the inclusion of women as confi-dantes for men and as model practitioners of friendship (13). Similarly, intending to write wholly about women's interracial friendships, I discovered that they could not be understood outside the mythology of male interracial friendship popularized in the work of James Fenimore Cooper, Edgar Allan Poe, Melville, Whitman, and Mark Twain that was elevated by later critics to "classic" status and inextricably linked with an American ideal of freedom and equality and the emerging nation itself. Furthermore, I discovered that these iconic male relation-ships have to be understood as part of a long transnational philosophical dis-course of friendship in Western thought from which women in their capacity as friends with men and with each other as well as friendships across differences of race and class were categorically excluded.

In this book, I take up the task of uncoupling friendship from its arranged

marriage with privacy, emotion, and derogated femininity by examining its classical, early Christian, and early modern sources. Rather than merely a form of or
vehicle for sensibility and sympathy, friendship, I argue, is a crucial and overlooked cultural practice and institution with a complex history not adequately
recognized in the emerging field of emotion studies. I take my cue from Aristotle,
who gathered up and systematized the extensive ideas circulating in the ancient
world about friendship and made them the linchpin of his teachings on ethics.
About this distinction he explained: "[F]riendly affection is like an emotion, but
friendship is like a state" because "people make a return of love out of choice, and
choice derives from a state" (*NE* 8:5, 8).

Working in the early modern period, Laurie Shannon adapts this distinction.
She describes the "discursive phenomenon" denoted by the conventional term
"Renaissance friendship" and characterized by "poeticized likeness" and pre-
liberal notions of "agency and polity" as proceeding from a "powerfully normative
homosocial bias" in literature and social practice (*Sovereign Amity* 1, 55). The
homosocial "normativity" of same-sex affiliations, she argues, served to critique
and both compete and coexist with heterosocial and hierarchical norms of affiliation like romantic love, marriage, erotic relations, and familial ties that enshrine
"gender difference as a law of subordination" (55). By contrast, the consistently
distinguishing feature of the ideal of perfect friendship inherited from the classical
model is its theoretical freedom from natural or biological obligation, social coercion, and institutional regulation.[12] Friends choose each other on the basis of
shared values according to the elemental principle that like attracts like. Thus,
friendship typically implies parity, symmetry, spirituality, and self-affirmation
through rational desire and free choice rather than hierarchy, physicality, and self-
loss or self-dilution through irrational and uncontrollable passion or forced alliance. Concluding his discussion of this distinction, Aristotle cites the proverbial
"saying" familiar to his audience and echoed by redactors of classical thought that
runs like a bright thread through this study: " 'Friendship is Equality' " (*NE* 8:5, 8).

For these reasons, classical as well as early modern thinkers considered friendship the most important and ennobling human relationship by far. More than the
connections of family or marriage, the voluntary, nonsubordinating affiliation of
friendship represented the highest ideal of ethical, political, and social development in the human sphere. In ancient Greece and in the Roman Republic, for
example, friendship among free-born male citizens was the basis of the polis and
all communal civic life. Plato considered friendship synonymous with the very
activity of philosophy, while Aristotle asserted that ties of friendship, because they
define what is just, precede and are necessary for justice (*NE* 8:1, 1).

In the early modern period, due in part to language instruction in Greek and Latin, the mainly aristocratic ideal of perfect friendship spread to encompass all social ranks. In 1531, Thomas Elyot published *The Boke Named The Governour*, England's first educational treatise, at the center of which is a section entitled "The true discription of amitie or frendship" in which he exhorts all "good men to seeke for their semblable on whom they may practise amitie" (161). Almost a century later, Robert Burton in *The Anatomy of Melancholy* likewise elevates friendship as the ideal human relationship: "As nuptial love makes, this perfects mankind, and is to be preferred . . . before affinity and consanguinity" (3:1, 31). In the eighteenth and early nineteenth centuries, radical thinking linked a universal though nominally masculine form of friendship and democracy through the notion of equality as exemplified by the motto of the French Revolution: *liberté, egalité, fraternité*. Striking a similar note, Whitman asserts throughout his writing that democracy is synonymous "with the lifelong love of comrades" and will be maintained by a homosocial force he calls "adhesiveness," defined as "the manly love of comrades" trilled in his "songs" (*Complete Poetry* 272).

Whitman notwithstanding, with the spread of romanticism in the nineteenth century, friendship as the privileged site of sympathetic attachment became increasingly feminized, privatized, and removed from the public sphere of republican and democratic politics. While elements of classical friendship remained influential, its power as a model for civic community waned in the face of liberal individualism, privatized domesticity, and the normativity of heterosexual marriage. By the twentieth century, Western culture developed an obsession with individual selfhood and sexual desire that marginalized friendship as a cogent social practice or civic ideal. Romanticism, modernism, existentialism, and poststructuralism made the intersubjectivity implied in classical friendship's face-to-face orientation unfashionable if not unimaginable. In his description of an ethics of reading based upon Aristotelian friendship, Wayne C. Booth confesses to be puzzled by the modern neglect of what had been "one of the major philosophical topics, the subject of thousands of books and tens of thousands of essays." He points out that while the fourth edition of the *Encyclopedia Britannica* (1810) had twenty long columns on "Friendship," they disappeared in the ninth edition (1879), and though an entry reappeared in the *Micropedia*, it did so only as a reference to Emerson's essay of that name. Nor is friendship a topic or index entry in *The Encyclopedia of Philosophy* of 1967 (170–71) or in the *Supplement* of 1996. (It appears, however, in the second edition published in 2006.)

The omission of considerations of friendship in important critical discourses like material determinism and psychoanalysis bears out this neglect. Karl Marx, for example, argued that human beings are defined, oppressed, and will be liberated primarily by their relations of production, not by their affective connections. Sigmund Freud's inattention to friendship as a shaping force in the human psyche is even more striking. Throughout his work, he stressed the importance of identification with others and the recognition of similarity for the formation of individual subjects as well as for social groups and politics in general. But he also understood identification as partly an unconscious and phantasmatic process, which he defined as the wish to *be* the other, to take his or her place. This wish could take the form of displacement, incorporation, and (often violent) appropriation of the other. Furthermore, Freud defined identification against desire—the wish to *have* the other—so that people achieve normative gender identity by identifying with the parent of their own sex and desiring the parent of the opposite sex. In this chiasmatic Oedipal model, which queer theorists have begun to challenge, one cannot in theory identify with (be similar to or the same gender as) a person whom one also desires (is different from). Homosocial affiliation as well as homosexual attraction are, in this understanding, non-normative.[13] Nor does Freud's or Jacques Lacan's discussion of the "neighbor" as the uncanny familiar stranger quite capture the social and psychic proximity or political centrality of the intimate friend.[14]

Several factors contributed to these changes. As it spread, Christianity's vertical orientation shifted the classical world's emphasis on lateral, interpersonal, and preferential bonds to relations with the divine and a nonpreferential, universal brotherhood. Augustinian theology's division of the world into spiritual and earthly realms also divided friendship into a sacred, quasi-monastic form, exemplified by the utopian community of friends Augustine gathered at his estate at Cassiacum, and a worldly, largely sinful one.

Maintaining this distinction, modern secular philosophy, especially liberal thought, emphasized individual selfhood and autonomy, relegating friendship and ethics to the private realm as issues of obligation rather than choice and leaving the public sphere to the dictates of self-interest and market economics. In the late eighteenth century, for example, the influential philosopher Immanuel Kant demoted friendship to a form of distant respect for others while advancing impartial rules to ensure justice (Dallmayr 105). Even democracy, the political theory enshrining equality, allegedly contributed to this failure: reporting to Europe on the experiment called "America" in the early nineteenth century, Alexis de Tocqueville argued that democratic structures attenuated, rather than encouraged, individual friendships (2:105). Until the 1970s and 1980s, scholars across many disciplines ignored friendship as a topic of inquiry while ethicists noted it only in passing. A theologian complained that writing about friendship in the latter half of the twentieth century most often took the form of "a collection of little sayings, attractively illustrated, meant as a gift, and sold in a drug store" (Meilaender 1).

In the wake of poststructuralism's decentering of the Cartesian ego, thinkers have begun to develop relational ethics and theories of intersubjectivity that challenge the traditional one-person focus of psychoanalysis, ego psychology, and liberal political theory as well as the spiritual and vertical orientation of some poststructuralist theories.[15] According to sociologists, the voluntary and egalitarian or "achieved" character of friendship makes it "an increasingly important form of social glue in contemporary society" challenging traditional and more conservative forms of affiliation and community based in formal, biological, or "ascribed" relationships (Pahl 2). Because of its "very fluidity as a cultural form," one sociologist dubs friendship "the relational genre of the future" (O'Connor 8–9). Popular culture of the late twentieth and early twenty-first centuries reflects this trend in the longevity of TV shows like *Friends*, *Seinfeld*, *Buffy the Vampire Slayer*, and *Sex and the City*, countless "buddy" films, and the emergence of Web sites like *Friendster*, a trendy Internet service that purports to broaden and virtualize one's network of connections by linking with friends and friends of friends.

Feminist and queer activists celebrate the emergence of "families of choice" in which friendship is the salient form of social affiliation, providing an alternative to hierarchical and potentially oppressive "communities of fate" (Pahl 3, 5). In an interview conducted in 1981, cultural historian Michel Foucault argued for the radical potential of homosocial friendship as a "relational system" that, operating "slant-wise" across the various power lines of society, could yield "a culture and ethics" that foster "the formation of new alliances and the tying together of unforeseen lines of force" ("Friendship" 136–38). Looking back in 2002 on almost a quarter of a century of feminist identity politics, Gloria Anzaldúa expressed the shift in theoretical terms: "Twenty-one years ago we struggled with the recognition of difference within the context of commonality. Today we grapple with the recognition of commonality within the context of difference." She dubs this redefined "inclusivity" the "new tribalism," a term we will see is borrowed and adapted from the history of friendship ("(Un)natural Bridges" 2–3).

Aristotle's *Philia* and the Politics of Mirroring

It is not only this renewed interest in friendship and concern with redefining ethics and revaluing relationality to produce new models of democratic community that have motivated this study but also the recurrence and underrecognition of representations of friendship as a phenomenon in American culture. In the following chapters, I offer an eccentric history of the dominant discourses of friendship as "a masculine political invention" that non-elites, people of color, and women in early American culture could and did appropriate. Through their adaptations, marginalized groups claimed admission to an exclusive discourse of affiliation, perpetuating but also, in turn, substantially and radically altering it.

I call my treatment of friendship "eccentric" because it runs counter to the prevailing critical emphasis on heterosexuality and elliptically deploys the discourse of friendship to illuminate privatized and sentimentalized spaces of intersubjectivity that shape public power structures. In doing so, I diverge from the approach of critics like Ellison and Shannon who highlight the *amicitia* of Marcus Tullius Cicero, a Roman statesman and orator whose treatise on friendship, *De amicitia*, was a popular text for teaching Latin.[16] In this study, I focus mainly on Aristotle's notion of *philia*, which recurs in various guises with remarkable frequency in early as well as in later and contemporary American texts.[17] As I discuss in more detail in chapter 1, Cicero incorporated ideas from Greek sources that reinforce the classical ideal as a heroic and spiritual connection (although eroticism and sexuality sometimes play central roles) freely entered into by virtuous men of relatively equal and elevated status who mirror each other. Cicero's account, however, is saturated with masculine political melancholia arising from the untimely death of his great friend Scipio and the loss of the Republic and its tradition of military and civic honor figured by that friendship. This compelling linkage of friendship and loss influenced other important contributors to the tradition such as Francesco Petrarch and Michel de Montaigne and set the overriding mood for postmodern conceptions of friendship epitomized by Jacques Derrida's 2001 collection of eulogies on friends entitled *The Work of Mourning*.

As Aguilar's savvy but untutored Mrs. Leslie confirms, however, there were other influential conceptions of friendship in circulation.[18] To recover these forms, in chapter 1 I offer an abbreviated history of friendship theory that highlights Aristotle's notion of *philia*, its sources in pre-Socratic ideas, its modification in Roman republican and early Christian thought, and its interaction with Scottish Common Sense philosophy and emerging notions of sentiment and sympathy. This account of friendship informs my reading of several representative early American texts in the following four chapters. I argue that for Aristotle, as for other classical thinkers, perfect friendship, though regarded as rare, was not impossible, appropriative, or fleeting. It was not, as Derrida implies in his centrifugal meditations on the friendship canon, only grasped at the moment of its loss, always a displacement of the other, or only enabled by the friend's absence and death. Rather, Aristotle theorized that friends lived together, shared all in common, and would, if necessary, die for each other (*NE* 8:3, 4–5; 9:8, 36). Most importantly, in this first chapter I trace the significance of tropes of equality and similarity in canonical friendship writing and consider their implications for later writers. These tropes, I argue, have had a powerful and uncharted effect on our ability to conceive of friendship across the lines of difference.

For the ancients, the friendship dyad was the building block of republican community. In this pair, the mirroring effect of friendship was so potent that it rendered the friends virtually and visually interchangeable. Aristotle reasoned that if the friend is "another self," then self-love is the model for love of the friend. But can people mirror each other and remain separate entities, resisting a narcissistic collapse into each other? Or are mirroring relations, as Lacan describes the "mirror stage" in childhood development, always misprisions and spatial projections of an "ideal-I" that in fact enclose and isolate the fragmented self "into mediatization through the desire of the other" (4–5)?[19]

The "passion" for friends, to use Socrates' punning phrase from *Lysis*, Plato's dialogue on the pederastic structure of Athenian male friendship, requires but also produces a moral "likeness" that writers often expressed through physical resemblance. In the classical model and its adaptations, friends had to be "like" each other in terms of rank, virtue, and temperament even to qualify for the ideal, but the affective "liking" that resulted from this equality and from long association and intimacy made friends "like" (similar to, resemble) each other. Sometimes, as we will see, physical similarity precedes and produces the affective liking of friendship. Frequently, the friends in question are not visibly interchangeable at all, but the idealized nobility of their friendship produces a likeness that, to amazed onlookers, overcomes perceived physical differences.

Examples of this slippage—closely related to the literary motifs of twinning, doubling, and mistaken identity—abound in the literature of friendship and have attained the status of legend.[20] Consider the story of two of Aristotle's well-known students, Alexander the Great and Hephaestion, Alexander's companion and comrade-at-arms. During his campaign for domination of Asia, Alexander defeated King Darius of Persia, who fled, allowing his family to be captured by the young conqueror. Fearing that they would be treated abusively, the queen mother, Sisigambis, is said to have thrown herself at Hephaestion's feet, assuming he was the famed general because he was the taller and more imposing of the two men. The Roman historian Quintus Curtius Rufus describes the emblematic moment: "Raising her with his hand, Alexander said, 'My lady, you made no mistake. This man is Alexander too'" (46). Curtius explains: "Hephaestion was by far the dearest of all the king's friends; he had been brought up with Alexander and shared all his secrets. No other person was privileged to advise the king as candidly as he did" (46).

Although scholars question the authenticity of this incident, which appears in numerous accounts of Alexander's life, its transmission through divergent sources is a telling index of its continuing cultural capital.[21] Compilations of proverbial wisdom like Erasmus's popular *Apophthegmes* published in English in 1642 and friendship archives like *The Oxford Book of Friendship* of 1991 cite it as an example of the ineluctable spiritual cohesion of classical friendship. Nicholas Udall, who translated Erasmus's collection, uses Aristotle's famous formula—the friend is another self—to explain the interchangeability of this famous pair and writes in a marginal gloss: "Alexander esteemed Hephestion a second Alexander, according to the prouerbe *amicus alter ipse*, that is, two frends are one soul and one body" (207). In her discussion of Renaissance friendship tropes, Shannon points out the errors here, as Udall confuses the proverbs and garbles the familiar phrase used extensively by early modern writers and distilled in this couplet from the poem "Of Frendship" in *Tottel's Miscellany*, "Behold thy frend, and of thy self the pattern see: / One soull, a wonder shall it seem, in bodies twain to be" (Rollins 106; Shannon, *Sovereign Amity* 4). But Udall's confusion is, as Shannon remarks, an intensification of the proverbial image since, in the example of Alexander and Hephaestion, even their bodies are rhetorically, if not literally, indistinguishable.

What affective or discursive force can render social and physical differences imperceptible, creating a single figuratively con/fused body as the dwelling for spiritually fused souls? To translate this into political terms, what affiliative mode can constitute "a single corporate or juridical body, a legal fiction creating an operative unity" (Shannon, *Sovereign Amity* 4), transforming the "many" of a diverse population into the "one" of a collective political body? These questions underscore friendship's proverbial association with utopia. Writers who deploy this classical discourse stake a claim to relations of similitude and parity—an "equality" that is not sameness but equivalence—as a way to imagine connection without hierarchy but also raise the perennial question of difference: what kinds of difference are bridgeable by the similitude of friendship, and what kinds of difference are nonnegotiable?

Despite its egalitarian premise, the classical ideal of friendship was not merely homosocial; it was in theory and practice specifically masculine and culture- and class-bound. Although some ancient thinkers considered women the moral equals of men, Aristotle believed them to be constitutionally deficient in the necessary rational faculties, discipline of appetites, and authority required for perfect friendship. Similarly, in his description of the household in book 1 of *Politics*, Aristotle propounds a theory of "natural slavery" that identified a category of people who, like women and children of all classes, did not possess rational faculties sufficiently developed to control the passions and, thus, could be neither citizens of the polis nor the friends of citizens (1130). Although slavery in the ancient world was not necessarily determined by skin color or ethnicity, medieval and early modern apologists for colonialism applied Aristotle's theory to the indigenous peoples of the Americas to justify social hierarchy, wars of conquest, and religious conversion by force. The idea of "natural slavery" operated like the inverse of perfect friendship and governed how many European explorers preconceived and later saw the indigenous people they encountered in the Americas.[22]

For writers drawing on these discourses, the emphasis on likeness to the point of interchangeability makes friendship across differences of gender, racial, and ethnic identity difficult if not ontologically impossible.[23] This difficulty is reflected in Western metaphysics, where difference inevitably produces opposition that culminates in hierarchy and domination.[24] It is possible to see the equality of perfect friendship emerging from the suppression of differences modeled by the exclusive androcentric homology of elite men, which nevertheless reinforces notions of masculine superiority. Read in this way, the homonormative principle governing friendship implies a fear of difference that characterizes the dominant Western intellectual tradition, concerned to the point of violence with unity, coherence, truth grounded in identity, and the idea of an autonomous, self-constituting subject.[25]

But friendship's insistence on likeness can also be a means of neutralizing differences and hierarchy and producing spiritual equality. Recall Addie Brown, who responded so powerfully to Aguilar's novel about women's friendships because, as I speculate at the outset of this introduction, it mobilized both possibilities simultaneously. Transgressive friendships, like Addie and Rebecca's, that cross social boundaries of gender, race, class, and sexuality radically challenge and reshape classical models. In this respect, friendship's emphasis on equality and likeness, as requirement or result, has special resonance in the Americas. In this space of conquest and encounter, the issue of racial difference more directly affected the equation of friendship and put stress on new points in the classical paradigm based on likeness, where before class and gender were the principal differences. Utility and necessity forged formerly unthinkable alliances that shifted the meaning of "likeness" and "liking" and helped to evolve new forms of friendship. This development is important in our understanding of affiliation in the

North American colonies, which became a proving ground for the ideals of liberty and democracy based in emerging notions of natural rights and universal equality.

Friendship in the New World

At the coastal fringes of the northern and southern hemispheres of America, Europeans arrived armed with ideas of friendship, equality, and natural slavery inherited from the ancients and abetted by fantasies of self-invention in what they regarded as uncharted lands. They encountered indigenous people who had their own notions of love, friendship, exchange, power, and otherness. In citing these confrontations as the founding moment of modern subjectivity, theorist Michel de Certeau uses tropes related to classical friendship. The Old World, he remarks, looked into "the mirror of savage society" created partly by its fantasy of the uniqueness of the New World (*Heterologies* 74). The images Europeans saw there more often than not confirmed their ethnocentric assumptions of cultural superiority and caused what Carla Freccero, in her study of Certeau's "psychoanalytics of historiography," describes as "the violent production of the same through the silencing of the other" ("Toward" 366). Occasionally, the images reflected Europeans' distance from their idealized innocence, creating a space of self-critique. Tzvetan Todorov calls the conquest of the Americas the most "extreme" and "exemplary" instance of the "discovery *self* makes of the *other*" that "heralds and establishes our present identity" (3 5; his emphases).

Europeans often cloaked their imperial projects in the noble characters of friendship or the related rhetoric of Christian brotherhood and an enlightened notion of natural rights. Though authentic relationships undoubtedly arose, European discourses of friendship helped to effect the reduction, submission, and in some cases eradication of indigenous populations across the Americas. Later, as the U.S. government pushed many native tribes west of the Mississippi to make room for expanding white settlements, early writers promulgated a fantasy of interracial friendship to disguise this checkered history, which they extolled as the epitome of the American democratic ideal.

Nothing more clearly illustrates the duplicitous use of friendship discourse than the "peace medals" distributed by colonial and government agents to native leaders. Striking commemorative medals was a tradition dating back to the early colonial era when the imperial powers of Spain, France, and Great Britain distributed them as an important element in their diplomatic negotiations with Indian nations. Peace medals eventually became essential ingredients in United States–Indian relations, so much so that in 1797, when their arrival from the issuing mint in England was delayed, Secretary of War James McHenry complained to the U.S. minister to Great Britain: "My poor Indians are very clamorous for their medals, more so indeed than for their plows" (Prucha, *Indian Peace Medals* 89). This patronizing language illustrates a pervasive attitude among officials who misunderstood the importance of symbols in Indian cultures and belied the message of friendship inscribed on the medals. Cast in different sizes of silver or bronze and, thus, virtually indestructible, these objects, even more than flags or "chief coats," which were also distributed as gifts to Indian leaders, embodied an enduring connection between donor and recipient.

The United States issued its first peace medals in 1789 as part of President Washington's campaign to placate tribes who had sided with the British during the Revolutionary War. To indicate their loyalty to the new Continental power, Indian chiefs ceremonially relinquished their old medals bearing the likeness of King George and received new ones bearing the likeness of George Washington (Prucha, *Peace and Friendship* 9–10). The great political significance of peace medals as markers of friendship and allegiance diminished after the Civil War as U.S. policy reduced the power of chiefs and tribal governments. Still, U.S. presidents continued to strike and distribute peace medals as rewards for service or even as prizes for "minor accomplishments" until 1881 (Prucha, *Indian Peace Medals* 59).

The design of the medals was standardized during Jefferson's presidency. The now familiar images included on the obverse a profile of the current president in the role of the new "great father" of the nation and on the reverse two hands, one with the cuff of a military jacket, the other with a presumably native wristband bearing an American eagle, clasped in the conventional gesture of unity under a crossed pipe and tomahawk and framed by the words "peace and friendship" (Ronda 33). This design constitutes an Americanization of the iconography of friendship discussed in later chapters, especially the emblem of the handclasp, which has a particular resonance in our uneasy history of interracial relations. Meriwether Lewis and George Rogers Clark carried medals of different sizes and grades on their famed expedition into Indian country at the turn of the nineteenth century and bestowed them on Indians they perceived to be leaders during formal ceremonies and negotiations. As ritual objects in a complex performance of power and allegiance, these medals underscore the close relationship of international diplomacy and friendship discourse, which, like pledges of romantic love, are secured through iconic tokens, special rituals, and formulaic language.

The peace medals had a diverse range of meanings. For Lewis and Clark and other government agents, they signified U.S. national sovereignty and a "bloodless conquest" that created a chain of allies and trading partners (Ronda 34). Native leaders, who were often depicted and later photographed wearing medals, saw them as "marks of respect and distinction," links to the material wealth of powerful white outsiders, as well as "conduits of spiritual power" and "medicine" of both the constructive and destructive kinds (34–35). Clark, for example, had trouble persuading a Cheyenne chief to accept the dangerously powerful token, and the Hidatsa supposedly gave the medals to their enemies, hoping to bring them misfortune (35).

The Washington medals are particularly noteworthy. In *The Pioneers*, the first Leatherstocking Tale, set in 1793–94, Cooper introduces a tragically diminished Chingachgook who is naked to the waist except for "a silver medallion of Washington . . . a badge of distinction" suspended on a buckskin thong around his neck (86). He wore this badge only for solemn occasions and donned it on the day of his death (400). This detail gains political significance with the knowledge that the individually engraved peace medals struck in Washington's first administration not only signified loyalty to the newly formed United States but also were rewards for assimilation to white practices (Prucha, *Indian Peace Medals* 8). The large and distinctive silver ovals depict George Washington handing a peace pipe to an eager Indian, whose naked chest bears a peace medal (figure 1). The Indian has cast his tomahawk away from him; behind the formally dressed and armed American president, a man tills a field with a plow and oxen, representing the settled and prosperous "civilized" future white leaders envisioned for and sought to impose upon nomadic hunting tribes (73–87). A lithograph by Charles Bird King for Thomas L. McKenney and James Hall's elaborate color-plate book *History of the Indian Tribes of North America* shows the Seneca leader Sagoyewatha or "Red Jacket" (c. 1758–1830) wearing a famous Washington peace medal dated 1792 (figure 2). This medal was passed down in his family and worn, in the words of descendant and Iroquois sachem Ely S. Parker, "as evidence of the bond of perpetual peace and friendship established and entered into between the people of the United States and the Six Nations of Indians at the time of its presentation" (328–29).

The native recipient of a bronze Jefferson peace medal on exhibit at the National Museum of the American Indian augmented it with quillwork and feathers, making it a hybridized object that visibly embodies its pledge of cooperation. But not every medal lived up to this promise. On their return journey in late July 1806 as Lewis and a small party explored the Marias River in what is now north-central Montana, they surprised some young Piegan Indians attempting to steal their horses and guns. Lewis shot and killed one youth while wounding others. Ac-

Figure 1. Obverse of Washington medal dated 1792, silver, 81×124mm. Courtesy of the American Numismatic Society, New York.

Figure 2. Sagoyewatha or "Red Jacket" (c. 1758–1830), Seneca leader, wearing the large oval Washington medal dated 1792 that became well known as the prototype. Lithograph from Thomas L. McKenney and James Hall, *History of the Indian Tribes of North America* (Philadelphia: J. T. Bowen, 1848), 1:9; courtesy of Dartmouth College Library.

quainted with the power of symbols in Indian country, Lewis stripped the sacred amulets from the Indians' shields, burned their weapons, and hung a peace medal around the neck of the corpse so, he explained in his journal, "that they might be informed who we were" (Moulton 8:135; Ronda 36). In this single gesture, Lewis identified the new United States not with the noble abstractions boldly engraved on the medals he was dispersing but with the violence of an imperial agenda.

Reading several early American texts through the lens of friendship discourses, I will show that colonial and early national writers continually drew upon classical, Christian, and Enlightenment notions of friendship to fashion their accounts of American culture and politics and to script new modes of affiliation in the new world of colonial settlements, republicanism, and liberal democracy. In chapters 2 through 5, I pair texts by male writers with texts by female writers in order to highlight the cultural conversation between gendered visions of friendship and their divergent political implications.

Chapter 2 examines John Winthrop's famous address, "A Modell of Christian Charitie," in which the shrewd leader of the Puritan émigrés en route to Massachusetts Bay outlines an ideal of affiliation for his exemplary community that continues to reverberate in our national imaginary.[26] Critics see the doubled perspective of Winthrop's foundational vision as characteristic of the Puritan desire to be in the world but not of it. Recently, in our efforts to expand the focus of early American studies, which has been trained almost exclusively on the religious "origins" of the American self, scholars have paid considerably more attention to the address's economic aspects. At the same time that Winthrop strives to unify his diverse followers through exhortations to spiritual love and self-sacrifice in the common endeavor of "visible saints," he also advances a hierarchical, profit-making commercial venture to reassure the gentry and entice wealthy backers. Though critics have explored the financial and commercial implications of Winthrop's stirring call to civic charity, they have not examined the sources for his understanding of Christian love. It is, I argue, a form of affiliation inextricably entangled with classical, early Christian, and Renaissance friendship discourses as well as the emerging legal and commercial language of contract to which these discourses give rise.

A version of classical friendship, shadowed by homosocial and masculinist undertones, grounds Winthrop's compelling blueprint for "familiar Commerce" in the "Citty upon a Hill" (*Winthrop Papers* 294–95). Winthrop masterfully manipulates these undertones to conflate friendship and Christian fellowship with the heteronormative and androcentric logic of marriage. This slippage subtly disarms friendship's lateral and egalitarian effects in order to advance a civic structure based on an analogy with an ideologically conservative and hierarchical (vertical) vision of marriage. In this vision, women and the unruly others associated with them—Nathaniel Hawthorne's infamous Hester Prynne serves as my concluding example—are a part but also set apart.

A century before Hester reenacted her tale of adulteration for antebellum readers, however, the American Revolution and its Enlightenment ideas were supposed to have swept away Puritan zeal, predestinarian gloom, and top-down relations of obligation in order to install rationalism, egalitarianism, and liberty in their place. During the eighteenth century, thinkers on both sides of the Atlantic began reconceiving bonds of passion and coercive authority, especially those between parent and child and husband and wife, as mutually sustaining, affectionate, and consensual "contracts" modeled on the voluntary egalitarianism of friendship. But as I show in chapters 1 and 2, women have been excluded historically and philosophically from friendship with men and have had their same-sex bonds trivialized. Even the Christian fellowship recommended by Winthrop oscillates between the exclusive dyad of ideal male friendship and hierarchical marriage.

In chapter 3, I examine the political implications of adopting a discourse of friendship in the early U.S. Republic. In particular, I argue that Federalists and apologists for the Constitution demonized the laterally organized "confederation" of states and strategically retooled and reclaimed Winthrop's analogy of hierarchical marriage, via Milton's popular paean to "wedded love," as an image for a nation of male citizens linked vertically to a single "executive" figure. This provides the backdrop for a reading of Hannah Webster Foster's 1797 epistolary novel, *The Coquette*, which, I argue, proposes same-sex and cross-gender friendship as a sociopolitical alternative to unequal and repressive Federalist notions of marriage. Faced with a choice between two suitors—a stuffy clergyman and a seductive libertine—Eliza Wharton chooses neither; rather, she rejects marriage in favor of a specifically American freedom of association and circulation, which the rake gives the appearance of modeling. Though Eliza's decision ultimately causes her ostracism, fall, and death in childbirth, she insistently disparages marriage as "the tomb of friendship" and elevates friendship as the most ethical and egalitarian relation of a public social sphere. Her failure helps us recover the existence of a social realm in which friendship functioned as a mode of affiliation across differences as well as an important trope of democratic possibility in the early American political imagination.

In the last two chapters, I look at representations of interracial friendship and the role they play in emerging forms of national identity in the early Republic. I pair an examination of two canonical narratives of interracial friendship, James

Fenimore Cooper's *The Last of the Mohicans* (1826) and Catharine Sedgwick's *Hope Leslie* (1827). Appearing within a year of each other, these historical frontier romances are part of the furious literary debate that took place in the early years of the nineteenth century between male and female writers over the nature of national identity and citizenship. Although they offer divergent visions for the new nation, both writers have inherited what I call "a semiotics of the other," which emerged with particular violence and clarity during Europe's conquest and exploration of the Americas. As I argue in chapter 1, Aristotle is a key figure in this discourse because he theorizes both extremes of encounter and affiliation: perfect friendship and natural slavery.

In chapter 4, I examine how Cooper repackages and disseminates these discourses in his depiction of the interracial friendship between the Anglo scout Hawk-eye and the Mohican chief Chingachgook that has come to represent for many readers the quintessential America. Read out of the order in which they were composed, as a chronological progression of snapshots in the entwined life stories of two men from different cultures, the Leatherstocking Tales subversively leave open the radical possibilities of interracial friendship—a reading that may have appealed to an aging Cooper. Reading the tales in the order of their composition, however, quashes this potential. Despite the sentimental pull of this interracial intimacy and its culturally hybrid values, the prevailing image of America it endorses is, ironically, white, autonomous, and, to reprise Hawk-eye's famous disclaimer, racially "uncrossed."

While dominant critical readings interpret this iconic interracial relationship in terms of a timeless, nostalgic, and violent "mythology" of the frontier, my reading positions the masculine interracial bond within the discursive history of perfect friendship and its emphasis on equality and interchangeability sketched in chapter 1 and within the religious and political adaptations of this discourse in early American writing treated in chapters 2 and 3. By excavating tropes of friendship, allegiance, and concord within *The Last of the Mohicans* and throughout the Leatherstocking Tales, I show how Cooper's heroic pair embodies central features of the classical, Renaissance, and Enlightenment notions of friendship that render homosocial attachment a powerful alternative to heterosexual marriage. Ultimately, however, Cooper recaptures and reverses the centrifugal force of this transgressive affiliation through tropes of symbolic cannibalism that Certeau associates with colonialism, imperialism, and the formation of hegemonic masculine subjectivities and their melancholic racial politics.

Sedgwick's frontier romance draws on all of the elements of friendship discourses discussed in previous chapters. In chapter 5, I show how she revisits many of the classical, Renaissance, and Christian tropes and adapts them to what can be described only as a feminine, if not proto-feminist, politics of affiliation. John Winthrop, for example, is a major character in *Hope Leslie*, a novel that scrutinizes and very deliberately *critiques* his famous "modell of Christian char-itie" as advancing an affiliative ethos that inhibits rather than promotes what Sedgwick understands as a specifically American independence of conscience and action. The novel's titular heroine, Hope Leslie, is both a historically posi-tioned precursor and literary descendant of the unruly Eliza Wharton. One could even say that Hope cites the rebellious Hester Prynne even before Hawthorne could imagine her.

While prevailing criticism argues that Sedgwick's narrative seeks the inclusion of white women, sisters, and Indians as citizens by equating them with white men and brothers, I argue that several intertextual references to Milton's *Comus* demon-strate the opposite: the failure of brothers and a hopeful (pun intended) counter-tradition of sisters "doin' it for themselves." Specifically, I focus on how Sedgwick's romance rewrites Cooper's *Mohicans* at every turn. Instead of epic nostalgia, Sedgwick produces a more nuanced, though still thoroughly sentimentalized, account of the challenges of interracial and cross-gender friendship that differs from Cooper's representation by its failure.

In the end, however, Sedgwick's Anglo-American protagonists cannot compre-hend—that is, incorporate—Magawisca, their native intimate and the true heroine of the tale. Magawisca, who is a rewriting of Pocahontas, resists assimilation into a monolithic (white, Christian) American identity and heterosexual romance and maintains her (and her tribe's) "sovereignty" by leaving the Puritan settlement. In doing so, she offers a salutary alternative—what I call "friendship-at-a-distance"—that constitutes a "friendly" critique of emerging U.S. politics. For, as feminist theorists Judith Butler and Drucilla Cornell argue, "the limit of recognition in the sense of comprehension" is a failure to appropriate and thus culturally cannibalize the other that signals, "paradoxically, the advent of ethical recognition" (Butler, "For a Careful Reading" 141).[27] From this failure, an ethics of friendship could emerge to ground a potentially more equitable notion of democracy.

By reclaiming the historical dimensions of friendship, this book aims to recast literary representations of friendship in early America as an underrated story of social and political life. This trajectory is, as my study suggests, less developmen-tal than recessional—at least till the end of the twentieth century, since the force of the classical ideal wanes in the face of romanticism, liberal individualism, and the normativity of heterosexual marriage. This story also illuminates how powerful voices that control the dominant cultural tropes shape national identities, further entrenching ideologies and quashing alternative expressions of equity. Despite its transnational history, friendship has a special resonance for the United States as the figure of our most cherished ideal of democratic equality and the emblem of our most egregious failures. This is not a figment of the "early" imagination alone. In 1962, John Glenn, the first astronaut to orbit the earth, named his spacecraft *Friendship* 7, as if this were the attitude most representative of the United States in the "final frontier" of space.[28] I believe we should celebrate and encourage the renascence of friendship in the new millennium as a means of reimagining equality and performing democratic values, since our fate as a global community depends on our ability to act on the similitude—however illusory or fantastic—of our shared humanity.

Friendship always either
finds or makes equals.
—Marcus Minucius Felix,
Octavius (third century C.E.)

The absence of women,
the presence of the question,
reveals that women call into
question the constitutive myths.
—Anne Norton,
Reflections on Political Identity

CHAPTER ONE

Smoke and Mirrors
A History of Equality and
Interchangeability in
Friendship Theory

I begin with a question that philoso-
phers have been asking for centuries: What does it mean for friends to be linked as
mirrors of each other? Understood in political terms, can individuals ever be
interchangeable or equal, and can we construct a community based on this reflective dyadic unit? As philosopher Paul Ricoeur remarks in his 1992 study of ethics
bearing the Aristotelian title *Oneself as Another*, this question is "in no way
rhetorical. On it, as [political theorist] Charles Taylor has maintained, depends
the fate of political theory"—that is, how we envision community, what constitutes
persons and their rights, and the mediating role of others in determining ethical
actions (181). Jacques Derrida, who examined the politics of friendship extensively in the late 1980s and 1990s, contends that "friendship is freedom plus
equality" and summarizes his complex musings in a similarly deceptively simple
question: "Is the friend the same or the other?" (*Politics* 282, 4). Perhaps the
crucial issue is not similarity or difference, however we construe these, but a
paradoxical postmodern form of both-and, the experience of being "in relation"
that is constituted precisely through separation. Near the end of his study of
friendship, Derrida quotes approvingly the words of fellow philosopher Maurice

Blanchot, who believed that friends "reserve, even on the most familiar terms, an infinite distance, the fundamental separation on the basis of which what separates becomes relation" (291; *Politics* 294).

Largely left out of this discussion, however, is gender, sexuality, racial identity, and class status. All of these identity markers complicate the vexed questions of sameness, difference, and equality that emerge in representations of friendship. In order to begin to understand how difference and these specific differences and their intersections function within and challenge theories of similitude, I offer in this chapter a history of friendship discourses that highlights tropes of similarity, equality, and interchangeability. Beginning with the preclassical sources for Aristotle's important notion of *philia*, we will see that equality and likeness are requirements for and thus constitutive elements of perfect friendship, which produce a fiction or illusion of interchangeability. Similitude, in different guises, continues to be a force in Christian adaptations of classical ideas; in the Scottish Common Sense philosophers whose theories inform modern notions of sociability, sympathy, and universal benevolence; and in postmodern and feminist conceptions of friendship.

Each age, no matter how different its vision of sociability, politics, or the role of affect, retains a version of dyadic friendship based on adaptations of the Aristotelian idea that "friendship is equality" (*NE* 8:5, 8). Other classical thinkers, such as Plato, Aristotle's teacher, and Marcus Tullius Cicero, Aristotle's Roman redactor, produced friendship discourses that shaped particular historical understandings of gender, identity, affect, and politics. As I mentioned in the introduction, the *amicitia* of elite men in the Stoic Ciceronian model underlies early Whig and later American republican notions of homosocial friendship, while Platonic ideas of transcendence shape homosocial friendships of the romantic era and help distinguish them from a sentimentalism increasingly associated with women's bonds. I argue, however, that the perfect friendship of second selves formulated in the *Nicomachean Ethics* exerts the most pervasive hold on our imagination of friendship and democratic politics and provides women and people of color with a conceptual means to produce rhetorical equality. We are then left with a question, the answer to which remains problematic: Can we have equality or equity within difference and differences within equality?

Classical *Philia* and the Requirement of Equality

By the time Aristotle delivered his great ethical treatises, he had inherited and systematized a long tradition of thought about *philia*.[1] This word—*philotes* in early Greek writing—has a range of meanings not completely synonymous with its most frequent modern translation as "friendship"; furthermore, writers often referred to more than one of its possible connotations.

As an adjective, *philos* means "dear" or sometimes "own," and as a noun it often connotes a broadly applicable "love." Writers in the preclassical world employed the word in several related ways: to designate the members of one's household to whom one was bound by ties of blood, law, or custom; to describe unrelated people whom one "loves," the meaning nearest to the "elective affinity" of modern friendship; and also to invoke a reciprocal, though not necessarily affective, "trans-generational" relationship known as "guest-friendship," a social institution that afforded hospitality to travelers of similar rank and status (Stern-Gillet 6). Thus, in the *Iliad*, Homer tells of Diomedes, an invading Greek soldier, and Glaucus, a Trojan defending his homeland. Upon entering the area for single combat on the battlefield at Troy, they realize that because their grandfathers were *philoi*, they are also bound by this connection though they are strangers and enemies. In order to publicly signify this status, they agree to exchange armor and to avoid each other's spears (*Iliad* 6:119–282). This practice lends later Greek *philia* its aristocratic character, since the extensive networks of guest-friendship that linked upper-class families within ancient Greece and beyond formed the foundation upon which the organization of the Greek city-state or polis was superimposed (Easterling 15). These powerful and extensive networks enshrined the value of reciprocity in rituals of hospitality, gift-giving, and wishing or doing harm to one's common enemies (a proverbial formulation) but were not necessarily relations of affection or individual choice.

This study focuses primarily on the second meaning of ancient *philia*, a personal relation of affection between unrelated peers. In Homer's works, such affiliation was closely associated with male comrades and family ties. Thus, when King Alcinous questions Odysseus about his sadness upon hearing of the fall of Troy, he asks,

> Did one of your kinsmen die before the walls of Troy,
> some brave man—a son by marriage? father by marriage?
> Next to our own blood kin, our nearest, dearest ties.
> Or a friend perhaps, someone close to your heart,
> staunch and loyal? No less dear than a brother,
> the brother-in-arms who shares our inmost thoughts. (*Odyssey* 8:652–57)

Homer's *Odyssey* also expresses, albeit ironically and in negative terms, the other important principle underlying this notion of *philia*. It occurs when Melanthius, an arrogant wooer of Penelope, reviles the disguised Odysseus as he and Eumaeus herd she-goats to the feast at Odysseus's house: " 'Look!'—he sneered—'one scum nosing another scum along, / dirt finds dirt by the will of god—it never fails!' " (17:236–37). In its positive form, classical writers considered this principle a general truth and cited it extensively. Erasmus includes it in his *Adages* as "God always leads like to like," pointing to its origin in this scene in the *Odyssey* and giving Aristotle's quotation of the proverb "Whence they say 'like will to like' " from book 8 of the *Nicomachean Ethics* (*Adages* I.ii.22, 168–69).

While this important notion suggests a divine or natural origin for human friendship as well as community, it also posits an ineluctable attraction between "likes" that becomes the basis for a principle of exclusion. The great friendship between Achilles and Patroclus depicted in the second part of the *Iliad* and held up by ancient as well as modern sources as the model of "devoted comrades" shows that a specific heroic and moral code had already grown up around dyadic friendships (C. White 14). Learning of Patroclus's death, Achilles calls him *philos hetairos*, "dear comrade . . . the man I loved beyond all other comrades, / loved as my own life" (*Iliad* 18:94–96; Konstan, *Friendship* 41). Through frequent citation, Homer's famous pair reinforces *philia*'s persistently homosocial, suggestively homoerotic, thoroughly masculine, and often military character. Despite these prevailing connotations, scholars speculate that friendships between women existed in early Greek culture and elicited similarly eroticized language, though we have little evidence of it except for the surviving poetic fragments of Sappho (Easterling 18–20; Konstan, *Friendship* 47–48).

Although Homer couches his preclassical example of "symbiosis" and "alter egos" in metaphors of physical similarity and interchangeability, Patroclus was not, according to Nestor, Achilles' equal in lineage or strength (*Iliad* 11:939–40). Familial obligation also shaped their connection. But as in the example of Alexander and Hephaestion discussed in the introduction, this "inequality" reveals an important aspect of *philia*. A few years older, Patroclus was adopted into Achilles' household as a youth and eventually became Achilles' "squire" (Stern-Gillet 16; Konstan, *Friendship* 40). Rules of hospitality, long acquaintance, and mutual affection and the exigencies of war coalesced to form this powerful bond (C. White 15).

The discrepancy in the heroes' status and Achilles' fervent expressions of love and grief over the death of Patroclus have led ancient and modern commentators to speculate about the homoerotic/pederastic nature of this early representation of friendship.[2] According to classical scholars, there is no evidence that erotic pederasty as later practiced in fourth and fifth century B.C.E. Athens existed in this early period (Konstan, *Friendship* 38), though this does not rule out behavior later labeled homosexual. Athenian pederasty clearly defined the roles of *erastes* (lover) and *eromenos* (beloved) as complementary and unequal: the older man desiring, teaching, and being sexually "active," and the beautiful youth receiving, learning, and being sexually "passive."[3] According to Aristotle, *erastes* and *eromenos* take pleasure in different things and, thus, are not equal and cannot be friends (*NE* 8:4, 6). Writers in this period described the roles of friends as "symmetrical" and saw friendship requiring mutuality and equality. A "jingle" thought to have originated with Pythagoras in the sixth century B.C.E., which later writers associated with his ideas, expresses these crucial characteristics: *philotes isotes* ("friendship is equality"), wittily rendered as "amity is parity" (Konstan, *Friendship* 38–39).

Pythagoras, like other early pre-Socratic philosophers, understood *philotes* as a principle operating in a vast context; in fact, he considered it the essential quality of the cosmic sphere. Although much of what we know about this legendary figure remains speculative, the innovative practical ethics and philosophical ideas, distilled in *acusmata* or *symbola*—oral maxims or sayings—and attributed to Pythagoras by later writers, strongly influenced the shape of classical friendship doctrine. A mathematician, astronomer, and musician trained in Persia and Egypt, Pythagoras was said to have founded an academy at Croton in southern Italy, whose inner circle, known as "Pythagoreans" and *mathematici* (advanced students), lived and studied communally, sharing all possessions, following a restricted diet, and seeking intellectual, moral, and physical excellence. Less stringent rules applied to the "Pythagorists" and *acusmatici* (probationers), members of the society's outer circle who did not live and study communally but received oral teaching. All members were bound by strict rules of secrecy and loyalty. There is no agreement on how large this school was, how far Pythagoras's influence spread, or how long it lasted. We do know that both men and women were members of the society, and several women followers became eminent philosophers in their own right (Iamblichus 259).

In his *De vita pythagorica*, composed as an introduction to a ten-volume study of Pythagoras's thought, the second-century C.E. Neoplatonist Iamblichus credits Pythagoras as the "discoverer and legislator" of a broad concept of "friendship" or universal harmony that governed relations between gods and humans, humans and each other, and humans and animals, as well as the "opposite powers concealed" in the human body (227). The governing principle in these related spheres was a striving for balance and a numerically based harmony through the avoidance of passion, dissension, and vice. Describing the "highest virtue," chapter 33 of *De vita pythagorica* begins by recommending "Friendship of all with all"

(227). While this ideal theoretically included everyone, reports suggest that the Pythagoreans practiced among themselves a radical mutuality, unselfishness, and loyalty that extended even to society members unknown to them but avoided relations with outsiders whom they considered immoral. These principles were epitomized in dramatic stories of emblematic friendship, most famously in the tale of Damon and Phintias (or Pythias), whose unswerving loyalty, discussed below, translated into physical interchangeability. The adage *koina ta ton philon*, "Friends have all things in common," repeated by later writers on friendship, expresses the principle of *koinonia* practiced by the *mathematici*. The "jingle" *philotes isotes* may also have referred to the society's practice of sharing property, but for later writers like Aristotle, it encapsulates the requirement of similar status, virtue, and temperament for the perfect friendship.

Other classical writers attributed to Pythagoras the popular image of the friend as a "second self" and the idea that in friendship, many become one. Because he envisioned friendship extending "to all," Pythagoras is said to have advanced a more humanitarian ideal of association—*philanthropia*, "the love of many"—than that which prevailed in Greek thought (C. White 19). His practice, to the extent we can determine it, implied that intimate relations of choice and mutuality best created the conditions under which humans could achieve "some kind of mingling and union with God, and . . . communion with intellect and with the divine soul. For," Iamblichus concludes in chapter 33, "no one could find anything better, either in words spoken or in ways of life practiced, than this kind of friendship. For I think that all the goods of friendship are embraced by it" (235). It is not surprising that the Neoplatonism of Iamblichus was a strong influence on early Christian thought.

By the time of Socrates, an ideal of friendship emerged as a primary personal connection that was separate from the exchange relations of marriage and commerce and vitally concerned the moral character and disinterested actions of the partners. This view of *philia* as a primarily affective affiliation revises the predominant view of classical scholarship, which holds that the Greeks understood friendship as a broadly applicable affiliation, deeply embedded in economic relations, while the Romans understood it in a narrowly political sense, shorn of emotion. Classicist David Konstan counters that despite cultural differences like the inseparability of economics and interpersonal relations and divergent notions of selfhood, Greek and Roman writers recognized a "domain of human sympathy" analogous to modern conceptions in which a specific facet of friendship operates. He makes this case philologically, distinguishing the broad meaning of the abstract noun *philia*, which like the verb *philein* connotes love and affection, from the concrete noun *philos* (plural: *philoi*), which means "friend" in a specific and restricted sense (and is not to be confused with the adjective *philos*, which when applied to family members means "dear") (*Friendship* 55–56).

The drama of the period, focusing on the lives of the Greek elite, illustrates the multiple meanings of friendship but also offers an example of dyadic male friendship that becomes as proverbial as the love of the Homeric heroes or Alexander and Hephaestion. In a tense scene from Euripides' *Orestes*, Orestes and his sister Electra, fearing Menelaus's vengeance for the murder of their mother Clytemnestra, resign themselves to suicide. Electra portrays their sibling connection with the words and imagery of *philia*, calling Orestes "[m]y dearest, you who have a name that sounds most loved and sweet to your sister, partner in one soul with her!" (1045–46). They are interrupted by Pylades, Orestes' childhood companion and comrade in war and matricide, to whom he has betrothed Electra "from a deep regard for [Pylades'] companionship" (1080), thus closing the circle of kin and friends. Bound by love and honor as well as by obligation, since he regards Electra as a wife, Pylades invents a plot to save them all. And when Pylades refuses to part from his friend, even in adversity, misfortune, and death (1095), Orestes extols the immeasurable value of intimate friendship between virtuous men: "Ah! there is nothing better than a trusty friend, neither wealth nor monarchy; a crowd of people is of no account in exchange for a noble friend" (1155).

In the *Lysis*, an early dialogue and the only one that focuses specifically on friendship, Plato depicts Socrates as failing to define the concept, though he declares his lifelong "passion" for "possessing" friends (Pakaluk, *Other Selves* 12). The dramatic setting of this dialogue is revealing. On his way from "the Academy straight to the Lyceum," Socrates is waylaid by Hippothales, an older man who insists that they stop at a new wrestling school to see his current favorite, the young Lysis. Lovesick and ridiculed by his companions for obsessively singing "unoriginal" poetic odes about his *enamorato*, which Ctesippus compares to "old women's spinning-songs," Hippothales asks Socrates to "demonstrate" how an *erastes* should approach his *eromenos*. Socrates agrees, and meeting Lysis and his age-mate Menexenus, another son of the nobility, leads them through a dizzying consideration of many of the commonplaces about friendship in circulation at the time: that friends have everything in common, that friends are primarily useful to one another, whether it is better to love or be loved, whether like is drawn to like or the opposite, whether friendship is reserved to the good, and finally, what is the nature of desire. While Plato may be merely clearing the ground for his later discussions of eros, his presentation of friendship as "aporetic" may be the point: like Socrates, we are forced by the desire of others out of our direct route and must accept that there is no one definition of friendship, a possibility supported by the different meanings of the word ("dear," "fond," and "friend") Socrates implies throughout (Price 14, 6–7).[4]

Furthermore, the detour Socrates takes, drawn by Hippothales' embarrassing pederastic desire, leads him to a pair of young friends who, upon close examination, are equals in all things and thus have what Socrates calls, somewhat incongruously given their youth, the "experience" (as opposed to the knowledge) of friendship. In questioning the pair about their experience in order, ostensibly, to determine "how one person becomes the friend of another" (Pakaluk, *Other Selves* 13), Socrates enacts a form of pedagogy-as-friendship, which stands in stark contrast to Hippothales' "gross misuse of language and music" (6). It is important to note that in fifth century B.C.E. Athens, erotic friendship between men coexisted with heterosexual marriage and the fathering of children as a carefully regulated set of pedagogical, pederastic, and social structures that linked young boys of the ruling class to older men who shaped them into citizens. Such strictly complementary erotic relations were meant to lead to a higher spiritual communion and the contemplation of the highest Good through Beauty.[5] The view emerging from the *Lysis*, as well as from Plato's later dialogues and letters, equates male bonds with the process and end of philosophy itself. Thus, the "utility" of friends has a higher function in Plato's view. And desire, arising from lack or loss, becomes a search for what is *oikeion*—that is, closely related to and like the self (C. White 23). Still, friendship is not an end or good in itself, as it would be in Aristotle's thought. In perhaps the only concrete assertion in this inconclusive dialogue, Socrates tells the youths that men are drawn to friendship in search of a dimly remembered "first principle" or "first friend," which is "truly a friend," while all the rest "may be deceiving us, like so many phantoms of it" (Pakaluk, *Other Selves* 23).

Plato's student Aristotle rejected pederastic friendship for a vision of *philoi* no less intensely connected but who were relative equals of long acquaintance. He places his discussions of friendship at the heart of his ethical system because *philia* is inseparable from his vision of social and political organization. Not only does he argue that sociability is an inherent human trait, but he asserts that "city-states too are held together by friendship, and that lawmakers are more concerned about it than about the virtue of justice," because civic "concord" resembles and flows from the highest form of individual friendships. Thus, Aristotle states at the beginning of book 8 of the *Nicomachean Ethics*, "[I]f people are friends there is no need for the virtue of justice, yet if they are just they still need friendship. Furthermore, among [types of] just actions, that which is most just is thought to be characteristic of friendship" (*NE* 8:1, 1). Aristotle refers to the highest form of friendship, which I call "perfect" or "ideal" friendship, to be distinguished from two lesser types, friendship that produces something useful, such as cooperation, and friendship that produces pleasure, such as leisure and companionship.[6] The two lesser friendships are instrumental processes (*kinesis*), what Aristotle calls "accidental." By contrast, the perfect or ideal friendship, which might include the two lesser types, is an intrinsically valuable, ongoing activity (*energeia*) whose end is the realization of individual human potential ("happiness") as well as the generation and maintenance of "the highest good of all"—the city (Stern-Gillet 42–46).[7]

Emphasizing two crucial requirements for the achievement of friendship's highest form—voluntary, rational choice and an equality between friends that makes such choice possible—Aristotle offers a definition that has dominated the long philosophical and popular discourse: "a friend is another self" (*philos allos autos*), so that "Equality—and likeness—is friendship, and especially the likeness of those alike in virtue" (*NE* 9:4, 29; 8:8, 12).[8] Philosophers have taken this to mean that what Aristotle understands as self-love is the best model for love of another, but to understand this we need to recognize that Aristotle has a notion of selfhood and self-awareness that differs significantly from modern conceptions.[9]

Aristotle's unsystematic account of selfhood begins with sense perception and turns outward to the ethical and social, rather than proceeding from self-awareness, as in the Cartesian notion of subjectivity, and turning inward to the personal and introspective (Stern-Gillet 15–16, 22–23). People, in Aristotle's view, strive for *eudaimonia* (happiness, well-being) by exercising the active principle or *nous*, variously translated as "intellect," "understanding," and "spirit," in imitation of the divine. While God is completely self-sufficient (*autarkia*)—"Thought that thinks itself"—humans can achieve self-awareness only indirectly through mediation by an other (Aubenque 25). Thus, friendship provides cognitive access to self-awareness that leads to moral "actualization" as friends perceive and know together (Stern-Gillet 54–55).

In the *Magna Moralia*, Aristotle offers the analogy of the mirror: "And so, just as when wishing to behold our own faces we have seen them by looking upon a mirror, whenever we wish to know our own characters and personalities, we can recognize them by looking upon a friend; since the friend is, as we say, our 'second self'" (2:15.7, 683).[10] Likewise, Cicero argues in his treatise on friendship in the Roman world that the highest virtue and best life can be achieved only in society. Human sociability, he speculates, was the invention of "nature," which hoped "that since virtue when solitary cannot arrive at the highest kind of life, it might do so when joined and shared with a companion" (xxii.83; 81). Thus, Cicero concludes, "the man who keeps his eye on a true friend, keeps it, so to speak, on a model of himself" (vii.23; 56).

Furthermore, in the Aristotelian scheme, the quality of the object contemplated determines human self-awareness. To obtain the most accurate self-knowledge logically requires that we contemplate an other that is most nearly identical to ourselves. Since Aristotle regards virtue as the quality most necessary for moral development, the friend who will most accurately reflect oneself is someone equal or similar in virtue. These friends don't "complete each other," as do the divided halves of the man/woman in the myth of love Aristophanes relates in Plato's *Symposium*. Aristotle's perfect friendship differs significantly in that these friends choose to join themselves to each other, while the Platonic lovers have no control over their division or the urge that irresistibly draws them together (Heller 11). By contrast, good men love the good in themselves, as they should according to Aristotle, and they freely choose a friend who reflects a similar good. When such friends find each other—a relatively rare occurrence, by all accounts—they desire to live together and share everything in common and will risk their lives for one another, since the love of *philoi* desires above all the highest good humanly possible for the friend (*NE* 8:3, 4–5; 9:8, 36). "Desire," Agnes Heller concludes, "enters the world and the works of friendship through freedom" (11–12).

For these reasons, Aristotle and many thinkers up to the early modern period considered friendship the most dignified form of human connection, ennobling and tempering the self through a voluntary, mutual affiliation. Laelius, the speaker of Cicero's *De amicitia*, begins with a declaration that rings with the force of common sense and popular wisdom: "All I can do is to urge you to put friendship ahead of all other human concerns, for there is nothing so suited to man's nature, nothing that can mean so much to him, whether in good times or in bad" (v.17; 53). Next to this, heterosexual erotic love, which was thought to be marked by the inequality and, hence, asymmetry of the lovers, or heterosexual marriage, also asymmetrical on account of gender, are forms of imbalance, even insanity as the Stoic philosopher Seneca wryly observes: "Beyond question the feeling of a lover has in it something akin to friendship; one might call it friendship run mad" (Letter IX, 49). On this understanding, the ideals of self-sufficiency and friendship, which seem at first contradictory, prove to be mutually reinforcing.

For his understanding of equality and similarity, Aristotle draws on well-established tradition—Pythagoras and Empedocles—that advances resemblance and unity as central principles of human consciousness. According to some scholars, this tradition indicates a fear of difference and diversity in Greek thought.[11] In his discussions of equality as a physical characteristic, Aristotle asserts in the *Physics* (7:4) that things that are equal can be different and that all relations of equality are symmetrical. Here, as in the *Metaphysics*, he classes equality and inequality with the terms "like" and "same" and explains that "things whose substance is one are the same, whose quality is one are like, and whose quantity is one are equal" (von Leyden 27, 33).[12] In his discussion of friendship, Aristotle uses the term "equality" in relation to justice and to denote political standing and shared interests and links types of friendships found in "households" with different political forms.[13] For example, he argues: "[T]he various friendships and justice exist even in tyrannies, but to a small extent, while in democracies they do so to a greater extent, because many things are in common, since the citizens are equal" (*NE* 8:11, 17). Equality in this sense derives from the minimum property qualification (*timema*) for citizenship, which defines the political structure Aristotle calls "timocracy" or "constitutional government" where the propertied majority shares rule and from which democracy, where "everyone . . . is on the same level," "deviates only a little" (8:10, 15).

Although Aristotle considers timocracy and its deviation, democracy, the "worst" political forms, with monarchy the best and aristocracy second, he links them with the friendship type that arises among brothers, also synonymous with the bond between comrades in arms that is closest in description to the highest form of friendship.[14] Because brothers and comrades "have *everything* in common," they are not bound by rules of obligatory reciprocity but share equally, live together, and will die for each other (*NE* 8:9, 13; his emphasis).

In his elaboration of fraternal friendship, Aristotle lists the major features through which similarity can produce the requisite equality or parity: brothers "are equals and similar in age"—that is, of comparable social standing and close in years but clearly not identical. Aristotle cautions, however, that "brotherly friendship will fail to develop when they differ greatly in age" (*NE* 8:10, 15). This suggests that physical aspects of equality are at issue. Furthermore, "such people are usually alike in feelings and in character" (8:11, 16). Putting aside the verifiability of these claims—for brothers can certainly be of different social status and age, contrary dispositions, and opposite sentiments—likeness in these four physical and developmental aspects of life form the ground on which perfect friendship and, by association, democratic structures can be built. These are precisely the categories enumerated by Mrs. Leslie in Grace Aguilar's novel discussed in the opening of my introduction. They are echoed in several of the examples from the early American sources I will examine later in this chapter, except that those examples make gender sameness an explicit criterion.

Implicit in the classical notion of likeness is an essentialized understanding of gender. Although Aristotle cites the powerful love of a mother for her child as the very model of *philia* in which loving and wanting good for the other is more important than being loved and wanting good for oneself, he excludes women from the category of *philoi*, believing them constitutionally incapable of a fully rational, appetite-controlling intellect. Men and women, husband and wife, can achieve a friendship including and transcending utility and pleasure "on account of virtue as well, if they are good, since there is a virtue for each," but these virtues are not the same or equivalent (*NE* 8:12, 19). Rather, marital association "is the same as that in an aristocracy," where a superior group rules "with more good to the better, and assigning what is fitting to each" (8:11, 16). These spheres are clearly gendered: a husband rules "in virtue of his worth," which is determined by his biological sex, but "only over those things which a husband should, and whatever is appropriate for a wife he hands over to her." Wives have dominion in the domestic sphere by virtue of their biological capacities. If the husband oversteps his sphere in a marriage and "dominates in everything, he converts it into an oligarchy" where he rules not by his worth but by force (8:10, 15).

In the case of relations between unequals—between father and son, older and younger men, husband and wife, ruler and subject—Aristotle argues that a compensatory proportionality, or "loving [that] reflects the comparative worth of the friends," can operate to "equalize" the parties (*NE* 8:7, 10; *Nicomachean Ethics*, trans. Irwin 25). Each party gives and receives what is appropriate to them and their differing "worth." Because the "better" person is more "beneficial" to the lesser person, he loves less and the inferior person loves more. This proportional equality, however, does not operate in the same way even in the closely related areas of justice and friendship, and the difference reinforces the literal, perceptible character of equality in friendship.

In his explanation of this equalizing process, Aristotle observes that in matters of justice, equality based on worth is primary, while equality based on "quantity" is secondary, because such determinations tend to bring differences among people to the foreground in the interests of allotting "goods" (that is, rights or privileges) on the basis of merit. Such equality, however, is practical, expedient, and metaphorical—that is, based on substitutions, additions, and subtractions that produce equity. Thus, proportional worth only approximates the "equality in quantity" or strict equation of virtues, powers, abilities, and sentiments of the friends, approaching a measurable perfection and balance that is proper and necessary to (in Aristotle's words, "seems indeed to be characteristic of") perfect friendship.

This kind of equality tends to "close differences" in its strict accounting and equalizing of the attributes and actions of the friends (*NE* 8:7, 10–11, 95–96).

As many scholars note, Michel de Montaigne adverts to "the common agreement of the ancient schools" on the unfitness of women for ideal friendship, even though Pythagoras admitted them into his academy, presumably on an equal basis (138). While neither Plato nor Aristotle categorically excluded women from friendship, citizenship, or political rule, their human ideal, as Elizabeth Spelman observes, "is above all else a masculine ideal" (54). The ways in which these thinkers perceived women to be different from men—as less innately capable of reason and discipline—are also inimical to classically defined friendship. Exiled domestically and thrown together in male-dominated cultures, women formed relationships with each other, but these could not achieve the visibility or cultural importance of male bonds. A few instances of female and cross-gendered friendships between husbands and wives occur in later Greek romances of the first century C.E., but these depend upon an equality of status, age, and education and the mutual passion of the spouses characteristic of ideal friendship between men (Konstan, *Sexual Symmetry* 7; Hock 161).

In later elaborations of Aristotle's ideas, writers on friendship magnify the equality necessary for perfect friendship into a requirement that restricts it not only to people of the same sex and predominately to men but also to the deceased. The key text is Cicero's *De amicitia*, a treatise on friendship written around 44 B.C.E. during his retirement from public life and after the fall of the Roman Republic. In this dramatic dialogue, Cicero claims to be transmitting his recollection of a conversation with his teacher and role model Q. Mucius Scaevola, who, on the occasion of several highly visible, politically motivated deaths, recalled a conversation *he* had had as a young man with his father-in-law, Gaius Laelius (second century B.C.E.), a Roman general and statesman. Laelius, who had been trained in Stoic philosophy, is the speaker of Cicero's dialogue, which is set just after the untimely death of Scipio Africanus, Laelius's military comrade and lifelong friend.

Through this complicated dramatic framework, Cicero suffuses a topic popular in Greek thought from which he borrowed liberally with a deep yearning for and idealizing of the absent beloved friend and personal/political concord that have come to define the discourse. The murderous political intrigues and the loss of republicanism against which it is set only enhance the "true and perfect" nature of this exemplary connection (vi.22; 56). The dialogue amplifies several key Aristotelian ideas about friendship, such as its requirement of similar aristocratic rank, temperament, and virtue, and repeats Aristotle's familiar formulation with an added emphasis on the virtuality of equality and merger: "[T]he true friend is, so to speak, a second self. . . . [T]hey become virtually one person instead of two" (xxi.80–81; 80). As Eleanor Winsor Leach points out, in discussing these commonplaces Cicero uses both the language of resemblance (*similitudo*) and the language of doubling (*alter idem*) (12). The "weakness" of women and their need for "protection" from rather than for spiritual mutuality with men prevent their inclusion in such a lofty enterprise (xiii.46; 67).

Centuries later, in the late sixteenth century, Montaigne crafts a romanticized version of Ciceronian friendship discourse in which "distance came to seem a permanent, almost a constitutive, element of friendship" (Weller 504). Montaigne places his essay "De l'amitié" about his "sovereign and masterful" connection with the deceased writer Étienne de La Boétie at the precise center of a collection of essays whose decidedly modern purpose was self-disclosure and self-perpetuation. Thoroughly familiar with the ideas of Aristotle, Cicero, and Seneca, Montaigne protests that "the very discourses that antiquity has left us on this subject seem weak compared with the feelings I have" (143). The key term here that makes this an early modern text is "feelings."

Friendship, Montaigne asserts, is the ultimate act of an unconstrained will, so that kinship relations implying "natural" obligation do not qualify. Such friends are not merely bonded but "fused" and "confused"; their "souls mingle and blend with each other so completely that they efface the seam that joined them, and cannot find it again" (139). But there is also a rapturous, erotically charged, consuming violence in this ineluctable force "which, having seized my whole will, led it to plunge and lose itself in his; which, having seized his whole will, led it to plunge and lose itself in mine, with equal hunger, equal rivalry" (139). While Montaigne does not completely rule out the possibility of cross-gender or female friendships, he declares that at the present moment, "the ordinary capacity of women is inadequate for that communion and fellowship which is the nurse [*nourrisse*] of this sacred bond; nor does their soul seem firm enough to endure the strain of so tight and durable a knot" (138). Despite women's current spiritual infirmity, the physically nurturing capacities specific to female anatomy provide Montaigne, as Aristotle, with a figure for an intensely spiritual, melancholic, and exclusively masculine friendship. In the context of this prevailing discourse, striving for the ideal renders women's friendships acts of resistance to assumptions of female difference and inferiority.

Because women are not equal with—that is, not like—men, they cannot function as the mirrors that accurately reflect a man's virtue. This failure, in Virginia

Woolf's acerbic analysis, has been instrumental to the very progress of civilization: "Women," she observes dryly, "have served all these centuries as looking glasses possessing the magic and delicious power of reflecting the figure of man at twice its natural size. Without that power probably the earth would still be swamp and jungle" (35). It is not coincidental that Aristotle's figure of the friend as mirror for the self plays on the double meaning of "reflection" as thought on the one hand and as resemblance or likeness on the other. The psychic symbiosis that for Aristotle signals an intellectual and affective equality, even despite obvious differences, is expressed as a visual likeness and interchangeability that serves to discourage friendship across differences, not only of gender, but also of class and ethnicity. As I mentioned earlier, this tendency appears in the early Homeric accounts of friendship where, for example, the way Achilles' immortal armor perfectly fit his comrade and squire Patroclus expresses the perfect consonance of their minds and hearts, despite their inequality in lineage and strength (*Iliad*, book 16). Patroclus dons this armor when he enters the battlefield before the walls of Troy to fight and die in Achilles' stead. When Hector, the foremost Trojan warrior, kills Patroclus, strips the famed armor from his dead body, and dons the armor himself, he requires divine intervention from Jove and Mars to fill it. Hector's literal unfitness for Achilles' armor signifies his psychological and spiritual dissonance with the Greek warrior-comrades (book 17; Stern-Gillet 16).

Not just resemblance or likeness but the interchangeability of friends becomes the signifier of their perfect connection. This is illustrated in the well-known emblematic story of the Pythagoreans Damon and Phintias, recounted by Iamblichus, who draws on earlier sources who claim to have heard it directly from Dionysius, the deposed king of Sicily and one of the participants. Egged on by jealous "associates," this local tyrant unfairly accuses Phintias of plotting against him and sentences him to death in order to test the Pythagoreans' legendary "dignity, pretended trustworthiness, and freedom from emotion" (Iamblichus 231).

Phintias calmly accepts the sentence, asking only "the rest of the day to settle both his own affairs and those of Damon. For these men lived together and shared all things, but Phintias, being older, had taken on himself the main management of the household"; he appoints Damon as his substitute and "security." Dionysius is amazed that anyone would agree "to become a security for death," but Damon readily agrees, amid the jeers of the false accusers. When Phintias faithfully returns at sunset to suffer his fate, "all were astonished and subdued." Moved by this display of loyalty and trust, Dionysius commutes Phintias's sentence and begs to be included in such a remarkable friendship, but the two Pythagoreans refuse on account of the tyrant's immorality (231).

Iamblichus cites this story to illustrate the importance of selecting friends carefully and the Pythagoreans' strict avoidance of affiliation with outsiders (229). Striking is the representation of "communalism," which Iamblichus invokes in its proverbial form (the men "lived together and shared all things") but apparently also applies to a pair of men of different ages and divergent responsibilities. Despite these inequalities, perfect friendship allows one person to substitute, even to the death, for the other.

In another version of the story, included by the first century C.E. historian Valerius Maximus in his collection *De Amicitiae Vinculo*, a compilation popular in the Middle Ages, the writer does not even specify who is arrested and who stands security, nor does he mention the men's difference in age. The friends, who are mere abstractions and representatives of Pythagorean practice, have become truly interchangeable while the friendship itself is held up as a heroic ideal. In contrast to Iamblichus, Maximus draws a moral that emphasizes "the powers of friendship . . . to humanize cruelty, . . . to which powers almost as much veneration is due as to the cult of the immortal gods" who ensure "public safety," because on friendship "does private happiness depend" (book 4, ch. 7; qtd. in Carpenter 33–34).

Cicero cites an even more extreme case of interchangeability in *De amicitia* when Laelius recalls a Roman audience's wild applause during the performance of a play by his friend the playwright Marcus Pacuvius that enacted the exemplary friendship of Orestes and Pylades discussed above. In Pacuvius's version of the Greek tragedy, when Orestes is sentenced to death for killing his mother, he and Pylades are captured and brought before the king, who "did not know which man was Orestes; thereupon, Pylades declared that he was Orestes, so that he might die in Orestes's place; but Orestes insisted that *he* was Orestes, as indeed he was" (vii.24; 57). The resemblance, interchangeability, and willingness of friends to sacrifice themselves for each other become dominant features of chivalric romance and set pieces in friendship narratives. James Fenimore Cooper, for example, includes a similar scenario in *The Last of the Mohicans*, the subject of chapter 4, in which the impetuous young American major, Duncan Heyward, thinking to protect Hawk-eye from his enemies, claims to be the famed sharpshooter. A spectacular display of marksmanship identifies the men—in both senses of this word—that is, simultaneously distinguishing them and confirming their true identities but also more nearly con/fusing and aligning them in terms of wilderness "gifts" and loyalties (295–300). In Cicero's treatment, Laelius declares emphatically that the Roman audience's unstinting approbation of the nobility of *amicitia* "is all I can tell you of my feelings about friendship" (vii.24; 57).

Christian Fellowship, Medieval Chivalry, and Renaissance Similitude

The moral nature of classical friendship appealed to early Christian thinkers who drew heavily on classical discourses, transposing earthly friendship to a spiritual plane. In terms of individual relationships, the emphasis of Christian friendship shifted significantly from rational desire and shared virtue to affective affinity and spiritual intimacy. However, Christian beliefs produced a more important change, directing believers away from exclusive dyadic friendships to a broader fellowship of the faithful and, finally, in a move reminiscent of the pre-Socratic idea of *philanthropia*, to a "brotherhood" with all humanity. Christian doctrine takes this to its logical conclusion, commanding us to love our enemies, a form of affection outside the pale of classical friendship.

The heady millennial atmosphere of the early church fueled the displacement of restrained dyadic friendship. There, fanaticism promoted an emotionally solidifying identification in a lay following under continual threat. Furthermore, sin, innate depravity, and injunctions to humility rendered human virtue completely dependent on the active work of God; thus, Christianity valued affiliations based not on the recognition of merit or deserts but on an imitation of God's free, equal, and boundless love to all. Early Christianity discouraged "particular" relationships, advocating a universal love enunciated in Jesus' "Golden Rule" and denoted by the use of the words *caritas* (dearness or charity) and *agape* (affection) rather than *philia* or *amicitia* and figured as "fellowship" or "brotherhood."[15]

Jesus himself echoed Greek and Roman thought by valuing friendship over marriage or kinship but routed the "love" of his band of male disciples for each other through his love for them: "This is my commandment, That ye love one another, as I have loved you. Greater love hath no man than this, that a man lay down his life for his friends" (John 15:12–13).[16] Thus, loving each other became a sign of loving God. Unlike *philia* or *amicitia*, *agape* did not require reciprocity or mutuality but forgiveness and bringing others to an experience of it in an expectation of its perfection in the hereafter. And because all people were, theoretically, equal in the eyes of God, social and moral inequalities did not have the same inhibiting force.

Furthermore, the early Christian sexual ethic, which tolerated marriage as necessary in the fallen state, proscribed extramarital relations and extolled celibacy, chastity, and even virginity, encouraging sex-segregated groups like monasteries and nunneries in which homosocial relations flourished. Though Augustine embraced Cicero's celebrated definition of friendship—*omnium divinarum humanarumque rerum cum benevolentia et caritae consensio* (complete sympathy in all matters divine and human with goodwill and affection [vi.21])—and applauded its reverent spirit, he nevertheless regarded individual friendships as pale imitations of the ultimate, always unequal friendship with God (C. White 50).[17] These were not primarily affectionate relations but spiritual bonds in which partners shared confessions of faith and the endless struggle to overcome earthly ties, like kinship, erotic love, and "worldly" friendships, that obscured the spiritual goal of union with the divine.

Two great medieval works on friendship that strive to marry classical and Christian ideas offer important background for the discussion in chapter 2 of the signal American text, John Winthrop's "A Modell of Christian Charitie." Deeply affected in his youth by his reading of *De amicitia*, a twelfth-century Cistercian abbot named Aelred of Rievaulx wrote a treatise entitled *De spiritali amicitia* (Of Spiritual Friendship) that attempts to define friendship for a Christian society. Aelred echoes the pagan writer he so admired in restricting "spiritual friendship" to the "just" and defining it as "born of a similarity in life, morals, and pursuits, that is, a mutual conformity in matters human and divine united with benevolence and charity" (par. 45, 60–61). The difference, he informs his fellow monk and interlocutor in the opening line of the treatise, is that two are never just two: "Here we are, you and I, and I hope a third, Christ, is in our midst" (par. 1, 51). Christ is, simultaneously, the principle of "friendship"—eternal, unconditional, disinterested love—and its fulfillment. Thus, Christian friendship is, paradoxically, unattainable except by Christ but also widely accessible, because everyone can and should aspire to that ideal (Pakaluk, *Other Selves* 129).

Furthermore, Aelred makes the important distinction, reinforced later by Thomas Aquinas, between friendship and the religious practice of charity that shapes the idea of a Christian "commonwealth." He begins by explaining that God created Eve "from the very substance of the man" to "teach that human beings are equal . . . and that there is in human affairs neither a superior nor an inferior, a characteristic of true friendship" (par. 57, 63). But the Fall "caused private good to take precedence over the common weal," corrupting friendship that formerly extended to all but is thereafter restricted to the faithful few. Charity, or universal love, pertains to everyone else, even sinners and enemies to whom "good" persons could never be linked in bonds of friendship (par. 58, 63–64). For Aelred, spiritual friendships are the only "true" friendships, producing "sweetness," the almost bodily or sensory experience of divine unity, and promoting intimacy between people—an intersubjective space in which "we can fearlessly entrust our heart and all its secrets" (par. 32, 58). This notion of interpersonal intimacy assumes an internal psychic realm that allows for the privatizing and romanticizing of friendship.

Aquinas, the eminent thirteenth-century theologian, extends the discussion of love and charity in the second part of his monumental *Summa Theologiae*, locating it specifically in the context of Aristotle's ideas on friendship from books 8 and 9 of the *Nicomachean Ethics*, which he cites extensively. He argues that charity is based on "communication" or "conversation," imperfect in its earthly form, with God. Thus, "charity is the friendship of man for God" and "extends to sinners, whom, out of charity, we love for God's sake" (Pakaluk, *Other Selves* 172–73). A particular kind of vicarious friendship, routed through God, becomes the anchor and guide of a Christian's moral life (148).

While monks wrote to each other in a fairly unrestrained language of spiritual love, another influential discourse of male homosocial bonding arose in the Middle Ages between warrior knights. Emerging as an honor code of the ruling class, chivalry took three distinct and competing forms: military, religious, and courtly, each with its specific literary expression. Warrior knighthood, celebrated in the early *Chansons de geste* and epitomized by the miraculous physical resemblance and beauty of the legendary Ami and Amile, privileged martial skills and exalted epic qualities like heroism, loyalty, and male camaraderie (Langer 234). Roland and Oliver, for example, are one of many pairs of knights attending King Charlemagne in the *Song of Roland*, an anonymous mid-eleventh-century French epic. Their deep love, expressed particularly in Roland's mourning for his fallen comrade, echoes the paradigmatic bond of the Homeric heroes Achilles and Patroclus.

By the fourteenth century, the popular romance of *Amadis de Gaule* was circulating through Europe and featured a similar friendship between Amadis and his brother Galaor. In an episode recalling the scene with Orestes and Pylades from Euripides' play discussed above, the French queen seats the brothers next to each other and asks the ladies of the court to tell them apart. Although they do differ slightly, these details are diminished by "the equalizing effect of knightly perfection," a quality also operating in other medieval romances that feature friends who are not brothers (Langer 233–34). A version of the common doppelgänger motif but "without anxiety," this doubling allows for heroic feats and "functions as a literalization of the equality that moral philosophy requires of friends" (235).

Wary of the worldliness of this model of male affiliation, the church advanced an ideal of knighthood that embraced the virtues of "chastity, austerity, humility, and righteousness" (Richards 97). Poems and legends about King Arthur, the

Knights Templar, and the quest for the Holy Grail exemplify this tradition. Lastly, a school of courtly love emerged to moderate the martial temper of knightly chivalry, whose object was winning the love of a noble, usually unattainable lady. Embodied in the romance genre and shaping prevailing Western traditions of romantic love, this heterosexual version of chaste chivalry co-existed alongside a homosocial ideal of male friendship.

At the end of the Middle Ages, writers attempted to meld these three traditions into a vision of perfect knighthood, which returns in the romantic revival of the nineteenth century, for example, in the novels of Sir Walter Scott and the poetry of Alfred Tennyson, influential touchstones of Victorian masculinity.[18] Cultural ideals of a spiritual love between men persist, according to Jeffrey Richards, because they are products of "an exclusively or largely male-dominated and male-centered society" (98).

The extensive Renaissance discourse on friendship that emerged from medieval chivalry and Christian monastic traditions revives and expands classical formulations. Erasmus, who brought classical learning to Europe, begins his collection of over four thousand adages with the maxim "Amicorum communia omnia" (Between friends all is common), remarking that "[s]ince there is nothing more wholesome or more generally accepted than this proverb, it seemed good to place it as a favorable omen at the head of this collection of adages" (*Adages* 29). His second entry is the familiar formula "Amicitia aequalitas. Amicus alter ipse" (Friendship is equality. A friend is another self) (29–50), which he ascribes to Pythagoras, equates with the Hebrew "law" commanding "us to love our neighbor as ourselves," and observes that Aristotle quotes it as "proverbial in his [*Nicomachean*] *Ethics*, book 9" (31). This classical formulation, as Laurie Shannon finds, was widely disseminated in early modern English culture and especially among the middle and upper classes through the pervasive use of Cicero's *De amicitia* as a "gateway text in Latin learning" both for its style and exemplary humanist morality (*Sovereign Amity* 27–28). Young boys studying a classical curriculum in the Tudor era would have been initiated into Latin grammar and friendship doctrine almost simultaneously.

These pedagogical and "interpellating structures" locate a rhetoric of likeness at the very core of Renaissance self-fashioning that reflects the dominant sixteenth-century episteme Michel Foucault describes as "resemblance" and Shannon translates into the affective social structures of "homonormativity" (*Order of Things* 17; *Sovereign Amity* 22, 19). For Renaissance thinkers, heterosexual love and marriage constituted something of "an intellectual problem: the mixing of disparate kinds" —here, genders—which they believed had a diluting effect on identity (Shannon,

Sovereign Amity 64). Writers often portrayed erotic love as an invasive, infecting, and disintegrative force and considered marriage a set of legal constraints that yoked spouses in unequal, unfulfilling, and, according to John Milton, "unmanly" relations (Shannon, *Sovereign Amity* 65–67; Luxon 128–29).

By contrast, homosocial friendship was thought to encourage tempered self-sufficiency, which Shannon punningly calls "sovereignty," and strengthen gender identity among elite men who then voluntarily consented to "bind," "knit," and "knot" themselves to another equally sovereign self in the "practice" of amity.[19] Their earliest schooling exposed young men of the educated classes to classical friendship doctrine in which they recognized its "laws" about virtue, honor, and mutuality as codes they could use to fashion and judge selves.[20] The law governing changing commercial relations in this period contributed to this trend. A legal contract required some kind of parity or similarity between its parties to ensure their competence to enter and understand the contract and their mutual consent to its terms. The parties would then seal the contract, agreement, or treaty with a "good faith" handshake.

This gesture originated in the early worship of Mithras, a Persian god whose name derives from the Indo-European root *mihr*, which means both "friend" and "contract" (D. Cooper 2–3). Believed to represent a system of ethics that encouraged brotherhood, Mithras became the patron of soldiers who developed the handshake as a token of friendship to indicate that one was unarmed. When Mithras later entered the Roman pantheon as a guardian of contracts, oaths, and pledges, Roman soldiers spread the handshake gesture throughout the Mediterranean and Europe (Vermaseren 96–97). Two emblems from George Wither's collection, published in London in 1635, illustrate the association of the hand-clasp and the two major and competing forms of social affiliation. The emblem for *Bona fide* (good faith) shows hands clasped around a flaming and crowned heart as an image for friendship conceived as the willing connection of two loving and sovereign selves (figure 3; Shannon, *Sovereign Amity* 38–39). But Wither also includes a strikingly similar image for the binding union of heterosexual marriage, suggesting the closeness of these forms of affiliation for early modern readers. Emblem 37, *Jusque a la mort* (until death), depicts hands emerging from clouds on either side, as in *Bona fide*, clasped over a flaming heart and topped by a death's head (figure 4). In this emblem, however, the hands are clearly gendered by the different cuffs, one plain and one ruffled (99).

Shannon argues for a generous reading of the central friendship trope of similarity. We should understand it not in the condemnatory terms of contemporary philosophical critiques of identity and sameness, where the equality of some

That's Friendſhip, *and* true-love, *indeed,*
Which firme abides, in time of need.

ILLVSTR. XXIX.   *Book.* 4

Figure 3. *Bona fide.* From George Wither, *A Collection of Emblemes, Ancient and Modern* (London: A. Mathewes, 1635), 237; courtesy of Dartmouth College Library.

requires the subordination of others. Rather, we should try to grasp the opportunities such rhetoric afforded early modern subjects: to imagine a secular, preliberal, private, and "sovereign" self, whose freely consenting relations with a similar, self-determining other forms a "micropolity" of affiliation without subordination that prefigures democratic relations (*Sovereign Amity* 21).

While Renaissance similitude links friendship with consensual, contractual, and democratic practices, it also emphasizes the literal aspects of likeness as "a wonder-generating physical fact" (Shannon, *Sovereign Amity* 43). This "fact," by encouraging interchangeability, inhibits differences. To expand on the example I

Figure 4. *Jusque a la mort*. From George Wither, *A Collection of Emblemes, Ancient and Modern* (London: A. Mathewes, 1635), 99; courtesy of Dartmouth College Library.

mentioned earlier, when Thomas Elyot enumerates the qualities of mind and body requisite for gentlemen of the ruling class in the first educational treatise published in England in 1531, he places at its center what he calls "[t]he true discription of amitie or frendship" (161). Elyot cites Cicero's definition, which he paraphrases as "a parfecte consent of all thinges appertayninge as well to god as to man, with bene-uolence and charitie" (162). But he augments it with his own expanded understanding that more nearly echoes Aristotelian notions: "frendshippe" is "a blessed and stable connexion of sondrie willes, makinge of two persones one in hauinge and suffringe . . . properly named of Philosophers the other I" (164).

Elyot then caps the familiar stories of "Horestes and Pilades" and "Piteas and Damon" with a detailed retelling of the exemplary tale of Titus and Gysippus. Brought together as boys, their "wonderful" physical likeness "in yeres, but also in stature, proporcion of body, fauour, and colur of visage, countenaunce & speche," not only prevents their "proper parentes" from discerning one from the other but *precedes* their acquaintance and *prepares* them for "such a mutuall affection, that their willes and appetites daily more and more so confederated them selfs" into indistinguishable, interchangeable doubles (166–67). Unlike twins, who passively bear a "natural" but incidental likeness, friends actively choose to fuse and, in Montaigne's words, "confuse" their wills, uniting parts of a whole that nature has perversely produced as separate parts. Elyot describes this process in political terms, as an intersubjective "confederation," a mutual alliance of equalized parts that is the initial structural embodiment of the United States.

The "consent," "confusion," "co(n)founding" of selves enacted in friendship, though distinguished from twinship by active choice, in later eras retain a strong, androcentric sense of kinship and interchangeability. By the eighteenth century, "fraternity," friendship's specifically gendered (though universally applied) term, famously constituted the end of the democratic process in which "liberty" and "equality" were the means (W. McWilliams 5). In the late nineteenth century, Walt Whitman adopts the early modern period's homonormative logic in "Democratic Vistas," when he anchors his radical understanding of mass governance in the "threads of manly friendship, fond and loving, pure and sweet, strong and life-long": "It is to the development, identification, and general prevalence of that fervid comradeship, (the adhesive love, at least rivaling the amative love hitherto possessing imaginative literature, if not going beyond it,) that I look for the counterbalance and offset of our materialistic and vulgar American democracy, and for the spiritualization thereof." In unabashedly passionate language, Whitman dreams of a spiritualizing "comradeship" that will rescue imaginative literature from its current unhealthy obsession with "amative love," "not only giving tone to individual character, and making it unprecedently emotional, muscular, heroic, and refined, but having the deepest relations to general politics." Finally, the "adhesiveness" that binds men to each other becomes itself interchangeable with, and the exclusively male generative source of, democracy: "I say democracy infers such loving comradeship, as its most inevitable twin or counterpart, without which it will be incomplete, in vain, and incapable of perpetuating itself" (2:414–15).[21]

Tribal (Br)Otherhood and Sympathy/Sentiment

Renaissance friendship discourses represent the flowering of an earlier, exclusive form of social affiliation Benjamin Nelson calls "tribal brotherhood" as well as the beginning of its eventual demise through universalization. Widening theological interpretations of the Deuteronomic law (23:19–20), which forbade the ancient Hebrews from charging interest on loans to their "brothers" but allowed it for "strangers," offer a model of egalitarian "fraternalism" adopted by kin groups in early European society. This type of social organization is characterized by a tradition of the chivalric devotion of pairs of male friends, which, along with arranged marriages, were the mortar of clan and aristocratic alliances.

Nelson's remarkable argument reveals the imbrication of this tradition of male friendship with socioeconomics. The ancient friendship doctrine that celebrates the interchangeability of Orestes and Pylades or Damon and Phintias translates into the tradition of "substitutes" in settling debts of honor through dueling as well as in the practice of men standing surety for one another in business transactions, as Antonio does for Bassanio in Shakespeare's *The Merchant of Venice*. In the early modern period, standing surety came under sharp attack, for different reasons, by Protestant reformers like Martin Luther and John Calvin and by representatives of the emerging merchant classes like Sir Walter Raleigh. These critiques were part of a larger shift Nelson discerns from the exclusive fraternalism of "tribal brotherhood" through a medieval Christian program of "universal brotherhood" based in the "Golden Rule" to a precapitalist notion of "universal otherhood," which stressed the rational and commercial pursuit of individual gain. The decentering of inherited status and consequent "expansion" of the moral community results, as Alexis de Tocqueville also perceived about the effects of "democracy in America," in a thinning of the moral bond because, as Nelson concludes, "all men have been becoming brothers by becoming equally others" (136).[22]

Taking his cue from Max Weber, Nelson blames the rise of "otherhood" on the dependence of emerging capitalist systems on stable and consistent social "rules" (xxiv). By the eighteenth century, features of classical friendship modified by the Christian notion of universal charity infused international law and became the standard language of treaties and negotiations (155). This was part of a quickly spreading "spirit of benevolence" promulgated by Scottish Enlightenment thinkers whose views on friendship, according to sociologist Alan Silver, diverged considerably from Nelson's picture of "universal otherhood." David Hume, a leading light among Scottish thinkers, for example, distinguishes between two forms of commerce: "interested" exchanges in which persons stood to gain or lose economically, and "disinterested" relations of sympathy and affection in which affiliation is its own reward (Silver 1480). Until the eighteenth century, both of these meanings co-existed in the definition of friendship, which could signify the relationship with a patron or sponsor, close or distant kin, or associates and advisors, as well as ties of warm affection (1487).

By midcentury, however, Dr. Johnson defines "friend" in personal and private —that is, modern—terms, as someone "with whom to compare minds and cherish private virtues" (Stone 79). According to thinkers like Hume and Adam Smith, it is the advent of commercial—that is, precapitalist—society that allows for the shift by confining economic relations of exchange to the market, thereby encouraging the flourishing of an independent moral realm, which frees "disinterested" friend-ships from the world of clan, patronage, obligation, or necessity. The Scots considered such "liberated" friendships to be morally superior to the honor-bound affiliation of "tribal brotherhood" because they are voluntary and inclu-sive, based on a "natural sympathy" that, according to Smith, "need not be confined to a single person but may safely embrace all the wise and virtuous, with whom we have been long and intimately acquainted" (224–25; Silver 1481).[23]

Smith's *The Theory of Moral Sentiments* (1759) is a work that, according to Julie Ellison, "confirms the affective ideals of republican discourse" (*Cato's Tears* 10). On its very first page, Smith lays out the problem: despite charges of selfish-ness, "man" harbors "principles" of sociability, later identified as the need for recognition, consolation, and approbation, "which interest him in the fortune of others, and render their happiness necessary to him, though he derives nothing from it, except the pleasure of seeing it" (9). Smith establishes the importance—in fact, the dominance—of visuality and spectacle from the outset. However, he continues, "we have no immediate experience of what other men feel . . . but by conceiving what we ourselves should feel in the like situation" (9). Thus, "the imagination" plays a crucial role in allowing us to "place ourselves in his situation . . . enter as it were into his body and become in some measure the same person with him" (9)—that is, we imaginatively experience a bodily likeness with another person that amounts to interchangeability based on a fantasy of affect. Despite this radical process of identification—"changing places in fancy with the sufferer"— we remain anchored in our separate selves, since "it is the impressions of our own senses only, not those of his, which our imaginations copy" (9). This difference produces the mediating and tempering effects of sympathy.

Smith continues to elaborate this complicated scenario of interdependent fan-tasies. As we try, but fail, to fully imagine the emotions of an other, even an intimate, "he" tries to imagine what we think "he" must be feeling and so "is constantly led to imagine in what manner he would be affected if he was only one of the spectators of his own situation" (22). In Smith's theory, the installation of internal distance and difference, of the "impartial spectator" or social conscience within consciousness, helps to moderate passions and encourage social "concord" but also constitutes experience as performance and makes it vulnerable to panoptic surveillance; we are always watching ourselves or imagining ourselves being watched.[24] Rather than objectifying the self, however, according to Smith this impartiality encourages us to see ourselves as others would—to become, in the language of amity, our own friend and moderating, corrective force. Furthermore, as a spectator of what Smith calls the "benevolent affections" in life or in art, we imaginatively enter into the feelings of the friend as well as of the persons who are the object of friendship and so experience a "redoubled" dose of sympathy (38).[25] Thus, reading about friendship, and sharing the experience of reading about friendship, constitutes a crucial element in the broad, cohesion-producing operations of sympathetic exchange.

Race and Friendship

This sympathizing sensibility, according to Ellison, found ready and powerful expression in dramatic spectacles and poetic accounts produced during the long eighteenth century in Britain. In particular, she argues that writers dramatized "cross-racial imperial relationships" in which characters from different cultures—most frequently European and Amerindian or African—struggle with inequality and "the legitimating rhetoric that evokes friendship between peers" (*Cato's Tears* 98). There is evidence, however, that from the very beginning of Europe's contact with the Americas, writers deployed various discourses of conquest grounded in classical notions of friendship and in what I call its obverse, a theory of natural slavery.

Tzvetan Todorov, for example, lays out the contradictory views entertained by Christopher Columbus of the native peoples he encountered on his voyages to the Caribbean, ideas shared by many people in Europe. The Indians were either "noble savages," gentle, innocent, and eager for conversion to Christianity, or "dirty dogs," lazy, ferocious, and fit only for enslavement. Both views, Todorov argues, "rest on a common basis, which is the failure to recognize the Indians, and the refusal to admit them as a subject having the same rights as oneself, but different" (49). We have seen that the early modern European mind, schooled in classical ideas of friendship, considered the equality of subjects synonymous with a notion of identification or mirroring that depends on a similarity bordering on sameness. According to Todorov, the perennial problems of equality, sameness, and difference also inform our own postmodern dilemma: "[W]e want equality without its compelling us to accept identity; but also difference without its degenerating into superiority/inferiority. We aspire to reap the benefits of the egalitarian model [democratic individualism] and of the hierarchic model [monarchic collectivity]; we aspire to rediscover the meaning of the social without losing the quality of the individual" (249). Thus, we study the history of cross-racial encounters in the New World in order to ask how we can find a "new way to experience alterity" that affirms the other's exteriority and recognizes the other as a subject in his or her own right (250).

A key moment in this history is the famous debate that took place in Valladolid, Spain, in 1550 over the question of "just war" and the morality of using force in the conversion of native peoples to Christianity. Ginés de Sepúlveda, the preeminent Aristotelian scholar of his time, drew his arguments from Aristotle's *Politics*, which he had translated into Latin. In book 1, chapter 5, of *Politics*, Aristotle explains that the theory of natural slavery originates "in the constitution of the universe," specifically that "the rule of the soul over the body, and of the mind and the rational element over the passionate, is natural and expedient." What follows from this is a "natural" principle of male superiority and dominance: "[T]he male is by nature superior, and the female inferior; and the one rules, and the other is ruled." The same gendered hierarchy extends to "the lower sort . . . those whose business is to use their body, and who can do nothing better. . . . For he who can be, and therefore is, another's, and he who participates in rational principle enough to apprehend, but not to have, such a principle, is a slave by nature" (1254b, 1132). Thus, natural slaves recognize and accept without question their need to be ruled and even welcome domination by those superior to them in reason.

This remarkable definition justified the Spaniards' use of the *Requerimiento*, an extraordinary document composed by the royal jurist Juan López Palacios Rubios around 1512.[26] Conquistadors were instructed to read the *Requerimiento* to the indigenous people they encountered, translated into their language and in the presence of a notary. Its promissory words, "we shall receive you in all love and charity" (Gibson 60), echo the friendship tropes of Christian fellowship. A swift acceptance of the document's terms won native auditors protection as vassals of the Spanish crown, while their "malicious" hesitation justified attack, enslavement, and murder.

Alvar Nuñez Cabeza de Vaca describes a scene at the end of his nine-year sojourn in the south and southwest of North America in which Melchior Diaz, the *alcalde mayor* or chief justice and civil official of the province of Culiacán, administers the *Requerimiento* through an interpreter to the assembled Indians. Diaz promises them "that the Christians [the conquistadors] would take them as brothers and treat them very well, and we would order them [the conquistadors] not to provoke them or take them out of their lands, but rather to be their great friends, but that if they did not want to do this, the Christians would treat them very badly and carry them off as slaves to other lands" (166). The Indians' immediate acceptance "occurred in the presence of the notary they had there and many other witnesses" (167). Supporters of Indian rights, like Bartolomé de Las Casas, discussed below, resolutely condemned the *Requerimiento* as a complete sham. However, its form and the stipulations of its performance (translated into the native tongue, witnessed and notarized like a contract) suggest that colonial policy-makers believed the Amerindians just rational enough to apprehend and accept the "natural" superiority of the Spanish crown and church in accordance with the Aristotelian definition of natural slavery.

Adopting Aristotelian principles, Sepúlveda declared political hierarchy to be the "natural" structure of human society and, using Aristotelian terms, declared Spanish rule over the Amerindians to be "the domination of perfection over imperfection, of force over weakness, of eminent virtue over vice" (*Democrates Alter* 20; qtd. in Todorov 152). Although Sepúlveda conceded that Aztec culture, the most advanced in Meso-America, contained what appeared to be "proofs" of civilization—public institutions such as extensive cities, appointed rulers, and commercial transactions—without having visited the New World he nevertheless concludes: "In wisdom, skill, virtue and humanity, these people are as inferior to the Spaniards as children are to adults and women to men; there is as great a difference between them as there is between savagery and forbearance, between violence and moderation, almost—I am inclined to say—as between monkeys and men" (*Democrates Alter* 33; qtd. in Todorov 153). According to this logic, Indians were the ontologically inferior term in a string of analogies that defined Indian men as infantile, feminized, savage, violent, and beastly. Thus, they were ineligible for natural or civil rights or friendship with European men; Indian women were doubly burdened and doubly ineligible. All deserved, even required, conquest and the imposition of the religion of "peace" and the "true faith."

The Dominican monk Las Casas, who first traveled to America in 1502 as a missionary and became one of the staunchest defenders of Indian rights, made the opposing case at Valladolid. In his five days of testimony, he rejected pagan philosophy and boldly asserted, "Aristotle, farewell! From Christ, the eternal

truth, we have the commandment 'You must love your neighbor as yourself' "
(*Apologia* 3; qtd. in Todorov 160). Under the Christian banner of the *potential*
equality of all people through their acceptance of faith, Las Casas attacked Sepúlveda's assertion of inherent good and evil, superiority and inferiority. Indians, he
argued, have the same "natural" rights as Europeans. Thus, he fiercely condemned the use of the *Requerimiento*, writing to Prince Philip in 1544, "All the
Indians to be found here are to be held as free: for in truth so they are, by the same
right as I myself am free" (qtd. in Todorov 162).

But this equality, as Todorov observes, is achieved only through the potentially
renovating operation of Christian faith. In his condemnation of Aristotle, Las
Casas failed to recognize that the biblical injunction to neighborly love he invoked
echoed Aristotle's pagan definition of spiritual friendship. The ontological "non-
difference" he advanced already assumed what Todorov calls "a kind of cultural
identity." While Sepúlveda's "prejudice of superiority" made knowledge of the
other impossible and large-scale genocide acceptable, Todorov finds Las Casas's
"prejudice of equality" a "greater obstacle" to knowledge of the other, one that is
perhaps "more attractive" but remains indisputably "colonialist" (165–167, 173).

Although the indefatigable Las Casas eventually discovers what Todorov calls
"perspectivism," a "higher form of egalitarianism" (192), a rhetoric of instrumental friendship enters Spanish colonialist discourse under the good friar's unwitting
sponsorship. In 1573, Juan de Ovando, the head of Spain's Council of the Indies,
drew up its definitive royal ordinances in the light of the Valladolid controversy,
recommending linguistic and amicable pretense in the service of "pacification":

Discoveries are not to be called conquests. Since we wish them to be carried
out peacefully and charitably, we do not want the use of the term "conquest" to
offer any excuse for the employment of force or the causing of injury to the
Indians. . . . [Erstwhile conquistadors] are to gather information about the
various tribes, languages and divisions of the Indians in the province and about
the lords whom they obey. They are to seek friendship with them through trade
and barter, showing them great love and tenderness and giving them objects to
which they will take a liking. Without displaying any greed for the possessions
of the Indians, they are to establish friendship and cooperation with the lords
and nobles who seem most likely to be of assistance in the pacification of the
land. . . . The preachers should ask for their children under the pretext of
teaching them and keep them as hostages; they should also persuade them to
build churches where they can teach so that they may be safer. By these and
other means are the Indians to be pacified and indoctrinated, but in no way are

they to be harmed, for all we seek is their welfare and their conversion. (qtd. in Todorov 173–74)

The rhetoric of peace, friendship, and Christian charity cynically advanced by Ovando encourages learning the natives' culture in order to eradicate it and stealing their children and thus their future—"benefits" that serve imperial designs as well as if not better than warfare and genocide.

Early modern French writing on New World encounters explicitly links colonialist discourses of friendship with Eurocentric insistence on Indian alterity and the consumerism of incipient capitalism (Bartolovich 207). Theorists call the structure of modern Western subjectivity emerging from these encounters "cultural cannibalism . . . the unethical reduction of the other to the status of 'me' or 'mine'" (Deutscher 162). The touchstone text in this tradition is Montaigne's "Des cannibales" (Of Cannibals, 1580). This French skeptic and intellectual was profoundly shaken by reports of the New World such as *Histoire d'un voyage faict en la terre du Bresil, autrement dite Amerique* (1578), penned by his countryman Jen de Léry, a Protestant who traveled to Brazil with the explorer Villegagnon. Léry's account records the shock he experienced witnessing the ritual cannibalism practiced by the Tupinamba Indians as well as the cannibalism of Europeans under duress in the New World. His account served as a source for Montaigne's essay, which holds up the American cannibal as a mirror for Europe and finds—a European cannibal. That is, by comparison with the idealized innocence and simplicity of the Tupinamba, the supposedly civilized culture of France appeared rife with violence, dogmatism, and unreflecting ethnocentrism. The fiercely defended Catholic doctrine of the "real presence" of God's body in the Eucharist and French Catholic persecution and genocide of the Huguenots lent weight to the charge.

For historiographer Michel de Certeau, Montaigne's account of the cannibalistic Tupinamba serves as "an allegory of the relation to the other in all its forms" (Freccero, "Toward" 365).[27] Certeau argues that while the European intellectual attempts to capture the exotic other in writing, a principal instrument of colonial mastery and of the production of knowledge, the Tupinamba described by Montaigne condemns French social inequities and corruption in speech that is "groundbreaking and organizing, pathfinding in its own space, it precedes us, moving, passing on. It is always ahead of us, and always escapes us" (*Heterologies* 78). This mobile "cannibalistic orality" serves the Western intellectual as a kind of Indian guide through the discursive wilderness and new epistemic territory opened up by cross-cultural contact. But in this guiding role, the other, with his powerful, threatening speech, faces exoticization and incorporation (cultural cannibalism) by the West (77). The problem for Montaigne and for European modernity is to innovate a noncannibalistic "ethic of writing" that recognizes the other's role in the constitution of his subjectivity while simultaneously acknowledging his separate and indigestible existence (78–79). This acknowledgment, for Certeau, grounds a modern metaphysics because, as he explains, "God and the cannibal, equally elusive," both occupy a space of radical alterity that precedes and authorizes but finally eludes "the modern European masculine subject of humanism" (69; Freccero, "Toward" 370).

The new ethic Certeau glimpses in Montaigne's writing of the other/Other turns on figures of mirroring and incorporation. Thus, we should not be surprised to find the lost friend also inhabiting this metaphorical space. In "De l'amitié," a key text in the friendship archive discussed earlier in this chapter, Montaigne pens a Ciceronian paean to his perfect friendship with the deceased writer La Boétie. Linking this essay with "Des cannibales," Certeau collapses the two figures of the other: "The cannibal (who speaks) and La Boétie (who listens) are metaphors for each other. One is near, one is far, both are absent, both are other. . . . The text is produced in relation to this missed present, this speaking, hearing other" (79).

By conflating the figure of the cannibal/God and the perfect friend as absent presences, Certeau links the incorporative thematics of cannibalism with a Ciceronian discourse of specifically male friendship as well as with Christian and chivalric discourses of sacrificial divinity and heroism. The famous "merging" that Montaigne extols between himself and his friend, as Carla Freccero demonstrates, relies on metaphors of "nourishment, hunger, tasting, communion" and replicates the incorporation of the loved and lost object in Sigmund Freud's description of mourning ("Cannibalism" 78). In this psychic process, the ego figuratively incorporates the lost or absent other in order to preserve (contain) or absorb (identify with) it. But the ego also resents and then denies the interior existence of the other. The inability to successfully mourn and let the other go produces what Freud calls "melancholia," a state of incomplete mourning in which a desired but lost and then denied love object returns as a ghostly trace within the self.[28]

Recent discussions of the ethics of alterity draw heavily on Freud's concept of mourning and melancholy and on the various meanings constellated around cannibalism. I mention a few of these here because the psychic structures of mourning and melancholy illuminate the dynamics of identification and projection within friendship discussed in the following chapters. Judith Butler, for example, argues that the affective foreclosures that result from having to choose between identifying with or desiring the other constitute all gendered subjectivity (*Bodies That Matter* 235–36). Anne Anlin Cheng links the disavowed identificatory structure of melancholy with the history of toxic American race relations (11). An "anticannibal ethics" has been drawn from Luce Irigaray's considerations of friendship and love in *I Love to You: Sketch for a Felicity within History* and *Etre Deux* (Deutscher 159).

Derrida offers an extensive examination of friendship and mourning, expanding the Freudian scenario in order to "generate a generalized concept of the cannibal or 'eating' subject" that transforms relational ethics into an ethics of successfully failed cannibalism (Deutscher 170). In an interview entitled " 'Eating Well,' or the Calculation of the Subject," Derrida argues that the "so called nonanthropophagic cultures construct their most elevated socius, indeed the sublimity of their morality, their politics, and their right," upon "the idealizing interiorization of the phallus" and its various signifiers, such as words, things, bread and wine, or "the breast of the other" (113–14). The resulting "carno-phallogocentrism" characterizes all subjects as "mourning subjects" noncoincident with themselves because they contain and are constituted by the other as ideal, memory, or love object (*Mémoires* 28). But even in the melancholy identification of friendship, our cannibalism always fails because, try as we might, we can never wholly assimilate or efface the other in us. "And inversely," Derrida concludes about the loss of his friend Paul de Man, "the failure succeeds; an aborted interiorization is at the same time a respect for the other as other, a sort of tender rejection, a movement of renunciation which leaves the other alone, outside, over there in his death, outside of us" (35).[29]

Getting a relatively late start in the business of colonization, the Protestant English fashioned their endeavors as antithetical to the "Black legend" of Spanish atrocities and the assimilationist strategies of the Catholic French. Nevertheless, their agenda also drew heavily on gendered discourses of friendship as exemplified with particular clarity in Roger Williams's Algonquian/English dictionary boldly entitled *A Key into the Language of America*. The very first entry in the first chapter, "Of Salutation," is the word "Netompaûog," Algonquian for "Friends" (93). Williams introduces this initial word with an offhand assertion of his belief in the "natural" (pre-Christianized) similarity of Indians and English: "The Natives are of two sorts, (as the English are)." However, he signals his skepticism of the English belief in native equality when he observes that "What cheare Nétop" is how settlers address natives they encounter "out of a desire to Civilize them" (93).

By contrast, the very structure of Williams's *Key*, with its two vertical columns of facing Algonquian and English words, suggests the face-to-face, dialogic interaction of friendship and its presumption or production of parity.[30]

Still, the relationship Williams describes in this first chapter is not the long-term intimacy recommended by the ancients as the basis for perfect friendship but an amicable predisposition that initiates dialogic recognition between ontological —and implicitly masculine—equals. These are relationships of utility and necessity—lesser forms of friendship in Aristotle's terms—that involve trade, exchange of goods and knowledge, aid in travel, and help in survival and crises. Some of these phrases ring with an autobiographical urgency. Exiled in 1635 from the Massachusetts Bay by his intolerant Puritan countrymen, Williams took wintry flight to Narragansett Bay. One can imagine him uttering several phrases in this chapter to the natives he met there who sheltered him: "I pray your favour . . . I came over the water" (94).

The moral lesson of this opening chapter provides Williams with the occasion to hold up, as Montaigne did, the savage mirror to so-called civilization. In this instance, it is the "courtesy" of the "Pagans" who, without the benefits of Christian conversion or European education, evinced a kindness and tolerance of differences that "condemns" by comparison the barbarities of "Uncourteous Englishmen," as Williams pointedly observes in the short didactic poem that concludes this first chapter. In testimony given in 1682, the year before he died, Williams was very clear about his affiliations. He recounted that "when the hearts of my countrymen and friends and brethren failed me, [God's] infinite wisdom and merits stirred up the barbarous heart of Canonicus to love me as his son to his last gasp." This providential affection ensured Williams the friendship of the Narragansett chief's nephew, the great sachem Miantonomo, and many other lesser sachems in the region (*Complete Writings* 6:407–8). The untutored "courtesy" of these "natural men" linked them to long-standing English discourses on honor and heroism running through texts like Chaucer's *The Knight's Tale* and Spenser's *The Faerie Queen*, in which the nobility of friendship plays a major role.[31]

Evidence that native peoples entertained their own ideas of friendship and could see through European professions of amity appears throughout early accounts. John Smith, the pugnacious captain of the Jamestown settlement who treated Indians cavalierly, reports being addressed in 1609 by a young Powhatan brave named Okaning who charged: "We perceive and well know that you intend to destroy us, that are here to intreat and desire your friendship" (2:210). Often, interracial marriages, like the one in 1614 between English planter John Rolfe and

Chief Powhatan's daughter, Pocahontas, temporarily facilitated amicable economic relations between groups of men otherwise hostile to each other (Calloway 153). There is some evidence that Indian sachems viewed the "gift exchange" of women through intermarriage as an expression of friendship among men, which English settlers, on the whole, rejected.[32]

Although specific native discourses on friendship are difficult to document, one prominent example is the Covenant Chain, a complex and shifting confederation of trade and military alliances that extended from the eastern seaboard to the Great Lakes region and was active from the early seventeenth century to the late eighteenth century. Originating in the Great League of Peace, a compact established among the five nations of the Iroquois by Deganawidah and Hiawatha before the appearance of Europeans, the Covenant Chains bound other tribes and European trading partners in bonds of "friendship" that ensured the stability of commerce between imperial powers who were hungry for furs and natural resources and native tribes who had come to depend upon trade for survival.

The term "covenant" may have come from the Protestant Dutch who first traded with the Iroquois. Since they did not have "chains" before contact, the Iroquois invented a word for this concept that, according to Cayuga chief Jacob E. Thomas, meant literally "arms linked together" (Jennings, *Ambiguous Iroquois Empire* 123). Through recurring performances of intercultural ritual dramas known as Condolence Councils, tribal representatives and colonial officials "polished" the chain, strengthened the links, or created new ones and renewed the covenant with "frequent meetings well-oiled with food and presents and laced with rum" (Jennings, *History* 22).[33]

The earliest recorded description of a Condolence Council, "The Mohawk Treaty with New France at Three Rivers, 1645," published in the *Jesuit Relations*, contains language and gestures of friendship that reappear in other reports of treaty negotiations as late as 1776 (Jennings, *History* 135). At the parley at Three Rivers, Kiotseaeton, the leading Mohawk spokesman, came arrayed completely in wampum (belts or "collars" of strung beads that were a means of exchange as well as a record of events) and rose dramatically from his approaching shallop to address the French and their Huron allies. Hailing them as "brothers," he later observed in the council meeting, "The minds and thoughts of men are too diverse to fall into accord; it is [he who is in] the Sky that will combine all" (qtd. in Jennings, *History* 137–38). During the ensuing ritual, this consummate performer employed eloquence and wit in the bestowal of seventeen "presents" of wampum, each accompanied by a dramatic reenactment of events significant to the participating parties. The tenth gift involved a binding ceremony, probably the

Adonwa or Personal Chant of adoption, one of the four most sacred of the ancient, pre-Columbian rites (Jennings, *History* 129). Father Barthelemy Vimont, the Jesuit missionary present at the parley who took copious notes, relates:

> He took hold of a Frenchman, placed his arm within his, and with his other arm he clasped that of an Algonquin. Having thus joined himself to them, "Here," he said, "is the knot that binds us inseparably; nothing can part us." This collar [of wampum] was extraordinarily beautiful. "Even if the lightning were to fall upon us, it could not separate us; for, if it cuts off the arm that holds you to us, we will at once seize each other by the arm." And thereupon he turned around, and caught the Frenchman and the Algonquin by their two other arms,— holding them so closely that he seemed unwilling ever to leave them. (qtd. in Jennings, *History* 141)

In his analysis of circum-Atlantic performance, Joseph Roach calls this gesture "the kinesthetic foundation of what was to become the concept of the Covenant Chain" (137–38).

Forged in "yron" between the Iroquois and the Dutch in the early seventeenth century and later between the Iroquois and French, after 1664 the chain was "reforged" by the English in "Pure Silver" according to Mohawk chief sachem Tahaiadoris, speaking on September 23, 1689 (Fenton 314). Addressing Governor Fletcher at Albany in 1694, the Indian spokesman Sadeganaktie explained the import of this imagery: "The least Member cannot be touched, but the whole Body must feel and be sensible; if therefore an Enemy hurt the least part of the Covenant Chain, we will join to destroy that Enemy, for we are one Head, one Flesh, and one Blood" (qtd. in Jennings, *History* 22). Sir William Johnson echoed these powerful sentiments in his negotiations with the Six Nations on April 25, 1748, recalling how their "Forefathers . . . made an offer to the Governour [of Albany] to enter into a Band of Friendship with him and his People which he was so pleased at that he told you he would find a strong Silver Chain which would never break, slip, or Rust to bind you and him forever in Brothership together, and that your Warriours and ours should be as one Heart, One Head, one Blood &c." (qtd. in Jennings, *Ambiguous Iroquois Empire* 145). This savvy royal agent, intent on consolidating the English crown's influence with the Iroquois during the Revolutionary period, repeats the near formulaic combination consisting of the assimilationist rhetoric of the French ("one Blood") with the spiritual figure of the Iroquois ("one Head") and the conventional early modern European image of friendship ("one Heart").

This "polishing" of the chain represented a new structure of association, which joined but did not merge the English and Iroquois, as the latter hoped, and in which "[d]iplomacy had replaced domesticity and kinship" (Dennis 269). In fact, some historians argue, as Johnson's words certainly intimate, that English treaty scribes may have unilaterally imposed the comparatively impersonal silver chain metaphor on native speakers, overriding the more traditional Iroquoian figure of clasped hands for any recognized alliance of friendship (Haan 45). As we will see in the following chapters, in the hands of white writers the figure of the chain connotes fixed and hierarchical *vertical* ranking, as in John Winthrop's invocation of the classical concept of "the Great Chain of Being." In Hannah Foster's novel, chains represent marital enthrallment, parental coercion, and chattel slavery. Steeped in the contemporary accounts of native traditions recorded by missionary and ethnographer John Heckewelder, James Fenimore Cooper prefers the hand-clasp as the performative gesture of friendship in his frontier romances, while Catharine Sedgwick attributes to her Pequot heroine as well as to her English characters a discourse of "chains" that connotes the deeply spiritual and lateral attachment of perfect friendship.

Manipulated by all parties to support their specific interests, a cross-racial discourse of friendship was part of the representational language that evolved in "the middle ground" of "accommodation" between Europeans and Indians in the early years of North American settlement. Studying the language of treaty negotiations, historian Richard White finds that until the mid-1790s, Anglo-Americans and Indians of both the Western Confederacy and the Six Nations used the metaphor of "brothers" sprung from "a common Mother" (the land) resisting a common paternal tyrant (King George III). While this fictional fraternity implies relations of equality important in the Revolutionary rhetoric of the time, each group understood the term differently. For Indians, White argues, "brother" was the diplomatic kinship term "least fraught with mutual obligation. . . . Brothers did not necessarily share warm feelings. Brothers could be less than friends" (68–69). After the Revolution, when shifting to a discourse of conquest failed largely because it could not be squared with notions of republican values and universal natural rights, U.S. negotiators adopted the more flexible rhetoric of benign patriarchy, whose logic of younger sons displacing older ones, as the biblical Jacob displaced Esau, foreshadowed the "vanishing Indian" of the early nineteenth century (72, 75).[34]

"Race," as Ellison observes about the period's literature of sensibility, "becomes a figure for emotion" and makes empire "a setting for men in crisis" (*Cato's Tears* 17). The racially marked other—now also including Africans—who earlier stood for an inassimilable savagery or intellectual incapacity that required removal, extermination, or paternalistic supervision becomes a nostalgic figure for the dangers *and* growing delights of heightened emotion produced by relationships across perceived gulfs of inequality and difference.

Women and Friendship

During the colonial period, classicism filtered through Christianity met Enlightenment thought in the American landscape. The English-dominated, Puritan-inflected culture of North America promulgated a Christian humanism in which a classical education remained an essential feature of a gentleman's profile. Renaissance republican theorists revived Greek and Roman ideas about the importance of the rational and "cooperative virtues" like friendship and justice, which filtered into the American colonies (Bloch 43). Thomas Jefferson jotted several maxims about friendship into his *Literary Commonplace Book* during the 1760s; one from Euripides' *Phoenissae* seems particularly prophetic: "Prize equality that ever linketh friend to friend, city to city, allies to each other, for equality is man's natural law" (71). Although by the early nineteenth century, incipient romanticism drove writers to prefer Greek ideals of beauty and spirit, the mid-eighteenth century extolled Cicero—orator, senator, resister of imperial tyranny, and advocate of ideal friendship—as the model citizen (Winterer 25). According to Ellison's history of emotion, Adam Smith envisioned moral sentiment arising from the bonds between "elite males" who replay "the neoclassical scenario of the Roman Stoic surrounded by his sympathetic friends" (*Cato's Tears* 10).

This classical republicanism posited an exclusively masculine public sphere insulated from femininity, which thinkers associated with uncontrolled passion, attachment to luxury, and economic dependence and considered the makings of political corruption (Winterer 22). But Protestant religious influences continued to shape moral thinking in this period and repudiated the classical ethics of Aristotle and the Stoics, including their ideas on friendship, for their failure to examine broader social values like benevolence or to include a psychology of the passions in theories of virtue (Fiering 5).[35]

In the turbulent wake of the religious revivals that swept the eastern seaboard, the ideas of the Scottish philosophers about the centrality of sympathy in the formation of moral society became widely influential, building on Protestant religious psychology, expanding and attenuating the domain of the classical model of dyadic friendship. The earlier transformation by Augustine and Aquinas of Greek *philia* and Latin *amicitia* into Christian *caritas* opened the way for the inclusion of women and cross-gender "spiritual" friendships, clinched in the late eighteenth and nineteenth centuries by the Scottish philosophers' emphasis on universal benevolence and sympathetic interchange. Women's friendships, particularly when expressed in conversation and letters, become the romantic era's cultural model for affective attachment and, as the nineteenth century progressed, were increasingly stigmatized as sentimental and "unmanly" (Ellison, *Delicate Subjects* 31–32).

The extensive conduct literature written during the early period, however, reveals not only that women as well as men were being instructed in current theories of amity but also the interesting amalgam those theories had become. An essay, "On Friendship," appearing in *The Lady's Magazine and Musical Repository* published in New York City in November 1801, illustrates how pedagogues at the turn of the nineteenth century adapted classically inflected versions of friendship to more contemporary theories of sympathy. Although this essay is not addressed specifically to women, its appearance in this popular periodical suggests its role in recommending a particular conception of homosocial friendship for "ladies."

The essay's first sentence alludes to a model of dyadic bonding inherited from the ancients but mostly shorn of their emphasis on rationality: "Friendship is an affectionate union of two persons, nearly of the same age, the same situation in life, the same dispositions and sentiments, and, as some writers will have it, of the same sex" (245). While this opens the door to cross-gender friendships, all the proffered examples—"of Achilles and Patroclus, in Homer; of Nysas and Eurylas, in Virgil; and of David and Jonathan in the Sacred Writings"—are men and warriors of epic, heroic, and ideal proportions.[36] In highlighting not only the strength of homosocial bonding but "to what a degree of enthusiasm this attachment is sometimes carried," the author emphasizes pair friendship's positive "force" as well as its potentially dangerous, blinding intensity, which can lead to abuses.

Indeed, the author complains that "some of the ancients go so far as to say, that we may be unjust to others for the sake of our friend."[37] This may be an allusion to the threat some people perceived women's friendship posed during this period to conventional, heteronormative morality. In 1778, for example, the dramatic elopement of Lady Eleanor Butler and Sarah Ponsonby, daughters of the Irish gentry, to a rural cottage in the Welsh vale of Llangollen, later dubbed "the Shrine to Friendship," called attention to women's "romantic friendship" as an alternative to marriage and potential social threat to male control of women (Taussig 72; Mavor 203).[38] The essay's proffered examples are striking in their insistently masculine character: Patroclus's death in battle taking Achilles' place and wearing his fabled armor produces a passionate revenge and pervasive melancholy; Nysas, a Trojan in Aeneas's army, dies attempting to save his "boyish" friend, Eurylas, whose unequal status recalls erotic, pederastic models of male love (*Aeneid*, book 9; Konstan, *Friendship* 38); while Jonathan's heralded attachment was, in David's words, "wonderful, passing the love of women" (2 Samuel 1:26) and constituted the age's epitome of "manly love" (Richards 93). How were women to find a place in these models?

In explaining why "friendship should form so conspicuous a part" in human character, the author of this essay shifts registers, alluding to Enlightenment views of human nature. In particular, the author alludes to the Scottish philosophers' ideas of a common "principle of benevolence and generosity" separate from market interests that attaches people to particular others "without any expectation of benefit from them" (246). In this view, the universal need for sympathy among "persons of sentiment" encourages friendship, for in this relation one "finds his joys so much encreased, and his sorrows so much alleviated, when shared by a sincere friend" (246). The stress falls on fellow feeling, grounded in the eighteenth century's "logic of affective androgyny, encompassing the republican discourses of both manly virtue and benevolent motherhood" (Chapman and Hendler 3), rather than on the ancients' emphasis on the mutual growth of virtue in restraining the passions and sustaining the stability of the city-state. The author also puts particular emphasis on "sincerity" and the disruption caused by excessive emotion or false friends. Thus, the short essay concludes by warning young, probably female readers against the dangers of forming early, exclusive, and passionate connections with insincere people—a persistent anxiety in classical and Renaissance friendship literature that was amplified by political fears about demagoguery, false appearances, and seduction in the new U.S. Republic explored by authors like Charles Brockden Brown.

The focus then shifts back to classically inflected concerns with making informed—that is, reasoned—choices in matters of the affections. As the opening examples of dyadic friendship from the Greek, Latin, and biblical traditions suggest, these can disrupt the status quo by uncontrollable "enthusiasm." This possibility is so worrisome that the author admits dolefully: "The moderns [that is, Renaissance thinkers], indeed, though they seem to have abated of this enthusiasm, have not been able to extinguish it" (245–46). A means of controlling these passions was to feminize and privatize them.[39]

According to the emerging histories of affect, by the mid-nineteenth century women were inextricably associated with emotion in general, so that sympathetic attachment became a feminine and largely domestic domain (Chapman and

Hendler 3). Still, as Anne McClintock demonstrates, "the cult of domesticity was a crucial, if concealed, dimension of male as well as female identities . . . and an indispensable element both of the industrial market and the imperial enterprise" (5). I am arguing that, conversely, aspects of public political culture in the form of friendship narratives permeate the domestic sphere. As the essay from *The Lady's Magazine and Musical Repository* suggests and Addie Brown's letter with which I began the introduction confirms, a version of the classical model of aristocratic dyadic friendship reserved for men persists in female culture, co-existing with neoclassical notions of sympathy, thus giving women at least a foothold in debates about equality, virtue, citizenship, and national identity.

Coda: Contemporary and Feminist Philosophies of Friendship

My research indicates that the role of women and differences of race, class, and sexuality became issues for philosophers of friendship only in the last quarter of the twentieth century, if at all.[40] For Derrida, "the double exclusion of the feminine"—the barring of friendships between females and friendships between males and females—from all the "great ethico-politico-philosophical discourses on friendship" is not only a crucial question for our time but leads to the chief concerns of "deconstruction." He identifies these as the discursive history of concepts and "history *tout court*" and the question of "phallogocentrism," a construction/constriction of meaning and monopolizing of power by the imposition of the phallus as center and authority (*Politics* 277–79).[41] Derrida adds that this double exclusion "even" raises the question "of sacrificial 'carno-phallogocentrism,'" the discursive dominance of an anthropophagic (symbolically cannibalistic) masculine Western subject discussed earlier in relation to Montaigne's melancholy alterity (*Politics* 307).

Derrida's complex musings and his fascinating deployment of Aristotle offer insights into the discursive nexus of gender and friendship and its political implications. Although the canonical discourses on friendship "from Plato to Montaigne, from Aristotle to Kant, from Cicero to Hegel" are not homogeneous, in Derrida's view they all "will have explicitly tied the friend-brother to virtue and to justice, to moral reason and political reason" (*Politics* 277). This canonical notion of friendship operates through "homology" and "reciprocity," structures of correspondence—like a common gender—and mutual exchange that produce symmetry between citizens. As we have seen, this "logic of the same" derives from the classical idea of "the true friend . . . his ideal double, his other self, the same self but improved" and for Derrida "would confer on friendship the essential and essentially sublime figure of virile homosexuality," thus privileging "the figure of the brother" (as opposed to the father) (*Politics* 4, 279). Derrida labels the result "fratriarchy"—"a *familial, fraternalist* and thus *androcentric* configuration of politics" that has characterized all of the major political settlements in the West (*Politics* viii; his emphases). Phallogocentrism returns as "phratrocentrism" (*Politics* 278).

It is not hard to imagine Aristotle's notions of similitude and presence in friendship as the bogeyman in this postmodern critique, but Aristotelian thought and Aristotle as signifier play a complicated and framing role in Derrida's argument. Every chapter in his book *Politics of Friendship* is an extended meditation on Aristotle's apocryphal pronouncement cited in Montaigne's famous essay "De l'amitié," "O my friends, there is no friend" (140). Thus, Aristotle's ghostly words frame each major topic Derrida considers. In his critique of Derrida's study, Fred Dallmayr observes about this talismanic remark, "The aporetic character of this statement (its invocation of friends whose lack it simultaneously affirms) provides in many ways the keynote or tenor of the entire argument" (107).[42] Continually turning over this phrase, Derrida finally demonstrates how "the Graeco-Roman model" governed by homology and reciprocity "bears within itself, nevertheless, potentially, the power to become infinite and dissymmetrical" (*Politics* 290)—that is, to be widely, even infinitely extended and to encompass differences like the difference of gender.

While Aristotle provides us with the lofty "idea" of perfect friendship, Derrida observes that this ideal is "contradictory in its very essence" and makes the reality of a friend in the present impossible. Thus, Derrida argues, rephrasing Aristotle, "*in the name of friendship* we must conclude, alas, if there is friendship, 'there is no friend'" ("Politics" in *Journal* 636; his emphasis). In this view, friendship is thoroughly deconstructive, the ultimate deferral: "Friendship is never a given in the present; it belongs to the experience of waiting, of promise, or of commitment. Its discourse is that of prayer and at issue there is that which responsibility opens to the future" (636). Here, the bright thread of Aristotle's *philia* takes on the darkening shades of Cicero's *amicitia*, since throughout Derrida embraces the elegiac "Ciceronian logic" that defines friendship as the ultimate space of loss through mourning the deceased friend that his countryman Montaigne honed to a fine melancholy point. The ability to talk about the friend, Derrida insists, implies his absence, his death. The temporality of friendship, then, signified by Aristotle's repeated framing address to friends who cannot/do not exist, is a paradoxical "future anterior" that always surpasses the present (637).

At issue from a political perspective is a version of the problem feminist theorists have identified as the "dilemma of difference" (Minow 21). If one argues for the inclusion of women on the basis of their theoretical equality with men, one reinscribes masculine norms and ignores differences, which, whether natural or socially constructed, characterize many women's realities. But arguing for and privileging sexual difference has often implied women's inferiority with respect to male norms and a harmful ignorance of racial/ethnic and class differences among women. Can we define "equality" not as sameness but as a parity or equity that rests fluidly or contingently on differences? Can we redefine the norms that determine inclusion and agency in society? Furthermore, how can we found a workable democracy on utopian promises of affiliation?[43]

To imagine such a friendship, Derrida draws on Friedrich Nietzsche's resignification of "good friendship" (a phrase that inverts Aristotle's notion of "the friendship of the good") as a bond that "supposes disproportion. It demands a certain rupture in reciprocity or equality, as well as the interruption of all fusion or confusion between you and me" that marks erotic relationships. This logic "calls friendship back to the irreducible precedence of the other," to "a sentiment even more sublime than the freedom or self-sufficiency of a subject"—that is, to "a friendship prior to friendships" that exists "in the being-together that any allocution supposes" (*Politics* 62–63; "Politics" in *Journal* 636). In this view, friendship constrains the ontological singularity of the self by its assumption and acceptance of the prior claims of the listening other.

Under the auspices of his contemporaries, philosophers like Maurice Blanchot, George Bataille, Jean Luc Nancy, and especially Emanuel Lévinas, Derrida argues for the emergence of "friends of an entirely different kind, inaccessible friends, friends who are alone because they are incomparable and without common measure, reciprocity or equality," friends who call on us "to share what cannot be shared: solitude" (*Politics* 35). Including "the double feminine" in a vision of democratic politics freed from "the homo-fraternal and phallogocentric schema," then, can occur only under the sign of radical "heterology, asymmetry, and infinity," which runs counter to the "homology," "symmetry," "immanence," "finitism, and politicist concord" of classical friendship (*Politics* 306; "Politics" in *Journal* 644). The "we" of human community is, therefore, always paradoxical, a "community of those without community" (*Politics* 63; see also 47n.15). Finally, however, Derrida cannot release but can only repeat and revise Aristotle. The last line of *Politics of Friendship* calls upon and thus constitutes this community of the bereft by playing on Aristotle's haunting apostrophe *minus* the second negating phrase, leaving it provocatively incomplete: "O my democratic friends . . ." (*Politics* 306).

Responses to this largely unsatisfying postmodern formulation of friendship often return to Aristotelian thought. In his critique of Derrida, Dallmayr argues not for the "wholesale retrieval" of the classical tradition but for the readmission of Aristotle's ideas about friendship and politics in particular. As the title of Ricoeur's study *Oneself as Another* implies, he explicitly reclaims aspects of Aristotelian friendship doctrine to counter the "irreducible precedence of the other," a notion Derrida borrows from Lévinas. Specifically, Aristotle's emphasis on activity (friends *doing* good things for each other) and mutuality (as opposed to the obligatory equivalence of reciprocity) enables Ricoeur to highlight ethics rather than morality—that is, goods and striving for a common good rather than individual rights and their protection and "solicitude" for others rather than duties and obligations (189). The editor of a 1994 collection of philosophical essays on friendship concludes that Aristotle is the thinker with whom most of the contributors wrestle and thus dubs him "the patron saint of this volume" (Rouner 10). One of the essays in this collection considers friendship across gender difference and sports a witty title that places director Rob Reiner's popular 1989 romantic comedy on the subject in direct confrontation with Aristotelian notions of friendship: "When Harry and Sally Met the *Nicomachean Ethics*."

Feminist philosophers, on the whole, have embraced a *revised* Aristotelian notion of friendship and community. Distinguished legal philosopher Linda Redlick Hirshman argues that his misogyny notwithstanding, "Aristotle's writings on virtue ethics are the most ambitious work in the philosophical tradition addressing the critical question facing feminism—and contemporary political theory generally—today: the purpose and limits of equality" (202). Martha Nussbaum, Janice Raymond, Julia K. Ward, Mary Dietz, and Lorraine Code all look to Aristotle's theory as an alternative to "autonomy-centered theories" of the liberal state that originated in Enlightenment thought and prevail in current moral and political discourse. These theories rest on a conception of subjectivity in which separateness and self-sufficiency are the highest goals and people are regarded as "rational, self-conscious agents" and "the bearers of rights" who must be protected from other "equally self-serving" individuals (Code 77). However, many commentators have noted that this nominal liberal subject, disembodied and "universal" in order to ensure a theoretical "equality" and interchangeability, nevertheless remains gendered, raced, and classed. Furthermore, they argue that the "formal sameness" that should guarantee "fairness" through interchangeability actually "impede[s] the development of conceptual tools for coping with politically and morally significant differences" by permitting only "a pale, pluralistic liberal toleration: a bare recognition of difference-in-isolation" (Code 80).

By contrast, feminist theorists argue that Aristotle's relational ethics allow for a reimagination of intersubjectivity and community on more egalitarian bases.[44] In her critique of Richard Rorty's "untenable" distinction between public and private, for example, Dianne Rothleder turns to Aristotle's notion of perfect friendship. Briskly discarding "the clear sexism and classism of this model," she highlights Aristotle's ideas of the "pleasure" in and "care" for others that inform her notion of "a friendship of play" (123). By modifying Aristotle, Rothleder seeks to avoid "the hyperindividualism" of liberal rights theory, especially the right "not to play" or exclude others, and its converse, "hypercommunitarianism," which privileges groups and rejects individual solitude or predilection (124–25).

A chastened Aristotle also returns in the work of Dietz, who rethinks citizenship from a feminist perspective, and of Code, who explores a postmodern feminist epistemology. Both consider and reject mother-child love as a model for ethical social relations, though it held significant sway in the 1970s and 1980s. They argue that the maternal model is asymmetrical, inextricable from the power relations and the history of the Oedipal family, and maintains a public/private distinction that keeps politics out of the family and women out of the public sphere. Both prefer an Aristotelian model of friendship that is based in equality or equity on the one hand and in particularity and sociability on the other and requires an epistemology or means of knowing ourselves as well as knowing others that is intellectual as well as affective (Code 99).[45] They recognize, however, that this requires a "generous" and "open" reading of Aristotle that involves seeing beyond his elitist and sex-specific strictures for citizenship (Dietz 27; Code 99). Taken in this light, Aristotle's ideas provide a paradigm for affiliation that is specifically situated (non-essential), politically and morally engaged, and anchored in the recognition of "second persons," a belief in the importance of other people in our development (Code 100–101) that echoes Aristotle's formulation of the friend as a "second self."

Burden not thyself above thy
power while thou livest; and have
no fellowship with one that is
mightier and richer than thyself:
for how agree the kettle and the
earthen pot together? For if the
one be smitten against the other,
it shall be broken. . . .
All flesh consorteth ac-
cording to kind, and a man will
cleave to his like.
What fellowship hath the
wolf with the lamb? So the
sinner with the godly.
What agreement is there
between the hyena and a dog?
And what peace between the
rich and the poor?
—Ecclesiasticus 13

CHAPTER TWO

"Familiar Commerce"

John Winthrop's "Modell" of American Affiliation

According to recent scholarship on both sides of the Atlantic, the "Age of Reason" is becoming a misnomer. Formerly, scholars of early America followed their English counterparts and viewed the long eighteenth century mainly through its idealization of and dedication to dispassion. Now they are beginning to chart what one collection somewhat infelicitously calls "an emotional history of the United States" beginning with the colonial period (Stearns and Lewis).

Scholars are also beginning to investigate the political implications of affect in early America. Peter Coviello, for example, argues that the "nation" emerges through the rhetoric of its important early polemical writers, not from particular "state dictates" or political theories but through the strategic evocation of potent emotions. He cites a rather odd group—Thomas Jefferson, Thomas Paine, and Phillis Wheatley—who, he contends, marshal strong feelings specifically of loss and separation in their writing that enable a quite disparate and widely separated colonial populace to bond together imaginatively as a unified whole (441–42). Such an "odd civic intimacy" not only precedes and makes possible the political constitution of the new nation but also establishes the capacity for impassioned response as a prerequisite for virtuous republican citizenship. To elevate the importance of this affective capacity, in turn, requires a reconsideration of the standing of women and people of color, who were traditionally excluded from participation in the public sphere because of their perceived link with untrammeled emotion (457, 443).

A "seminal" precursor of this particular emotional collectivity, according to Coviello, is John Winthrop's famous address "A Modell of Christian Charitie," delivered in the spring of 1630 to a band of Protestant dissenters on the eve of their departure to establish a purified commonwealth in the New World.[1] What the deist Jefferson surprisingly "retrieves" from this lay sermon by the arch-American Puritan, in Coviello's account, is an early blueprint for American exceptionalism in which affect is central "to the mutuality that defines a civic body" (462). While "exceptionalism" may be more a legacy of the scholarly interpretation of this Puritan leader's words,[2] and while Winthrop did marshal strong emotion in his sociopolitical cause, Coviello is incorrect when he implies that Winthrop dwells on the "agonizing affection" for lost English brethren which Jefferson invokes at the dramatic climax of his initial version of the Declaration of Independence. I also suspect that women and minorities, represented in Coviello's argument by Wheatley, would not want to give up inclusion in the public realm as rational beings or give up reason as part of their rhetorical arsenal. Furthermore, Coviello's argument masks the very real struggles, not to mention the imposed silence, of women and minorities in their bid to reshape nationalism in meaningful and inclusive ways.

Rather, Winthrop highlights a form of Christian love and fellowship in the creation of a social and political commonwealth. But as I argue in this chapter, his version of Christian "affection" is indissolubly entangled with classical, early Christian, and Renaissance friendship discourses and—more surprisingly—the legal language of contract to which these give rise. As Laurie Shannon observes about early modern English culture, the "similitude" or "utopian parity" of "the other-self logics of friendship" is necessary for what emerging contract law calls a " 'meeting of the minds.' Equality between agreeing parties suggests a balance of wills, and only that parity can ensure that a contract has been freely entered" (*Sovereign Amity* 39). At the time, such "utopian parity" did not include women or people of color. Similarly, Winthrop does not diverge from the teachings of Ecclesiasticus, who asserts that there can be no "fellowship" or "peace" between rich and poor. The Hebrew sage's formulation of the principle of similitude, "a man will cleave to his like," illustrates how slippery the notion of "like" can be. On the one hand, it cites the ancient proverbs, examined in the previous chapter, that define friendship as the natural attraction of like to like, while on the other hand, it echoes the prelapsarian marriage vow of Genesis 2:24: "Therefore shall a man leave his father and his mother, and shall cleave unto his wife: and they shall be one flesh." Does "like" denote the likeness of same-sex friendship (one soul in two bodies), marriage (two souls becoming one flesh), tribal kinship, sectarian uniformity, similarity of class status, or something else?

Taking advantage of this instability, Winthrop recommends to his followers a form of exchange he extols as "a most equall and sweete kinde of Commerce."[3] In this he ironically (though perhaps unwittingly) presages the imperial economic vision Paine vividly painted for indecisive colonists in 1776 in his widely circulated pamphlet, "Common Sense." In passionate prose, Paine urges separation from England so that the colonies can free themselves from a heartless "Parent Country" to become a "continental" nation able to "carry our friendship on a larger scale [and] . . . claim brotherhood with every European Christian" and whose master "plan is commerce" (19–20). For Paine, and for many eighteenth-century treaty-writers, "amity" between nations not only indicated the cessation of conflict but was the necessary precursor of America's real purpose: economic development through trade.

A close examination of the sources and dynamics of Winthrop's "charitie" reveals the imbrication of friendship, understood as social and spiritual affiliation, and commercial relations. It also discloses the related strategic slippage characteristic of early Protestant culture between the homonormative logic of friendship and the heteronormative logic of marriage. We can glimpse this slippage in the tension that pervades Winthrop's address between different and competing models of community: covenantal and contractual models of social organization reflect friendship's "ideal" (though) masculine egalitarianism while corporeal models based upon the figurative "body politic" reflect the gendered hierarchy characteristic of even Protestant notions of companionate marriage. This association of social and commercial models with modes of affiliation illustrates how cultural institutions such as friendship and marriage can be used to naturalize gender differences and inequality.[4] The vision of a diverse "commonwealth" united by common beliefs and moral values may have had a radical, even democratic, tinge in Winthrop's day. But as we will see in chapter 3, this vision ratified for later generations of the early Republic a conservative social agenda in which women were the "equals" of men in neither marriage nor friendship.

Contexts for Winthrop's "Charitie"

John Winthrop based his famous "modell" for the "Citty upon a Hill" he envisioned in New England on an understanding of Christian "love" he absorbed from his father's generation of upstanding Protestant reformers. In a new biography of Winthrop pointedly subtitled *America's Forgotten Founding Father*, Francis Bremer draws a detailed picture of the mainstream Puritan "social gospel" that flourished among Winthrop's forebears in the Stour river valley in East Anglia during the late sixteenth century. In this region, eminent men of the community, such as Winthrop's father, Adam, and the like-minded clergymen he entertained at his estate at Groton, resisted the radical sectarianism spreading through England, advanced education as essential to a Christian commonwealth, and believed they could inculcate proper godly behavior by modeling it in their own lives ("Heritage" 533–35).

But under the reign of James I in the early seventeenth century, efforts to further this moderate Puritan vision met growing impediments from the church and crown. By 1617, Bremer finds, the maturing John Winthrop "saw the progress of reform slowed, halted, and then reversed" (540). When he finally decided to remove to New England, Winthrop's plan was to revive the waning social vision of his father's generation, which he outlined in his lay sermon to his fellow immigrants. Although we have elevated this address as "a kind of Ur-text of American literature" (Delbanco 72), its ideas and language closely echo many Puritan ministers and writers from his southeast corner of England.[5] In fact, Bremer surmises that Winthrop's contemporaries in New England almost completely ignored the address—he finds only one reference to it—which did not appear in published form until the late nineteenth century, because "the ideas which have struck so many later commentators as original and influential were commonplaces of the time" (*John Winthrop* 175).

One of the most important commonplaces for these men was the renovating power of the special love they called "charity." The influential Suffolk minister John Knewstub, a friend of Adam Winthrop's from his years at Cambridge, closely anticipates the theme of "A Modell" in his *Lectures on Exodus* (1579): "The lord to maintaine brotherly love among his, hath made one the store house of necessaries of another: So is the welfare of every man laid out of himself that love may by such means rather be maintained" (qtd. in Bremer, "Heritage" 536). The "love" both Knewstub and Winthrop refer to is a translation of the original Greek *agape*, which early church fathers called Christian "brotherhood" or "fellowship." The Vulgate renders this form of affiliation as *caritas*, while the Geneva and King James Bibles translate it variously as "love" and "charity."[6]

What emerges from the scholarly debate over nomenclature is an understanding of Christian *agape* and *caritas* that is tangled up in the shifting and diverse meanings of the ancient Greek term *philotes* and the *philia* and *amicitia* of later classical philosophers, not to mention the other prominent human affect the Greeks called *eros*.[7] Classicist David Konstan argues that Christian writers generally preferred metaphors derived from kinship relations (brothers, father-son) to distinguish spiritual and universal love from the particular, worldly though ideal affiliation often denoted by *philia* and *amicitia* and from the irrational passion of *eros* (*Friendship* 156–57). Historian Carolinne White counters that due to the classical training and sensibility of early Christian writers, "in reality the two [sets of] terms not only overlap in meaning to a large extent but are often used interchangeably" (54). As evidence, she cites Chrysostom's use of *philia* in referring to Matthew 22:37–40 where Jesus sums up his teachings for the wily Pharisees in two commandments to love, first, "the Lord thy God with all thy heart, and with all thy soul, and with all thy mind," and second, "thy neighbor as thyself." The common element in these sets of terms is a "liking" based on or achieving "likeness," which, as we will see, all too easily slides into notions of sameness and often underlines understandings of equality. Although the Christian pair *agape*/*caritas* differs from the classical pair *philia*/*amicitia* at least during the fourth century, which is the period White scrutinizes, "the two appear to merge in certain respects, with the result that friendship could be regarded as part of love of God rather than love of something merely mortal" (54–55).

The apostle Paul gives a source for these kinds of "love" in his first letter to the Corinthians, from which Winthrop draws extensively for his address's imagery. Paul concludes his frequently cited passage on love by asserting that of the three "gifts" available to believers—faith, hope, and charity—"the greatest of these is charity" (13:13). The Geneva Bible's marginal commentary, paraphrasing verse 10, explains that while faith and hope are promises that will be fulfilled on earth, charity "ceaseth not in the life to come, as the rest doe, but is perfected and accomplished" (86). In other words, charity is not just a human affection, it is also divine; moreover, its exercise on earth provides a foretaste of heaven.

The adjective Paul uses to describe this love, *teleios* (perfected, complete), is the same word Aristotle employs to describe the highest form of *philia*, a "perfect" friendship based on virtue and mutuality that obtains between brothers or military comrades who hold all in common and give their lives for each other (*NE* 8:9, 13).[8] As I discuss in chapter 1, Cicero uses a similar phrase in *De amicitia*, his dramatic dialogue on friendship in the Roman Republic, when his speaker Laelius says of his incomparable friend Scipio, "we shared the one element indispensable to friendship, a complete agreement [*summa consensio*] in aims, ambitions, and attitudes" (iv.15; 52). The apostle John echoes Paul's language when he famously declares in his first letter: "God is love" (1 John 4:16). Jerome renders the original

Greek *Ho theos agapê estin* into Latin as *Deus caritas est*. John continues his letter: "Herein is our love made perfect [*teteleiôtai, perfecta*], that we may have boldness in the day of judgment: because as he is, so are we in this world" (1 John 4:17). Other New Testament versions of the injunction to love the other as oneself also conclude with exhortations to achieve "perfection" akin to the divine (see, for example, Matthew 5:43–44, 48). They have their source in Leviticus 19:18, a text that predates classical writers like Aristotle on friendship.

In their extrapolation of charity as the basis for a Christian commonwealth, Puritan writers drew upon Thomas Aquinas's discussion, which primarily engages Aristotle's notion of *philia* in the *Nicomachean Ethics*. Even more striking, however, are the echoes in Winthrop's address of the twelfth-century Cistercian abbot Aelred of the Rievaulx monastery in Yorkshire, whose profound youthful regard for Cicero's *De amicitia* led the monk to compose a Christianized account of friendship suitably entitled *De spiritali amicitia*. Friendship, Aelred explains by paraphrasing Cicero, originates in the will of "Sovereign Nature" that "peace encompass all his creatures and society unite them; and thus all creatures obtain from him, who is supremely and purely one, some trace of that unity" (Pakaluk, *Other Selves* 141). For this reason, every creature, including angels, seeks and thrives in "society with its own kind" (141).

According to Aelred, the creation of Eve "from the very substance of the man" epitomizes this desire for unity in the human realm (142). While this idea reinforces what for Aelred is the central lesson of friendship, "that human beings are equal and, as it were, collateral" (142), it conflicts with Christian doctrine's understanding of the wife's necessary marital subjection to her husband's earthly authority.[9] The fall allowed "private good to take precedence over the common weal," thus corrupting friendship, which can only exist among virtuous people. Thereafter, what Aelred calls "spiritual friendship," the classical dyad of moral equals augmented by God, was confined to "the few good" believers "who bound themselves together by a closer bond of love and friendship" while they exercised charity in the form of "the natural law" of earthly morality to everyone else (143). Aquinas expanded on this distinction in his *Summa Theologiae* and concludes, "[C]harity is the friendship of man for God" and "extends to sinners, whom, out of charity, we love for God's sake" (Pakaluk, *Other Selves* 172–73).

In strikingly similar terms, Winthrop reminds his listeners that they are bound by "natural law" that requires mutual ethical treatment, an imperfect form of "brotherhood" to be superseded by the anticipated heavenly "friendship" with Christ.[10] We should remember that the Puritans undertaking this special endeavor often referred to themselves as "visible saints"—men and women who had given a public narrative of their conversion and faith acceptable to the congregation and thus came as close as possible on earth to membership in the "invisible church" of purified saints predestined by God before history. Winthrop implies that they have a particular obligation to exercise "mercy" toward one another (*WP* 283–84). This "special relacion" binds believers into a single "body" that transcends time, space, and death, as Cicero implies perfect friendship does. In fact, Laelius, the speaker of Cicero's dialogue, uses language close to Winthrop's purposes when he asserts that "the finest thing of all about" perfect friendship is its provision of a "model" for the virtuous self:

> [T]he man who keeps his eye on a true friend, keeps it, so to speak, on a model of himself. For this reason, friends are together when they are separated, they are rich when they are poor, strong when they are weak, and—a thing even harder to explain—they live on after they have died, so great is the honor that follows them, so vivid the memory, so poignant the sorrow. That is why friends who have died arc accounted happy, and those who survive them are deemed worthy of praise. (vii.23; 56)

Furthermore, this model relation dictates the "rules" governing the various levels of members' interactions with each other and those outside their congregational structure (*WP* 289).

Winthrop goes on to outline his rationale for translating the original royal charter of the Company of the Massachusetts Bay, a commercial enterprise, into a theologically based social, economic, and political program for the new commonwealth in New England. The import of this crucial vision, however, is still under debate.

Scholars in the pioneering generation of New England studies and their students emphasize Winthrop's bold invocation of a shared "federal" covenant to create unity and laud his vision as "representative" and "proto-democratic." Edmund S. Morgan, of course, uses Winthrop's life and thought to epitomize what he calls "the Puritan dilemma"—that is, the perennial question of "what responsibility a righteous man owes to society" when, in Winthrop's particular case, his rigorous faith commands him to be in the world but not of it (*Puritan Dilemma* xxi, 7–8). According to Morgan's reading, Winthrop resolved this dilemma, almost inadvertently and against his temperamental bias as a member of the landed gentry, by establishing a form of representative government. Perry Miller, whose evocation of the Puritans' epic "errand into the wilderness" spawned a myth of origins that scholars only recently have begun to dismantle, emphasizes how Winthrop's vision resolves social differences in the almost ecstatic mutuality of the shared covenant (*Nature's Nation* 6–7). In the next generation of scholars, Andrew Delbanco offers what may be the most extreme formulation of this interpretation when he dubs Winthrop's address a "communitarian statement" (74).

More recent commentary draws on our expanding knowledge of early transatlantic economic and legal spheres. Scott Michaelsen, for example, explores the legal contexts of Winthrop's address. Sacvan Bercovitch, who reads the entire Puritan New England and later American tradition as founded on a seductive form of ideological consensus in which dissent is constitutive, disarmed, and thus truly impossible, offers a *re*reading of Winthrop's address focused on its rhetorical "moves." Both Michaelsen and Bercovitch use the phrase "sleight of hand" to describe how Winthrop elicits the conformity of his diverse audience in his thinly veiled attempts to preserve social hierarchy (Michaelsen 90; Bercovitch 36).

These critics, however, do not advance a monolithic reading of Winthrop's text; rather, they uncover multiple and contending pressures at work in the address, which rendered it amenable to ideological appropriation by various interpretive camps. For example, although Michaelsen considers "A Modell" "economically progressive" and Stephen Innes goes so far as to call its economic program "moral or communal capitalism" (44), the address remains in their respective views "psychologically pre-modern" and "politically conservative" (Michaelsen 95; Innes 44). Similarly, along with the address's sources in the "traditional Christian religious teachings" of Winthrop's father's generation, Bremer cites the influence of "English commonwealth ideas as they had recently been modified to emphasize both the hierarchical and communal elements" (*John Winthrop* 176).

Hugh J. Dawson also emphasizes these contradictory aspects because, he argues with some compelling evidence, the address was probably delivered in England *before* the departure of the fleet. According to this reading, rather than speaking only to the storm-tossed company on the decks of the *Arbella*, Winthrop offered his striking vision of a purified commonwealth to a large audience of émigrés, their families, potential planters, those being left behind, and especially the endeavor's financial backers, who were necessary to the success of the enterprise and, furthermore, wanted to reap economic rewards. To reread the address in the context of this performance, Dawson concludes, reveals "a deeper sense of its conservative reaffirmation of established ways" ("'Christian Charitie'" 135). As we will see below, "the ligatures of contract and the ligaments of the body," Dawson's terms that I have adopted for the major rhetorical figures Winthrop employs in his address, serve in Dawson's view as "images of constraint and cohesion" (135). We should also note that Puritan culture already had an established theory of interconnection on which Winthrop could draw for his vision of society as an integrated organism in which each person played a different but vital role. In this worldview, all knowledge—the social and scientific as well as the theological and faith-based—was tied together under the rubric of "technologia" to form what thinkers of the age called "encyclopedia," the great circle of knowledge (P. Miller, *New England Mind* 161).[11]

How do we reconcile these disparate and conflicting readings of Winthrop's foundational text and the vision it promotes? What is at stake for scholars who see in Winthrop's address the nascent liberal politics of later New England and the United States? This is an issue of interpretation whose outcome can challenge prevailing understandings of America's "origins." I am arguing that to read Winthrop's address through the lens of friendship discourse will provide fresh insight into this problem and so intervene in this debate.

Creating a Corporate Conscience

Not under debate is the power of Winthrop's vision, which derives from his adept use of rhetoric and reliance on "polysemy" to yoke together two contradictory images of "Christian Charitie" that operate simultaneously in the secular, social world of business, law, and personal relations and in the sacred, theological realm of regenerate saints (Dawson, " 'Christian Charitie' " 120). The phrase "a familiar Commerce" is Winthrop's brilliant figure for this conflation, drawing attention to the Latin root *merx* (commodity or merchandise) of both "commerce" and "mercy"[12] and mobilizing the meaning of "commerce" as any communication or exchange in economic, sexual, and divine spheres. The adjective "familiar" characterizes such exchanges as familial or "tribal," occurring between intimates or within a small, local circle of insiders.

These meanings are important, because during the seventeenth century, England's economy shifted decisively away from personal transactions based on trust and limited credit to impersonal negotiations through middlemen, courts, and contracts based on what economic historians call "rational calculation" in the emergent transatlantic markets. Invoking biblical guidelines for ethical economic practice, dissenting English clergy in the early seventeenth century roundly condemned individual profit-making, which they regarded as usurious, sinful, and disunifying, and sought desperately to counteract it by inculcating "a corporate conscience" (Valeri 25). In his examination of "Puritans in the Marketplace," Mark Valeri argues that early-seventeenth-century English dissenting preachers used the term "usury as a synecdoche for the abuse of nearly every form of credit . . . as a form of exchange that disregarded the moral dynamics of neighbor-to-neighbor relations and looked instead to rational laws of supply and demand . . . [and] as a complete reversal of the true meaning of commerce, which was communication and union within the body social" (13–14).

By the 1620s, these clergymen were promoting settlement in New England as an opportunity to reform the corrupt economic practices of old England (Valeri 27). In fact, once they settled in Massachusetts Bay, Winthrop and the Puritan leadership had no qualms about strictly controlling trade, setting price limits, and punishing "sins of the market" as they would other forms of "social disintegration" (33). They may have been guided by William Bradford's troubled experiment in communalism at Plymouth Plantation, which in his famous account he called the "common course and condition" (120). Although it was "tried sundry years and that amongst godly and sober men," by 1623 Governor Bradford had to end the practice in order to placate discontent and avoid starvation (120). The earlier English settlement at Jamestown in the Chesapeake Bay was similarly threatened with calamity when many of the aristocratic members of the party refused to plant corn to augment the common stores and a drought hit the region. Captain John Smith, who was forced into hard and desperate negotiations with the Powhatan Indians for supplies, finally had to enforce a no-work-no-food policy to avert impending disaster.

Later plantations, like Plymouth, learned from this precarious attempt and brought over entire families and artisans united by a common set of beliefs and goals. Bradford recounts how when men were given separate plots of land in proportion to their family's needs to set corn and till "and in this regard trust to themselves," they had more success, "for it made all hands very industrious" (120). The settlers' refusal to work for the common good, which Bradford did not blame on "men's corruption" but saw as God's "wisdom" in choosing "another course fitter for them," nevertheless proved to the disappointed social architect "the vanity of that conceit of Plato's and other ancients applauded by some of later times; that the taking away of property and bringing in community into a commonwealth would make them happy and flourishing" (120–21). The equality of situation (rather than inherited status) that the physically challenging colonial experience produced among men—"they thought themselves in the like condition, and one as good as another"—in Bradford's view "did at least much diminish and take off mutual respects that should be preserved amongst them" (121).

How could later plantations avoid the pitfalls experienced at Plymouth Plantation? How could they create a deep commitment to a common endeavor and yet retain the impetus of individualism and preserve the distinctions of station that seemed to early modern pilgrims like Bradford to be "relations that God hath set amongst men" (121)? In a sermon preached in Dorchester, England, soon after the departure of Winthrop's fleet, Puritan minister John White used the same kind of "corporatizing" language and moral rationale we see in Winthrop's address to promote New England colonization. A fervent supporter of settlement, White published his sermon with the title *The Planter's Plea: or the Grounds of Plantation Examined* (London 1630), in which he develops corporate imagery in terms of mothers and children: "[A] Colony is a part and member of her [the 'mother' state's] owne body. . . . When the frame of the body is thus formed and furnished with vitall parts, and knit together with firme bands & sinews, the bulke may be filled up" (34).[13] It was most likely White, acting as negotiator for Winthrop's group, who drew up the royal charter that was granted to the Company of the Massachusetts Bay in New England (Michaelsen 88).

Winthrop needed to marshal authoritative, persuasive, and familiar figures of collective responsibility and cohesion, because according to the opening proposition of his address, the earthly social order is, by divine fiat, hierarchical: "God Almightie in his most holy and wise providence hath soe disposed of the Condicion of mankinde, as in all times some must be rich some poore, some highe and eminent in power and dignitie; others meane and in subjeccion" (*WP* 282). In the next breath, however, Winthrop amends this starkly feudal division, explaining that by "rich" "are comprehended all such as are able to live comfortably by theire owne meanes duely improved" (283). This definition encompasses precisely the "middling sort" of hardworking planters and farmers made possible by colonizing ventures, which provided them with the land and opportunity lacking in England.

Still, Winthrop's clarification does not dissolve the practical distinction between the small group of gentlemen stockholders who literally owned the "Company" holding the royal charter and stood to reap any financial profits, or the ten "undertakers" appointed to manage it, and all the other colonists. Although Winthrop believed, like other Puritans, that superiority of position as well as talents and achievements were all gifts of God, and that all suffered equally under the burden of sin, he supported to the end of his life the distinction between leaders—ministers, magistrates, and "men [gender specific] of partes"—and followers (*Winthrop's Journal* 2:238). As we see in chapter 4, believers in traditional republicanism and relations of deference, like James Fenimore Cooper, continued to maintain this distinction as well. Not only are people ranked in the social order, according to Winthrop's view, but "the riche and mighty" have a penchant for exploiting "the poore, and dispised," who want, in turn, to "rise upp against theire superiours, and shake off theire yoake" (*WP* 283). This socially calamitous contention occurs because after Adam's fall, "every man is borne with this principle in him, to love and seeke himselfe only" (290).

Echoing Aelred on the origins of friendship and its distinction from charity, Winthrop proposes several "reasons" for the existence of inequality in wealth and power, the last and most important of which undoes it: "That every man might have need of other, and from hence they might be all knitt more nearly together in the Bond of brotherly affeccion" (*WP* 283). The gendered language covers over inequalities in the "universal" bond that appear in Aelred's citation of Eve's creation as friendship's "lesson" of equality and will reappear later to further trouble Winthrop's rhetoric. Here the "bond" of fraternal love, especially between regenerate Christians who considered themselves "one in Christ," is theoretically a relation of equality. Yet how were the Puritans to manage this structural contradiction, especially when different rules governed the socially stratified body, the commercially incorporated body, and the spiritually egalitarian one?

For his answer, Winthrop turns to the doctrine and interpretation amassed in the previous half century by dissenting ministers concerned with teaching their charges how to live in the world but not be of it. In the first two cases, Winthrop hurries to assure his listeners, some of whom have invested heavily in this risky enterprise, that all worldly "Commerce" between rich and poor—giving and lending of money and forgiving debts—is governed by "justice," the "natural," postlapsarian moral law laid down in Deuteronomy and embodied in the "Golden Rule" and other biblical precepts. In this way, ideas of Christian friendship serve multiple purposes, schooling not only prospective community members in the Christian exercise of charity but investors, merchants, and moneymen as well. A higher law obtains between "brothers" in Christ, even those widely separated by the Atlantic expanse, one that overrules the fair but fallen accountability of justice: it is the rule of mercy, the gospel law of grace, which requires an "exercise of this love" resembling divine forgiveness (*WP* 290).

First Figurative Ligament: The Body

After addressing practical questions about conducting worldly business in an otherworldly way, Winthrop mobilizes two figures—body and covenant—to describe the relationship between saints. Both figures trouble his opening assertion of inherent social hierarchy and eventual spiritual equality. In his exposition of love as "the bond of perfection," Winthrop draws on Paul's description in Ephesians 4:16 and paraphrases his explanation that the church like "the body is one, and hath many members, and all the members of that one body, being many, are one body" (1 Cor. 12:12). Redundancy is the only way to express this paradoxical and mystical equation, which has a long history in Christian thought.[14] Renaissance friendship theory offers a secular and inverted version of this paradox in its fondness for the other Aristotelian formulation of perfect friendship, cited in the introduction and quoted from a poem in *Tottel's Miscellany*, "one soull . . . in bodies twain" (Rollins 106). Politicized, this paradox anticipates the future motto of the United States: *e pluribus unum* (Shannon, *Sovereign Amity* 44). Spiritualizing Aristotle's conception of "civic" friendship, Paul explains that each part of the body, like each member of the church, is different in "gifts," "administrations," and "operations," but each is equally valuable: "For by one Spirit are we all baptized into one body, whether we be Jews or Gentiles, whether we be bond or free" (12:4–6, 13). The "equality" of members of quite different social ranks—slaves and free—is, thus, a spiritual calculus that does not fully succeed in repressing or erasing the traces of earthly social hierarchy that render them unequal and unassimilable.

Spirit "perfects" this uneasy bond, which like Aristotle's *agathôn philia* is virtuous, mutual, and complete and like Aelred's spiritual friendship is "sweet," sympathetic, and intimate but not confined to the traditional dyad. According to Winthrop, the ligament of spiritual love "knitts these parts together" into a "perfeccion," making "eache part soe contiguous" that they "do mutually participate with eache other, both in strengthe and infirmity in pleasure and paine" (*WP* 288). "Perfection" figures the achievement of equality through sympathy across difference. Christ, of course, is the ultimate "model" or "pattern" of a body of perfected parts and is also the means of perfection or the "knitting" together of "contrary quallities or elements" into a cohesive whole (288). The resulting "mutual participation" of the parts requires not just reciprocated feelings—an affective "Sympathy of partes"—but a proximity and nearly physical or, more properly, metaphysical touching or overlap ("soe contiguous") in order to overleap the abyss of contentious differences separating people. This sympathy counteracts the fallen principle of selfishness so that we "seeke" others instead of only ourselves and "make others Condicions our owne" (289, 294).

How does one make another's condition one's own? Can one so fully identify with another or achieve a likeness that authorizes interchangeability? Are crisis or plight necessary to initiate the process, or does it originate in an ongoing, loving attention and selfless desire? Winthrop insists that saints must "feel" what others feel, not only in times of crisis and need but as the primary ontological condition of visible sainthood. Even though others may be in very different social circumstances, they are part of the special circle of Christian fellowship, part of the variegated but unified church body.

To achieve this interchange through sympathy, Winthrop appears to be recommending the exercise of the wildly unstable, dangerous but potent force of the imagination. Returning to Coviello's argument about early American affect cited at the opening of this chapter, Winthrop's recommendation anticipates the imaginative/affective operation that writers like Paine urged and performed for their readers, shaping them through the vicarious experience of loss and suffering into a unified, though not uniform, political body. Paine's imaginative exercises are explicitly gendered and intended, as he says, "to awaken us from fatal and unmanly slumbers" that cloud a true perception of Great Britain's "unnatural" treatment of its colonies (23).[15] Winthrop's call to sympathy works across different registers, revealing a spiritual, heavenly commonality clouded by earthly social differences. The Fall isolated people in bubbles of self-interest and self-pleasure. Only a renovating power like the imagination is strong enough to take us out of ourselves, overcome fallen selfishness, reveal common spiritual ground, and produce the selfless action Winthrop calls a "Sympathie of affeccions" (*WP* 290). This affective sympathy in turn produces a love that is "reciprocall in a most equall and sweete kind of Commerce" (291) and motivates daily self-sacrifice: giving monetary charity and forgiving debts.

It is a telling notion of reciprocity and "equal" exchange, however, that equates forgiving debts and other monetary sacrifices with the receipt of spiritual benefits associated with advancing communal welfare. The two sides of Winthrop's account book record expenditures and profits from different spheres or registers; he has to work hard rhetorically to calculate the "conversion" of one into the other. To this end, he follows Augustine and Aelred who also use the adjective "sweet" to qualify the Christian love Winthrop figures in his address as an "equal and sweete kind of Commerce." The entirety of his argument is epitomized in this phrase. Not only is this exchange "equal" in the sense of being mutual and reciprocal and occurring among those equated through Christian love, but it is pleasing in a very significant way.

The adjective "sweet" implies that the thing described is agreeable to a variety of fallen human senses—taste, smell, hearing, and sight; that it is "beloved" or "dear," which connects it to one of the ancient meanings of *philos* discussed in chapter 1; that it is attractive, delightful, free of impurities, and uncorrupted; and is an object of affection (*OED*).[16] Almost a century after Winthrop gave his address, the New England Puritan poet-minister Edward Taylor uses the adjective "sweet" to express the same heightened feelings of divine love he experienced meditating

on the sacrament of the Lord's Supper where salvation comes in distinctly gusta-
tory and gendered terms. Composed at the end of his life, the last sequence of his
poetic meditations all employ imagery from the Song of Solomon, the biblical
book Puritans read allegorically as a celebration of the mystical marriage between
Christ and his Spouse (the church). In these final, quietly ecstatic poems, the
ailing Puritan minister speaks in the feminine voice of the Spouse and calls Christ
"the best of sweeting" (2.163.4). In his extensive exploration of this theme, Taylor
rewrites the scenario of catastrophe—Eve's eating from the tree of knowledge and
falling from grace—as the very locus of his spiritual apotheosis in taking the
sacrament:

> While I sat longing in this Shadow here
>> To tast the fruite this Apple tree all ripe
> How sweet these Sweetings bee. Oh! Sweet good Cheere
>> How am I filled with sweet most sweet delight.
> The fruite, while I was in its shady place
> Was, and to mee is now sweet to my tast. (2.163.61–66)[17]

Taylor's usage presages Jonathan Edwards's frequent employment of "sweet" as
an adjective that calls attention to the sensory delight and specifically experiential
nature of religious faith. Winthrop anticipates this when he emphasizes the "sensiblenes" of the "speciall relacion" (*WP* 289) among Christians, which he protests
is "a reall thing not Imaginarie" (292).

But this affective identification—not just imagining but literally putting oneself
in another's place and practicing the financial liberality to prove it—cannot hap-
pen until the fallen self itself is forcibly displaced and replaced, until "Christ
comes and takes possession of the soule, and infuseth another principle love to
God and our brother" (*WP* 290). Thus, the "familiar Commerce" Winthrop
advocates has a physical, almost erotic quality reinforced by the sensory and
sacramental implications of Winthrop's vision of Christian love as "a kind of
socialized Eucharist" (S. Foster 44). In an essay written before Dawson's argument for the English context of "A Modell," Morgan speculates that the address
"preceded or accompanied the taking of the sacrament among the passengers
during one of the Sunday shipboard services" and shows its connection to other
addresses offered by ship captains or ministers during colonizing voyages of that
era that employ similar language of "Christian charity," "knitting," and "uniformity of consent" to "foster subjection to authority and to discourage dissension
that must imperil the mission" ("John Winthrop's 'Modell'" 145–46). Winthrop
brilliantly brings these two meanings together when, after he rises to his warning

that the "breache of such a Covenant" as the Puritans have made will surely call down God's wrath, he opens his final paragraph by soothing ruffled feathers and advising coolly, "Now the onley way to avoyde this shipwracke . . . we must be knitt together in this worke as one man . . ." (*WP* 294).

These sacramental implications also had important political ramifications. Admission to communion as the early New England churches conceived and rigorously practiced it became the basis for free*man*ship and male franchise in the fledgling commonwealth. This made spiritual election and political citizenship "mutually reflexive" and tied the "origin" of the "American" nation to a special covenant with God (Lang 31). Despite his rhetorical exertions and his strategic yoking of "sweet" and "equal" to describe the mutuality of "Commerce," Winthrop's spiritual body remains hierarchical, just as the corporate church has Christ at its metaphorical head while the members make up the clearly subordinate body. Even his example of the mouth's function in "the naturall body" displays an Aristotelian notion of "proportionate" or "distributive" justice that obtains between unequals: while this organ receives and minces food to nourish all the parts, they "send back by secret passages a due proporcion of the same nourishment in a better forme for the strengthening and comforteing the mouthe" (*WP* 291–92). The parties to this exchange, which Winthrop wittily calls a "labour of love," are *equalized* in value but are not equals or valued equally.[18]

Second Figurative Ligament: Covenant and Contract

It is not until the highly rhetorical "application" of his conclusions toward the end of the address that Winthrop unveils his other figure for mutuality in his performative declaration of incorporation: "[W]ee are a Company . . . knitt together by this bond of love" and "by a mutuall consent through a speciall overruleing providence" are sent to "cohabit" and "consort" in the New World under a duly established civil and ecclesiastical polity (*WP* 292–93). Subtly, through the strategic repetition of the first person plural pronoun and verbs enacting connection ("knitts," "bonds"), the elite stockholding "company" dissolves into a diverse but now unified spiritual elite. In his constitution of this new entity, Winthrop conflates civic rule with the private sphere's heterosexual order as he builds on the imagery of "Cohabitation and Consorteshipp" by invoking "the more neare bond of marriage" to describe the obligations binding God and the saints. In the next paragraph, however, the marital tie morphs into "a special Commission," which God "lookes to have . . . strictly observed in every Article," and a few lines later it becomes the vaunted "Covenant" that, Winthrop informs his audience, God will ratify and seal by bringing the saints safely to the New World, tolerating no failure or "breache" (294). In this, Winthrop depicts God as exercising none of the "mercy" he exhorts his wealthy Puritans to practice!

Scholars have extolled this audacious use of covenantal language, which draws on a long history in the Old and New Testaments but also appears to bind God in promises that imply an Arminian and Socinian—that is, from the Protestant perspective, heretical—quantity of human "will" and agency. Legally speaking, covenant is a feudal arrangement implying "a medieval sense of power relations" between unequals and the imposition of formal responsibilities (Michaelsen 87). However, Winthrop's notion of "covenant" absorbs the connotations of several of the terms that precede it in his address, from the common law he practiced as manager of his father's estate at Groton and in London's Court of Wards and Liveries, terms like "Company" and "Commission" that invoke the laws and "rules of incorporation" for joint stock ventures and other enterprises of the "commercial body" (89).

Another understanding of "covenant," especially in its political context, is "contract," a term that does not appear in the address but more accurately describes the "speciall Commission" the Puritans under Winthrop's leadership "have taken out." Winthrop expands this metaphor: "[T]he Lord hath given us leave to drawe our owne Articles wee have professed to enterprise these Accions upon these and these ends" (*WP* 294). The attribution of activity and human agency is unmistakable here and suggests that Winthrop may be referring to a new theory of contracts emerging in the seventeenth century as European thought shifted the basis of social relations from status to rights and from the patriarchal family to the individual. Contracts differ from legal covenants in understanding the specified obligations as "acts of will" that are mutually binding and entered voluntarily (Teeven 181; qtd. in Michaelsen 87).[19] In order to promote free and uncoerced consent, contractual mutuality requires a likeness or parity between parties that renders them competent to agree on fair terms for the transaction. On the heels of this modern legal understanding of contract would come the social contract theory of writers like John Locke, Thomas Hobbes, Jean-Jacques Rousseau, and others who posit that human beings are in possession of varying amounts of "natural rights," though women's inclusion in these theories is ambiguous.[20] Furthermore, these thinkers assert that some parity among men—gender specific—is necessary to uphold their contractual promises of money, goods, or labor and, more important, their voluntary submission and (in Hobbes's view) suspension of those natural rights to the greater good of civil government.

The inequality implied by the biblical and feudal notions of "covenant" as well as the leveling implications of Protestant salvation helped soften a position Winthrop must have known would sound to some like an Arminian bargain with God. At the same time, the language of contract served his urgent need to foster a sense of equality among the conglomerate members of the company in terms of their spiritual mission while leaving the door open to progressive financial practices.[21] Their "mutual consent" to "the worke wee have in hand" (*WP* 293) was crucial, because Puritan theology required, paradoxically, that conformity to God's will be voluntary, a willing subjection to sanctioned authority.

In his famous last speech to the General Court in 1645, Winthrop figures this consent to subordination as the "liberty" with which wives "chose" to subordinate themselves to husbands and church members submit themselves "wherewith Christ hath made us free" (*Winthrop's Journal* 2:239). This language refracts Renaissance discourses of amity, where consent is the means of bonding between equals, through the crucial difference that the friends are "sovereign"—that is, selves unsubordinated to another earthly power. Thus, the horizontal "fastening" handclasp of amity (as opposed to the vertically positioned "helping hands") becomes the emblematic "good faith" handshake of equals sealing a contract or business deal. What friends consent to, in the words of Thomas Churchyard, whose *A sparke of frendship and warme goodwill* (London 1588) was one of several treatises on friendship in circulation at the time, anticipates Winthrop's Christianized "liberty": "a willing bondage that brings freedom for ever" (qtd. in Shannon, *Sovereign Amity* 38).[22]

Winthrop was no stranger to these discourses and their formulaic language of specifically male affiliation.[23] Just before leaving for the New World on the *Arbella*, the usually tempered stylist penned a letter to his old friend Sir William Springe that rehearses the "knitting" language of his address in terms of a personal, sympathetic masculine amity. To modern ears, Winthrop's letter, like his unabashedly intimate missives to his third wife, Margaret, seems blushingly sentimental with its passionate confessions, its pious reference to the Bible's most famous pair of male friends, and its requisite "bedewing" tears:

> I loved you truely before I could think that you took any notice of me: but now I embrace you and rest in your love: and delight to solace my first thoughts in these sweet affections of so deare a friend. The apprehension of your love and worth together have overcome my heart, and removed the veil of modestye, that I must needes tell you, my soule is knitt to you as the soule of Jonathan to David: were I now with you, I should bedowe that sweet bosome with the teares of affections: O what a pinche will it be to me, to parte with such a friend!

If any Embleme may expresse our Condition in heaven, it is this communion in love. (February 8 1629/30, *WP* 205–6)

Letters lend themselves superbly to the melancholy produced by the separation of friends, as John Donne remarked wittily in his verse epistle "To Sir Henry Wotton" (c. 1598) that begins: "Sir, more than kisses, letters mingle souls, / For thus, friends absent speak" (214). Earlier, I cited Paul's letters as a source for Winthrop's rhetoric of love and the perfected body, but similar terms characterize Renaissance friendship discourse and the "confederated" polity it presages. They blend in this passage almost seamlessly, as Winthrop resolves initial anxieties about his worthiness (his equality with Springe) by recognizing the "sweetness" of affection and the mutuality of "love and worth" captured in an appropriate biblical exemplum of Jonathan and David. He reaches a rhetorical and emotional climax in his apostrophe to the bittersweet pain of separation, which he assuages with the abstracted visual "emblem" of an earthly Christian communion so powerful that it obviates time and space and, thus, offers a palliative foretaste of paradise.

The important point for my argument is how the unabashed emotionalism of Winthrop's language anticipates the recommendations he makes later in his address upon the departure of the *Arbella*. The grandson of a self-made member of the landed gentry, Winthrop may have consulted Thomas Elyot's 1531 treatise on the education of gentlemen at some point and, if so, would have come across this paraphrase of Cicero in Elyot's account of the exemplary bond between Titus and Gysippus at the book's center. "Friendship is none other thinge, but a parfecte consent of all thinges appertayninge as well to god as to man, with beneuolence and charitie" (162). Later writers on friendship echo a similar rhetoric of conjoining and similarity—even interchangeability—evoked by William Dorke in *A Tipe or Figure of Friendship* (London 1589) and other contemporary publications.[24] In his earlier translation of this passage from Cicero (London 1481), John Tiptoft employed Winthrop's favorite image of "knyttyng to gydre" the consonant wills in friendship (Shannon, *Sovereign Amity* 41). In his address, Winthrop puts this rhetoric to work when he asserts that "the way to drawe men to the workes of mercy is not by force of Argument from the goodness or necessity of the worke," which appeals to the "rationall mind." Pagan writers like Plato and Aristotle give pride of place to "rational desire," while Winthrop seeks to woo his listeners "by frameing these affeccions of love in the hearte" (*WP* 288). The affections he would "frame," I contend, are a Christianized and emotionalized version of perfect friendship.[25]

Christian "Commerce" and the Classical Ideal

In his long explanation of the "inward" exercise of love, Winthrop cites "that maxime of philosophy, *Simile simili gaudet* or like will to like," to argue that Christian love is the result of a perceptible, almost physical resemblance. God loves the natural world and his elect to the extent that they reflect his image, just as a mother loves her child for that child's resemblance of her. Likewise, "betweene the members of Christ, each discernes by the worke of the spirit his owne Image and resemblance in another, and therefore cannot but love him as he loves himselfe" (*WP* 290). These spiritual powers of "discernment" do not merely enable the elect to detect reflections of their redeemed Christlike selves in others but compel such recognition as an ineluctable call. Redeemed self-love is the model for the special love of an other who is (redeemed) like the self. Classical friendship doctrine and its Renaissance redactions inform this formulation.[26] Most obviously, the source of Winthrop's "maxime" is Erasmus's *Adages* (I.ii.21, 167), a popular collection of ancient wisdom that appeared in Nicolas Udall's English translation in the mid-sixteenth century and identified the source of this commonplace as book 8 of the *Nicomachean Ethics*, Aristotle's extended discussion of friendship. Elements of Aristotelian friendship transmuted into the topoi of Christian love appear throughout Winthrop's address, but, as the following discussion illustrates, from the outset they begin to slide into a discourse of marriage.

In the opening section of the address, Winthrop explains that the saint must perform the commandment "to love his neighbor as himselfe" that grounds "all the precepts of the morrall lawe, which concernes our dealings with men, . . . out of the same affeccion, which makes him carefull of his owne good according to that of our Saviour Math: [7:12] Whatsoever ye would that men should doe to you" (*WP* 283–84). The idea of other-directed love based on the regard for one's own worth and virtue, which is neither selflessness nor the egocentric desires of the fallen self, echoes the Aristotelian notion of *philia* or love of the second self. Generalized to all humanity, it becomes the "Golden Rule." The version of this central precept that Winthrop cites from Matthew 7:12 does not mention love at all but rather refers its authority to "the law and the prophets." Winthrop begins his discussion with a paraphrase of Matthew's first formulation of this rule, "to love his neighbor as himself," calling it "the first of these lawes . . . by which wee are regulated in our conversacion one towardes another" (*WP* 283). This version with its appeal to a universal love appears earlier in Matthew 5:43–44 as an amendment of the tribalistic Hebraic law that teaches a more exclusive love of kin and neighbors and hatred of enemies. Grounding his notion of charity in both the law and love is crucial for Winthrop's particular vision.

Chapter 5 of Matthew is an important source for Winthrop, since it also contains the phrase that will become the famous watchword of his address: "Ye are the light of the world. A city that is set on an hill cannot be hid" (5:14). These apparently diverse formulations of the "Golden Rule" come together in Matthew 22:37–40 when a "lawyer" from among the threatened Pharisees, thinking to "tempt" Jesus into heresy, asks, "Which is the great commandment in the law?" Jesus answers, much like a seasoned rabbi, by amending the question. He cites the first commandment to love God wholly but also insists that there is another "great" commandment, to love one's neighbor as oneself, not specifically part of the Mosaic law but also—equally?—fundamental. In fact, these two commandments are themselves like mirror images, associated by and with similarity: "This," Jesus says about loving God, "is the first and great commandment. And the second is like [*homoios*] unto it," so that loving God and loving the other as oneself are homologous, collateral. He then grounds the ethical treatment of others as second selves and the commandment's authority in *both* love and law: "On these two commandments hang all the law and the prophets," he asserts (Matt. 22:40). In Michael Colacurcio's deft reading of Winthrop's address as a source for Nathaniel Hawthorne's Puritan Boston, this conflation represents the crucial significance of his "utopian 'Model'" to the later New England writer, which "had implied that law was just like love, that civil combinations were but reflections of that more ideal union of man and woman" (124).

Winthrop echoes and adapts classical friendship doctrine in other ways. He holds up the "primitive Church" in which members "had all things in Common" —Aristotle's description of the sharing between brothers and comrades—as a model for the "liberality" Puritans must exercise "in cause of Community of perill," his term for a group like the English Puritans, émigrés, and their supporters living under extraordinary circumstances (*WP* 287). Like Aristotle, Winthrop gives active, unstinting maternal affection, based on the perception of similarity— the mother's recognition of herself in her child—as the earthly pattern of Christian love (290). Echoing John 15:13, "Greater love hath no man than this, that a man lay down his life for his friends," Winthrop exhorts Puritan saints "to lay downe your lives for the brethren" (*WP* 289), to "doe good" for each other without expectation of reward except the recompense of exercising mercy (291). He asserts that this love is "free, active strong Couragious permanent" (292), characteristics that all echo classical descriptions of male homosocial friendship based in and productive of virtue. Winthrop echoes the language of mutual attraction that pervades Cicero's *De amicitia*, especially Laelius's assertion that "there is nothing that so attracts and draws anything to itself as likeness of character does friendship." The result is "a compact of friendship" (*contrahat amicitiam*), a term that means both a collection and assemblage as well as a financial or business transaction, which is formed "when some indication of virtue shines forth; the heart fastens and yokes itself to this as to something like itself, and when this happens, love is bound to arise" (xiv.48; 68).

"Charitie"/Friendship as Heavenly Marriage

Although Winthrop imagines Christian saints practicing a version of antiquity's ideal of friendship as a wider but no less spiritually intense affiliation with a select group, the models he offers his listeners are all dyadic. In a long and quite remarkable passage that prepares his audience for his duly famous "Conclusions" in which he hails them in the gospel's words as citizens of "a Citty upon a Hill" (*WP* 295), Winthrop delivers a lyrical paean to the "inward" exercise of mercy—the spiritual love of one soul for another—in the form of an extended description of the soul's "doing good" for its beloved. He genders the soul of the Christian saint female, as was conventional in Christian writing, partly because the Latin word for soul, *anima*, is feminine. But this also reflects classical philosophy's gendered divisions of mental capacities and the association of femininity, appetite, and passion. For example, Cicero attributes the irresistible attraction of likeness cited above to *natura*, a feminine noun: "Now nothing is so eager, so greedy for its like as nature" (*Nihil est enim appetentius similium sui nec rapacius quam natura*) (xiv.50; 68). Winthrop's "soul" is not necessarily the opposite of the body, which is feminized in that binary; rather, it is the spiritual organ of saints making up the church, which, as we saw in Edward Taylor's poetry quoted above, he figures as the feminine "Spouse" in relation to Christ the bridegroom.

Unified by a rhythmic repetition of the pronoun "shee," the passage from "A Modell," which I quote at length below, echoes the language of spiritual avidity and craving for likeness. It begins with an extraordinary simile whose theme itself is "likeness," comparing the soul's *caritas* to Adam's prelapsarian experience of innocent yet insistent desire for Eve:

Now when the soule which is of a sociable nature findes any thing like to it selfe, it is like Adam when Eve was brought to him, shee must have it one with herselfe this is fleshe of my fleshe (saith shee) and bone of my bone shee conceives a greate delighte in it, therefore shee desires nearnes and familiarity with it: shee hath a great propensity to doe it good and receives such content in it, as feareing the miscarriage of her beloved shee bestowes it in the inmost closett of her heart, shee will not endure that it shall want any good which shee can give it, if by occasion shee be withdrawne from the Company of it, shee is still lookeing towardes the place where shee left her beloved, if shee heares it groane shee is with it presently, if shee finde it sadd and disconsolate shee sighes and mournes with it, shee hath no such joy, as to see her beloved merry and thriveing, if shee see it wronged, shee cannot beare it without passion, shee setts noe boundes of her affeccions, nor hath any thought of reward, shee findes recompence enoughe in the exercise of her love towardes it. (*WP* 290–91)

This intensifying catalog encompasses a wide variety of types of "love," somewhat like the early Greek notion of *philia*: heterosexual and erotic passion that desires physical closeness and cannot brook separation, protective maternal and parental love bordering on sacrifice; amicable desires to "do good" for one's friend without reciprocity but also to share affectively in the other's "conditions"; a humane instinct for justice; a sense of possessively holding the other close ("in the inmost closett of her heart"); and yet a primal "oceanic" sense of oneness, expansiveness, and dissolving boundaries in which to give all freely and happily is to receive all back in even fuller measure. This is, as Winthrop indicates at the conclusion of this long paragraph, his understanding of Christian charity, "a most equall and sweete kinde of Commerce" based in the recognition of spiritual resemblance, which produces mutual sympathy and "boundless affeccion" (291).

The initial reference to the first couple connects such commerce with a heterosexual love modeled on the example of *unfallen* marriage whose performative words the soul utters to its beloved "likeness": "fleshe of my fleshe . . . bone of my bone." In the Hebrew account of creation (Gen. 2:23), Adam addresses these words to Eve, whom God has created out of his body, when she is brought to him, giving a literal basis to the injunction in the next verse that in earthly marriage, a man "shall cleave unto his wife: and they shall be one flesh" (Gen. 2:24). But in putting these words into the mouth of the feminine "soule," Winthrop routes his reference through Paul's spiritualized reading of the Genesis passage as "a great mystery . . . concerning Christ and the church" (Eph. 5:32). In Paul's reworking, "flesh" comes to stand for the spiritual "body" of the church, its members whom Christ loves as his "bride."[27] While "likeness" produces "liking" in Winthrop's example, gender difference, which Puritans translated into gender hierarchy and many believed existed even in paradise, colors heterosexual relations with an understanding of "difference" as inequality that gets translated into social and political terms.

Despite its language of sexual difference, scholars have understood Protestant marriage as promoting equality between heterosexual partners. Edmund Leites, for example, argues that classical friendship models informing "the aristocratic idea of friendship among males gave way to the love between husband and wife" (393–94). But as several scholars point out, for Protestants, "companionship" did not merely describe marital compatibility and conversation but connoted "a sexual division of labor within the household" (Dillon 130).[28] As I argue in the introduction, marriage competes with and ultimately overshadows friendship, both as a model of political consent and, as Elizabeth Maddock Dillon argues, as "a model of privatized subject ratification" (129). Sexual difference and gender hierarchy remain marriage's salient characteristics. Later in his address, Winthrop invokes "the more neare bond of mariage, betweene [God] and us," positioning the Puritans as the collective, clearly subordinate "bride" of Christ who is the superior, clearly dominant "husband" (*WP* 293).

In the address's final admonition, Winthrop urges his audience, by "cleaveing" to God, to "choose life" and thus—significantly for the "commercial" multivalence of his dominant imagery—"prosperity," the final word of the address. Marriage, no longer a sacrament but a blessing of the Reformed church, was still referred to as a "covenant."[29] The "spousals," a formal verbal exchange before witnesses, acted legally like a contract but occurred most often among the upper classes between arranging families (Stone 30–32). In the marriage ceremony, the "good faith" handshake of the business contract takes the revealing form of the father "giving away" the bride to her new male authority by laying her hand in his. Reformed Protestant thought attempted to link the three major affective modes of kinship, love, and friendship in the internally skewed notion of "companionate" marriage: spouses were to be lovers and friends, but wives remained subject to the rule of husbands, just as saints of both genders willingly subordinated themselves to the rule of monarch and God. So Winthrop argued in his famous final speech before the Massachusetts General Court in 1645 on "the quasi-marital nature of 'liberty' and 'authority'" (Colacurcio 124). Because the Puritans believed in a "natural" and divinely sanctioned hierarchy of gender, they preferred marriage as the analogy for human-divine relations.

Despite the considerable rhetorical slippage between affective modes in his address, Winthrop's insistence on resemblance as the grounds of Christian love and his emphasis on an "equal" exchange between saints strongly suggest that his paradigm for *caritas* in the purified commonwealth is not marriage—even unfallen marriage—but a version of homosocial friendship. Through this slippage, Winthrop floats the general idea of spiritual egalitarianism while he subtly reintroduces androcentrism and male dominance. For example, Winthrop brings the long, breathless sentence with its accumulated proofs of the soul's passionate and generous loving to a close in a telling biblical climax: ". . . wee may see this Acted to life in Jonathan and David" (*WP* 291). Winthrop's biblicism would have led him to invoke the most frequently cited scriptural ideal of male friendship, as opposed to any of the classical pairs preferred by humanist writers, in his public address as well as in his private communication of affectionate leave-taking to Sir William cited earlier. While this is perhaps a conventional allusion, Edward Johnson's use of the trope in his *Wonder-Working Providence: 1628-1651* (London 1654) has the same sentimental force as in Winthrop's address. A zealous member of Winthrop's émigré community, Johnson describes the emotional farewell at Southampton of two Puritan leaders, one of whom was most certainly Winthrop (and the other may have been John Cotton), in terms of passionate male friendship: "Both of them had their farther speech strangled from the depth of their inward dolor, with breast-breaking sobs, till leaning their heads each on others shoulders, they let fall the salt-dropping dews of vehement affection, striving to exceede one another, much like the departure of David and Jonathan" (52). Thus, a male friendship embodies the feminine soul's longing for her spiritual counterpart. This exemplary pair serves Winthrop's multiple purposes in other revealing ways.

Jonathan was the son and heir of Saul, king of the embattled Israelites. Winthrop reads this Old Testament figure typologically, characterizing Jonathan as "a valiant man" and one "endued with the spirit of Christ"—that is, as a precursor of the Christian dispensation. Discovering the same spirit in the young David, Jonathan "knitts" his heart to the youth, "loved him as his own soule," strips himself of his finery to adorn David, desires to please him, converses with him rather than with his father's courtiers, protects him from dangers, and cannot bear to be parted from his friend without "aboundance of Teares" (*WP* 291). In other words, the extended paraphrase of 1 Samuel 18 that Winthrop offers here essentially repeats in length and intensity and, we might say, complements and competes with the inventory of the feminine soul's loving actions on behalf of her beloved in terms of male friendship, complete with the "teares of affections" Winthrop depicts himself shedding over his separation from Sir William. The soul's love finds its exemplary expression in male homosocial friendship.

The political dimensions of this male friendship also serve Winthrop's corporatizing purposes. After Saul welcomes David as a "son" and gives David his daughter in marriage, the two young men, who should be rivals as heirs to the kingship, instead make "a covenant" (1 Sam. 18:3). This pledge binds them to each other like brothers (via the flesh) but also like spouses (via the affections). Although Jonathan cannot completely discount his obligations and loyalty to his father and king, he protects David from his father's murderous jealousy and also prevents David from killing Saul. Reluctantly, Jonathan agrees to separate permanently from David in order to serve his father but refuses to breach the terms of their covenanted friendship. His love was, as David later explains in his often-repeated lament over his fallen friend, "wonderful, passing the love of women" (2 Sam. 1:26). That is, it was not the disrupting ephemeral passion of *eros* or strategic connections arranged by parents but the freely chosen, tempering, undying loyalty of *philia*. Their covenant, we learn, also extends to their progeny, binding them likewise to God, as the third partner in the Christian conception of spiritual friendship, and to each other in metaphorical marriage/kinship. In fact, this friendship does the work that arranged exogenous marriages were supposed to do: guarantee beneficial and stabilizing alliances between families and clans. In so doing, this marital-like covenant materially shapes the political leadership of Israel, just as male friendship shaped the republic of Athens and Rome and would—so Winthrop hoped—shape the commonwealth of Puritan New England.

In rehearsing the terms of this covenant, Jonathan repeats the performative phrase, "The Lord be between me and thee, and between my seed and thy seed for ever" (1 Sam. 20:42). Their friendship produces an interchangeability that casts David as the adopted "son" of Saul and thus the heir to the kingship of Israel. Jonathan's "spirit" is mirrored in David, who, we learn before they even meet, has been "chosen" by God and on his commandment anointed by the prophet Samuel, thereby replacing Jonathan as Saul's political heir. Thus begins the "messianic" line, culminating with the birth of Jesus.[30] Jonathan's choice of an "other self" is God's choice of a king, just as Adam chooses the "helpmeet" God creates for and from him, and the regenerate soul recognizes other members of the elect. This emblematic friendship also reflects God's "choice" of the Puritans as the vanguard of a new Israel and the Puritans' "choice," which Winthrop prays will be like Jonathan's, "to keepe . . . the Articles of our Covenant" with God (*WP* 295) and so establish in the New World a biblically based social, political, and economic structure purified of selfishness and immorality.

Winthrop offers only one other specific example of this kind of "affeccion," also from the Hebrew scriptures—the love of Ruth and Naomi. Although it is a friendship between women of different ages, status, and cultures, this relation serves Winthrop's purposes in being homosocial, dyadic, and intensely self-sacrificing. Ruth is a young Moabite woman who married Naomi's son when Naomi and her family took refuge in the neighboring region during a famine in Israel. However, after all the men in the family die, Ruth chooses to return with her mother-in-law to Naomi's homeland. Not only does Ruth pledge her love to Naomi when the obligations of marriage and kinship no longer require it, but she refuses to return to her own family, as does Naomi's other Moabite daughter-in-law, and chooses to accept Naomi's God and kindred. Back among Naomi's people, Ruth marries Boaz, her mother-in-law's wealthy kinsman, and bears a son whom she gives to the older woman to raise and who is the grandfather of David (Ruth 4:17). The women's relationship, like Jonathan and David's, also performs a kind of exogamous function in terms of the messianic line. Although Ruth is often taken as a conventional figure of selflessness, it is her voluntary choice of spiritual allegiance to Hebrew monotheism that distinguishes her, finds divine favor, and echoes classical friendship doctrine. Despite differences in background, age, and standing, the love Ruth and Naomi have for each other renders them interchangeable, even, in this case, as child bearers, so much so that an outsider and "Moabitess" can fill Naomi's place in the Davidic line that will eventually produce Jesus.

Although Winthrop mentions Ruth and Naomi only in passing as one of many other instances of "reciprocall . . . Commerce," this example picks up the unsettling theme of gender difference. The relationship between Ruth and Naomi fits uneasily into the classical friendship tropes that David and Jonathan's bond epitomizes. Not only are they women and, thus, excluded from ideal friendship because of the prevailing belief that, being ruled by passions and appetites, females were incapable of the highest forms of spirituality, but they are of widely divergent ages and cultures. Rather, this relationship reinforces Winthrop's key point that Christian love transcends such differences and creates the "likeness" necessary for *caritas* on the basis of spiritual resemblance and the overmastering desire to do good for the other. Jonathan gives unstintingly to David, but it is their similarity of status that authorizes their interchangeability; the mutuality of *philia* continues to shape their affiliation. Ruth's love slips into an almost selfless Christian *agape*; furthermore, she is interchangeable with Naomi because of a specifically female ability to bear children. Thus, their "spiritual" affection brings them back to "nature" and the flesh, precisely what spiritual friendship was thought to transcend.

It is the evasion of the material and fleshly that drives Winthrop's utopic vision and, we might say, ensures its failure. Such selfless giving, he insists, enraptured with his own rhetoric, yields a "pleasure and content" that is "the soules paradice, both heare and in heaven" (*WP* 292). Such spiritual mutuality far outstrips the joys of earthly marriage, destined, so Paul teaches, to dissolve at death anyway. Clinching his lengthy disquisition on the spiritual "marriage" to come in heaven that can be glimpsed in and most suitably emblematized by homosocial friendship, Winthrop declares: "In the State of Wedlock, there be many comfortes to beare out the troubles of that Condicion; but let such as have tried the most, say if there be any sweetnes in that Condicion comparable to the exercise of mutuall love" (292). Speaking as a man who found many comforts in his three marriages, Winthrop still propounds that earthly marriage is, finally, not quite as mutual or as satisfying as the "most equal and sweet kinde of Commerce" tasted in spiritual love illustrated by perfect (male) friendship.

This "charitie," a metaphorical love-based-in-law, was to be the foundation of Winthrop's exemplary "commonwealth." In searching for the Puritan sources of Hawthorne's *The Scarlet Letter*, Colacurcio cites Winthrop's "Modell" and finds particularly relevant the extended "loving outburst" of the feminine soul, quoted earlier, which "Hawthorne seems to have recognized . . . as Winthrop's own theme song for New England" (125). Although this gendered rhetoric may suggest that "Winthrop were bidding to become a sort of theological feminist," its wholly metaphorical nature actually discloses the persistent inequality of women in this rapturous vision. Winthrop's love, Colacurcio observes, "is the love of the citizen, under the law," the Puritan's "renewed spiritual ability to love the law as the unfallen Eve once so fully loved" Adam, or as the saved soul loves Christ (126). It is the love of law and love as law that Hawthorne's passionate Hester Prynne— walking in the footsteps of Anne Hutchinson and blazing a path for later American rebels and dissidents—"flatly rejects" (124). Unlike the tremulous Dimmesdale, who allows his theology to force him to choose between love and law, Hester rejects this Christian allegory. She rejects it because, as Colacurcio observes, recalling Winthrop's feminizing of Puritan subordination as the wife's freely chosen subjection to her chosen husband in his final speech to the General Court quoted earlier, it was created by men "arguably for the same (Platonic) purpose of escaping 'the woman,' by becoming her themselves . . . allegorically, by submission" (124, 128).

More than a century and half later, Eliza Wharton, another (not completely) fictional nonconformist and Hannah Webster Foster's famous "coquette," would suffer a personal and social defeat with distinct political overtones at the hands of a startlingly similar hierarchical and slippery vision of social relations. Beset with (bad) choices for her future affiliations, Eliza seeks maternal advice. When she rightly complains that the prevailing Federalist vision of marriage casts women in an unsupportable "dependent situation," her mother, a tepid clergyman's widow, counters by asking: "[W]hat one is not so? Are we not all links in the great chain of society, some more, some less important; but each upheld by others, throughout the confederated whole?" (XXI, 136). As Sharon M. Harris observes in her astute political reading of Foster's novel, which I expand on in the next chapter, Mrs. Wharton's comment does not envision a democratic society based in equality but instead "recalls more closely the hierarchical social order of John Winthrop's 'A Model of Christian Charity,'" delivered over a century and a half earlier (14). Ironically, Eliza embraces homosocial friendship as a more authentic, egalitarian relationship and, thus, echoes the other side of Winthrop's vision. But as she will discover—and it is a fatal discovery—Federalist culture may have lost the "sweetness" of Puritan zeal but shed little of its hierarchical, and from the standpoint of differences, hypocritical tenor.

I long to hear that you have declared an independency—and by
the way in the new Code of Laws
which I suppose it will be necessary for you to make I desire you
would Remember the Ladies, and
be more generous and favourabler
to them than your ancestors. Do
not put such unlimited power into
the hands of the Husbands.
Remember all Men would be
tyrants if they could. If perticuliar
care and attention is not paid to
the Ladies we are determined to
foment a Rebellion, and will not
hold ourselves bound by any Laws
in which we have no voice, or
Representation. That your Sex are
naturally Tyrannical is a Truth so
thoroughly established as to admit
of no dispute, but such of you as
wish to be happy willingly give up
the harsh title of Master for the
more tender one of Friend.
—Abigail Adams to John Adams,
March 31, 1776, in
The Book of Abigail and John

CHAPTER THREE

Hannah Webster Foster's *Coquette*

Resurrecting Friendship
from the Tomb of Marriage

By the mid-eighteenth century, politi-
cal and pedagogical writers in the American colonies were rethinking traditional
relations of authority—parents over children, husbands over wives—in terms Jay
Fliegelman identifies as the era's promotion of "rational, protective, and mutually
satisfying contracts of friendship" (41). Neither required by custom, like familial
duty, nor dangerously passionate, like erotic love, "equalitarian friendship" was
thought to temper and ennoble while it opened the self to sensibility, sociability,
and mutuality. In the eyes of many writers of the time, it was "the ideal relationship" (41).

This development was politically momentous, since, according to Fliegelman,
"the struggle for American independence and for subsequent federal union was
intimately related to, and ideologically reflected in, a national affirmation of the

sacred character of affectional and voluntaristic marriage" (129). Spouses were to be like friends, freely chosen, and their "reasonable liberty" to enter into matrimony and dissolve infelicitous bonds became a powerful argument for separation from England (125). There are, however, important differences between friendship and marriage as consensual relations, which republican apologists sought to downplay and which historians have ignored. As we have seen in previous chapters, "rational equalitarian friendship" was a form of affiliation adapted from classical *philia* and early modern discourses of "amity" that historically excluded women or limited their participation on the basis of their alleged emotionalism, while "consensual marriage" in this era, no matter how affectionate and voluntarily embraced, did not consider or render the spouses legally or socially "equal."

The evidence Fliegelman offers in support of his claims, from the poetry of John Milton, shows the same kind of slippage I explored in chapter 2 in John Winthrop's deployment of classical friendship tropes. In the practiced hands of these Puritan polemicists, the rhetoric of contractualism disarmingly embraces consensual if not egalitarian modes of affiliation but retains a gender hierarchy that disavows its hegemony.[1] Fliegelman cites how frequently, in the last quarter of the eighteenth century, colonial North American newspapers reprinted and political writers alluded to Milton's "hymn" to "Wedded Love" from *Paradise Lost*, book 4 (ll. 750–67), often blithely changing phrases to fit more closely the colonial situation (127). An examination of the verses Milton *did* write suggests that, like Winthrop, he viewed specifically *prelapsarian* heterosexual love as the basis for more profound, specifically masculine, and even civic ties:

> Hail wedded Love, mysterious Law, true source
> Of human offspring, sole propriety
> In Paradise of all things common else.
> By thee adulterous lust was driv'n from men
> Among the bestial herds to range, by thee
> Founded in Reason, Loyal, Just and Pure
> Relations dear, and all the Charities
> Of Father, Son and Brother first were known. (ll. 750–57)

These opening lines of the "hymn" do not extol all matrimony, only the "wedded Love" in paradise between unfallen Adam and Eve. Milton considers this foundational, because it remains the only instance of a pure but earthly "relation" between humans.

These innocent beings, though literally the same flesh, were not in Milton's mind ontologically equal, nor was their unfallen relation free from coercion.[2] Eve herself echoes Paul's teaching on marital gender hierarchy in 1 Corinthians when she acknowledges Adam "My Guide / And Head" (*Paradise Lost* 4:442–43). Although Adam's avowal, "Part of my Soul I seek thee, and thee claim / My other half," uses a Christianized discourse of friendship—the soul "seeking" its equivalent part or reflection, modified by the Platonic/Diotimic notion of love as the reunion of an originary whole—the "halves" are not equal and certainly not the same: what delights Adam most are Eve's "submissive Charms" (8:487–88, 498). Furthermore, Eve's first impulse, upon awakening after her creation, is to embrace her own pleasing reflection she glimpses in a "pure" pool, which she innocently equates with "th' expanse of Heav'n" (4:456). This is her first mistake, signifying her need for interpretive redirection to the "true" heaven. The watery being she spies in the pool returns her gaze "with answering looks / Of sympathie and love," an allusion to the primacy but misprision of narcissistic female homonormativity (4:464–65). God must purposely tear Eve away from her own image and lead her to Adam, whom she at first regards as not only "less faire, / Less winning soft," but less "amiablie mild" than her same-sex reflection—that is, less like herself and thus less likely to be a true friend (4:478–79). With a "gentle hand," Adam nevertheless "seizes" Eve's hand, who then "yields" and thereby learns to

> see
> How beauty is excelled by manly grace
> And wisdom, which alone is truly fair. (4:489–91)

Although instinctively drawn to homosocial affiliation and thus illustrating the principle of visual "likeness" advanced by classical and early modern writers, Eve must ultimately renovate her very perceptions so that she can "choose" a heterosexual relationship defined by gender. In this relationship she is subordinate and, because literally downward-looking, considered inferior. Eve's pre-heterosexual encounter with desire allegorizes the threat female friendship poses for heteronormative social orders, even nominally "enlightened" and "liberal" ones, as well as the way republican marriage subsumes what Fliegelman calls the "equalitarian" nature of friendship. In his support of gender hierarchy (though not monarchism), Milton echoes the royalist theory of Sir Robert Filmer, whose *Patriarcha, or the Natural Power of Kings* (1680) linked social and political power in the rule of Adam, the first father.

Similarly, Milton implies that the first couple's unfallen connubial relations serve as the basis for exclusively masculine civic affiliations. In the final lines of the passage quoted above, Milton contends that in unfallen marriage, "first were known" (that is, imagined and made possible) "all the Charities" (that is, the disinterested relations of Christian *caritas* and civic mutuality extolled by Winthrop in his famous "Modell of Christian Charitie" of 1630 discussed at length in chapter 2) that characterize the relations of "Father, Son and Brother." These are the specifically homosocial, exclusively masculine, and, Milton implies, superior and preferable affiliations of paternal kin and civic community. "Founded in Reason, Loyal, Just and Pure," these "Relations" not only encompass the noble characteristics of ideal male friendship enumerated most famously by Aristotle, Cicero, and Michel de Montaigne but are qualified by the adjective "dear," which the classically trained Milton would have known is rendered in Greek as *philos*, a word that as a noun also means "friend" (Konstan, *Friendship* 56).[3]

The view from the distaff side, even when penned by a man, was quite different. As one "maid" mused in the heavily freighted language of another frequently reprinted poem of the Revolutionary period: "For the great end of nature's law, is bliss. / But yet—in wedlock—women must obey . . . I wed—my liberty is gone for ever" (Lauter 1:774).[4] Despite a compelling nationalist rhetoric of "sacred" consensual marriage based on an Enlightenment discourse of contractualism in which wives willingly subordinate themselves in sentimental unions, many contemporary writers recognized and bemoaned the continued legal and political subordination of women as *femmes couvertes*, a situation that did not substantially change until the mid-nineteenth century (Kerber 155).

Dana Nelson argues that coverture contained a gendered logic that allowed white men to address growing fears during this period over masculine identity in the family, male rivalry in the market, and representation in the political arena. Politically, citizens of the newly confederated states began to insist on "*actual* representation," expressed in a range of local democratic practices that "echoed the one-state, one-vote rule under the Articles of Confederation" (*National Manhood* 32; her emphasis). Against this laterally organized and "more explicitly confraternal model" of political affiliation, supporters of a strong centralized government proposed the Constitution, a hierarchical structure for government that anchored masculine familial authority, market competition, and virtual political representation in "a symbolically fraternal, reassuringly 'common' manhood" posited against unruly or vulnerable femininity (34, 37). Thus, the emerging liberal ideology Nelson identifies as "national manhood" exchanged relatively egalitarian modes of affiliation and a public sphere of diverse local relations embodied in the Articles of Confederation for a vertical, abstracting, and uniformalizing structure of governance enshrined in the Constitution and based on the analogy of the male-headed family (45).

Excluded from marital equality as well as from peer relationships with men in politics, business, and the professions, women of the emerging middle class took up the elaborate rituals of homosocial friendship with enthusiasm.[5] By the early nineteenth century, the "interlocking ideologies of the separate spheres (domesticity, sentimentalism, woman's fiction)" identified by scholars were fully established (Davidson, Preface 451–52). Women's friendships, frequently fired by evangelical spirituality, became synonymous with sentimentality, sensibility's often derided second act. However, the early republican era produced narratives that oppose the "political coverture" of the Federalist marital model, which made women legally invisible and feminized men as brides of the state.[6] In this chapter, I will argue that Hannah Webster Foster's epistolary novel, *The Coquette*, published in 1797, proffers a discourse of "equalitarian friendship" as a social alternative to unequal and privatizing Federalist marriage. Though Foster's heroine is ultimately *not* sustained, socially or psychologically, by this alternative, she insistently appeals to friendship as the principal moral and egalitarian relation of a public social sphere. Her failure is, I think, meant to be instructive.

Enormously popular when it appeared in 1797 and reprinted repeatedly until 1870, *The Coquette* draws on the unfortunate history of Elizabeth Whitman (1752–88), educated daughter of a deceased clergyman from a solid New England family who was an active member of large social circles in Hartford and New Haven, Connecticut. An accomplished poet who was courted for a time by the young Joel Barlow, Whitman was engaged to a clergyman who died in 1775 and later broke off an engagement with another well-respected cleric. In 1788, she fled from her family to an inn where she gave birth to a stillborn child, whose father was unknown, and died of puerperal fever, alone and among strangers.[7]

Whitman's story circulated widely in New England newspapers and became what Cathy Davidson describes as "an object lesson on the dangers of female rights and female liberty" (Introduction ix). These popularized versions stressed Whitman's marital and heterosexual dilemmas. Foster, by contrast, embeds the story of her fictional Eliza Wharton in an exchange of letters among a close circle of female friends who correspond, advise, and condole with each other. Their interactions constitute what critics have identified as "the female plot" of a novel otherwise seemingly dominated by heterosexual concerns (Pettengill 186). To follow this often overlooked companion story of female affiliations, according to Janet Todd, is "to discover a different fictional trajectory" that frequently opposes the main one, "embittering the comic end or mitigating the tragic" (6).[8]

Critics who follow this plotline in Foster's narrative argue, however, that the female community, before and after Eliza's death, is not only ambivalent about her discordant desires but downright murderous.[9] Julia Stern, for example, contends that Foster's female circle is not the nurturing sororal world described in Carroll Smith-Rosenberg's classic essay on women's friendships of the period but is fully "penetrated" by the intolerant patriarchal values of the elite Federalist culture it ventriloquizes (139). In Stern's forceful reading, the contradictions of female friendship incarnate "the same repressive principle" as the libertine who causes the heroine's "fall" and produce "sadistic" impulses symbolically linked to his demonic machinations (140–41). The tyrannous quashing of differences by this "moral majority," like the bitter political factionalism of the 1790s it allegorizes, renders female friendship, and friendship in general, completely unrecuperable. What is missing from the novel, Stern concludes, is "precisely . . . a female world of love and ritual," a segregated, privatized sphere in which Eliza "would revel" (268).

This seems unlikely, however, given Eliza's overriding hunger to cut a public figure, a key aspect of her nonconformity. Stern locates Eliza's unabated yearning for "female communion" as one of two forms of "sympathy" that compete in the new Republic and reflect the political and philosophical differences bitterly dividing early national culture. The dominant mode of sympathy proceeds from "republican ideology" and is public and political, promoting community interests over individual gain and personal sacrifice in the service of a greater collective good. Stern links this reigning form of republican sympathy with "the feminized patriarchal chorus," which ultimately and tragically enforces hegemonic values, making Eliza its scapegoat (72–73). The second, less visible, largely privatized form of sympathy proceeds from "then-emerging liberal modes of thought" and emphasizes the autonomous person, the unrestrained pursuit of economic gain, and civic health through the protection of individual rights. According to Stern, Eliza is the only character in Foster's novel who exercises this proto-liberal individualism but, lacking an Adam Smithian "empathic respondent to reflect much-needed compassion . . . remains ideologically isolated, socially invisible, and emotionally erased" (73). Although aware of the binarism of this framework, Stern maintains that Eliza fails because she has "no access to a normative form of liberalism" with which to challenge conformist Federalist ideology, no "democratic and individualistic Jeffersonian universe" to embrace her sensibility (107). But has liberal individualism provided women, or people of color, for that matter, full access to the public sphere as anything but autonomous and isolated free agents—as honorary white men?

Eliza's unruly desire is threatening to the male status quo *and* its female enforcers, it seems to me, because she wants both—liberty, in the form of a literal and imaginative freedom to dispose of oneself that is restricted to white men, and connection, in the form of dyadic intimacy and larger sympathetic networks, as well as the ability to circulate freely in both the private/domestic world and the public/social sphere. Even the censorious Mr. Selby, deputed by Eliza's buttoned-up clergyman suitor to spy on her in his absence, recognizes her superior public social skills. Captivated almost against his will, he reports that in "general conversation . . . Miss Wharton sustained her part with great propriety. Indeed, she discovers a fund of useful knowledge, and extensive reading, which render her peculiarly entertaining; while the brilliancy of her wit, the fluency of her language, the vivacity and ease of her manners, are inexpressibly engaging" (XXIV, 140–41).[10] In fact, Eliza excels in the "rational discourse" associated with republican era print/text culture identified by Michael Warner as well as in the more affective, bodily based vocal performances of nation propounded by Fliegelman and Christopher Looby. It is precisely the "contraction," "retirement," and "confinement" of a private, domestic marital sphere *separate* from a public social sphere that she most fears and resists.

From this perspective, Stern's categories of reigning repressive republican sympathy and emerging expansive liberal sympathy are reversed: Eliza appears to be the champion of an inclusive, even feminist "civic republicanism," the antithesis of the elite, narrow, and conformist politics Stern rightly associates with Federalism, while the female "chorus" presages the more rigid separation of the sexes and women's exile from the social to the domestic sphere ushered in by liberalism.[11] As Gillian Brown argues, historians began to advance an "attractive vision of civic republicanism," bolstered by the compelling work of J. G. A. Pocock in the 1970s, which did not, like liberalism, compartmentalize the personal and the public spheres but treated these as continuous and interdependent. The "civic sense" promoted by this understanding of republicanism, Brown concludes, derives from rather than counters the Lockean liberalism that took root in early American thought (8–9). Stern dismisses Eliza's "fancied" vision of a "collectivity in which virtue and interdependence are the hallmarks of social relations" as "elite" and suffused with "nostalgia" (131). In order to explore the social and political tensions dramatized by Foster's novel, it is necessary to shift focus from Stern's central term, "sympathy," to the word most frequently employed by Foster's characters to describe their social relations—that is, "friendship"—in order to recall the historically utopian and theoretically egalitarian tenor of this mode of sociality.

Discourses of Friendship

Dualistic notions of "sympathy" linked to contending political philosophies obscure the overlaps and continuities that characterize affective regimes, even competing ones. With its roots in classical and Renaissance humanism, republicanism embraced historical forms of friendship such as civic or political friendship, defined as the practice of virtuous alliances for public good, not encompassed by Stern's use of terms from Scottish philosophy like "sympathy," "compassion," and "fellow feeling."[12] Furthermore, as I argued in the introduction, friendship is not a feeling but an institution—what Laurie Shannon calls a "normativity"—that in the early modern world competed with the institutions of heteronormativity (erotic love, marriage) and promoted what for classical thinkers was the most important and ennobling human relation characterized by equality and mutuality (*Sovereign Amity* 55). As I explained in chapter 1, although the major writers on friendship differ in specifics, Aristotle, Cicero, and Montaigne all describe its "perfect" or "ideal" form occurring only between elite, educated, and self-possessed men of virtue in dyadic relations that are quintessentially voluntary (unlike kinship relations), are equal and tempering (unlike marriage), and display a reflective homonormativity that borders on interchangeability: the friend is "another" or "second" self, and friends are, in the conventional phrase, one soul in two bodies.[13] The study of the Latin language and classical culture and the use of translated and "modern" texts, like Shakespeare's plays, to teach rhetoric by recitation helped to disseminate the ideal of Greek *philia*, Roman *amicitia*, and early modern "amitie" in colonial and republican America. Early modern redactors emphasize the mirroring, twinning/twining, and "confederating" elements of ideal friendship.

Scottish philosophy retooled the rational basis of classical friendship and its emphasis on virtue into the idea of "sympathy," an affective means of shaping and moderating sociability.[14] By the turn of the nineteenth century, sympathy as a feminized and feminizing form denoted the major affect of affiliation in Anglo-American culture, elevating but also trivializing women's expressive relations in the broad cultural work of sensibility. Intimate dyadic friendships became associated with the domestic and increasingly private social sphere but remained an important cultural institution, characterized by "mutuality" and derived from a constellation of structural similarities—age, gender, class, temperament, beliefs—that conspired to produce the psychic and social ensemble of rituals that define friendship.

Despite lingering associations with privilege, rationality, and exclusive masculinity, friendship in the republican period constituted an affective *ideal* linked with local, intersubjective, tempering, and above all equalizing affiliations, as opposed to the tyranny of the passions or the rhetorically consensual hierarchy of marriage. The language and governing structure of the Articles of Confederation enshrined the political version of this ideal. Despite the colonies' differences of size, population, and importance, the Articles bound them as political equals in "a firm league of friendship" (*Federalist Papers* 500). This "more explicitly confraternal model" of political association came under sharp attack by Federalist polemicists and was ultimately replaced by the centralizing and abstracting structure of the Constitution (D. Nelson, *National Manhood* 34).

Constraints on women's affective and affiliative opportunities echoed this political foreclosure. In the heterosexual plot of Foster's narrative, Eliza's father, a clergyman, narrowly determines his daughter's social future and imaginative horizon by choosing another clergyman as her marriage partner. Eliza accepts, but only because she perceives that Mr. Haly, her father's choice, is not long for this world, and she nurses him dutifully. When both her father and fiancé die, Eliza is released and resurrected, as it were, from what she calls the "slavery" and "entombment" of coercive paternal authority, arranged marriage, and privatized domesticity. Reentering society and anticipating the pleasures of free circulation, Eliza promptly encounters two suitors who, presenting her with the illusion of choice, merely intensify her earlier dilemma. The respectable, stodgy, and self-satisfied Reverend Boyer offers her a replica of her mother's stultified life, while freedom and pleasure beckon alluringly in the company of the insouciant, unmistakably dangerous Major Sanford.

Ironically, for a novel of seduction, marriage is one of the principal temptations the heroine must struggle to avoid. Eliza's exasperated remark on Boyer's unremitting courtship—"I don't know but this man will seduce me into matrimony" (XXXIII, 156)—reverses the genre's conventional plot and hints that the usual allegorical valences do not apply. By contrast, the homosocial plot offers Eliza another choice altogether, which her women friends cannot perceive and perversely conspire to prevent her from making—that is, to reject the terms of Federalist marriage or extramarital passion and choose friendship, a historically rooted social alternative and the contemporary political equivalent of independence. The Declaration of Independence specifically cites "happiness," in the broader Aristotelian sense of self-realization, as one of the "unalienable rights" of all "men," the gender position Eliza will have to identify with in order to pursue that right.

In the very first letter she writes, Eliza admits to her confidential friend Lucy the giddy, almost guilty sense of "pleasure" she feels on being liberated from her engagement to Mr. Haly, a man "of real and substantial merit" but not a mate of her choosing, and from the "paternal roof" (and her weak, collusive mother) with its "melancholy," "gloom," and "condolence." From the outset, Eliza associates "melancholy" with coercion and confinement, while she associates pleasure with freedom from constricting arbitrary power—a specifically "American" sort of freedom.[15] At the end of the first letter, Eliza firmly announces her own desires: "Calm, placid, and serene; thoughtful of my duty, and benevolent to all around me, I wish for no other connection than that of friendship" (I, 107–8).

While Eliza will report, in the very next letter, that "the opposite disposition"—"Naturally cheerful, volatile, and unreflecting"—has taken hold of her mind and will confess to Lucy her enjoyment of romantic "conquests" (II, 108–9), she remains determined to resist entanglements and to freely participate in "those pleasures which youth and innocence afford" (V, 113). For example, after her initial rejection of Boyer's precipitous declaration of love, Eliza echoes the very word "zest" that Grace Aguilar's Mrs. Leslie used to describe the essence and enjoyment of friendly intercourse between virtuous people cited at the beginning of my introduction. Eliza reports to Lucy with relief that, after Boyer finally mastered his emotion, they had tea, "during, and after which, we shared that social converse, which is the true zest of life, and which, I am persuaded, none but virtuous minds can participate" (XIV, 127). "Perfect harmony" is how Eliza characterizes a long afternoon outing on horseback and dinner in mixed company (XVI, 129).

Repeatedly, Eliza expresses the desire to engage "placidly" in "social conversation" while the unsolicited "ardor" of the men around her threatens everyone's full engagement in this social benefit (XVI, 129). Furthermore, because republican "liberty" in the classical sense depended on the possession of inalienable private property, which ensured the possessor's freedom to act with disinterest in the public good, Eliza has to found her freedom in her social/affective possessions. Presuming, she quips significantly, "on a large stock in the bank of friendship," Eliza enters the unstable Federalist social market with Hamiltonian "credit" based in the affection, support, and solidity of her family, circle of intimates, and virtuous reputation (III, 110). But can friendship rooted in local material relations function as abstracted fungible funds with which to trade?

As indicated in her first letter quoted above, Eliza regards "friendship" as a relation characterized by balance, cognizant of duty, and suffused with "benevolence" or disinterest. Not merely personal or private, it is the paradigmatic "social" relation and society's cohering force. This understanding reflects contemporary thinking shaped by Scottish philosophers earlier in the century who defined "society" as combining aspects of the public and private spheres. In the nineteenth century, these spheres became more rigidly opposed and more exclusively gendered. According to historian Jan Lewis, society occupies "the space between the solitary individual and government . . . [which] included all those institutions and places where men and women came together . . . and realized their human potential" (" 'Those Scenes' " 57). Reading the letters of early thinkers as theoretically divergent as Thomas Jefferson and Alexander Hamilton, Lewis finds that they both redefined friendship "by removing patronage from [its] obligations." Thus, they divested friendship of its formerly "instrumental, political dimension; it now entailed only sociability and affection" (61).

As a consequence of this shift, Lewis argues, women of the upper classes were "being stripped of the only significant political power they had held, the ability to call friends—in the older meaning of the term—and kinsmen to account." In this way, "democratic politics" ironically limited women's political participation to moral suasion in the social sphere and revalued female emotion as volatile affection requiring management (61). Women of the rising middle class, like Eliza, and their male counterparts never even had the power of instrumental friendship Lewis describes to intervene politically by calling in "favors." Neither were the politics shaped by Hamilton or Jefferson truly democratic with regard to women and people of color. Emotional management, though different for the sexes, gained a special importance in the new American Republic where proliferating conduct books, like the list of rules composed by none other than George Washington, retooled aristocratic codes of courtesy for the middling class and defined social success as "self-madeness" and "self-possession" (Hemphill 34).

The ennobling, self-possessing, but also other-embracing effects of friendship Eliza solicits in her newly liberated state recall the central features of aristocratic courtesy and genteel pedagogy, which drew on classical models of friendship. For Aristotle and other classical philosophers, friends act as disinterested mirrors for each other, encouraging moral growth through mutual love of what is good, offering frank criticism (the opposite of flattery), and sharing affection and goods. While the ancients believed that only the elite and mostly men could even aspire to, let alone achieve, friendship's highest form, early modern conduct books exhorted "good" men of all ranks to "seeke for their semblable on whom they may practise amitie"—a call that was heard by, if not aimed at, women (Elyot 161). By the mid-eighteenth century, the Scottish philosophical school secularized Christianity's fellowship of faith and universal benevolence into a widely applicable, potentially democratizing principle of sociability on which Eliza's conception draws. Adam Smith, for example, distinguishes his understanding of "sympathy" from classical Greek *philia* or Roman *amicitia* by remarking, "They who would confine friendship to two persons, seem to confound the wise security of friendship with the jealousy and folly of love" (225). The "reflecting" function best served in classical friendship by a single friend or small circle of intimates is, in Smith's conception, served much better by "a mere acquaintance" and best of all by "an assembly of strangers" (23).

Both of these understandings are at work in the world Foster delineates. The term "friend" encompasses family, parents, advisors, and protectors (supervisory and ascribed relations of inequality) as well as intimates, social acquaintances, and even conjugal partners (achieved relations, if not of equality and mutuality, then nominally, of consent). Although the dynamics of these various types of friendship differ, for Eliza the moral, moderating, and supposedly strengthening effects are the same. The "calmness," "serenity," and "mindfulness" she seeks at the novel's opening are products of friendly sociability—that is, seeing oneself and one's opinions reflected generally, but also specifically, in the people around you.

Eliza recounts her attempts to achieve this reflective balance during her first venture into society at the commodious estate of her cousins, aptly named the Richmans, after a period of mourning for her fiancé. As the "gates of a spacious garden" are dramatically thrown open, inviting Eliza into a new world, she remarks: "Mirth, and hilarity prevailed, and the moments fled on downy wings; while we traced the beauties of art and nature, so liberally displayed, and so happily blended in this delightful retreat" (III, 110). Although Eliza's monitory friends will soon begin to upbraid her for what they judge a dangerously escalating taste for "mirth, and hilarity," in this instance it is Eliza who leaves off participation in the mirth to be a spectator of this characteristically neoclassical scene. Eliza relates how she "had rambled some way from the company" to better admire the spectacle when she is accosted by the intrusive Mrs. Laiton, who rudely reminds Eliza of her recent loss (110). Julia Stern observes that "waywardness and eccentricity ultimately become [Eliza's] characteristic spatial patterns," figuring her escape from "the Augustan scenery of post-Revolutionary Connecticut" to a more hospitable "realm of heightened emotion" associated with the "fervor that marks the Great Awakening" (80). But Eliza signals both an affinity with heightened emotion *and* her need for distance from it when she confesses to being an "*enthusiastic admirer* of scenes like these" (my emphasis). She forgoes the company's "mirth, and hilarity" for the momentary quiet of detachment and solitude. Mrs. Laiton's condolences threaten to drag her back into the thrall of arranged matrimony.

Eliza's spatial "waywardness" is also an affective eccentricity. She wants to be simultaneously independent and attached, admiring spectator and enthusiastic participant, aware of the center but not—as we will see below—centered or fixed. Sleepless, because her "imagination is so impressed with the festive scenes of the day," Eliza writes that night to Lucy of a renewed sense of integration, which is mirrored for her in the external world: "[A]ll nature is serene and harmonious; in perfect unison with my present disposition of mind" (III, 109–10).

Friendship's Clouded Mirror

While Eliza's witty and incisive letters to Lucy detail what readers recognize as doomed attempts to forge tempered friendships with men, they constitute the textual embodiment of more intimate exchanges with her female circle. This divide characterizes the entire narrative and raises questions about the discursive parameters of friendship in this period. Eliza and her suitors are each paired with homosocial correspondents to whom they open their minds, while Eliza also corresponds with a wider circle of intimate women friends who pen the majority of the letters. Letters rarely cross the gender divide, and when they do, they are stilted, desperate, or high-handed. Significantly, Sanford's egocentrism exiles him from the "emotional-disciplinary circuit" of mirroring sociability exercised, in particular, by Foster's female characters (Pettengill 194). Thus, the responses of his correspondent, a Mr. Charles Deighton, if they exist, never appear in the text.

The primary exchange of letters, between Eliza and Lucy, is necessitated by their physical separation for most of the narrative. They are reunited briefly, in the middle of the story, so Eliza can be made to bear witness to Federalism's normative pageant, Lucy's wedding, which signifies the female friends' definitive division. This separation may simply be the device Foster used to generate the main body of letters, but it also foregrounds how marriage can isolate women from supporting networks and make them dependent on textual exchanges. In this period, women were not self-determining, and their reliance on family and marriage often meant separation from same-sex friends and sources of emotional support. Conversely, epistolary relations allowed women to participate in forms of textual expression. Eliza's long letters read like minidramas with astute characterization (including self-description), dialogic interchanges, and multiple voices and show off her discernment and nimble style. Rather than moralize and chastise, as all her women friends do, Eliza *narrates*, sometimes with commentary, sometimes without, so that her letters resemble third person literary (not merely literate) accounts. Ironically, Eliza's entangling heterosexual relations involve her physical presence and face to face engagement, while her homosocial relations are largely textual, narrative, and deferred, captive to other social obligations. Even when her final melancholy causes her to lose interest in writing letters, at the moment of crisis Eliza reverts to composing a long missive to her mother rather than endure a painful confrontation with her. Can friendship, as a social and political mode of democratic relation modeled by educated women, be maintained across distance and through textuality, Foster seems to be asking, and what does this mean for an alternative vision of republicanism?

For Aristotle, who was influenced by the radical friendship doctrines of Pythagoras, the highest form of friendship required that friends live together and share everything in common. Thus, the brotherhood of comrades in arms, which Aristotle associates with the political form of democracy, is his paradigm for the most complete friendship in which the mirror of self and other is never clouded by distance or absence (*NE* 8:9, 13–14). When Cicero set his dialogue on friendship at the moment of the disintegration of the Roman Republic and placed it in the mouth of the Stoic-trained statesman Gaius Laelius, who had recently lost his lifelong friend Scipio, not just discourses about friendship but the institution of friendship itself became linked to absence and loss, personal and political.[16] This linkage became inextricable after Montaigne wrote his influential treatise on friendship describing his incomparably sublime connection to his deceased friend Étienne de La Boétie. A major concern of Jacques Derrida's extensive meditations on "the politics of friendship" has been the way canonical friendship discourses encompass oppositions like presence and absence.

Christian friendship, whose spiritual character is reflected in its deferral of fulfillment until after death, was more amenable to physical separation. Early Christians, scattered far from each other but united by a common faith, adapted the classical and pagan belief that letters could make absent friends present and raised the practice of epistolary friendship to new heights (C. White 8). A powerful spiritual sense connected these correspondents, much like the feelings of "charitie" John Winthrop recommended to "the household of faith" in his lay sermon "A Modell of Christian Charitie." Winthrop exhorted the departing Puritans and those remaining behind that "though wee were absent from eache other many miles, and had our imploymentes as farre distant, yet wee ought to account our selves knitt together by this bond of love, and live in the exercise of it" (*WP* 292). As I observed in chapter 2, critics have taken Winthrop's call as a precursor of the collective emotional responses evoked by republican-era writers to unify the disparate colonial population. The responses produced an "odd civic intimacy" associated with a specifically American national identity (Coviello 457). But what are the effects of this spiritualization and abstraction on civic identity and community?

By contrast with Eliza's embodied practice of "social converse," Lucy drives the stakes of friendship higher into a rarefied sphere. In Lucy's heightened rhetoric, friendship is "that heavenly passion," and she questions whether it can "reside in a breast"—Major Sanford's—"which is the seat of treachery, duplicity, and ingratitude? You are too sensible of its purity and worth, to suppose it possible," she chastises Eliza sharply (LXI, 212). Lucy links her transcendent notion of friendship not merely with moral virtue, social conversation, or "the true zest of life," as Eliza (not to mention Adam Smith) does, but with a more stringent, almost Puritanical, and bodily "purity," a quality that suggests its opposite: moral or physical contamination. In this respect, Lucy anticipates the sentiments of nineteenth-century apologists of gender difference and female "superiority," a social "fiction" one historian of emotion describes as a "token compensation for [women's] continued inequality in the bourgeois public sphere" (Hemphill 46).

As friendship became more spiritualized and apolitical in the course of the nineteenth century, women receded further into domestic obscurity. Lucy's stridency may be fueled by her own impending nuptials, which require, as we will see, the total transfer of her desires not only from homosocial to heterosexual objects but from social visibility and, within her female circle, relatively egalitarian relations to domestic invisibility and consensually hierarchical ones. While Lucy is sobered by this prospect, she cannot imagine, as Eliza does, refusing it. Despite their differences, it is the loss of Lucy as moderating mirror, frank correspondent, and reflecting consciousness that forces Eliza to seek for an answering image in the accommodating and unscrupulous Major Sanford.

Sanford incarnates self-centered passion. He declares several times about Eliza: "Though I cannot possess her wholly myself, I will not tamely see her the property of another" (XVIII, 131; XXVIII, 148). Regarding women as disposable assets, he can contemplate Eliza's "possession" by another—even herself—only with feelings of incipient violence whose depths are suggested by his menacing use of the word "tamely." In the text's economic vocabulary, Eliza has become an "engrossing" mental image, what Sanford in his extremity calls "the *summum bonum* of my life" (XLII, 181). Although this phrase, Latin for the "greatest good," implies that possessing Eliza has become the final end of Sanford's actions, it has unmistakable connections to ethics and politics. For Aristotle, the *summum bonum* is happiness achieved by restraining the passions, not by gratifying them. From Plato's *Republic*, modern republicans borrow the idea of the greatest good to the most people as a principle of civic virtue. For Aquinas and Christian thinkers, it is the love of God. Sanford's perverse appropriation of the term highlights the ineffectiveness of his "gentlemanly" education by the way he individualizes and hedonizes the concept, since the "good" he seeks pertains only to himself and his erotic desires.

Often identified with political factionalism, Sanford embodies a more dangerous tendency—anarchy—duly feared during the volatile decade of the 1790s. In the narrative's one explicit discussion of politics in Letter XXIII, General Richman enacts his duty as host and former military leader one evening by chiding the rebellious Sanford for carrying on a competing conversation with several of the women about the theater. A master of performance, the seductive Sanford thus divides the guests into "parties," a term that implies both political factions as well as parties of pleasure. The general's chastisement draws the social renegade back into the majority orbit, while "the gentlemen" applaud Mrs. Richman, who claims to speak for a silent Eliza, for her insistence upon women's visible but completely subordinate role in republican politics (139). But Sanford is not so easily controlled or disarmed. At the height of his obsession with Eliza, he declares, "[M]y mind is all anarchy" (XLI, 177). Without any governing system or set of moral controls, Sanford can eschew all responsibility for his actions and wreak social and personal havoc.

Mr. Boyer represents a contrasting affiliative tendency. Hoping that "I am, and ever shall be a reasonable creature" acting "upon just and rational principles," he fails utterly (VIII, 117; IV, 111). His overpowering emotions might qualify him as the vaunted "man of feelings," a cultural figure that emerged earlier in the eighteenth century, except that Boyer attempts to conceal his feelings beneath a veneer of reason and views the sensibility produced by his passion as dangerously feminizing. At the height of his infatuation with Eliza, he exclaims: "My heart is in her possession. She has a perfect command of my passions. Persuasion dwells on her tongue. With all the boasted fortitude and resolution of our sex, we are but mere machines. Let love once pervade our breasts; and its object may mould us into any form that pleases her fancy, or even caprice" (XXXIX, 165). Political writers of the time echo this sentiment, particularly fearing the passions demagogues could whip up in an ill-educated general populace whose effects would be precisely a dangerous loss of control, making men into "machines" easily manipulated. Boyer's abject confession contradicts and renders hypocritical his many assertions to Selby, his confidante, that justify his "regard" for Eliza as "not of that passionate kind" but "governed by reason . . . excited by the appearance of excellent qualities" (XLVII, 188).

Despite his lip service to current discourses of friendship, Boyer is finally incapable of a truly mutual "regard" for Eliza that would allow for the necessary "reflecting" of one equal in another. In his rejection letter to her, he self-righteously (and in self-justifying hindsight) portrays courtship as "the rational interchange of affection" and marriage as "the calm delights of domestic life" (XL, 166). Earlier, he quoted to her lines from James Thompson's poem "Spring," which characterize "the matchless joys of virtuous love" as "Content, retirement, rural quiet, friendship" (XXII, 137), and assured Eliza that "far is the wish from me to restrain your person or mind" (XIV, 126). However, mental and physical restraint is precisely what Boyer, and the societal/political principle he embodies, seeks. As husband and moral monitor, he imagines himself supplying Eliza's "gay disposition" with "discretion sufficient for its regulation" (IV, 111). Moreover, he fantasizes about not just regulating but channeling Eliza's gaiety to the amelioration of his own dreary situation: "A cheerful friend," he tells Selby, "much more a cheerful wife is peculiarly necessary to a person of studious and sedentary life. They dispel the gloom of retirement, and exhilarate the spirits depressed by intense application" (111–12). This mirror, however, looks all one way.

Erotic love not only overthrows reason, making Boyer proverbial putty in his beloved's hands, but also, in his own words, "unmans" him (XL, 169). "The tear of sensibility" Eliza mockingly spies "sparkl[ing] in his eye" (XIV, 127) feminizes Boyer, robbing him of discretion, opening him to dangerous emotional and political manipulation. Sanford has a similar reaction to the reconciliation he effects with Eliza after a long absence, though not without a note of sardonic self-irony. He declares archly to Deighton: "I never knew I had so much sensibility before! Why, I was as much a woman as the very weakest of the sex!" (LVIII, 205).

Reviled by Selby as a female rake (XXVII, 146), Eliza desires to freely circulate in a visible social sphere, which masculinizes her. Sensing the danger in her friend's trespasses on masculine privilege, Lucy counsels Eliza to stay within her social sphere and seek a "modest freedom" (XIII, 125). This is not surprising coming from a character who rejects as "truly disgusting" the "masculine habit and attitudes" adopted by female equestrian performers she sees in the circus at Boston (LII, 196). But Eliza does not want half-measures, feminine difference, or a diluted version of independence. Later, she self-consciously appropriates male prerogative, even embracing a "double standard" for sexual behavior when she jokingly quips that she might consider marriage "when I have sowed all my wild oats" (XXXIV, 158). This expression, usually reserved for men, links Eliza with indulgence, anarchy, and the dubious gender "privileges" exercised by Sanford.

The unsettling similarities between these characters point to a pattern of imagery in which Eliza finds her reflection in Sanford rather than in the circle of female friends around her. In stark contrast to the "prudish" Mrs. Richman, whose "contracted ideas confine virtue to a cell" (V, 114), the "monitorial lessons" of absent Lucy (II, 109), and the self-deluding hypocrisy of Boyer, Sanford represents the free pursuit of pleasure, bolstered by (the appearance of) affluence that Eliza mistakes for the pleasurable pursuit of freedom. In relation to the disapproving Richmans, Sanford imagines himself "independent of their censure and esteem" (XVIII, 131) and thus insulated from the Smithian stings of regulating morality. The experience of "independence," however, is precisely what, as an American, Eliza craves.

It is ironic that the one way Eliza thinks she can achieve this independence is to imagine herself on a par with the seemingly aristocratic Sanford. Eliza tells Lucy that she only considered marrying Sanford "from a predilection for his situation in life"—that is, for the "independence, which [she] fondly anticipated" his affluence and tastes would afford her (LV, 201). In several cases, they echo each other uncannily: Sanford is the only other character in the novel that describes marriage as a "noose" and the submission "to be shackled" (XI, 122; XVIII, 131). His use of these metaphors confirms his egotistical blindness to the situation of real slaves in the new Republic as well as to the subordination of white women in post-Revolutionary marital arrangements where their biological difference—resulting in pregnancy—prevented them from enjoying the same freedom as men. But his deployment of these figures gives Sanford a superficial congruence of interests with Eliza that he can use to build up his case for their similarities and, hence, their friendship.

The echo that most captivates Eliza occurs when Sanford cleverly enumerates the "restraint, the confinement, the embarrassments to which a woman, connected with a man of Mr. Boyer's profession, must be subjected; however agreeable his person might be" (XIX, 132). Alluding flatteringly to Eliza's "generous mind," Sanford asks whether she "could submit" to such surveillance and constraint, and playing on her social ambitions, he wonders whether she might not "find greater sources of enjoyment in a more elevated sphere of life, or share pleasures better suited to [her] genius and disposition, even in a single state" (132). While this last suggestion serves his purpose by increasing her isolation, it strikes a deep chord in Eliza, who puts Sanford's blandishments in starkly political terms: "He warmly applauds my wish, still longer to enjoy the freedom and independence of a single state, and professedly adopts it for his own" (XLI, 174). Sanford is the only character who even entertains the idea that a woman might want to remain, and might benefit from being, single—a "sovereign" self/state, treating with other sovereign entities.[17]

Finally, Sanford wins Eliza's confidence by making "the most ardent professions of friendship[,] . . . solicit[s] a place in [her] friendship and esteem," and asks to "be admitted to enjoy [her] society . . . as a brother, if no more" (XIX, 132–33). Sanford's wily and ingenuous request to play the role of brother to Eliza seems innocent and protective. Yet it masks an illicit and potentially anarchic sexual attraction that Foster's readers would have recognized from William Hill Brown's epistolary novel *The Power of Sympathy*, published eight years earlier. In that story, tragedy ensues and incest is narrowly averted when the young lovers discover that they are, in fact, brother and sister.

We are not surprised, therefore, when Sanford almost immediately breaks this promise to treat Eliza as a sister because, he confesses, he is "not stoic enough, tamely to make so great a sacrifice" (XXVI, 144). In this chilling admission, he differentiates himself explicitly from the classical, self-disciplined ("stoic") practitioners of perfect friendship and affords us a glimpse of the brutality of his selfish desires. Still, in these finely tuned machinations, Sanford astutely "reads" Eliza, providing us with an index of her desires, which points to the centrality of friendship in her mind. The language of siblings he employs offers Eliza the illusion of horizontal, egalitarian relations rather than the hierarchical, unequal, and male-dominated relations of erotic love and marriage.[18]

In fact, Eliza repeatedly asks her clergyman suitor, Boyer, to change his rhetoric of love to "some more indifferent epithet" such as "esteem, or friendship" (XII, 123). The language of love and marriage, she declares, does not strike her "fancy." By contrast, Eliza admits that "her ear was charmed with [Sanford's] rhetoric, and [her] fancy captivated by his address" (XIX, 132). What proves so "captivating" and potentially ameliorating to Eliza's fancy that it succeeds in overcoming her heart's disapproval of his questionable sentiments is Sanford's discourse of "freedom and independence" with its implications of sovereignty and equality, couched in the rhetoric of friendship.[19] He manipulates this rhetoric brilliantly, first flattering the vulnerable Eliza, then confessing his "guilt," and finally petitioning her to reform him as an act of "benevolence": "[L]et the kind and lenient hand of friendship assist in directing my future steps" (133).

Not just once in the course of the narrative but twice Eliza "falls" for Sanford's professions of friendship, even though both times she has ample evidence that they are dissimulations. However, they offer her something she cannot find anywhere else in the world of this novel. In the first half of the narrative, Eliza longs for a vision of freedom and equality in the public social sphere actively opposed and stymied by her female circle; and in the second half, she misses the "consoling power of friendship" in the private realm, which her mother fails to provide and which her erstwhile confidante Lucy actively and selfishly withdraws (LXVI, 222). Lucy claims to be motivated "by real friendship," and the substitute she sends in her place, the unmarried and uptight Julia Granby, likewise dismisses Sanford's professions as "mere hypocrisy, and deceit." Julia portrays her own solemn warnings as part of the "duty of the friendship and affection I bore" you (LX, 210).

Why doesn't Eliza heed these warnings from her closest friends? In a devastating revelation of the psychological as well as social failure of female friendship, Eliza confesses to Julia that although fully apprised of Sanford's character, "I embraced with avidity the consoling power of friendship, ensnaringly offered by my seducer" (LXVI, 222). The choice between "real" friends who offer astringent criticisms and a constricted vision of female opportunity and the false, flattering, deliciously amoral deceiver offering an elusive, degendering, masculine freedom seems absolutely clear—but is it? And if it is so clear, why can't the brilliant Eliza—why can't we as readers—make that choice? I argue that Eliza can no longer "see" herself in these upstanding, upbraiding women; the "mirror" of friendship they provide offers a view of "virtue" that demonizes Eliza's progressive desires.[20]

Federalist Marriage Entombs Friendship

In a crucial interchange with Mrs. Richman, recounted to Lucy in Letter XII, Eliza parries the older woman's unsolicited recommendation of Mr. Boyer as a suitable match for her with the emblematic declaration, "[M]arriage is the tomb of friendship." She goes on to observe, "It appears to me a very selfish state," and asks, "Why do people, in general, as soon as they are married, centre all their cares, their concerns, and pleasures in their own families? . . . The tenderest ties between friends are weakened, or dissolved; and benevolence itself moves in a very limited sphere" (123). In Eliza's experience, marriage "centers" the affections on a small, private group, excludes all but the closest intimates, and "limits" what should be the "universal" effects of sociability.

Mrs. Richman counters by offering a defense of marriage but in terms of friendship. The circumscription of intimacy to a few, she argues, "refines . . . our enjoyments" by concentrating them; this suggests the intensity of classical friendships that were dyadic or limited to a very small group. But in the next breath, Mrs. Richman reveals her true point: "Here we can repose in safety" (123). The social world, she implies, is dangerous on many levels for women; only in the privacy of marriage can they find a protection whose very necessity underlines their vulnerability to and inequality with men. Centering, circumscribing, concentrating, refining: this language echoes the warnings of the writers of *The*

Federalist Papers against "diffusion," "dismemberment," and the "eccentric tendency . . . to fly off from the common center" for which the "blessings of union"—metaphorical marriage between the states and the federal government, (male) citizens and the representative executive—is the proper, Federalist antidote (7).

To illustrate her point, Mrs. Richman quotes the following lines from Joseph Addison's *Cato, A Tragedy* (1713), act 3, scene 1, part of an exchange between Cato's sons, Portius and Marcus:

> The friendships of the world are oft
> Confed'racies in vice, or leagues in pleasure:
> Our's has the purest virtue for its basis:
> And such a friendship ends not but with life. (XXII, 123)[21]

As I discussed earlier, Julie Ellison demonstrates in her study *Cato's Tears* how this play, popular on both sides of the Atlantic, established the influential paradigm of a heroic, republican, and sentimental *masculine* affect within homosocial friendship. The male-identified and patriotic Mrs. Richman is more than eager to appropriate this vision of affiliation. Worldly friendships, the citation suggests, allow people to collude or conspire in "confederacies" based only in vice or pleasure; the latter experience always has a negative connotation for the "prudish" Mrs. Richman.[22] Private relations, such as marriage, can be based not only in virtue but in "the purest virtue," a phrase implying that only pleonasm can express the benignity and safety women apparently require. In fact, according to Mrs. Richman, superintending the "little community" of the private, circumscribed family rather than masking women's political contributions "renders us more beneficial to the public" since "benevolence," even though it changes its "objects" (husband and children for same-sex friends or community), remains "true" and "unlimited by time or place." "Its effects," Mrs. Richman concludes, invoking the signal phrase of classical friendship, "are the same, and aided by *a second self*, are rendered more diffusive and salutary" (123; my emphasis).

The citation from *Cato* is a strategic choice, for it deploys republican male and brotherly friendship in the service of romantic passion: in this speech the impassioned Marcus reminds his brother, Portius, of their undying loyalty to each other in order to secure Portius's help in winning Lucia's love. Even Eliza appears to contribute to this logic when she describes her friends' marriages in terms reminiscent of classical homosocial friendship. Of Lucy and George's union, she says: "The consonance of their dispositions, the similarity of their tastes, and the equality of their ages are a sure pledge of happiness" (XXXVI, 160). Eliza implies, however, that the qualities necessary for an enduring friendship make a strong basis for marriage, while Mrs. Richman subsumes the egalitarian aspects of friendship within the hierarchical structures of Federalist matrimony. Without the possibility of an independent exercise of friendship, Mrs. Richman's logic transforms women's submission to marital subordination, legal and political invisibility, and a restricted (soon to be self-effacing, self-sacrificing) notion of selfhood into a veritable public service and civic duty.

Lucy strenuously reinforces Mrs. Richman's view of marriage in Letter XXIX, where she perceives Eliza balanced precariously on a "precipice," having been led "from the path of rectitude and virtue" (accepting the marriage proposal of Boyer) by the "*ignis fatuus*" of the artful Sanford. Marriage, Lucy argues, is not, and has never been, Sanford's intention; rakes like him are, she asserts, "steeled against the tender affections, which render domestic life delightful; strangers to the kind, the endearing sympathies of husband, father, friend" (150). By contrast, as I showed in chapter 2, the Protestant notion of companionate marriage recommended that the categories of "lover, husband, or friend" unite, as they appear to do in the figure of the respectable clergyman Boyer (XIII, 124). Thus, Lucy counsels Eliza not to fear losing her "freedom" when married to a man like Boyer, whose "honor and good sense will never abridge any privileges which virtue can claim" (XV, 128). In other words, allowing women's "modest freedom" depends entirely upon the honor of husbands who grant it as a "privilege" to women, not as a "right."

But there is more than a note of guilt in Lucy's high-minded prating, since in the course of the narrative, she will reenact the effects of marriage Mrs. Richman exemplifies and celebrates: not only woman's heterosexual "domestication" and subordination but the decentering of primary, homosocial friendship that is its inevitable but disavowed consequence. Both women repeatedly protest that privatizing marriage does not force them to exclude friends from their "affection or society" (XLIII, 182). Mrs. Richman's declaration rings particularly hollow next to the account of her "natural" and "easy" transition from being "a gay, volatile girl; seeking satisfaction in fashionable circles and amusements"—and sounding uncannily like the pleasure-seeking Eliza she chastises so energetically—to being "thoroughly domesticated. All my happiness is centered within the limits of my own walls; and I grudge every moment that calls me from the pleasing scenes of domestic life" (182). More ominously, Lucy reveals that though her fiancé is pressing her to set an early date for their wedding, she insists on waiting for Eliza's return to Hartford. "Such is my regard for you, that a union of love would be imperfect, if friendship attended not the rites" (XV, 128), she explains. Friendship has become a required "attendant" to the central and centering rite of marriage, subsumed by the normalizing *centrality* of heterosexual relations. Eliza must bear painful witness to the "rite" by which her special intimacy with Lucy—and friendship as an equalizing principle more generally—is entombed.

It was not always so. Even the unromantic Lucy admits ruefully that marriage has removed her from her "native home" and its special joys. In promising—herself as much as Eliza—to visit Hartford "when the summer returns," Lucy offers a glimpse of their girlhood affection: "Again, my Eliza, will we ramble together in those retired shades which friendship has rendered so delightful to us" (LII, 196). These words call up the innocent "sisters' vows" invoked by Helena, Shakespeare's heroine of *A Midsummer Night's Dream*, in a passage that would have been familiar to Foster's audience as a mainstay of eighteenth-century rhetorical training through recitation from the classics and "moderns." Stung by her friend Hermia's apparent "confederacy" (l. 192) with (the now magically enchanted) Lysander and Demetrius in making cruel sport of her, Helena chides:

Is all the counsel that we two have shar'd,
The sisters' vows, the hours that we have spent,
When we have chid the hasty-footed time
For parting us—O, is all forgot?
All school-days friendship, childhood innocence?
We, Hermia, like two artificial gods,
Have with our needles created both one flower,
Both on one sampler, sitting on one cushion,
Both warbling of one song, both in one key,
As if our hands, our sides, voices, and minds
Had been incorporate. So we grew together,
Like to a double cherry, seeming parted,
But yet an union in partition,
Two lovely berries moulded on one stem;
So with two seeming bodies, but one heart,
Two of the first, like coats in heraldry,
Due but to one, and crowned with one crest.
And will you rent our ancient love asunder,
To join with men in scorning your poor friend?
It is not friendly, 'tis not maidenly.
Our sex, as well as I, may chide you for it,
Though I alone do feel the injury. (3.2.198–219, 269–70)

This evocation of early modern girlhood is perhaps the most lyrical extrapolation of the classical ideal of perfect friendship. In these lines, Helena echoes

Aristotelian ideas in the phrase "two seeming bodies, but one heart," suggesting that the socially diverse audiences for Shakespeare's plays would have been familiar with these concepts. The strategic substitution of "heart" for the more conventional "soul" signals the increased emphasis on the emotional, rather than rational or spiritual, qualities of friendship that began to characterize Renaissance representations of amity and the depictions of female same-sex affiliations. Helena describes the metaphorical "sisters" not only as ripening fruit vulnerable to sexual and marital plucking but as inseparable and interchangeable: "a double cherry, seeming parted . . . [t]wo lovely berries moulded on one stem." Even the physical separation and palpable divergence of their bodies—much comedic wordplay springs from their noticeable difference in height—is a deceptive appearance, as the repetition of "seeming" suggests; in the real world of their girlhood love, they are almost undifferentiated and physically merged and constitute an ontological and political paradox, "an union in partition." The irony or comedy (depending on your viewpoint), of course, is that this idyllic, innocent oneness has been broken by the women's own socially requisite heterosexual desires, which can be reconciled only through Puck's enchantment.

Likewise, Lucy's condescending nostalgia for "home" conceals a deeper connection—and more painful separation—she wishes to obscure: Lucy and the brilliant Eliza as "mirror" images, just as Mrs. Richman's self-representation as "a gay, volatile girl" suggests youthful similarities among all the women of this circle. Furthermore, in her comments Lucy discloses that as girls they both "rambled"— that is, wandered and perhaps imagined freely without constraint, enjoying the "eccentric" waywardness that, in Eliza's return to society at the beginning of the novel, signifies her resistance to Federalist norms and her fatal desire for freedom. The key difference is that as girls they rambled in "retired shades," frequently secluding themselves in "the little arbor" in the Whartons' garden where, Eliza recalls, they "spent so many happy hours" (XLI, 178), while her later rambles, literal and symbolic, take place in the unforgiving glare of a censorious public eye.

It is Eliza's reaction to Lucy's marriage that offers the most extensive hints about their early friendship and what its loss entails. Letter XXXVI begins with Eliza congratulating Mrs. Richman on the birth of her daughter Harriot and saluting the newborn—"Hail happy babe!" These words echo the Miltonic apostrophe, "Hail Wedded Love," from the "hymn" discussed at the beginning of this chapter that republican writers used to persuade American men and women of the necessary, centering "blessings of union." This innocent girl child, Eliza implies, will also be subject to such mixed "blessings" (159). Lucy's circumscription through marriage compounds the strictures on women's "circulation" Mrs. Richman earlier recommends and practices. This event, Eliza reports, fills every on-looker with "pleasure" and moves every tongue to "wishes of benevolence. Mine only was silent" (160). The "idea of a separation; perhaps of an alienation of affection, by means of [Lucy's] entire devotion to another" casts "an involuntary gloom" over Eliza's mind. Boyer, who is attending Eliza, pompously offers "to lead you to your lovely friend" in order to ensure Eliza's "participation"—that is, her symbolic witnessing of the marital pageantry and Lucy's "natural" transition from an egalitarian feminine circle and homosocial dyadic friendship to a private, domestic, hierarchical heterosexual one. But Eliza resists and retorts: "Oh no. . . . I am too selfish for that. She has conferred upon another that affection which I wished to engross. My love was too fervent to admit a rival" (160). In desiring a homosocial emotional "monopoly" over Lucy, Eliza's use of commercial language recalls Sanford's rhetoric of possessive individualism and invokes the "freedom" he only seems to offer, associated with emerging capitalist endeavors and "paper" money. Incapable of "hearing" Eliza's complaint and thinking to turn her desolation to his own advantage, Boyer suggests, "Retaliate . . . this fancied wrong, by doing likewise" (160), revealing not only his self-centeredness but his inability to "credit" the salience of female attachment.

According to social historians, Eliza's "fervent love" and "engrossing" desires accurately reflect the emotions characteristic of women's homosocial relations in this period, while the loss of primary affective connection through marriage often provoked similar crises (Chambers-Schiller 173). Claire C. Pettengill reads Eliza's account of Lucy's marriage as the "climax of the drama of feminine bonding that runs through the novel." Forced to completely "reformulate her sense of self and sense of purpose" to conform more nearly with her friends' expectations that she settle respectably, Eliza falls into a "depression" that causes her "fatal hesitation" to accept Boyer's proposal and his rejection of her. This, in turn, causes her social ostracism, which leads to her secret liaison with Sanford (who is married to another woman), her sexual fall, and her death in childbed (196–97). However, Pettengill does not mention that before the narrative even begins, threats to female homosocial bonding surface in the arranged engagement to Mr. Haly in which Eliza would have been forced to "sacrifice [her] fancy" to the will of her parents and probably experienced her first real separation from Lucy, who was also entering the marriage market. Although Eliza's fortuitous "liberation" from paternal and marital coercion temporarily stayed this depression, it returns upon Lucy's marriage, and when Eliza's attempts to conform to expectations fail, it finally defeats her.

More threats resurface when Eliza realizes that, even though after Lucy's wedding she will accompany her friend to Boston "and spend a month or two in her family," a decisive shift in Lucy's focus has occurred that will never be reversed (XXXVI, 161). In fact, after her marriage, Lucy does not respond to several of Eliza's long letters, including the missive detailing the crucial events leading up to and following Boyer's final rejection. Lucy's damaging silence continues until Eliza writes and encloses the humiliating letter of "expiation" Mrs. Richman urged her to send *a year after* Boyer's departure and Boyer's self-congratulatory response, which spells Eliza's social doom (Letters XLVI–XLVIII).[23] The loss of Lucy as "correspondent" represents Eliza's loss of "correspondence," not only someone to communicate and "answer the world with" but one who is similar, equivalent, agreeable, matching. Marriage silences, because it centers even the willing Lucy, leaving Eliza with no one "with whom I could freely converse, and advise" (XLVIII, 190). Sanford, Lucy's demonic other, is also absent at this time, trawling in the South for a rich wife to amend his embarrassing financial situation. Finally, Mrs. Wharton's inadequacy as an advisor or mirror prompts Eliza to write again and beg Lucy to allow their mutual and unmarried friend, Julia Granby, to come to Hartford. Although Lucy is unable to attend Eliza because of her "engrossing" domestic obligations, she is also strangely reluctant to let Julia go, as if her own marital situation requires the presence of another woman to make it bearable.

Not only is Julia a substitute for Lucy, but she represents, in Eliza's own words, "all that I once was; easy, sprightly, debonair," combining the heroine's former vivacity, intelligence, and sociability with Lucy's "moral hygiene" (Stern 141). Urging Eliza "to revisit the scenes of amusements and pleasure," Julia "likes neither to be secluded from them, nor to go alone" (L, 192), participating gladly in post-Revolutionary sociability while benefiting from a network of women's dyadic intimacies. Unhampered by Eliza's "fanciful" notions about "freedom" and happily imitating Lucy's "discreet and modest behavior in a single state," Julia announces she would also "take [Lucy] for a pattern should I ever enter a married life" (LXIII, 214). Lucy is her "modell of charitie." Even Sanford, who finds Julia "a most alluring object," recognizes her virtue as unassailable and her "honor" as impregnable (LXV, 218). According to early modern "homonormative logic" discussed in chapter 1, these qualities offered women limited access to the "masculine" virtues of autonomy, self-disposition, and homosocial friendship (Shannon, *Sovereign Amity* 69) but within a severely contracted sphere. Willing to pay the price of "limitation," Julia enters the narrative as an imitator of Lucy, the "pattern" for republican womanhood, and as an "improved," politically acceptable replacement for Eliza.

Initially buoyed by Julia's friendly ministrations, Eliza shares a bed with her, as women friends often did during this period, until Eliza's secret liaison with Sanford begins to "bear fruit." Eliza also reports that they "have been rambling in the garden," even straying, on Julia's insistence, into the retired "arbor" (L, 192–93). Once the favored retreat of Eliza and Lucy, a privileged, sheltered site of girlhood rambles, the arbor and its healing privacy, which Julia thinks to recapture, have been fatally contaminated by Sanford's "ensnaringly" and doubly false vows of friendship offered there. Though Julia perceives the weakness of Eliza's resolve in relation to Sanford and has fresh evidence of his schemes to isolate his victim (Letter LX), she nevertheless departs for a visit to Lucy in Boston, which Eliza's depressed state prevents her from joining. During Julia's absence, Sanford achieves "the full possession of my adorable Eliza!" (LXV, 217). When Julia returns, she finds Eliza irreversibly altered and beginning to recede into a melancholic silence. Later, Eliza indirectly indicts her female circle of friends and lays the blame for her dependence on Sanford on their failure to truly respond or correspond to her: "I had no one to participate my cares, to witness my distress, and to alleviate my sorrows, but him" (LXVI, 222).

Eliza's "settled melancholy" ironically produces the domestic confinement and social silence she earlier feared as a consequence of marriage to a clergyman (LI, 193), and in essence, she has linked herself with the soul-killing social customs represented by both Boyer and Lucy. However, her melancholy points to a form of loss that is both psychological and political. According to Sigmund Freud, melancholic depression is a product of the incomplete mourning of a loved, narcissistically chosen but lost object by a psyche already ambivalent about object relations. In a movement Freud describes as "regressive," the ego identifies with the lost object and incorporates it, hoping thereby to redress the loss to the id and in this process shapes the ego's sedimented "character" (19). Thus, Eliza's excessive mourning for the loss of Boyer's suit suggests her identification with and incorporation of the repressive masculine/paternal figure and the values he represents.

There is, however, a more interesting way to look at the collapse of desire and identification in this process. In her revisionist psychoanalysis, Judith Butler argues that gender identity, understood as a cultural "accomplishment," not a natural "disposition," is also a melancholic effect, produced through cultural prohibitions that operate according to a double negative: not only the denial of same-sex attachments but the disavowal of those losses, which amounts to a "foreclosure of possibility . . . understood as unlivable passion and ungrievable loss" ("Melancholy Gender" 24). In other words, society not only denies the significance of same-sex relationships but forbids us to mourn the loss of this source of affection. Butler refers specifically to "homosexual desire," but the intensity of homosocial friendship blurs the self's object of desire and object of identification in similar ways. Eliza's friendship with Lucy represents a form of homosocial affiliation linked to self-possession, imaginative freedom, and lateral, egalitarian relations. Eliza cannot grieve her loss of Lucy—as the object of her affections *and* identification, the person who mirrored and rambled with her— because heterosexual marriage has subsumed friendship and has become Federalist culture's horizon of personal, social, and political stability. Unlike her female peers, Eliza cannot accept the loss of homosocial affiliation, which is also a loss of self-possession, or function in its absence and seeks substitutes who might reopen the foreclosed possibilities of identification and desire that are not routed through heteronormativity. Thus, Eliza's disavowed "anger at the other" is, in Butler's words, "turned inward and becomes the substance of self-beratement" ("Melancholy Gender" 29), a source of Eliza's self-blame and repeated sense that she has "forfeited" her friends' love and trust (XLVIII, 190).

In the end, no longer able to conceal her pregnancy and unable to face what she imagines will be her mother's condemnation, Eliza flees her home and censuring community to even deeper "retirement" in "Salem," a town in Massachusetts with an indelible history of the suppression of unruly women. Ironically, Sanford begs to visit her "not in continuation of our amour, but as a friend," and Eliza, who has been reduced to complete silence, "only bowed assent" (LXX, 234). Her "fall" transforms the seducer, who defended his "inability to possess her in an other way" into someone "solicitous to know her situation and welfare" (233–34). He now realizes that in being "shunned as the pest and bane of social enjoyment," he is "debarred from every kind of happiness" (LXXII, 239).

After her death, Lucy and Julia make the requisite visit to Eliza's grave so that it "shall not be unbedewed by the tears of friendship" (LXXIV, 241), and they erect a tombstone whose inscription is reproduced in the last letter Julia writes to Mrs. Wharton as a kind of relict (242). The spectacle of "weeping friends," as they describe themselves, mourning over a fresh grave is a staple of sentimental literature and draws on the association of friendship with absence and death. However, the reconsolidation of the female circle over Eliza's death is self-consciously belated and its effect mixed. Meant to memorialize not only the precipitate passing of Eliza but the sorrow of her friends, the stone and its inscription reveal instead their failures—or rather, the failure of their contracted conception of friendship to sustain a figure of difference like Eliza. These "weeping friends" who invoke themselves in the fourth line of the epitaph were, as they report, absent when Eliza "sustained the last painful scene, far from every friend," and this occasioned a sentimental horror: "[T]he tears of strangers watered her grave" (242).

In order to recuperate Eliza as worthy of memory, her eulogizers invoke "candor," the unflinching honesty that friendship doctrine recommends as one of friendship's more important ingredients. But instead of embracing Eliza with all her faults and "waywardness," these friends beg candor to "throw a veil over her frailties," thinking thereby to enact the same Christian kindness they attribute to Eliza: "for great was her charity to others" (LXXIV, 242). But is charity synonymous with a refusal to see the shortcomings and blasted dreams of others, or our own failures and mistakes? In this tragic moment, we are far from even a skewed Winthropian notion of heavenly mutuality or civic intimacy. This metaphorical veiling covers affective failures that result from the Federalist elite's refusal to accord everyone an equal stake in the post-Revolutionary settlement.

Because Eliza's alternative vision never had a chance to flower, we as readers cannot accurately judge the soundness of a renovated public social realm in which women could freely circulate like men and imagine a truly egalitarian sociopolitical ethos. In their need to veil Eliza's eccentricities, Lucy and her ilk become the harbingers of a separate and unequal private domestic sphere collusive with masculine privilege from which women would not emerge until the end of the nineteenth century, perhaps not even until the "Roaring Twenties." Conversely, even in failure Eliza Wharton remains a champion of the political and social in(ter)dependence signified by friendship—buried but by no means dead.

I hear colored men speak of their "white friends." I have no white friends. I could not degrade the sacred name of "Friendship" by associating it with any man who feels himself too good to sit at a table with me, or to sleep at the same hotel.
True friendship can only exist between men who have something in common, between equals in something, if not in everything; and where there is respect as well as admiration.
I hope yet to have a friend. If not in this world, then in some distant future eon, when men are emancipated from the grossness of the flesh, and mind can seek out mind; then shall I find some kindred spirit, who will sympathize with all that is purest and best in mine, and we will cement a friendship that shall endure throughout the ages.
—Charles Chesnutt,
The Journals, March 1882

Queequeg was George Washington cannibalistically developed.
—Herman Melville, *Moby Dick*

The parable of Pythagoras is dark, but true; *cor ne edito*; eat not the heart. Certainly, if a man would give it a hard phrase, those that want friends to open themselves unto, are cannibals of their own hearts.
—Francis Bacon, "Of Friendship"

CHAPTER FOUR

Eat Your Heart Out

James Fenimore Cooper's Male Romance and the American Myth of Interracial Friendship

One of the themes running throughout these readings of early American narratives is how structures of friendship— ontological, epistemological, and sociopolitical—haunt dominant forms of heterosexual affiliation. In the previous chapter, I argued that the Federalists' use of hierarchical marriage as a figure for democratic political relations murdered and entombed friendship, thereby promoting its return as a ghost. Then, the differences (of sex, gender, sexuality, race, and class) suppressed in and by the classical ideal of male homosocial affiliations unsettled later conceptions of friendship. The specific case I consider here is romance, the genre of U.S. literature many critics consider its defining form. In its nineteenth-century incarnation, the romance famously highlights representations of friendship between males across race, class, and age: Arthur Pym and Dirk Peters, Ishmael and Queequeg, Huck and Jim, with James Fenimore Cooper's famous pair, Hawk-eye and Chingachgook, often regarded as the archetypal model, not merely of male homosocial bonds but of an affiliation that shapes an emerging, ironically monoracial American national identity. The cross-racial character of these bonds is crucial, serving as fictional embodiments of the Revolutionary ideal—however far from the reality—enshrined in the Declaration of Independence: "all men are created equal."

But an insistent, monolithic whiteness anchors formulations of early U.S. national identity and belies the interracial intimacy celebrated in these male romances. Furthermore, the "invention" of white America disavows its multicultural, multilingual, and heterogeneous origins, producing a toxic culture of denial and resentment Anne Anlin Cheng calls "the melancholy of race." To explain this phenomenon, Cheng cites Freud's description of melancholy as a form of mourning that reprises the oral stage of development in which the ego devours its lost objects in order *not* to lose them, thus becoming haunted—the embodiment of ghostly others. In chapter 1, I examined a similar convergence of friendship discourses, cannibalism, cross-cultural encounters, and masculine subjectivity exemplified by Michel de Montaigne's essays. This psychic dynamic is relevant to American racial politics because, as Cheng reminds us, "social and psychical cathexes work in collaboration," not just for individuals but in the broader sense understood by psychoanalysis in which personal desires are inextricably entangled in social relations (27). Cheng reasons that the dominant "racial imaginary" of the United States "may be said to operate through the institutional process of producing a dominant, standard, white national ideal, which is sustained by the exclusion-yet-retention of racialized others. . . . Dominant white identity in America operates melancholically—as an elaborate identificatory system based on psychical and social consumption-and-denial" (10–11). She offers the example of blackface minstrelsy, an "entangled network of repulsion and sympathy, fear and desire, repudiation and identification" (12), and cites Toni Morrison's description of founding U.S. literature as a body of work haunted by dark presences it "excludes but cannot forget," rendering it, in Cheng's resonant words, "a melancholy corpus" (12).

The romance epitomizes this corpus. More specifically, the frontier romances of Cooper popularize a racial imaginary that typifies the "exclusion-yet-retention" of native Americans—excluded from citizenship and ejected beyond the boundary of the nation west of the Mississippi, yet retained as noble and demonic in so-called historical fictions. Through intimacy with his native counterpart, Hawk-eye, Cooper's white scout, stakes out a liminal position in which he is both inside and outside dominant culture. In identifying with/desiring/incorporating the "gifts" of the "savage other" and the "naturalness" he represents, Hawk-eye resists re-absorption into white hegemony and offers an insider's critique of the violence of intercultural relations and imperial projects. His liminality is glamorous, but its alienation also neutralizes the force of any substantive critique. Like Huck and Jim "lighting out for the territory," Ishmael and Queequeg aboard the *Pequod* (a name that vehicularizes the fierce northeastern Indian tribe supposedly exterminated in the colonial wars), and Pym aided by Dirk Peters strangely passing into whiteness, such liminality produces a resignation that moves into a mythic realm, an ever-receding space of dislocation, ambiguity, and longing. This purportedly "new" epistemic space is, nevertheless, drenched in "imperial nostalgia" for the very world that has been destroyed, a mood that is the stock and trade of historical romances (Rosaldo 69–70). These narratives generate and reinforce a dominant white national ideal that, even in the face of colonization, imperialism, slavery, and the genocide of indigenous populations, allows its readers to sustain inclusive and egalitarian American ideals.

In this chapter, I examine Cooper's depiction of the interracial friendship of his emblematic duo in *The Last of the Mohicans* in the light of the history of friendship I have provided in the preceding chapters. There is evidence to suggest that Cooper's vision of this friendship and of affiliation across ethnic differences in general evolves over the course of his writing career.[1] Nevertheless, I focus on *Mohicans* because, as Leslie Fiedler argues, it "defined almost perfectly the basic myth of Leatherstocking" in which the necessary elements of the four other books in the series are gathered together and "presented in their pure essences" (*Love and Death* 200). In response to this distillation, the long popular and critical histories of *Mohicans* demonstrate a persistent myopia about the presence and function of friendship as a structuring affiliation in "the basic myth." For example, Michael Mann's acclaimed 1992 film adaptation of *The Last of the Mohicans* dispenses with the famous friendship altogether, focusing attention on Nathaniel, the Hawk-eye character in this version, who is the adopted "white son" of a considerably older Chingachgook and the spiritual brother of the chief's biological son Uncas. The plot's emphasis, along with Nathaniel's steamy romance with Cora, whose racial background is unproblematized, falls on the interracial family. In this way, the film "consumes" Indianness—that is, identifies with a phantas-

matic indigenous America and denies white domination bent on destroying it—
even more seductively and unapologetically than its novelistic original.[2]

Critical myopia about the novel's friendship discourses is also revealing. In
1955, R. W. B. Lewis hailed Hawk-eye in his various guises as the quintessential
American hero, a solipsistic and alienated Adamic figure practically incapable of
affiliation. This view ignored the interracial friendship and buttressed an excep-
tionalist notion of an originary American individualism. D. H. Lawrence in 1923
and Fiedler some forty years later resituated Cooper's hero in an interracial
friendship, but one that takes on "mythic" proportions.

For Lawrence, the "immortal friendship" of these characters embodies Cooper's desire to escape repressive, Europeanized civilization symbolized by "the
wife" and provides a Whitmanian "clue" to a future beyond white ethnocentrism
and rampant American materialism (52, 59). Fiedler pathologizes Cooper's escap-
ist wish as a refusal of adult male heterosexuality (which Mann's film cleverly
restores for the 1990s) but nevertheless elevates what he calls the "pure marriage
of males—sexless and holy, a kind of counter-matrimony" that reunites the white
man with "nature and his own unconscious" in the form of the "dark brother"
without the loss of his freedom (*Love and Death* 211). The male interracial friendship plot, symbolized melodramatically by "two lonely men, one dark-skinned,
one white, bend[ing] over a carefully guarded fire in the virgin heart of the
American wilderness," represents for Fiedler a "national archetype . . . the most
deeply underlying image of ourselves" that figuratively and affectively reconciles
the history of American racial conflict (192, 182, 390). This reconciliation serves
mainly to re-center white male subjectivity, highlighting male interracial friendship
only to alienate it from the historical, political, and specific cultural contexts in
which, I argue, it is embedded.[3]

Similarly, Richard Slotkin's mythopoetic reading of the Leatherstocking cycle
focuses exclusively on the moral quest of its white hunter hero, Natty Bumppo,
never once considering the mythopoetic trope of "brothers" from different cultures journeying together (Gilgamesh and Enkidu, for example). For Slotkin,
Natty's only affiliative choice is "sacred marriage" with a female anima figure.
When, in *The Deerslayer*—Cooper's account of Natty's "initiation" into manhood
—the youth refuses to accept Judith Hutter's offer of marriage, he achieves a
"moral purity," but the cost is, according to Slotkin, affiliative failure, "self-
defeating" sacrifice, and "impotence" (*Regeneration* 502–3).

What these divergent readings have in common is a withdrawal from history
into the refuge of mythology. By contrast, Robyn Wiegman argues that by re-
capitulating "the narrative trope of America"—the confrontation and transcen-

dence of difference—early romances of interracial male bonding like Cooper's provide an important index, not of "the mythic mass mind, but of the political, social, and economic tensions underwriting masculine relations in their various historical configurations" (*American Anatomies* 132, 159).[4] In fact, the post-Revolutionary generation faced tensions produced by the centralization of governmental authority and challenges to that power posed by the War of 1812. According to historian Ruth Bloch, when the "quest for heroic mastery associated with the early war effort" ended, political reform and nation-building began. This required a curtailment of independence and "a greater acceptance of institutionalized public order" symbolized by the ratification of the Constitution (55).

In chapter 3, I explored the ramifications of this curtailment for the immediate post-Revolutionary social scene. Cooper's generation expressed these tensions in the field of historical fiction, which in this period took the form Nina Baym dubs "Indian stories." As she and others have shown, Cooper's early frontier romances are part of a furious literary competition between male and female writers of the 1820s and 1830s over the status of Indians and racial mixing, gender politics, the definition of citizenship, and the ownership and tenor of American history itself.[5] In the next chapter, I consider Catharine Sedgwick's *Hope Leslie*, a historical romance published the year after Cooper's *Mohicans* as a direct response to his masculine vision of national identity. Reading these two romances back to back gives us a snapshot of the cultural issues at stake in this period.

Allegories of Affiliation: Friendship and Marriage

No scene is more closely associated with interracial friendship than the conclusion of Cooper's *The Last of the Mohicans*. All the characters surviving the final chase to the cliff's edge gather around the funeral biers of the "ardent" Cora and noble Uncas, who are being buried as royalty, since Uncas has revealed himself as the noble scion of the Delaware nation. The six Delaware maidens performing the funeral rites acknowledge the pair's superiority and eulogize them as if "the will of the Great Spirit" intended them to be united in the afterlife and "be forever happy" (*LM* 342–43).[6] Natty Bumppo, referred to as "Hawk-eye" in the narrative, is an American-born scout serving under the British and the only white person who understands these songs. He firmly rejects the women's implication, shaking "his head, like one who knew the error of their simple creed" (344). After Cora's people depart, the scene shifts to Chingachgook, who breaks a protracted silence only to refuse to mourn the son whose premature death renders him "the last" of the ancient Mohican line. Hawk-eye, Chingachgook's longtime companion, interrupts him to offer consolation as a spiritual father to Uncas and fellow sufferer, finally pledging his undying friendship, as if to fill the place of the lost son. I quote the passage in full, beginning with Chingachgook's speech:

"Who can deny it? The Manitoo had need of such a warrior, and he has called him away. As for me, the son and the father of Uncas, I am a 'blazed pine, in a clearing of the pale-faces.' My race has gone from the shores of the salt lake, and the hills of the Delawares. But who can say that the serpent of his tribe has forgotten his wisdom! I am alone—"

"No, no," cried Hawk-eye, who had been gazing with a yearning look at the rigid features of his friend, with something like his own self-command, but whose philosophy could endure no longer; "no, Sagamore, not alone. The gifts of our colours may be different, but God has so placed us as to journey in the same path. I have no kin, and I may also say, like you, no people. He was your son, and a red-skin by nature; and it may be, that your blood was nearer;—but if I ever forget the lad, who has so often fou't at my side in war, and slept at my side in peace, may He who made us all, whatever may be our colour or our gifts, forget me. The boy has left us for a time, but, Sagamore, you are not alone!"

Chingachgook grasped the hand that, in the warmth of feeling, the scout had stretched across the fresh earth, and in that attitude of friendship, these two sturdy and intrepid woodsmen bowed their heads together, while scalding tears fell to their feet, watering the grave of Uncas, like drops of falling rain. (349)

The relational dynamics of this highly charged moment bear close examination. Hawk-eye's preemption of Chingachgook's invocation and intended application of the unforgettable "wisdom" of his tribe sums up the ideological "argument" of Cooper's narrative. Indian spokesmen at the time had delivered similar warnings. In 1781, for example, the Delaware war chief Pachgantschihilas exhorted the Indians at the Moravian village of Gnadenhütten, sixty miles north of Philadelphia, not to trust white men who "will say to an Indian, 'my friend, my brother!' They will take him by the hand, and at the same moment destroy him. And so you will also be treated by them before long." Within the year, ninety-six members of that band of Christian Indians had been slaughtered at that very spot (Heckewelder 81).

Although Cooper set his story in 1757 during the French and Indian War, this incident at Gnadenhütten was part of the imaginative context for his romance. He would have read about it in his primary source for Indian history and culture, John Heckewelder's *An Account of the History, Manners, and Customs of the*

Indian Nations, Who Once Inhabited Pennsylvania and the Neighbouring States (1819). A Moravian missionary, Heckewelder lived with various tribes for almost sixty years and staunchly supported the preservation of their cultures, a sentiment reflected in his widely popular and unusually sympathetic history of the North American Indians. Why does Cooper depict Hawk-eye's heartfelt offer of interracial love as preventing his grieving friend from calling on this proleptic tribal "wisdom" that from experience counsels the falsity of professions of white friendship? Do these two figures and their friendship represent alluring mythical exceptions that prove the historical rule of white genocide of native peoples?

It is important to note that Hawk-eye's act of "friendship" supersedes at the same time as it also re-invokes the "blood" logic he himself has professed—to excess—throughout the narrative. Although a self-proclaimed bibliophobe, Hawk-eye outlines the precise characteristics of the classical ideal of perfect friendship most famously articulated by Aristotle: sharing values (journeying in the same path), living together (sleeping side by side), risking lives for one another (fighting side by side).⁷ His untutored frontier "philosophy" even follows the elaboration of Aristotle's formulation of classical friendship by Cicero and Montaigne by arguing that the spiritual kinship between the two "stoical" scouts competes with and is superior to relations of biological kinship.⁸ And like Aristotle's Roman and Renaissance redactors, Cooper links friendship discourse and loss by triangulating Hawk-eye's bond with Chingachgook through the slain Uncas and the defeated Indian world.⁹ When Chingachgook grasps the scout's outstretched hand, he signals his acceptance of Hawk-eye's offer of consolation and pledge of companionship. Cooper's source for this imagery was the Covenant Chains, discussed in chapter 1, originating in Condolence Councils and adoption ceremonies that were specifically intended to redress the loss of loved ones through sickness or war. Chingachgook reconfirms this connection with his white friend as spiritual kin and accepts Hawk-eye as a (pale) replacement for the slain Uncas.

While the handclasp was a traditional gesture of confirmation for the tribes of the Iroquois, it also expresses the salient requirement of classical friendship in the Western tradition—similarity or equality. The gesture probably originated in the worship of the Persian god Mithras, an ancient mystery religion that spread throughout the Roman empire during the first century B.C.E., vied in popularity with early Christianity, but disappeared after the Theodosian decrees of 391 banning all pagan rites. A relief in Rome shows Mithras grasping the wrist of another figure, probably the god Sol, in order to make a small incision with a knife and seal their pact with blood (Vermaseren 97). Early English representations of friendship depict hands clasping around or beneath a crowned and flaming heart to signify affection, mutual consent, and shared sovereignty, such as the emblem for *Bona fide* (good faith) from George Wither's collection published in London in 1635 (see figure 3). In the early modern period, this image symbolized the "knot" binding two equal and consenting selves into a new, essentially democratic entity: out of many, one.

The "fresh" grave, fallen Indian brave, and "scalding tears" of Cooper's scene, however, are familiar props of the sentimental mode and indicate a historically and ideologically specific locus for the friendship it depicts. Furthermore, Cooper's handshake is interracial, perhaps the inaugural literary instance of this gesture's contentious history in American race relations.[10] In Cooper's narrative, this handshake implies a linkage radical for the time: the moral equality of a white man and a member of a "savage"—in some contemporary eyes—uncivilizable people that was rendered unthreatening by being set in an evanescing world. Hawk-eye himself invokes the friends' racial difference in his speech quoted above through his often-repeated allusion to the varied "gifts of our colours" but implies that their friendship, secured by time and trials, overcomes without denying these differences. Even as he acknowledges the priority of Chingachgook's biological connection to Uncas, Hawk-eye qualifies it by remarking ambiguously, "and it *may be*, that your blood was nearer" (my emphasis). Whether Hawk-eye accepts that the kinship relation *is*, in fact, nearer or speaks in spite of that priority, he insists on an equally strong *spiritual* affiliation with Uncas, "one who might, in some degree, be called the child of his adoption," as the narrator observes earlier (*LM* 265) and to whom the childless and unmarried scout feels he owes the offices of a "friend" (266).

In this concluding scenario, we can trace the play of sameness and difference operating through competing narrative plots of affiliation. Cooper's earliest critics puzzled over "the perplexingly mixed nature of Cooper's art itself," which used American materials and advanced republican values in literary forms, like the historical romance and the novel of manners, that have conservative ideological charges (Dekker and McWilliams 1–2). What these critics considered "generic" problems, Ross Pudaloff recasts as "ideological" issues specific to the early American Republic, which produced "the bifurcated goals" of Cooper's fiction—a commitment to republicanism, which he expressed in masculine adventure plots of "fraternal relationships" on the one hand, and a belief in conservative social arrangements symbolized by hierarchical marriages on the other (712).[11] In his examination of the English novel, Joseph Allen Boone argues that the essentially conservative and ultimately hierarchical love and marriage plot, which is coincidental with the rise of the form itself, produces a subversive "counter-narrative" that is often couched in terms of homosocial friendship (2–3). Broadly speaking, marriage and erotic love represent relations of inequality in terms of gender difference, social position, or sexual power, while homosocial friendship, even across its long and divergent history, has been characterized by some form of equality or similarity. In his study, Boone proposes to listen to the "too often ignored" dialogue between these divergent "responses to love and marriage" (3).

In my reading of friendship discourses, however, homosocial friendship is not a "response" to the assumed norm of heterosexual coupling. On the contrary, as I argued in chapter 1, for the ancient world and into the early modern period, homosocial friendship, especially among males, was, morally speaking, the privileged and dominant affiliative mode. It has a long canonical history with important implications for notions of politics, community, personal agency, and the production of literature through patronage. It takes historically specific forms, operating sometimes in tandem with family, marriage, and erotic love and sometimes in competition with them.

While critics have explored the ideological implications of the courtship, marriage, and miscegenation plots in *The Last of the Mohicans*, they have either ignored or downplayed the interracial friendship plot. Or they have highlighted the interracial male bond only to mythologize and thus de-historicize it. In both cases, what they overlook is the ideological stakes, for the new nation and for current questions about ethical relational structures involved in the contestation between the two affiliative plot resolutions. For example, in a reading of the novel that discloses Cooper's "habits of simultaneous acknowledgement and denial, seeing and not seeing," Forrest G. Robinson argues that Cooper doubles the sanctioned romantic pairing of Alice and Heyward (representing the triumph of white patriarchal values) with the transgressive pairing of Cora and Uncas (a multiracial egalitarian fantasy), both of which "compete for center stage, and for the reader's attention and approval as the novel closes" (27, 16). This reading fails to see the other "romantic" pair that remains onstage at the novel's close, has long occupied the popular imagination, and, furthermore, achieves singly the effect the other pairs produce jointly: the fantasy of a passionate bond across racial and cultural differences that simultaneously assures, even vindicates, if not white supremacy, then white hegemony.

Cooper himself stages this contestation toward the end of the narrative. In a long speech, Hawk-eye justifies his "desperate" intention to rescue Uncas, who has been captured by their Huron enemies in his attempt to rescue Cora, to a protesting Duncan Heyward, who has just rescued his beloved Alice from captivity: "I have heard," Hawk-eye begins laconically, "that there is a feeling in youth, which binds man to woman, closer than the father is tied to the son. It may be so. I have seldom been where women of my colour dwell; but such may be the gifts of natur in the settlements! You have risked life, and all that is dear to you, to bring off this gentle one, and I suppose that some such disposition is at the bottom of it all" (*LM* 265). In his attempt to understand Heyward's similarly perilous behavior, Hawk-eye reveals that erotic passion and romantic heterosexual love are, for men of his ilk, like rumors that circulate in the distant, gender-mixed "settlements" but do not hold sway in his predominately masculine wilderness.

The Pathfinder, a later novel in the Leatherstocking series, illustrates the inherency of this disposition when a slightly older Natty Bumppo falls in love with Mabel Dunham, an officer's daughter. In rebuffing him, Mabel helps Natty see that his heterosexual desire is "unwise" and even "unnat'ral" because it interferes with his near-sacred homosocial "calling" as scout and woodsman (271). In explaining his romantic failure to Mabel's disappointed father, Sergeant Dunham, Natty invokes the ancient principle of similitude: "Like loves like," he observes (278), implying that he and Mabel are definitely not "alike." Similarly, in rejecting the romantic advances of the "erring" but beautiful and courageous Judith Hutter in *The Deerslayer*, the last novel in the series, a very young Natty (re)asserts his initial preference for masculine friendship. In explaining why he must aid his friend Chingachgook in recovering his betrothed, who has been captured by the Huron, he tells Judith: "Then, if love does count for so much with some people, particularly with young women, fri'ndship counts for something, too, with other some" (273).

In the explanation of his disposition in *Mohicans*, Hawk-eye first invokes the father-son tie but quickly shifts to the ideal "friendship" rhetoric outlined in his final pledge to Chingachgook. It is a rhetoric Hawk-eye repeats in all the "farewell" speeches he delivers to his Indian friends at various points in the narrative when death seems imminent: "As for me, I taught the lad the real character of a rifle; and well has he paid me for it! I have fou't at his side in many a bloody skrimmage; and so long as I could hear the crack of his piece in one ear, and that of the Sagamore in the other, I knew no enemy was on my back. Winters and summers, nights and days, have we roved the wilderness in company, eating of the same dish, one sleeping while the other watched" (265). This argument has the desired effect. Just as Hawk-eye earlier withdrew his resistance to Heyward's reckless plan to rescue Alice from Huron captivity, Heyward finally drops his objections to the scout's intentions to rescue Uncas. In doing so, Heyward acknowledges the legitimacy of Hawk-eye's vow that Uncas will not "perish for want of a friend" (266). More important, Heyward's acceptance of Hawk-eye's sense of obligation places it on an affective par with white heterosexual relations. Not merely a nostalgic desire for egalitarian bonds between warriors, the claims of masculine interracial friendship that motivate Hawk-eye combine elements of erotic, romantic, and paternal love. Heyward's acknowledgment of this bond's centrality for Hawk-eye suggests the text's qualified recognition of male homosocial relations as a viable affective and social alternative or complement to marriage, as well as a more threatening democratic vision of parity across difference.

Critical myopia with respect to friendship themes suggests the powerful totalizing effect of heteronormativity. Even historicized readings like Slotkin's preserve a split view that discounts friendship. In his introduction to the Penguin paperback edition, Slotkin argues that the "bifurcation of *Mohicans* is crucial, for with the massacre [of English settlers retreating from Fort William Henry] we leave the stage of 'history' and firmly enter the world of myth" as the heroes pursue Magua and the kidnapped Munro sisters fleeing north to a "deeper and darker wilderness" even more removed from contemporary contexts (xx).

Friendship discourses and motifs, however, persist across this crucial bifurcation. For example, in the very first skirmish between Magua's warriors and the party protecting the Munro sisters, which has taken refuge in a cave under Glenn's Falls, Uncas saves Heyward's life. As they regroup and take stock before another attack, Heyward acknowledges this "debt" by offering his friendship, which Uncas readily accepts; the two young men from seemingly antithetical cultures perform the same "act of friendship"—grasping hands—that their older counterparts enact at the tale's sobering denouement. Hawk-eye presides over the young men's pledge, regarding "this burst of youthful feeling with a cool but kind regard" and comments, "Life is an obligation which friends often owe to each other in the wilderness" (*LM* 73).

Having his life saved by a "savage" stranger opens up for Heyward the *possibility* of cross-racial friendship, providing, at the outset of the narrative, a crucial experience for him—and for the white readers for whom he serves as the determining viewpoint. This moment "civilizes" the Mohicans in the white readers' imagination through a strategic repression of difference, preparing them for the more dramatic pledge at the end. Thus, the narrator observes: "During the act of friendship, the two young men exchanged looks of intelligence, which caused Duncan to forget the character and condition of his wild associate" (73). The mutual exchange of "intelligence" that is requisite for friendship overcomes Heyward's white presumption of red "savagery." In stark contrast to the interracial violence and mayhem saturating his tale, Cooper offers a performance of male friendship that requires, and thus confers, equality and similarity across what his contemporary readers may have assumed to be an abyss of racialized differences.

I am arguing that Cooper employs friendship discourses, and especially interracial friendship, to explore the types of affective bonds linking people of different backgrounds in the new nation. As a traditional republican, Cooper was attracted to the mixture of elite and egalitarian elements in the classical formulation of friendship as an intimate and ethical attachment based on notions of virtue, equality, personal sovereignty, rational choice, and generosity inherited and adapted by European culture from Greek, Roman, and humanist thought. He would have been familiar with the pervasive early modern trope of homosocial amity through the plays of Shakespeare, which serve as a frequent source for many of the chapters' epigraphs in *Mohicans*. In her study of "figures of friendship in Shakespearean contexts," Laurie Shannon stops short of adducing specific political implications in these figures, characterizing them as a "pre-liberal, utopian discourse" that begins to imagine "a politics of consent" based on voluntary connection between free and "sovereign selves" (*Sovereign Amity* 10). The political allegory in Cooper's representations of friendship, as we will see, is more explicit. Although he represents various types of friendship among a variety of characters, Cooper's ideal is an enduring, mutual affection between men without the connotations of feminizing or "unmanly" sentiment that represents, at its most ideal, the same promise of democracy Walt Whitman saw in the love of "cameradoes" or Herman Melville saw in the "marriage" of Ishmael and Queequeg.

Cooper, however, advances this ideal and at the same time disarms it. As I will show, in borrowing and reconfiguring the terms of Aristotle's famous formulation of perfect friendship, Cooper mobilizes a principle of equality (likeness) through liking that allows him to circumvent his own strictures about miscegenation. But he keeps his heroic pair rooted in a past and dying world. In this reading, the "vanishing Indian" Lora Romero teaches us to see becomes a version of Cicero's "lost friend" and Montaigne's "cannibal," canonical figures of the masculine beloved other. Cooper produces his ideal of homosocial bonding by setting it in sharp contrast to the corrupt aristocratic notions of "tribal brotherhood" practiced both by Indians and by the colonizing Europeans at war in America. Originating in medieval chivalry, this specifically masculine code of honor and allegiance crumbles under the exigencies of wilderness life. Alongside these competing representations of friendship Cooper lays discourses of Christian benevolence and the sympathy of secular humanism that could, in the fantasy meritocracy of the wilderness, temporarily overcome class, gender, and ethnic boundaries. The incongruous mouthpiece for these discourses, psalmist David Gamut, however, proves comically ineffectual in promoting universal Christian love. Finally, I return to the melancholic friendship with the raced other explored in chapter 1 to underscore the cannibalistic implications of Cooper's narrative that both confirm and challenge the unifying—that is, whitening and nationalizing—effects of same-sex affection.

Ennobling Effects of Perfect Friendship

Hawk-eye's final pledge of loyalty to Chingachgook includes all the preliminary "offices" of "sacred" friendship enumerated by antebellum black writer Charles Chesnutt—such as sharing meals and physical proximity—as well as the more crucial elements Chesnutt adds of "respect," "admiration," and, finally, "equality in everything" (172). In fact, Hawk-eye acknowledges Chingachgook "as the oldest and highest in rank" in their quasi-military undertakings (*LM* 198) and continually affirms the "differences" between—though not necessarily the hierarchy of—the "gifts" of their natures and cultures. Nevertheless, like Montaigne's explanation of his passion for La Boétie ("I think it was by some ordinance from heaven" [139]), Hawk-eye reckons their friendship divinely ordained and sanctioned: "God has so placed us as to journey in the same path" (*LM* 349), he reminds the bereft Chingachgook.[12] Their mutual trust and understanding are so profound as to appear telepathic. After the friends frustrate an ambush by Oneida snipers, the uninitiated Heyward wonders whether "the foresters had some secret means of intelligence, which had escaped the vigilance of his own faculties" (195). Despite their differences, which Hawk-eye attributes to "blood" or "natur," these men meet in the wilderness as equals and freely choose to bind themselves to each other, as in the Aristotelian model of perfect friendship.

Their association contravenes the kinship logic of "tribal brotherhood," since the Delaware, as the ancient chief Tamenund reminds Uncas when he recognizes Hawk-eye as "La Longue Carabine," are allied with the French against the English. "My son has not done well to call him friend!" upbraids the aged sachem. But in a rare instance of (Cooper's version of) an Indian perspective on interracial friendship, which is also an uncharacteristic moment of self-assertion, Uncas contradicts the venerated wisdom that dictates amity collectively and abstractly through political treaties by replying firmly, "I call him so who proves himself such" (311). It is perhaps not surprising that a character often compared to a classical Greek statue would enunciate Aristotle's dictum that friendship is self-determining, consensual, and virtuous and renders the friends nearly interchangeable: "If Uncas is welcome among the Delaware, then is Hawk-eye with his friends" (312).[13]

These men call each other "friend" but also "brother," a term that, in the white imagination of the time, connotes the fraternity of democratic relations. This imports the intensity of kinship ties into elective affinities, ultimately modifying even the rhetoric of a "blood" purist like Hawk-eye. In stark contrast to the hierarchical organization of the European military controlled by invisible though frequently invoked monarchs, as well as to Hawk-eye's "long and habitual deference to the mandates of his superiors" in rank and class (209), the three scouts model a democratic "micropolity" in which age, experience, and cultural origins are acknowledged but not deciding factors.

For example, when the rescue party finally picks up the trail of the kidnapped sisters after the fatal retreat from Fort Henry, the scouts formally "deliberate" to determine their course of action. Heyward participates as a "spectator" and one largely reliant on visual and tonal cues since he does not understand the Delaware tongue. As seen through his eyes, the untutored "disputants" comport themselves "with so much gravity and decorum" as to appear more like Roman senators or enlightened republicans, offering an example of "moderation . . . forbearance and courtesy" from which "the most decorous christian assembly, not even excepting those in which its reverend ministers are collected" could learn "a wholesome lesson" (198). Hawk-eye eventually wins his friends over to his plan by abandoning "the cold and inartificial manner, which characterizes all classes of Anglo-Americans," and adopting "all the arts of native eloquence," a strategy associated in Cooper's narrative with the cunning and vengeful Magua (199). In this case, like Magua, Hawk-eye uses a native form of eloquence to unify many divergent wills to one purpose, but because the scout's motives, unlike Magua's, are "amicable"— that is, disinterested and rooted in a clearly established accord—the wills of those he converts are not enslaved or imbruted but elevated and tempered.

The ennobling effects of friendship encompass political concord and social and domestic harmony, as exemplified by the extraordinary scene that immediately follows the deliberations of this "council." Uninterested in reaping approbation (from Heyward, the only onlooker) for his triumph, Hawk-eye unceremoniously retires, while Chingachgook and Uncas "seized the moment to devote some attention to themselves" by engaging in an hour of affectionate play, which the narrator characterizes as "the indulgence of their better feelings." Without missing a beat and in full view of the "unconscious multitude" slain in the recent massacre at the fort, the Indians shift easily from the ferocity of war and austere gravity of political deliberation to "the soft and playful tones of affection" (199–200).

This scene is the "double" of another family gathering, also observed by Heyward, in which Colonel Munro and his daughters engage in "the soothing indulgence" of familial interaction, taking advantage of a temporary truce and lull in hostilities during the siege of Fort Henry "to devote an instant to the purest and best affections" (156). In this scene, however, the anxious Scotsman "affected to frown" as Alice "sate upon his knee, parting the gray hairs on the forehead of the old man," while the soberer Cora sat apart. Chingachgook, by contrast, "never failed to smile in reply to the other's contagious, but low laughter," whose "wonderful" musicality the narrator finds it impossible to describe (200). Far less saccharine and associated through the allusion to musicality with the notions of concord and harmony, the intimate view of "noble" Indians is the most "domestic" scene in the text.

The ennobling effects of friendship even moderate the seemingly inflexible rhetoric of difference that Hawk-eye gives much lip service to throughout the narrative. Although he regards his final offer to Magua—to give his life in exchange for the release of Cora—as profoundly "unequal" in "frontier" terms, everyone else approves of "the manliness of the intended sacrifice" justified by the manly love Hawk-eye bears to his Indian friends with no expectation of reward. According to the ancient thinkers and Christian doctrine, giving one's life for one's friend is the act most characteristic of perfect friendship and Christian love. In explaining his decision and publicly bidding his friends farewell (yet again!), Hawk-eye noticeably qualifies his earlier, sharply essentialist position on the differences between himself and his Indian companions. In doing so, he draws as near as possible to a Renaissance similitude of amity without erasing differences altogether: "I loved both you and your father, Uncas, though our skins *are not altogether* of a colour, and our gifts *are somewhat* different" (315; my emphases). At the apparent moment of reckoning, Hawk-eye retreats from the language of blood purity and racial separation and finds refuge in the tropes of manly love.

Tribal Brotherhood: The Demise of Masculine Codes of Honor

This remarkable interracial accord runs like a bright singular thread through the dark weave of *The Last of the Mohicans*. Cooper sets the tale in the third year of the French and Indian War, a bitter contest between the European powers of France and England for dominance in North America "that neither was destined to retain" (*LM* 12). This "bloody arena," with its pronounced interracial hostility and violence, was in reality a product of the breakdown of European codes of masculine amity and honor in the American wilderness. This context underscores

Cooper's concern with codes of friendships as metaphors for political and national cohesion; the failure of elite codes of honor sets up the conditions by which egalitarian, interracial "American" friendships can prevail.

The text's opening sentences announce this breakdown by framing the plot with a vow that is the horrific *inversion* of the pledge of friendship between Hawk-eye and Chingachgook performed at the novel's conclusion: "[I]n time," the narrator recounts, "there was no recess of the woods so dark, nor any secret place so lovely, that it might claim exemption from the inroads of those who had pledged their blood to satiate their vengeance, or to uphold the cold and selfish policy of the distant monarchs of Europe" (11). The personal vengeance mentioned here refers to Magua's vow to recoup the loss of his family, tribal position, and dignity due to drunkenness overzealously punished by Colonel Munro, the commanding British officer at Fort William Henry. It is rhetorically interchangeable in this sentence with the "cold and selfish" policies of the imperial European powers. These policies licensed Munro, acting as the representative of his king, to dispense "justice." But as Magua shrewdly observes, "is it justice to make evil, and then punish for it!" (103). It was, after all, the Europeans who brought hard liquor to the Indians of the northeastern forests and disrupted their lifeways. Furthermore, Magua implies that European greed for land and power produces the thirst for interracial revenge white men consider an "innate" part of Indian character and forms the implacable force that drives Cooper's dark plot.

A second pledge made by the French commander, the Marquis de Montcalm, to Colonel Munro for honorable withdrawal and safe conduct from the besieged Fort Henry literalizes this self-generating violence. "Distinguished as much for his attention to *the forms* of courtesy, as for [his] chivalrous courage," Montcalm is the product, Cooper implies, of hypocritical European "civility" (153; my emphasis). Gallantly assuring Munro and his officers of their safety in the overblown language of aristocratic amity, he offers them "the plighted faith of 'un gentil-homme Français'" (162). Performed ceremoniously by high-ranking military officers and members of their nation's nobility, this agreement is promptly violated by the Indian allies of the French, who are incensed by their exclusion from the action. Unchecked and secretly encouraged by Montcalm, the Huron, led by Magua, commit the interracial massacre and ferocious cannibalism at the book's center. Munro's literal but also psychological and cultural defeat is ensured when his fellow commander General Webb, at neighboring Fort Edward, refuses to send reinforcements to Fort William, another fatal instance of what the narrator characterizes as the "imbecility" of England's military leaders (13). The once fiery Scotsman bemoans having lived so long to see what he never expected and casts war tactics in terms of personal allegiances: "An Englishman afraid to support a friend, and a Frenchman too honest to profit by his advantage" (165). Webb's betrayal brings "dishonor" and heaps "shame" on Munro's "gray hairs" (164) and is only magnified when Montcalm's surprising generosity proves fatally perfidious.

In this moment, not just Old World military conventions but an entire class-inflected cultural identity is shaken to its foundations. When so-called gentlemen in high positions flout the civilized codes of behavior signified by war and personal friendship, Munro's lament implies, what structures of affiliation remain? It is this betrayal, the failure of elite masculine connection, *not* the resulting loss of his daughters, that weakens the sturdy Scotsman's spirit: "From the shock of this unexpected blow the haughty feelings of Munro never recovered; but from that moment there commenced a change in his determined character," which renders him distinctly passive for the remainder of the narrative and "which accompanied him to a speedy grave" (165).

Cora, Munro's older daughter and the product of his liaison with a West Indian woman "descended, remotely" from slaves, inherits her father's courage and fortitude (159). Although every male character recognizes this fact, Cora can act only within narrow feminine bounds, for she is also a creature of this elite masculine code. As she herself confesses, the prospect of her father's defeat at Fort Henry weighs heavily on "the daughter of a soldier, whose greatest happiness is his honor and his military renown!" (150). The ambiguity of the referent for "whose" renders the father and daughter equally dependent on "*his* honor and his military renown," making their "happiness" indistinguishable.

The real inheritor of these codes, Virginia-born Duncan Heyward, attempts to apply them in the New World; his failures are revealing. For example, despite his knowledge of Magua's history with Colonel Munro, Heyward chooses the Huron defector to guide the group escorting the Munro sisters to Fort Henry. When the three scouts encounter this party, lost and weary, Hawk-eye immediately recognizes Magua's treachery. By birth, Magua is a member of the Huron tribe which is allied with France. But Heyward assures Hawk-eye that Magua is now, through adoption, "a Mohawk, and that he serves with our forces as a friend" (37).

Heyward repeats this error in the second half of the narrative, when an Indian sniper attacks the party pursuing Magua and the kidnapped Munro sisters. Uncas kills the sniper and identifies him as Oneida, a tribe loyal to the English. Unaware of the traditional enmity between Mohican and Oneida and assuming the "white quarrel" to be at the center of Indian actions, Heyward observes naively: "The poor fellow has mistaken us for French . . . or he would not have attempted the life of a friend." When Hawk-eye retorts that Heyward was just as likely to "mistake them white coated grenadiers of Montcalm, for the scarlet jackets of the 'Royal Americans,'" and that his allegiance to his Mohican friends would have prompted him to attempt to kill the sniper, Heyward invokes inapplicable Old World standards of "sacred" amity: "That would have been an abuse of our treaties, and unworthy of your character," he upbraids Hawk-eye (196). In this exchange, Heyward's ignorant and arrogant nationalism ("our treaties"), which underlies the ruthless colonial project, directly confronts Hawk-eye's historically specific understanding of American alliances and classically informed notion of friendship. This combined knowledge has, in fact, saved all their lives. Even so, Hawk-eye fails to make Heyward comprehend the "local" American situation. Thus, "the honest but implacable woodsman turned from the fire, content to let the controversy slumber" (197). Clearly unsatisfied with Heyward's obtuseness, however, the narrator continues to explain to his readers the painful confusion of the Indian tribes produced by colonization.

Impeding Heyward's comprehension is his association with ancient codes of chivalry. These unwritten rules of comportment provide seductively romantic models of manliness but prove unrealistic in the American scene. Colonel Munro explicitly endorses this antique and very elite form of public honor when he disparages Montcalm's pedigree and boasts, "The Thistle is the order for dignity and antiquity; the veritable 'nemo me impune lacessit' of chivalry! Ye had ancestors in that degree, Duncan, and they were an ornament to the nobles of Scotland," he reminds the young American (157). Munro refers to "the Most Ancient and Most Noble Order of the Thistle," the Scottish order of chivalry (second in precedence to its English equivalent, "The Most Noble Order of the Garter"), which includes only a handful of "knights" and "ladies" appointed by the sovereign. Though the original date of its foundation is unknown, James VII of Scotland (also James II of England) instituted the Thistle in its modern form in 1687.

The motto of the order, from the Latin quoted above, is "No one provokes me with impunity." This threatening sentiment is especially applicable to the villains in the narrative. In fact, Cooper associates the duplicitous Montcalm as well as the demonic Magua and other Indian tribes who stand perhaps too strongly on matters of honor with these antique and outmoded codes of chivalry (157). William P. Kelly argues that the whole discourse of chivalry in Cooper's narrative only serves to "mask" the "savage enterprise" of colonial conquest with a patina of honor (57).[14] It is perhaps a mark in his favor that Heyward cannot quite live up to the unrealistic expectations of a chivalrous knight, although he tries. Alice Munro, whose hand in marriage Heyward requests from her proud, beleaguered father, flirtatiously chastises Heyward as a failure in this discourse when she hails him in the besieged fort: "Ah! thou truant! thou recreant knight! He who abandons his damsels in the very lists" (*LM* 149). Heyward's aspirations and failures in chivalry reinforce his southern birth and connection with America. In his self-imposed attempt to guard the tent of his beloved Alice on a wild hilltop in the northeastern forests, the young suitor falls asleep at the watch; only in his dreams can he successfully be "a knight of ancient chivalry" (129).

Heyward's southern connections reveal much about his relation to codes of honor. Like the other aristocratic Europeans, Heyward assumes that "those natives who dwelt within our boundaries had found us too just and liberal, not to identify themselves, fully, with our quarrels" (197). Not only do his comments indicate his ethnocentric ignorance of the moral hypocrisy of which Magua is a victim, but his use of the word "liberal" offers an interesting self-revelation. Hawkeye identifies him on first meeting as "a young gentleman of vast riches from one of the provinces far south" (38). Heyward has most likely inherited his father's slave-worked plantation. This is further supported by his bigotry against people of color. In preferring the pallid and racially "pure" Alice to her older and darker sister, Heyward reveals a "prejudice" against blacks the narrator describes "as deeply rooted as if it had been engrafted in his nature" (159).

Later, we learn about the sobriquet Heyward has earned in the wilderness, bestowals Cooper strongly emphasizes throughout the Leatherstocking Tales: "[T]he appellation of the 'open-hand' was a name his *liberality* had *purchased* of all the friendly tribes" (199; my emphases). Many elements attest to Heyward's generosity: he naively clings to European standards of honor, is unpracticed in deception, and has an "open countenance" (42). Another meaning of "liberality," however, suggests he may also have used bribery to "buy" the natives' loyalty. In several sticky situations, he offers Magua rich rewards for his consideration or as "ransom" for Cora (313). Believing that avarice drives the Indians, he emphasizes the importance of Munro's daughters to their father and the "liberal" recompense Magua will receive if he returns them, thereby inadvertently suggesting the more sinister means the Huron employs for luring the doting father into his power (101). Despite his pact of friendship with Uncas, Heyward's assumption both of native simplicity and baseness replicates the binary Eurocentric view of the other offered earlier by Tzvetan Todorov. Neither essentialist attitude accords Indians depth or complexity of character (individual or collective).

Furthermore, Heyward is the only Anglo character in Cooper's novel to engage in the pretense of friendship—a tactic characteristic of Magua and second only to his malignant use of eloquence. This raises the specter of feigned amity and affective dissimulation.[15] In his initial negotiations with Magua, for example, Heyward heeds Hawk-eye's advice to "use Indian fashions," by which he means cunning and deception: "[T]alk openly to the miscreant, and seem to believe him the truest friend you have on 'arth" (40). Hawk-eye may recommend this ploy, but he never practices it. Amid this performance and verbal profession of friendship in which Heyward attempts to get close enough to "seize his treacherous companion," Magua "even suffered their hands to meet" in a truncated version of the friendly handclasp, but sensing a trap, he darts suddenly into the underbrush (43). When they negotiate again during a subsequent captivity, Magua takes the moral high ground and rightly upbraids Heyward for his hypocrisy, saying that his "tongue was peace, while his heart was colored with blood!" (90). Later, encountering several French sentinels on the dangerous approach to Fort Henry, Heyward uses his knowledge of French to impersonate, first, a "capitaine de chasseurs" and then an "Ami de la France" (137, 144).

Finally, Heyward's reckless plan to rescue Alice from the Huron camp involves disguising himself as an Indian "juggler" from the French-held fort at Ticonderoga. He persuades Chingachgook to paint him with "the fantastic shadow that the natives were accustomed to consider as the evidence of a friendly and jocular disposition . . . those conceits that might be construed into amity" (229). This willingness to take on an Indian identity suggests both the possibility and futility of a deeper, more meaningful cultural synthesis, since it is inextricable from Heyward's willingness to pretend friendship—both are, in the end, purely expedient, serving to advance the hegemonic white identity Heyward's marriage to Alice portends.

The breakdown of "tribal" codes of "brotherhood" affects the Indian allies of the European powers as well. In a tense conversation with Montcalm the night before the fateful surrender of Munro, Magua confronts his "French father" with the fact that "not a warrior has a scalp, and the pale faces make friends!" (169). Montcalm explains that the goal of the French was "to drive off these English squatters. They have consented to go, and now he calls them enemies no longer." Using the discourse of amity overlaid with a paternalistic rhetoric, Montcalm reminds Magua of the Huron's pledge "not to sully the lilies of France. The enemies of the great king across the salt lake, are his enemies; his friends, the friends of the Hurons" (170). Magua regards this strategic shifting of allegiance as hypocritical: " 'Friends!' repeated the Indian, in scorn," as he takes Montcalm's hand and draws it over his many scars from bullet wounds and beatings suffered at the hands of the English (170). Magua's experience of friendship and enmity can be read on his body.

Although Magua assumes a demonic stature in the narrative, Cooper makes this same point through the "unassailably honest" words of Hawk-eye, who responds to Heyward's naive insistence on European morality by arguing "that white cunning has managed to throw the tribes into great confusion, as respects friends and enemies . . . [arming] friend against friend . . . thus throwing every thing into disorder, and destroying all the harmony of warfare" (196–98). In Native America, as in the sophisticated metropols of Europe, men regarded warfare as an "orderly" and noble means of masculine interaction, epitomized in the Indian world by the "*chivalrous* scalping tuft . . . the only admissible trophy of victory" (29; my emphasis). In that world, Magua remarks, if Indians "fought among themselves, it was to prove that they were men" (301), and one could tell one's friends from one's enemies. But the advent of the Europeans has, according to Cooper, destroyed even that cold, oxymoronic comfort.

Concord, Christian Benevolence, Sympathy

According to Susan Cooper, the author's daughter and manager of his literary estate after his death, the formative kernel of *Mohicans* came to her father during a bout of fever and delirium brought on by sunstroke, during which he dictated the outlines of the dramatic account in chapter 12 of the whirling combat between Chingachgook and Magua (Philbrick 27). Thomas Philbrick's influential 1971 reading of *Mohicans*, which shifted the interpretive emphasis away from the "myth and symbol" school, takes its cue from this encounter.[16] It is not surprising that Slotkin's largely unchallenged study, *Regeneration through Violence: The Mythology of the American Frontier, 1600–1860*, first published in 1972 and reprinted in 2000, has N. C. Wyeth's depiction of this crucial moment on its cover. As the paradigmatic instance of the "disintegration of order in confusion and obscurity," this scene, according to Philbrick, "sounds the keynotes of the book" by staging bloodletting before which "the gentler emotions—'filial affection, friendship, and gratitude'—give way" (28, 30; *LM* 113). This imposes a reading of *Mohicans* that becomes, in Slotkin's handling, the standard approach to frontier narratives based on a dialectic in which Christian "civilization" and social order appeared out of and against Indian "savagery" and chaos; "tales of strife between native Americans and interlopers, between dark races and light, became the basis of our mythology and . . . the Indian fighter and hunter emerged as the first of our national heroes" (*Regeneration* 18). But this "regeneration-through-violence" thesis of American literature obscures the complexity and historicity of early views of ethnic and cultural identities and their dynamic play in literary representations of the national imaginary. Thus, in Philbrick's and Slotkin's readings, the interracial friendships threaded throughout *Mohicans*, as well as the final pledge of loyalty between Hawk-eye and Chingachgook, go completely unremarked.[17]

While instances of enmity and violence frame, and even dominate, Cooper's narrative, countervailing allusions to friendship appear throughout. Philbrick argues that Cooper reinforces the centrality of violence by his use of the signal words "blood" and "bloody" that "recur with numbing frequency," appearing "at least ninety-five times, an average of one every four and a half pages" (29). If this is any measure, we should point out that the words "friend," "friendly," "friendship," and "amity" occur over 150 times, six times on one page alone (*LM* 229). A key question of the narrative turns on the co-implication of identity and allegiance: "Who comes? . . . Speak! Friend or enemy?" Heyward demands anxiously on being awakened after failing to keep a chivalrous night watch over his beloved Alice (129). This question recurs as the protagonists stumble through literal and epistemological fogs (137, 144) and is magnified by the many disguises of the second half of the narrative.

Predilection in the human sphere is such a powerful organizing force in the novel that it characterizes the natural and material realms. The "ramparts" of Fort Edward and the "works" of Fort Henry are "friendly" (60, 143); "rocks and shrubs" provide "friendly shelter" from enemy attacks (71); and "kill deer," Hawk-eye's deadly rifle, is an "invaluable friend" from whom he parts only under extreme circumstances (295). These personifications serve to heighten the dramatic tension in this tale of colonial warfare and recapitulate Cooper's schematizing habit of doubling. As signifiers of amity and concord, though, they call attention to the nagging subtext of the narrative: how can a diverse group of people hope to live together and achieve harmony, much less form a community? And what, then, are their social and political obligations?

The Scottish philosophers of the eighteenth century adopted ancient Greek theories of "natural sympathy," which they understood as the primary mechanism or vehicle of human sociability. Adam Smith, for example, defines "sympathy" as denoting "our fellow-feeling with any passion whatsoever" (10). As discussed earlier, these thinkers believed that sympathy's complicated, reciprocal, and performative action facilitated the formation of a moderated, collective morality through the perception of similarity with others. Smith theorized that in societies no longer unified by powerful monarchies, churches, or influential nobility, sympathy between people produces, not perfect "unisons," which he implies are unrealistic, but "concords" among multiple and divergent sentiments. These are the minimum necessary for what he calls the "harmony of society" (22).

While readers have argued for the importance of spectatorial sympathy in *Mohicans*, I want to focus on Cooper's employment of Smith's aural metaphor, since, according to Aristotle and other friendship writers, "concord" is the political embodiment of amity (*NE* 8:1, 1).[18] Philbrick argues that music and especially the psalms sung by David Gamut throughout the text function as the antithesis of bloodshed and disorder, offering temporary interludes of beauty and peace. Not only is Gamut "the man of peace, the man of God, and the man of art" and culture in Philbrick's view, he is also the only figure of "concord" and remains "Cooper's chief vehicle for delineating, sustaining, and finally diminishing the values that lie at the opposite pole from the prevailing struggle and confusion of the narrative" (36). While it is true that Gamut is a pacifist, neither his "God" nor his "art" go unchallenged as absolutely positive visions. The Christian "sympathy" he represents is also, finally, "diminished," but as I show below, it is not the only form of "concord" the text offers as an alternative to the prevailing discord it describes.

The feckless psalmist decides to join the ill-fated party escorting the Munro sisters to Fort Henry in order, he declares affectedly, to "partake of social communion." When asked about his profession, he recommends psalmody as "a consoling communion" and one that requires four voices of different timbres to sing in unison for "the perfection of melody" (*LM* 24–25). To reinforce his point, the first hymn he offers to exemplify his "art" is Psalm 133 from the twenty-sixth edition of the venerated *Bay Psalm Book* published in 1744, for which he pompously gives the entire, lengthy title. The psalm expresses divine pleasure at the spectacle of human, specifically masculine, concord:

> How good it is, O see,
>   And how it pleaseth well,
> Together, e'en in unity,
>   For brethren so to dwell. (*LM* 26)

This is not far from the vision John Winthrop offered the Puritans in his "Modell of Christian Charitie." Through the amazed responses of Heyward and the Munro sisters, however, the narrator mocks Gamut for wasting his "full, sweet, and melodious tones" on the jarring, slavishly literal biblical translations of the Puritan fathers. This may be Cooper's jab at the artlessness of New England's "native poets," but it is also a critique of the hypocritical "unity" their religious doctrines advanced (26).

Furthermore, the humorous "unfitness between sound and sense" (27) demonstrated in this performance characterizes all aspects of Gamut. "The same contrariety in his members, seemed to exist throughout the whole man," so that his opening hymn to the blessings of unity itself becomes not just comical but discordant and strangely premonitory of its exact opposite: the displeasing enmity the "brethren" of the frontier suffer (26). Yet Alice's spontaneous enthusiastic response mistakes Gamut for "a disciple of Apollo" and thus a devotee of foundational Greek thought; she desires to "take him under my own especial protection" and enlist him as a "friend"—that is, as a potential protector against Magua, the Indian guide engaged by Heyward whom she finds completely unnerving (24–25). The most naive and fearful of the group, Alice mistakes Gamut's shallowness and contradictory performance as an index of Western culture and authentic amity, a Eurocentrism that only serves to reinforce enmity and disunion.

As the "muse" of a universal Christian "social communion," Gamut casts suspicion on the very concept, especially when the first person he addresses reflexively as "friend" is the "stoic" and "sullen" Magua (17).[19] By contrast, the relationships among the major Euro-American characters and their native associates evince a basic form of benevolent sociality. Not only Hawk-eye and Chingachgook but all the major characters are connected through this trope, signified by their use of "friend" as the general term of address. Hawk-eye addresses Heyward, Gamut, and even the Munro sisters by this term, and they return the favor. For example, before they are even introduced, Hawk-eye offers Gamut a taste of home-brewed spruce beer to assuage his sadness over the necessary killing of his noisy colt and says heartily, "I drink to our better friendship, hoping that a little horseflesh may leave no heart-burnings atween us" (57). When Heyward, awakened suddenly on his watch, asks the signal question, "Who comes?" Chingachgook answers softly, "Friend" (129) to indicate the absence of enmity and immediate danger.

The extensive use of this term of address temporarily suspends the obvious racial, class, and gender distinctions among the major protagonists. Although all the whites acknowledge Hawk-eye's expertise as guide and "friend"—meaning, here, protector—he "defers" several times to their higher rank and status. The term "friend" encompasses the varied meanings of family, extended kin, protectors, and associates, as well as private connections and intimates, and involves the major characters in a network of differentiated but connected relations based in moral and sympathetic, as opposed to commercial or self-interested, exchange. In fact, in this war-torn world, amicable relations play an intensified role as a requirement for survival: when one of the elderly Delaware chiefs demands of Heyward, "What has brought the white man into the camp of the Delawares?" (their supposed enemies), he answers, "My necessities. I come for food, shelter, and friends" (296).

This relational network of "disinterested" amity is perfectly illustrated in the scene Philbrick finds singly emblematic of chaos. Weary and bloodstained from a battle in which they rescued Cora, Alice, and Gamut from impending death at the hands of Magua's band, the trio of Uncas, Hawk-eye, and Heyward watch anxiously as Chingachgook and Magua "twisted together, like twining serpents" in a furious combat that "seemed to incorporate their bodies into one." "Urged by the different motives of filial affection, friendship, and gratitude," the three men hang over the combatants eager to intervene, but "the friends . . . knew not where or when to plant the succouring blow" (113). Cooper juxtaposes the disturbing "confusion" and even merging of the noble and demonic Indians with the onlookers' different relational responses, all encompassed under the eighteenth-century category of "friend." Rather than "giving way" before the rampant violence and disorder, however, instances of these "gentler emotions" often follow bloody engagements, come into prominence in response to them, and serve to counter the "savagery" exhibited throughout by Indians and whites alike.

Nor do the characters distinguish friendship in this general sense along gender lines. When, for instance, the gunpowder runs out during the battle in the cave at Glenn's Falls, Cora makes the generous suggestion that her male protectors escape in order to bring more help. Impressed with her courage, Hawk-eye takes her aside, instructs her how to mark a trail so they can follow it, and declares gallantly (if platonically): "[D]epend on having a friend who will follow to the ends of the 'arth afore he desarts you." As if to ratify this rather hefty vow, Hawk-eye "gave Cora an affectionate shake of the hand" in a muted but nevertheless unmistakable repetition of the text's signal gesture of friendship (79). This is not quite the mutual "exchange" that binds the male characters, but it draws the courageous Cora into the web of amicable male promises.

Ultimately, however, this equalizing benevolence and moral sociability fail to insulate the protagonists against the overriding violence of colonial warfare, the savagery of imperialism, or the hierarchy of masculine domination. Gamut's specifically Christian vision of "universal brotherhood" proves inapplicable even to his own person and impractical in the wilderness. His "art" not only fails in his attempt to "heal" Magua and convert the Indians but also does not help him fulfill the function of friend as "protector" that first Alice and later Cora and Heyward assign to him (172–73). Every time Gamut raises his resonant voice, though he once brings "scalding tears" to Hawk-eye's eyes with his "friendly manner of saying goodnight" reminiscent of the scout's childhood, he also brings danger. Gamut's singing alerts Magua and his band to the Munro sisters' hiding place in the cavern under the falls and, later, to their whereabouts during the melee of the retreat from Fort Henry (58–59, 177). In brief moments, Gamut embodies the Christian charity he idealizes, as when he selflessly takes the place of Uncas to allow him to escape from Huron captivity, or when he and Hawk-eye achieve friendly relations despite their vast, irreconcilable differences.

Nevertheless, the narrative implies that the psalmist's hypocritical Christian benevolence and narrow bibliocentric perspective cannot be the harbingers or guarantors of a general concord among people, nor can they equal or replace the transcendent quality of Hawk-eye and Chingachgook's enduring friendship.

"A Blazed Pine"

The only untarnished image of concord the text offers is the orderly and peaceful deliberations of the racially mixed band of scouts. But in the end, Uncas detaches himself from this dignified interracial fraternity and dies, not only because his desires cross boundaries of racial identity and court the mixed and "impure" but because he leaves the all-male family. The paradigm that remains is the nostalgic ideal of perfect homosocial friendship between Hawk-eye and Chingachgook, recapitulated in various guises throughout *Mohicans* and reaffirmed in the final moments of the narrative.

From a historical perspective, as Geoffrey Rans concludes in his antimythic reading of the series, this "is not merely a gesture of human fraternity but an embrace of defeat" and offers a consolation that is "profoundly qualified" (129–30). No matter how sincere and consoling, an alliance with Hawk-eye cannot assuage Chingachgook's many-layered grief, distilled in his final speech in his self-representation as "a blazed pine, in a clearing of the pale-faces" (*LM* 349). In this phrase, set off as a citation with no clearly discernible origin, Cooper encrypts a complicated narratorial wish for the proud Mohican's realization that interracial friendship requires his death as an agent and his final, willing resignation, like one of Aristotle's "natural slaves," to being marked by a dominating, if not superior, whiteness.

In the edition of 1831, published in London for English readers, Cooper appended the following gloss to the term "blazed": "A tree which has been partially or entirely stripped of its bark is said, in the language of the country, to be 'blazed.' The term is strictly English; for a horse is said to be blazed when it has a white mark" (318). Blazes mark a trail; they indicate direction; they "proclaim" the way (*OED*). In this sense, Chingachgook represents himself as the lone remnant of his noble race reduced to a signpost in a land "cleared" literally and figuratively by and for white men. A form of "cultural" castration, this figurative whitening overshadows "the bright blue blazonry of his race, that was indelibly impressed on his naked bosom," the tattooed mark of the Mohican's clan and noble lineage (*LM* 340).

Suffused with loss, individual as well as collective, this self-image is also a reminder of Chingachgook's future—but already accomplished—humiliation as the drunken "John Mohegan" of *The Pioneers*. That novel, the first of the Leatherstocking series, published in 1823, is set in the thriving post-Revolutionary settlement of Templeton in 1793, more than three decades after the events of *Mohicans*. In his waning years, described in *The Pioneers*, Chingachgook is converted to Christianity by Moravian missionaries and dies in a fire wearing a "medallion" of George Washington around his neck yet invoking "the Great Spirit" and anticipating his long-awaited return to his people (400, 419, 421).

Though unquestionably admirable and even heroic, Chingachgook is, as Cooper's first feverish dream of *Mohicans* reveals, inextricable and ultimately indistinguishable from the deeply wronged and malevolent Magua. In the account of their epic encounter in chapter 12 that grew out of his initial vision of the story, Cooper uses Miltonic diction to describe the native antagonists as "twisted together, like twining serpents, in pliant and subtle folds," a kind of satanic doubling (*LM* 113). Without the "perspectivism" Todorov earlier specified as its antidote, the same objectifying and reductive logic of otherness governs the dominant culture's perception of the noble as well as the ignoble "savage." In this sense, then, Cooper links his idealized Mohicans to one of the excesses with which the European colonial imagination defined and distinguished itself from the New World other. For at the heart of *The Last of the Mohicans*, a demonic act of cannibalism grips the Huron warriors incited by the vengeful Magua. Their unmotivated attack on unarmed mothers and infants retreating from Fort William Henry unleashes a "crimson tide" of blood from which "many among them even kneeled to the earth, and drank freely, exultingly, hellishly" (176). In Mann's film, Magua alone dramatizes this moment of excess when, during the massacre, he unhorses the proud, bewigged Colonel Munro and cuts out his still-beating heart, holding aloft the bloody trophy as if he now possesses the very soul of his enemy. It is not necessary to show Magua actually eating Munro's heart to make the point. This is the demonic form of identificatory incorporation that Michel de Certeau uncovers in Montaigne's conflated representations of the New World cannibal and the perfect Ciceronian friend explored in chapter 1.

Even this historically unfounded "bloodbath" is a form of "blood brotherhood." Shirley Samuels calls the massacre the "most appalling" example of a series of taboo cultural crossings proposed by *Mohicans*, which moves "beyond graphic descriptions of battles into an emblematic and terrifying fantasy of the 'unnatural' mixing of blood in which the Indians violently reproduce miscegenation by killing" ("Generation" 103–4). Cooper's identification of male Indians and generating women, in Samuels's view, justifies "the elimination or replacement of both by a fantasy of national identity" embodied in the "uncrossed" Natty Bumppo (108).

But in focusing on the Anglo scout outside of his relationships, Samuels ignores the profound spiritual and symbolic "crossing" or miscegenation (Fiedler's "male marriage") enacted in his friendship with Chingachgook. This friendship is profoundly Ciceronian in its pervasive melancholy, complex relation to history, and immersion in loss. From his first appearance in the narrative comparing the "histories" of white and red people in chapter 3 of the novel, Chingachgook elicits spectral imagery: "[H]is body, which was nearly naked, presented a terrific emblem of death, drawn in intermingled colours of white and black" (*LM* 29). Soon after, in the cave under Glenn's Falls, he appears to the frightened Munro sisters as "a spectral looking figure . . . this appalling object" (54). Though he wears symbols of hybridity and miscegenation ("intermingled . . . white and black") and of the death he would deal to others, Chingachgook is himself marked and defined by an affective interracial crossing that proves deadly. This crossing produces his own symbolic demise, the death of his son and people, his way of life, his agency. Finding Chingachgook "appalling" (from the Old French root *apalir*) signals not only his figurative whitening as a "paling" and "loss or change of color" but also his "dimming," "fading," and "weakening" (*OED*)—that is, his vanishing as the "palefaces" achieve ascendancy.

As other fictional Indians of the time, Chingachgook agrees to "vanish," forced like Aristotle's "natural slaves" to accept the superiority of the Europeans. But while Aristotle posited natural slavery on the basis of the slave's recognition and acceptance of the master's apparent superior reason, Chingachgook bows only to the whites' superior force. Therein lies his critique of colonialism. For this reason, Hawk-eye's devotion to Chingachgook is undiminished, and Chingachgook remains the moral polestar of his fleeting wilderness world. In *The Deerslayer* (1841), the last novel in the Leatherstocking series, Cooper describes the origins of this epic relationship as a kind of capstone to it. In this story, the untested young friends embark upon their "first war-path" together, Natty earns his mature appellation of "Hawk-eye," and he comes into possession of his famed firearm, "kill deer." Purporting to illuminate retrospectively Natty's moral development, which is fully displayed in *Mohicans*, *The Deerslayer* offers us a glimpse of Cooper's final thoughts on Natty's original choice of male friendship over marriage and, perhaps more important, of interracial friendship.

The story opens as Natty, called "Deerslayer," and his companion, Harry March, journey through the forest to numinous "Glimmerglass," later renamed Lake George and the milieu of Cooper's boyhood. Eliciting many interpretations, this mystical setting can also stand for the "mirror" of perfect friendship. "Hurry Scurry Harry," a handsome giant of a man so called for his "dashing, reckless, off-hand manner, and . . . physical restlessness" (*D* 20), is traveling to the home of an eccentric family of settlers who live on an island in the lake: a former pirate known as "Floating" Tom Hutter and his two daughters, the beautiful, high-spirited Judith, object of Harry's romantic interest, and her simpleminded, pious sister, Hetty. Natty's object is a rendezvous with Chingachgook in order to help him retrieve his betrothed, a feisty Delaware maiden who has been coveted and captured by their Huron enemies.

At first, Harry, the rugged and experienced frontiersman, appears to be the perfect male companion for the still-unproved Deerslayer, but their palpable moral differences make this friendship impossible. While Harry is handsome, impulsive, self-centered, and an inveterate Indian-hater, Natty is plain, deliberate, generous, and highly appreciative (not to say imitative) of "red gifts." Unthinkingly, Harry shoots at a deer out of season when there is no need for food, while his insatiable greed drives him to join Tom Hutter on a raid of defenseless Huron women and children in search of scalps they can redeem for money from the colonial governor. By contrast, despite his Delaware sobriquet, Deerslayer's central moral principle is never to take a life unnecessarily. Furthermore, when Judith definitively rejects Harry because she recognizes Natty's moral superiority and wants to interest him in marrying her, Harry leaves the orphaned Hutter sisters to their fate. In this and other ways, Cooper deliberately sets up Hurry Harry as the false (though white) friend against Chingachgook, who, though similarly concerned with his romantic pursuits, nevertheless remains Deerslayer's true friend. Chingachgook is the figure who most accurately (though not thoroughly) reflects back to the young hunter the moral clarity and virtues he strives to embody.

The choice between corrupt white settler values and the natural morality of noble Indians like the Mohicans and Delawares is not the only one Cooper offers his maturing hero. Like Eliza Wharton in *The Coquette*, Deerslayer also has a choice of mates who represent divergent ideological positions. Judith Hutter is a worthy match for Deerslayer in courage and innate nobility and proves herself over the course of the narrative willing to give up a glamorous life with the officers of a nearby garrison, one of whom has "tainted" her. This single moral "impurity," however, makes her unacceptable to the upright Deerslayer.

Her sister, Hetty, by contrast, is undeniably pure but simpleminded. She, like David Gamut, represents a shallow Christianity that is almost comical in wilderness encounters. Although the Huron chiefs accord her the privileges and protection of one who "possessed a mind that was constituted differently from those of most of the human race," allowing her unmolested access to their encampment where her father and Harry are captives, they reject her biblical exhortations to interracial fellowship as hypocritical. With no sense of irony or reality, Hetty recommends that the Huron follow the great Christian commandment to "love thy neighbor as thyself." The perceptive Wah-ta!-wah, Uncas's captive betrothed who has befriended Hetty and acts as translator, immediately responds, "Neighbor, for Injin, no mean pale face" (192–93). Although they share an abiding spiritual innocence, Deerslayer never seriously considers Hetty, who is smitten with Harry's comeliness and dies at the end of the narrative, collateral damage in the final defeat of the Hurons. Deerslayer also categorically rejects the Hurons' offer that he marry and provide for the widow of a warrior he has killed in self-defense.

Like Eliza Wharton, Natty does not so much choose between these possible spouses and the different "paths" they represent; rather, he chooses friendship and the masculine honor of the wilderness as his defining affiliative mode. Captured in the raid that frees Wah, Deerslayer is let out on "furlough" by the wily Huron chief to negotiate a settlement with his white friends. In returning to captivity to face impending torture and death, he rejects marriage, trusting in his simple belief, which he expresses in his farewell speech, that "fr'inds can scarce be separated [in the afterlife], though they are not of the same race on 'arth" (436).

Strongly encouraged by the courageous Wah, Chingachgook promises not to abandon his imperiled friend. Just as the young Mohican recognizes his new obligations to his betrothed, she honors the importance of his friendship with Deerslayer and argues that they both must act on the white man's behalf; marriage and friendship are not mutually exclusive for this Indian husband and wife, as they are for their white friend. In fact, in soliciting Wah's counsel, Chingachgook treats her like a moral equal and implies that their indistinguishable sentiments render them friends: "Good! The husband and the wife will have but one heart; they will see with the same eyes, and feel with the same feelings" (430). Deerslayer cannot imagine such mutuality across gender. Nevertheless, while Eliza Wharton falls into a killing melancholy and dies as a result of choosing the unsubordinated sovereignty of friendship, Natty not only lives but is rewarded with the status of hero and American icon.

Still, even in this initiation/conclusion to the Leatherstocking series, Cooper remains bound to his earlier published depictions of the male friends in their maturity and old age. In the final pages of *The Deerslayer*, the pair returns fifteen years later to the breathtaking Glimmerglass without Wah, who has died, but with Uncas, just entering manhood. Loss and lost opportunities suffuse this visit by the male companions, anticipating the ultimately melancholic nature of Cooper's representation of male interracial friendship we see in *Mohicans*. Bringing together New World cannibalism and Ciceronian *amicitia*, this pairing echoes the sacrificial form of Certeau's identificatory incorporation and does important cultural work. Both exemplary and ideal, masculine friendship allows readers of *The Last of the Mohicans* to identify with the epic figures' shared spiritual values and sentimental connection, exclusive of women and sexual generation, and to simultaneously disavow the narrative's justification of white domination and imperialist logic. Although, in a perverse twist, over the years Natty Bumppo has become an icon of a monoracial American national identity, in *Mohicans* at least he is not its champion. Along with the Indians, he is also the victim of American nationalism, longing for a vanishing world he has helped to defeat. In his intimate association with Chingachgook and his deliberate choice of masculine interracial friendship over heterosexual marriage or intraracial alliance, Hawk-eye imbibes certain "red" values that oppose and reject the encroaching settler world and its implicit national identity signified by Heyward's marriage to Alice. Hawk-eye "eats the other," participating in a Derridean "symbolic anthropophagy" (" 'Eating Well' " 113).

"Eating the other" is a notion that feminist critic bell hooks applies to contemporary popular culture's complicated racial dynamics. Focusing on the "pleasure" of transgressing boundaries, hooks wonders if late-twentieth-century "consumer cannibalism" opens the possibility of a critical resistance that more often than not reinscribes a racist status quo (31, 22). In a similar way, readers of Cooper's nostalgic fantasy of history continue to identify with and consume this pleasurable story of interracial friendship that simultaneously appalls and ennobles us.

Thus, in a move which appears at first to be in tension with received notions of equality, [Drucilla] Cornell will argue that ethical recognition will always consist in a failure to comprehend the other. The limit of recognition in the sense of comprehension is, paradoxically, the advent of ethical recognition, understood as the recognition of the limits of comprehensibility.
—Judith Butler,
"For a Careful Reading"

CHAPTER FIVE

The Ethical Horizon of American Friendship in Catharine Sedgwick's *Hope Leslie*

A year after the appearance of *The Last of the Mohicans*, Catharine Sedgwick published her third novel, *Hope Leslie; or, Early Times in the Massachusetts* (1827), which Nina Baym quips "might have been subtitled *The Last of the Pequods*, so closely did it invoke its precursor while at the same time challenging it" (81).[1] Set on the New England frontier in 1637, immediately after the first Pequot war, *Hope Leslie* takes up the debate over the definition of the new Republic, waged through the cultural medium of historical romance, where Lydia Child's *Hobomock* (1824) left off.[2] As liberal America struggled to emerge from its republican origins, the implications of traditional republicanism remained open to nostalgic and strategic re-presentation by romance writers attempting to influence the shape of the evolving political settlement. Baym sees these romances as part of an intertextual "network" in which male and female writers "revised each other from gendered perspectives" and in the process revealed "the self-conscious merging of gender and Indian issues" that characterizes the genre and the era (68). These issues included whether the Republic, after its first half century, would recognize women, Indians, and people of color as fully fledged citizens. This question gained urgency in the 1820s as states began to abolish property requirements and religious restrictions on voting, giving the franchise to all white males (as well as some naturalized immigrants). Andrew Jackson expressed his position by beginning the process of Indian removal west of the Mississippi.

Sedgwick's complex treatment of these issues, like Child's and James Fenimore Cooper's, hinges on the dynamics of cross-racial relations. Like *Hobomock*, Child's fictional response to Cooper's first frontier romance, *The Pioneers* (1823), Sedgwick's *Hope Leslie* features a headstrong English girl who comes to the struggling New England colonies and chafes against repressive patriarchal authority and Puritan ethnocentrism. In different ways, both heroines pioneer what some readers consider progressive proto-feminist alternatives to Cooper's conservative republicanism and masculinist vision of American national identity.[3] The dilemma and rebellion of Child's heroine, Mary Conant, however, revolve around marriage choices. These feature an Episcopalian suitor whom Mary's doctrinaire Puritan father rejects on religious grounds and a Wampanoag brave beyond the wildest paternal imagination conjured up by an infuriated Mary who chooses him purely to spite her intolerant father. In this scenario, women in America and, by association, American women win human rights as a subset of the right to freely contract marriage, while the sensational specter of miscegenation defines intercultural relations in the New World.

By contrast, Sedgwick's narrative decenters and deflects (but cannot completely evade) the marriage plot and gives a more historically accurate portrait of interracial marriage based on the experiences of Sedgwick's extended family.[4] As a deliberate challenge to Cooper's celebrated interracial male friends in *The Last of the Mohicans*, Sedgwick pairs her heroine, Hope Leslie, with Magawisca, the estimable daughter of the Pequot sachem Mononotto. This female friendship embodies the conflicting qualities Sedgwick's text struggles to integrate: on the one hand, a disinterested loyalty to community and nation (a discourse of "civic" responsibility derived from classical republicanism) and on the other, an independent conscience and unswerving commitment to impartial justice and equality (a discourse of rights derived from liberal theory).[5]

Like Cooper's famous homosocial pair, Sedgwick's heroines struggle to create a relationship within a historically specific discourse the narrative labels "friendship." However, a profound affinity that springs up in the initial scenes between Magawisca and Everell Fletcher precedes and mediates their homosocial bond. Everell is the oldest son of William Fletcher, a disaffected Puritan émigré who adopts Hope and her younger sister, Faith, when their mother, Alice Leslie, his cousin and first (thwarted) love, dies on her arrival in Boston. As Fletcher travels to Boston to meet his new charges, Magawisca and her brother Oneco arrive at Bethel, the Fletcher homestead near the frontier settlement of Springfield, as "servants"—captives, really, placed there by Governor Winthrop after they are taken prisoner along with their mother, Monoca, in New England's first military engagement against the indigenous people. Historical accuracy drives what critics see as Sedgwick's clever reversal of the captivity of white women, a trope Cooper and other writers used strategically to create compelling, ultimately hegemonic frontier narratives of male heroic quest, female passivity, and the American penchant for "regeneration through violence" hailed by critics like Richard Slotkin. Intent on rescuing his children from English captivity, Mononotto raids the isolated homestead, murders Mrs. Fletcher and her infants, and takes Everell prisoner in order to execute him in revenge for the murder of his oldest son, Samoset, by the English during the recent war. Magawisca clinches her role as a model of commitment to interracial friendship and impartial justice by risking her life to preserve Everell from her father's obsessive vengeance.

The triangulated ties among Sedgwick's three young protagonists allude to but significantly revise Cooper's dyadic interracial male friendship. Like Cooper, Sedgwick advances a spiritual ideal of friendship, but does not exclude women or disarm it by association with mythic or nostalgic presettlement innocence. By contrast, Sedgwick grounds her spiritual friendship on romantic notions of "nature" and "instinct" that diverge significantly from the ideas of the classical writers Cooper invokes and adapts in *The Last of the Mohicans*. Furthermore, Sedgwick explicitly links this form of affiliation with radical republican politics. Setting her narrative in the early years of the English Puritan settlement in New England, she links Anglo-America with the Puritan revolution in England while critiquing the elitism of its colonial manifestation. She begins her story a year after the Pequot war, in 1637, and concludes it in 1644, two years after the beginning of the English civil war between King Charles I and the Puritan parliamentary forces. Thus, Sedgwick uses the theme of English dissenters' resistance to monarchical tyranny to mount a fictionalized and anachronistic—really, allegorical—challenge to the patriarchal authoritarianism of the early Puritan settlement.

With its emphasis on freedom of conscience, civic virtue, and principled action, English Puritan republicanism signifies egalitarian ideals that are both nourished and impeded in the theocratic atmosphere of the New England colonies. To expand the notion of civic virtue to include women, Sedgwick revises canonical friendship doctrine by demonstrating that all women have the potential for self-possession and spiritual nobility required for friendship's highest form. She goes further in positing friendship between virtuous women as a model for egalitarian relations. In her boldest move, she juxtaposes an interracial, female-derived model with John Winthrop's elite masculinist perspective on models and charity in his foundational address of 1630, "A Modell of Christian Charitie." Like Cooper, her contemporary and competitor in the "culture wars" of the early Republic, Sedgwick advocates friendship as a specifically American form of democratic and sympathetic affiliation, but she does not limit it to same-sex relations or to males.

Friendship, I am arguing, is one of several affiliative discourses Sedgwick engages more than critics have recognized, which structures relationships and politics in her narratives in ways critics have not thoroughly explored.[6] In her influential analysis of Sedgwick's rhetoric in *Hope Leslie*, for example, Judith Fetterley marshals the unrelievedly gendered terms "sisterhood" and "brotherhood" to designate the dominant relationships Sedgwick represents in her narrative. These abstract terms mask the historical contours of the complex affinities between characters across gender, race, culture, and class encompassed by the term "friendship" and cloaked by the easy clichés of romance or miscegenation. Thus, Fetterley highlights the implied "sisterhood" between Hope and Magawisca and defines it in terms of Hope's biological connection to her younger, less evolved, and far more passive sister, Faith.

In claiming that Magawisca is the "real" sister for whom Hope obsessively pines throughout the narrative and whose "redemption" actually drives her thoughts and actions, Fetterley limits this important cross-racial relationship to one of obligatory kinship or mere political alliance, not ethical or spiritual consonance. Sisterhood, in this context, is both a familial sororal tie and a metaphor for political affiliation based on a consciousness of common female experiences that does not depend on or necessarily generate intimate personal bonds. Biological and even political sisters do not necessarily "choose" each other. Nor does sisterhood require, encompass, or produce virtue—the all-important ethical quality that for Sedgwick, as for the ancients, was requisite for and the result of perfect friendship. As I will show, Hope's obsession with redeeming her sister from Indian captivity has more to do with her own unexamined assumptions of cultural superiority and inferiority, her uninspected acceptance of "nature," and her inability to tolerate differences. These ethical shortcomings were characteristic of her era and prevent her, until the very end of the narrative, from thoroughly engaging in egalitarian friendships with any of the "sovereign selves" who offer themselves as her spiritual equals. This includes her presumptive "sister" Magawisca, who, in the final analysis, models an indigenous and open-hearted "American" friendship.

The Failure of Brothers

Hope's failure, Fetterley contends, is a necessary corollary of Sedgwick's discursive strategy for the inclusion of privileged white women, like herself, in republican citizenship through the deployment of an Enlightenment discourse of identity between brothers and sisters. Playing on Linda Kerber's well-known formulation of "Republican motherhood" to describe the sole political role available for women in the early national period, Fetterley identifies Sedgwick's argument for "Republican *sisterhood*" (495).[7] Having watched the suffering and painful demise of her own "republican mother," Sedgwick explores a different basis for women's political inclusion, not merely as dependent citizens in their roles as mothers, wives, or invisible daughters, but as sisters and unmarried women (or women married to their metaphorical brothers) who can pass morally and legally as men. Fetterley uncovers this logic in the "rhetoric of sameness" that characterizes the descriptions of Hope and Everell as physical and moral equivalents. At the same time, this cross-gender logic competes with the progressive notion of cross-racial parity based also in the "enlightened" belief in the shaping influence of material conditions rather than in fixed and inherent "nature," expressed in Sedgwick's preface to *Hope Leslie*. There, she addresses her reader as "an impartial observer" and "liberal philanthropist"—terms that invoke Smithian sympathy and Pythagorean *philotes*—who "will admit that the difference of character among the various races of the earth, arises mainly from difference of condition" (*HL* 6).[8]

But the equation or "homology" between elite men and women produced by cross-gender sibling identification fails to address the problem of recognizing differences within equality. Taking the brother as norm creates what Jacques Derrida describes as a "fratriarchy," a nominally democratic rule of men whose political homology makes them metaphorical "brothers." "The fratriarchy may *include* cousins and sisters but," Derrida cautions, "including may also come to mean neutralizing," since women and others can only be homologous and friends with brothers if they cease being (regarded as or making claims for) women and others (*Politics of Friendship* viii; his emphasis).[9] This is precisely why, in Fetterley's reading, Sedgwick finally has to banish both Hope's metaphorical though "real sister" Magawisca, as well as Faith, her biological sister, who "faithlessly" refuses to be redeemed from her cultural conversion to Indianness and her marriage to Magawisca's brother Oneco. The argument for racial equality "hopelessly" compromises the argument for gender equality through the identification of sisters and brothers.

Another way of reading the text's disfiguring obeisance to frontier and romance conventions turns on Sedgwick's awareness of the limits of Enlightenment rhet-

oric and liberal discourse as well as the necessity of incommensurate differences—
what Derrida and others call "heterology"—for the achievement of gender equality and the inclusion of others in a truly democratic state. Fetterley's reading
assumes that Sedgwick does not or cannot imagine beyond "the rhetoric of
liberalism" in which "white men are understood as grounding all claims for
equality, [so] those who cannot be equated with them by either race or gender
have no basis for their claims" (507). Critics have read *Hope Leslie* as positing an
alternative, heteronomous notion of community, modeled not on an abstracted
white male but on negotiated alliances and relationships forged among female and
male characters who attempt to resist or subvert both patriarchal tyranny and
Puritan theocracy, as well as the liberal individualism emerging in the Jacksonian
era.[10] In these readings, the character of Everell does not ground a liberal norm of
rights but rather is a brother who must be converted into a metaphorical sister and
friend in order to become an active partner in an interracial, intercultural, and
interclass network of alliances and affiliations. As the chief inheritor and future
manager of the patriarchy's privileges, the "brother" figure is key. His sympathy
for the perspective of the person lowest in the dominant cultural hierarchy—the
woman of color—models for readers what now we call the process of coming to
consciousness about the unearned advantages some receive simply because of the
accidents of birth (MacIntosh 100). The brother's rejection of patriarchal and
fratriarchal norms allows a redefined heterological "norm of rights" to emerge.

Everell is the major brother figure in *Hope Leslie*. His conversion, which
subalternist theorists describe as the psychic and ideological displacement or
"repositioning" that results when one "shifts location," occurs in several ways.[11]

Endowed with a strong sense of justice, Everell from the beginning meets
Magawisca on equal terms. Despite regarding her condition as "savage"—that is,
unconverted and uneducated, in which he echoes even the most progressive
thinkers of his time—Everell recognizes Magawisca as a moral being like himself.
He defends her and her people from ethnocentric and paternalistic attitudes like
that initially expressed by the family's retainer, Digby, who in an early scene gives
his opinion of Indians: "They are a kind of beast we don't comprehend—out of
the range of God's creatures—neither angel, man, nor yet quite devil" (*HL* 42).
Later in the narrative, Sedgwick sums up the relationship that emerges between
the English settler's son and the Pequot daughter: "He opened the book of
knowledge to her—had given subjects to her contemplative mind, beyond mere
perceptions of her senses." Most important, "he had gratified her strong national
pride, by admitting the natural equality of all the children of the Great Spirit; and
by allowing that it was the knowledge of the Englishman—an accidental superi-

ority" that reduced and subjugated the Indians (263). Thus, Everell is prepared to "hear" Magawisca's wrenching recital of the English attack on the mothers, children, and elderly of her tribe in the recent Pequot war, which unmasks the ethnocentrism of the official Puritan account.

Upon hearing this version, "Everell's imagination [is] touched by the wand of feeling," and he dashes away sympathetic tears that signify the authenticity of his vicarious feelings (54). The powerful "wand" Magawisca wields—her performance of recent history from a native *and* female standpoint—produces an affective response that induces Everell to reject the official Puritan histories. Composed by men and echoed by Digby in his recollections of the war, these accounts characterize the massacred Pequots as "sullen dogs" and call their deaths "a sweet sacrifice" (54). Everell's experience of "feeling with the other" helps to jump-start the process of seeing the world differently, of seeing from the perspective of difference; the relationship that emerges "has the power to deconstruct practices of racism . . . without promoting paralyzing guilt or denial" that often accompanies the jolting recognition of one's witting or unwitting participation in unethical structures of thought or behavior (hooks 177). When his mother is killed in Mononotto's raid on the Fletcher homestead, Everell literally joins the ranks of the bereft female characters—Magawisca and Hope—who have also lost mothers to analogous forms of paternal/patriarchal violence. Finally, Everell's narrow escape from Mononotto's ritual execution renders him symbolically reborn through Magawisca, the "sister" who sacrifices herself to save him (*HL* 93).

Sedgwick foregrounds the disarming of brothers and the concomitant empowering of female alliances in the epigraph to the first chapter of *Hope Leslie* from John Milton's *A Mask Presented at Ludlow Castle, 1634*. More familiarly known as *Comus*, after its intoxicating villain, the mask was written to honor John Bracly, Earl of Bridgewater, on his installation as Lord President of Wales. As part of the celebration, the mask included major roles for the earl's three unmarried children, a teenaged daughter and two younger sons. Its theme is the necessity of trial for the triumph of true moral goodness, as summed up in the passage Sedgwick chooses as her epigraph:

> Virtue may be assail'd, but never hurt,
> Surpris'd by unjust force, but not inthrall'd;
> Yea, even that which mischief meant most harm
> Shall in the happy trial prove most glory. (ll. 589–92)

Spoken by the "elder brother," these lines refer specifically to the threatened chastity of his sister, called "the Lady." As she and her brothers were crossing a "drear Wood" on the way to their father's installation, the powerful necromancer Comus, villainous offspring of Bacchus and Circe, kidnapped her and imprisoned her in an enchanted chair. Like his transfiguring mother, Comus lures travelers with offers of refreshment, only to give them a magical draught that transforms their "human count'nance . . . / Into some brutish form" (ll. 68–70). But unlike the Circean transformation, Comus's spell causes his victims to

> boast themselves more comely than before
> And all their friends, and native home forget
> To roule with pleasure in a sensual sty. (ll. 75–77)

Indulgence of the animal nature, Milton suggests, encourages dangerous self-misrecognition and the abandonment of all "friendly" affiliation and moral restraint. But the Lady possesses a "hidden strength" and is, thus, "clad in compleat steel"—that is, she has a full set of moral armor (l. 421). Through this mental fortitude, she manages to resist Comus's blandishments to drink from his magical cup and become the "Queen" of his riotous troops.

The "chastity" Milton extols as "saintly" and characterized by a punning "Sun-clad power" (ll. 782) does not merely connote sexual purity. That meaning of chastity, which early modern writers considered one of the "passive," specifically female virtues along with silence and obedience, was firmly in place by the time Sedgwick composed *Hope Leslie*. For Milton, however, chastity in this context connotes, as the Lady explains to Comus, "the freedom of my minde" (l. 663), a spiritual, ethical, and ultimately political power to judge and reject specious and dangerous ideas. The Lady illustrates this power in the bantering discussion on the correct use of "nature," a theme also central to Sedgwick's argument in her novel against authoritarianism. With a masculine Marvellian logic, Comus reasons that "[female] beauty" is a part of nature's bounty and, if not consumed, goes to waste and rot; "the good thereof," he concludes rakishly, "Consists in mutual and partak'n bliss" (ll. 740–41). Of course, Comus craftily ignores the power differential of consumer and consumed and the social "double standard" applied to them, expertly manipulated by Hannah Webster Foster's Major Sanford in his seductively "mutual" vision of libertine pleasure.

The Lady strenuously objects to Comus's distorted notion of "the good," which finds reason for license and gluttony in material abundance. The right use of nature, she counters, is available

> onley to the good
> That live according to her sober laws,
> And holy dictate of spare Temperance. (ll. 765–67)

The problem with indulgence, she continues, lies not in nature but in humanly derived, hierarchical social arrangements and could be addressed

> If every just man that now pines with want
> Had but a moderate and beseeming share
> Of that which lewdly pamper'd Luxury
> Now heaps upon som few with vast excess. (ll. 768–71)

The key words here, "good," "just," and "moderate," curb and Christianize the surprisingly anti-aristocratic, even democratic implications of this argument while also aligning it with early modern discourses of perfect friendship. Friendship that tempers and centers the self is an important element of traditional republicanism and necessary for the production of civic virtue, which can only obtain between good men.

In her study of these early modern discourses, Laurie Shannon argues that notions of perfect friendship converge with the "even more rhetoricized and heavily invested ideal" of female chastity around resistance to personal and political subordination in the forms of marital heteronormativity and political tyranny. Writers advancing male homosocial friendship as "a private sovereignty resistant to subordination" often denied the ideal to women who were not considered self-disposing. It was, however, available to them as a social form through female sexual chastity, which writers frequently represented in allusions to the virgin goddess Diana and her followers as "associative"—that is, productive of female bonds and elective communities. Both discourses configure a form of "political chastity" (Shannon, *Sovereign Amity* 57) with strong spiritual overtones that appealed to the republican strains in writers as different as Milton and Sedgwick.

The word "virtue," however, derives from the Latin *vir*, meaning "man." Historian Ruth Bloch argues that the "highly gendered" and specifically masculine attributes embedded in the classical republican concept of public virtue have their origin in "the Homeric idea of *aretê* or human excellence (later translated as 'virtue'), which stressed physical strength and bravery in athletic contests and in battles . . . and later fused with Greek and Roman ideas about the intellectual and cooperative virtues (such as judgment, justice, and friendship) that bind men in citizenship with the polis" (42–43). Sedgwick must have had this meaning in mind, since the unassailable virtue described in her first chapter, which the epigraph from *Comus* opens, is not a woman's sexual purity but the ethical stamina of William Fletcher, Everell's father. Fletcher's tyrannical uncle Sir William tempts him to renounce his commitment to Puritan dissent and liberty of conscience in order to marry his beloved cousin Alice and become his heir.

Not only does a female figure—Milton's morally unassailable Lady—stand behind Sedgwick's embodiment of Puritan and proto-American political virtue, but brothers fail to protect and preserve it. A second epigraph from *Comus* in *Hope Leslie*'s second volume, chapter 6, reminds us that both of the Lady's brothers have managed to "lose" her in Comus's wood (*HL* 236).[12] An "attendant Spirit" in the guise of their father's shepherd, Thyrsis, comes to their aid, giving them a potent herbal charm and specific instructions on how to defeat Comus and release their sister from captivity. The otherwise valiant brothers fail, however, because they neglect to "sease" the villain's powerful (dare we say phallic) "wand." In the end, the Spirit must call upon "Sabrina," patron of besieged virgins, who, from sisterly sympathy engendered by her own transfiguring experience of domestic abuse, frees the Lady from Comus's spell, much like Magawisca's "wand of feeling" frees Everell from the thrall of ethnocentric Puritan and patriarchal rhetoric. The female chastity invoked here is, also, in Shannon's terms, "associative"; after liberating the Lady, Sabrina hastens away "to wait in *Amphitrite's* bow'r" (l. 921) as a member of the retinue of Neptune's bride (who married despite a vow of perpetual celibacy). Thus, a specifically feminine power, derived from turning victimization into protection and suggesting the existence of a kind of mythical sisterhood, replaces the brothers' ineffectual use of arms and their inability to capture the destructively phallic magic wand. This second epigraph introduces a scene in which Hope, threatened by drunken sailors on Governor's Island and beyond masculine protection, uses her wits to free herself.

A third reference to *Comus* in *Hope Leslie* comes from the Lady's gender-bending description of her youthful brothers, about whom she says: "As smooth as Hebe's their unrazor'd lips" (l. 290; *HL* 127). This comparison to Hebe, the goddess of youth and cupbearer of the Olympian gods, somewhat explains and excuses the young brothers' ineptitude. But it also adds to the novel's comically subversive subtext of the blurring of gender roles, since Sedgwick applies the phrase to an evocation of her gender-bending transvestite character, Roslin/Rosa. To complete the displacement of brothers with sisters, Sedgwick also compares Hope to Hebe (*HL* 122). In doing so, Sedgwick suggests that sisters can replace and subsume brothers as the embodiment and protectors of virtue, while the chaste associations they form can serve as a norm that grounds more inclusive claims to natural rights and equality. In her witty and complex allusions to *Comus*, Sedgwick ties Milton's figure of female virtue and associative feminine triumph over immorality to political virtue, collective struggle, and an "American" love of liberty and justice.

By contrast, for Fetterley, sisterhood arises only in relation to a brotherhood in which it is subsumed and "however powerful it may become, begins with the recognition of mutual misery" as the common female condition (511). According to historian Nancy Cott, Sedgwick's readers would fully comprehend the notion of a sisterhood based on the belief "that women were different from but not lesser than—perhaps better than—men" (*Bonds* 160). These readers may have been practitioners of the "newly self-conscious and idealized concept of female friendship" that blossomed in the late eighteenth through mid-nineteenth centuries among middle- and upper-class women (160). Such homosocial bonds "expressed a new individuality on women's part, a willingness and ability to extract themselves from familial definition and to enter into peer relationships as distinct human beings" (190). Bolstered by evangelical Protestant notions of women's moral superiority and the superiority of sensibility over rationality, this notion of female friendship also expressed a form of gender identification Cott describes as "the consciousness of 'womanhood'—so thickly sown and vigorously cultivated in contemporary social structure and orthodoxy" (194). Although this new "group consciousness" often buttressed the idea of the complementarity rather than equality of the sexes, which mainstream thought easily translated into the inferiority, subordination, or domestication of women, it also fueled the idea of a powerful "women's culture" that did not originate in "mutual misery" but in mutual joy and passionate attachments that fostered the development of women's political consciousness (194).[13]

Sisterhood describes the consciousness of a specifically female commonality, based on experience and expressed through a kinship metaphor that does not depend on or necessarily generate intimate personal bonds. It remains an important social and political affiliative mode in *Hope Leslie* and in nineteenth-century women's literature and culture, despite critiques of its forced universalism, "whitewashing," and re-centering of the Oedipal family.

Mounting similar criticism about the ubiquitous discourse of sisterhood in feminism's second wave, philosopher María Lugones defines friendship as "a kind of practical love that commits one to perceptual changes in the knowledge of other persons" and offers it as a more viable theoretical alternative, especially for relations between women across differences ("Sisterhood" 411). Lugones specifies a practice she calls "pluralist friendship," a "very demanding feminist ideal" that involves "an understanding of the realities of the friend" as well as "a dislodging of the centrality of one's position in the racist, ethnocentric, capitalist, patriarchal state in one's own self-concept," the epistemic "dislocation" I mentioned earlier (411).[14]

In the spirit of this difficult ideal, I propose that we shift our attention from discourses of sisterhood in *Hope Leslie*, which are grounded in biological relations of "blood" and familial kinship, and examine Sedgwick's use of popular discourses of female friendship as well as a variety of discourses of spiritual or sympathetic affiliation based in similarity and equality that ground social relations as well as ethical, political action.

The "Theory of Affections": Revising Canonical Friendship

Evidence abounds in *Hope Leslie* that Sedgwick advances friendship as a superior form of affection and affiliation associated with disinterest and justice and condemns romantic love as a weakness causing psychic and social chaos. Hope signs the long, newsy letter she writes to Everell, who is finishing his education in England, "thy loving friend and sister" (*HL* 115). Using the familiar imagery of attachment, Everell describes his bond with Hope as "the chain of affection wrought in youth, and rivetted in manhood, and whose links seemed to him, to encompass and sustain his very life" (280). Their love has less of the "selfish," "engrossing," and ultimately tragic qualities of romantic love that overtakes other characters. The severe, puritanical Esther Downing, for example, smitten with unrequited love for Everell, finds it a "degrading experience," a "sinful dream," and the product of her "weakness" (134–35). Likewise, the unfortunate Rosa cannot extricate herself from what she describes as a form of emotional enslavement because, as she tells a sympathetic Hope, "I have not a friend in the wide world" to offer an alternative. "My heart," she confesses, "is steeped in this guilty love. If my master but looks kindly on me, or speaks one gentle word to me, I again cling to my chains and fetters" (244). Rosa's emotional "chains," unlike Everell's, enslave her because, as we will see, they are not forged with the angelic quality of "disinterest." At the lowest extreme is Sir Philip Gardiner, the Cavalier masquerading as a Puritan who prates of chivalrous love but whose "face was deeply marked by the ravages of the passions" (124). Hope explicitly characterizes the romantic love he peddles as "an inferior passion" when compared to "the fervour of devotion, and the tenderness of friendship" (217).

Allusions, epigraphs, and citations in the text indicate Sedgwick's awareness of classical, Christian, and early modern friendship discourses. But her use of these discourses reveals significant reversals and adaptations of classical ideas. For example, Sedgwick sets up Hope as the novel's principle of sociability and succor, a point Hope's younger sister, Faith, makes in the only English words she utters in the narrative. As the inhabitants of the isolated Fletcher homestead eagerly await Hope's arrival at the beginning of the narrative, Faith declares, apparently unaware of the implications of her words: "[E]verybody loves Hope. We shall always have pleasant times when Hope gets here" (60). Barnaby Tuttle, the elderly jailer Hope convinces to "relinquish . . . the letter of his duty" in order to facilitate her plan to free Magawisca from prison, identifies Hope's universal and irresistible charm when he muses, "I think she keeps the key to all hearts" (314). And yet, Hope's repeatedly expressed desire "to have my own way" seems to counteract the mutuality of society and friendship. Fearing this tendency in herself, Hope turns to Digby, a trusted friend, who offers a long explanation that redefines what looks like spoiled self-centeredness as the freedom of self-disposition.

Digby aligns his position with the "blunt" William Blackstone, a nonconformist Episcopal minister who in 1625 fled the religious intolerance of Archbishop Laud in England only to find an overdiscriminating theocracy in the Massachusetts Bay and finally settled in the Cumberland region of what is now northeastern Rhode Island (225). Having our own way, Digby assures Hope, is "the privilege we came to the wilderness world for. . . . Thought and will are set free. . . . Times are changed—there is a new spirit in the world—chains are broken—fetters are knocked off—and the liberty set forth in the blessed word, is now felt to be every man's birth-right" (225). And every woman's, apparently. To have one's own way is the basic liberty of conscience Digby locates, somewhat optimistically, in the holy scriptures; it is the privilege Hope wants for herself and strives, in theory, to extend to everyone else. However, even Hope, everyone's favorite, proves to be flawed, as we will see. In fact, Sedgwick's most daring revision of canonical friendship is to embody its earthly perfection not in her titular heroine but in Hope's idealized double, the Indian character Magawisca.

At their baptism in Boston "by the Reverend Mr. [John] Cotton," the orphaned Leslie sisters received the allegorical names of "Faith" and "Hope" "in commemoration of the Christian graces of their mother" (29). These names suggest the existence—and current absence—of the third and "greatest" term in the Pauline vision of spiritual graces, love or "charity." Without this virtue, according to the apostle, faith and hope as well as all "prophecies . . . tongues . . . knowledge" are ineffectual. And without charity, Paul finally admits, "I am nothing" (1 Cor. 13:8, 2), as if loving others and being loved are necessary to existence itself. As I discussed in chapter 2, this kind of "perfected" love is the "charity" John Winthrop holds up as his "model" for the Puritans emigrating to the New World in 1630, hoping that they will combine to create a Christian commonwealth defined by charity for all the world to see and emulate. The graces of hope and faith, Paul implies, are fallen, earthly props and therefore partial: "when that which is perfect is come," he explains, partiality will give way to the fullness of knowledge that is divine love. Paul describes this fulfillment as seeing "face to face" and knowing another "even as also I am known" (1 Cor. 13:10, 12), a profound mutuality characteristic of classical Greek *philia*. Sedgwick tempers her critique of Puritan religious zeal and patriarchal authority by embracing the *spirit* of their original utopian vision of community, epitomized in Winthrop's exhortation to the Puritans to "knit together" in love. She thoroughly radicalizes her representation of "charity," however, by embodying the third, most heavenly term of the Pauline trio in the character of Magawisca, as I will show below.

Sedgwick's revisions of canonical friendship are especially apparent in her representations of classicism. When Hope finally admits to her romantic feelings for Everell, the narrator intones, "It has been said that the love of a brother and sister is the only platonic affection," but calls this into question in the next breath by commenting, "This truth (if it be a truth) is the conviction of an experience far beyond our heroine's" (*HL* 224). Whatever the "truth" about "platonic affection" is, Sedgwick pronounces it beyond Hope's fanciful ken.

The same bemused tolerance characterizes Hope's playful indulgence of Master Cradock, her infirm but dedicated tutor. Though a comic figure, Cradock is a classically trained scholar who "not only wrote Greek and Latin and talked Hebrew like the Rev. Mr. Cotton, but . . . was skilled in Arabic, and the modern tongues" (342). As with the elderly jailer Tuttle, Hope can easily bend her tutor and his "little classical notices" to her often extravagant will. But like a true *philos*, or a bumbling "knight errant" to which Hope compares him, Cradock would willingly sacrifice himself for his young charge. "To her simple tutor, she seemed to embody all that philosophers and poets had set down in their books, of virtue and beauty," a description that positions Hope as the *eromenos* (beloved boy) of the older *erastes* (male lover) more than the untouchable "lady" of courtly love (123).[15] In either case, Cradock's adoration of his charge is comically overblown and masks a stronger criticism. Sedgwick frequently juxtaposes the dryness of "philosophers," whose inquiries "into the process of nature . . . will turn out like the experiment of the inquisitive boy, who cut open the drum to find the sound," with Hope's "winged . . . fancy" and joyful "imagination" (99). Her preference for the latter is unmistakable.

In Sedgwick's fictional universe, classicism requires naturalizing by an innocent and feeling heart, a principle represented by Hope. Even the pious Governor Winthrop chastises Master Cradock's "foolishness," calling him "an old man, whose original modicum of sense was greatly diminished by age, and excess of useless learning" (342). Hope adeptly utilizes this "useless learning" when she enlists Cradock in her plan to release Magawisca, who is captured during the reunion of the sisters she has engineered and is imprisoned in the Boston jail on charges of conspiracy against the Puritans. Luring Cradock into the privacy of Winthrop's study, Hope delights the aged scholar with "her seemingly profound attention" to a "difficult passage" in "her Italian author" (who appears to be a conflation of Dante, who composed *The Divine Comedy*, and Ariosto, who composed *Orlando Furioso*) in which "Orlando hesitates whether to go to the rescue of Beatrice." This passage conveniently reminds Hope "of a duty to a friend who sadly needs my help—and thine too, my good tutor." It is an association that alludes to and blurs chivalric, romantic, and charitable Christian impulses. Flattered to be asked, the obtuse Cradock exclaims, "My help!—your friend! It shall be as freely granted as Jonathan's was to David, or Orpheus' to Eurydice" (304). At this jumble of references, Hope "could not forbear laughing at Cradock's comparing himself to the master of music." This is one of several comments paralleling Sedgwick's figure of comic relief to the psalmist David Gamut, his counterpart in Cooper's *The Last of the Mohicans*. Hope good-naturedly responds that their task "is not very unlike that of Orpheus" (304).

These playful ripostes subtly re-center Sedgwick's friendship discourses. Cradock's mention of Jonathan and David is the only direct allusion in the narrative to the Bible's most famous pair of friends, so central to Winthrop's address.[16] Cradock's confused scholarship juxtaposes this masculine exemplum of friendship with one of the most tragic heterosexual love and marriage stories in Greek tradition, the futile attempt of bereft Orpheus to bring his adored Eurydice back from Hades with the power of his song. Furthermore, Jonathan succeeds in protecting his beloved friend from his father's murderous rage, though they must ultimately separate, while Orpheus fails to retrieve Eurydice (who, incidentally, dies of a snakebite, a fate Cradock only barely escapes because of Hope's solicitation of old Nelema's intervention). The heterosexual failure of this story installs absence, loss, and female silence at the heart of the Western lyric tradition (Joplin). Quite deliberately, Sedgwick replaces the Bible's signal pair of male friends, Greek mythology's premier heterosexual couple, and the Renaissance's epitome of courtly males rescuing endangered women with an interracial female friendship. To clinch the comparison, Sedgwick has Magawisca dramatically describe herself at her trial as immured, like Eurydice, in "that dungeon—the grave of the living, feeling, thinking soul, where the sun never shineth, where the stars never rise nor set, where the free breath of heaven never enters, where all is darkness without and within" (*HL* 293).

Moreover, Sedgwick allows Hope to reverse Orpheus's failure and succeed in "resurrecting" Magawisca. Ironically, humorously, Hope leads the slender Pequot woman up from the dungeon dressed like the hulking Master Cradock—charity inhabiting the form of pagan scholarship! Hope's charm and persuasive abilities are her Orphic "song," which she uses *not* in the service of individual heterosexual love or marriage but in the service of politically progressive, same-sex interracial friendship. In case her readers miss the allegorical meaning of this moment, Sedgwick has Magawisca conclude her eloquent plea to the Puritan court in which she refers to captivity as living death by echoing the rallying cry of American revolutionaries only fifty years earlier—or several centuries in the future: "I demand of thee death or liberty" (293). These women are either precursors of the American rebels or their true inheritors—or both.

Similarly, Sedgwick is aware of the classical requirement of equality of status and temperament for perfect friendship but applies it in revisionary ways. Early in the narrative, as Everell and Digby stand watch over the Fletcher homestead the night before Mononotto's attack, they disagree over Magawisca's allegiances. Digby argues that more worldly experience would teach Everell not "to trust a young Indian girl just because she takes your fancy." Everell retorts hotly that Magawisca engages his fancy "because she is true and noble-minded," an estimation later affirmed by her many attempts to avert danger from the Fletcher household. Insisting on Magawisca's "natural" loyalty to her people, Digby invokes the ancients' central principle of *philia*, also given prominent position in Winthrop's address in his description of the special community of saints: "The old proverb holds fast with these savages, as well as with the rest of the world—'hawks won't pick out hawks' eyes.' Like to like, throughout all nature" (42–43). Although Digby includes "savages" in the human family, he uses the proverb to argue for tribalism and the unnaturalness of cross-racial friendships. Magawisca will shortly upstage this limited view and the victors' account of the recent Pequot war Digby offers in this scene as evidence against the Indian character by her eloquent "recital" of the catastrophe from an Indian and maternal/feminine perspective.

While the cross-gender and cross-racial affiliations of the main characters require their possession of similar ethical qualities, Sedgwick deliberately inverts this in sketching the attachment of Hope and Esther. Hope is, in Miltonic terms, "an allegro to [Esther's] penseroso. They were unlike in every thing that distinguished each; and it was therefore more probable, judging from experience, that they would become mutually attached. Whatever the theory of affections may be, the fact was, that they soon became inseparable and confidential friends. . . . [H]owever variant their dispositions, they melted into each other, like light and shade, each enhancing the beauty and effect of the other" (139). Hope and Esther seem like two complementary halves of one whole, Diotima's image for heterosexual love described in Plato's *Symposium*, rather than the "one soul in bodies twain," which was the popular Renaissance figure for friendship. Even Governor Winthrop comments, using his favorite image for affiliation from "A Modell of Christian Charitie," that "their hearts appear to be knit together" (*HL* 153). But when it comes to putting their beliefs into action in planning the rescue of Magawisca, Esther's refusal to diverge from the "narrow" path of obedience to Puritan and patriarchal authority drives a deep wedge between the female friends and between Everell and Esther. This failure of ethical likeness suggests that only an intrinsic consonance in character will allow the fullest expression of private sentiment in public action. In this passage, Sedgwick refers to a reigning "theory of affections" whose emphasis on likeness is suggested, if not confirmed, by this exception to the rule.

Sedgwick's revision of classical notions of friendship not only encompasses women but includes them under a specific understanding of feminine connection, thus making women's bonds exemplary of the spiritual friendship her age regarded as its purest form. This is confirmed by the epigraph Sedgwick chooses for the last chapter of her narrative in which she wraps up the loose ends, gives extremely (and significantly) short shrift to the details of Hope and Everell's wedding, and sketches the subsequent history of Esther, whom she promotes as a marriage resister. The aphorism is from *Maximes*, a collection of reflections first published in 1665 by François La Rochefoucauld, the brilliant French aristocrat and epigrammatist, and summarizes much of traditional friendship theory: "Quelque rare que soit le véritable amour, il l'est encore moins que véritable amitié" (However rare true love may be, it is still less rare than true friendship) (*HL* 336). The emphasis on "*véritable* amité," on its extreme singularity and its implied superiority even to "le véritable amour," indicates that Rochefoucauld finds inspiration in the canonical friendship discourse of his countryman and precursor Michel de Montaigne, discussed in chapter 1. A "disciple" of Rochefoucauld was Lord Chesterfield, the influential English writer Jay Fliegelman credits as a spokesman for the "rational pedagogy" and "redefinition" of authoritarian relations on the basis of friendship and contractualism so popular in pre- and post-Revolutionary American culture (40–41). Sedgwick cites Rochefoucauld rather than Montaigne or Cicero because she wants to avoid the elegiac and nostalgic mood conventionally associated with ideal friendship by these writers. Unlike his predecessors, Rochefoucauld did not explicitly and categorically exclude women from "véritable amité" as Montaigne did. Moreover, Rochefoucauld had deep, abiding, and intellectual friendships with prominent women of the day, including Madame de Sablé and Madame de Lafayette, author of the landmark French novel *La Princesse de Clèves*, with whom he established a distinguished literary circle.

Revising the "Modell" of Puritan Charity

Closing her novel with an aristocratic French skeptic's assertion of friendship's superiority measures the philosophical distance Sedgwick travels from the opening account of the immigrant generation that frames her tale of their "American" children. In this framing story we learn that Sir William, the royalist uncle of William Fletcher, wants his nephew as heir and husband for his only daughter, Alice, but fears Fletcher's dissenting leanings. Admonishing Fletcher's father about his son's education, Sir William declares, "I would that all our youths had inscribed on their hearts the golden rule of political religion," which accepts unquestioningly the central authority of the "sovereign's laws and injunctions." He rails against cramming "our lads' heads with philosophy and rhetoric and history of those liberty-loving Greeks and Romans" whose "pernicious lore . . . has poisoned our academical fountains" (8). Prominent among this contamination is the thought of Plato, Aristotle (though he actually preferred monarchy as a political system), and Cicero, all who place friendship at the foundation of the republican polis.

In advancing what amounts to a political baptism (inscription on/circumcision of the heart) and transposing the "Golden Rule" of the Gospels to the realm of contemporary politics, Sir William trades the lateral mutuality of loving neighbors and treating others as oneself for a vertical relation in which subjects can never be friends with or equals of their monarch. He especially targets "puritans," those "mad canting fools" he would ship off to the New England colonies "where they might enjoy with the savages that primitive equality, about which they make such a pother" (8).[17] Personifying "Liberty," and by association equality, as feminine, Sir William derides these as the "[d]aughter of disloyalty and mother of all misrule," casting them as the very temptations that caused Adam and Eve to fall from paradise. "Awed" and somewhat mystified by his nephew's "lofty independence," but observing "that love was a controlling passion" for him, Sir William uses the affection he has fostered between his nephew and Alice, who were childhood companions, to pry Fletcher away from "the principles of civil and religious liberty" that imbue his young mind (9–10).

Though uncle and nephew are almost diametrically opposed, both of them regard affection, religion, and politics as inseparable, so that loving others is tantamount to according them a "natural" right of legal, though not social, equality. Sir William associates this "primitive equality" with both the dissenting Puritans led by John Winthrop, "a notable gentleman" who "doth grievously scandalize his birth and breeding" by embracing "these scurvy principles," and the "savages" of the New World, whom the "young zealot" and "fanatical incendiary" John Eliot would attempt to convert to Christianity (8). Sir William's machinations to "reduce . . . his nephew to dependence on his will and whims" confirm that personal alliances are always subject to political and public pressures (9–10).

When Fletcher's attempts to elope with Alice and evade this parental/political tyranny fail, he turns for advice to Winthrop, his "confidential friend" and the stand-in for his deceased father. Sedgwick characterizes Winthrop as "a man of the most tender domestic affections and sympathies," who at the same time possesses "that characteristic zeal which then made all the intentions of Providence so obvious to the eye of faith, and the interpretation of all the events of life so easy" (11). When Sir William forces Alice to marry the man of his choice, Winthrop convinces Fletcher that it is the "design" of heaven and encourages the desolate lover to wed a devout young woman who has been Winthrop's ward and join him by taking passage to the New World on the *Arbella* in 1630. Thus, the opening chapter of *Hope Leslie* advances, in stark contrast to Sir William's cynical Old World authoritarianism, a progressive understanding of what Sedgwick calls, somewhat ironically, "the apostolic principle of community of goods" based on the affiliative paradigm Winthrop outlines in "A Modell of Christian Charitie."

Sooner than expected, however, Fletcher becomes disillusioned with the Puritan experiment, which he regards as "sometimes perverted to purposes of oppression and personal aggrandizement" (16). Sedgwick neatly deflates the lofty Puritan project when she depicts the merry seaman ferrying Everell and Sir Philip Gardiner to Boston blessing Governor Winthrop's "piece of christian love" in "not joining in the hue and cry against the good creature tobacco" (125–26). Moreover, Sedgwick imbricates Fletcher's disillusionment with a deep personal loss caused by his adherence to principles that ties it inseparably to issues of public and political moment. In 1636, Fletcher moves to the outlying settlement of Springfield, building his homestead a mile from the village to escape "the surveillance of an inquiring neighbourhood" (17).

But even the "visionary" and "idealistic" Fletcher illustrates some of the narrowness of his age. In quelling Mrs. Fletcher's fears about his former lover's daughters joining their family, Fletcher invokes the discourse of companionate marriage. He assures his wife that though the "affection I gave to [Alice], could not be transferred to another," and though even she begged him to "yield my integrity . . . there was a principle in my bosom that triumphed over all these temptations. And think you not that principle preserved me faithful in my friendship to you?" (20). Fletcher invokes the Protestant view of marriage that appropriated the language of classical friendship and also implies that his unwavering republican principles are the foundation of his "egalitarian" marital affections. We learn in his next comments, however, that his "friendship" for Mrs. Fletcher derives not from a recognition of parity between them but from "your obedience, your careful conformity to my wishes; your steady love" (20)—a belief in the husband as "benevolent" sovereign.

In this attitude, Fletcher follows the pattern set by his "friend" John Winthrop. Although Sedgwick describes Winthrop's public mien as colored by the "solemn and forbidding aspect of the times in which he flourished," she also gives him a benignant side: "[W]e know him to have been a model of private virtue, gracious and gentle in his manners, and exact in the observance of all gentlemanly courtesy" (144). Winthrop begins as a character that embodies the gendered separation of the public and private. Illustrating a key term in the title by which his lay sermon became known, Sedgwick's Winthrop is the "model" of the qualities early modern writers thought requisite for perfect friendship: virtue, nobility, and "courtesy." In his *Essays*, Francis Bacon gives the last of these qualities a specifically Christian character, likening "courtesy" to "St. Paul's perfection, . . . a kind of conformity with Christ himself" (41). Likewise, Sedgwick portrays the governor's wife, Madam Winthrop, as a fit helpmeet, modeling for "matron and maiden, the duty of unqualified obedience from the wife to the husband, her appointed lord and master; a duty that it was left to modern heresy to dispute" (*HL* 144). This female paragon has so internalized her subordination that her "matrimonial virtue . . . was prompted by feeling," not merely obedience or obligation. Sedgwick even risks giving offense by comparing Madame Winthrop to "a horse easy on the bit" and, relishing the metaphor, adds, "it sometimes appeared as if the reins were dropped, and the inferior animal were left to the guidance of her own sagacity" (145).

A few pages later, Winthrop reinforces this view of women and marriage when he discloses to Fletcher his desire to consign Hope, whom he calls "this lawless girl," to "the modest authority of a husband" because "she hath not, I speak it tenderly, that passiveness, that next to godliness, is a woman's best virtue" (153–54). His private "tenderness" toward Hope or her guardian, however, does not mitigate the misogyny of his coercive designs. Masking gender hierarchy as "the modest authority of a husband," he echoes Lucy Freeman's recommendation of "consensual" Federalist marriage to Foster's Eliza Wharton, who accurately recognizes it as a woman's consent to be shackled. Fletcher diverges from the "narrow" Puritan path by responding, "I should scarcely account . . . a property of soulless matter, a virtue," confirming that for him, activity and agency are important virtues not only for Puritan men but also for Puritan women. In case her readers do not immediately recognize the contradictory nature of Puritan marital doctrine in a theoretically republican polity, Sedgwick comments acerbically that "our pious fathers, or even mothers, were so far from questioning [it], that the only divine right to govern, which they acknowledged, was that vested in the husband over the wife" (144). The radical implications of this argument are unmistakable. If Fletcher and the dissenting Puritans can find moral and spiritual grounds on which to resist the divine right of the English king and justify immigration and even regicide, why should wives still bow to the divine right of husbands?

Winthrop's patriarchal attitudes do not, however, prevent him from fulfilling the private offices of friendship. At the opening of the scene described above, in the privacy of his study, Winthrop hands Fletcher a letter from Esther's father detailing Everell's activities in England. Downing suggests that his pious and obedient daughter would be a better match for the "high-metalled youth" than the wealthy Hope, "reported here, to be wanting in grace." Downing further insinuates that because Fletcher's fortunes need mending, he seeks the match for his son from mercenary motives (151). Using the language of his correspondent's famous address, Downing reminds Winthrop, "you in the new world, are as a city set on a hill. . . . [A]ll appearance of evil should be avoided" (151). Deeply wounded by the impugning of his honor, his virtue, his civic loyalty, and his favorite, Hope, Fletcher begins to weep. "Governor Winthrop laid his hand on his friend's arm, and by a gentle pressure, expressed a sympathy that it would have been difficult to embody in words" (152). Although Winthrop usually enacts friendship somewhat like a doctor probing a wound and "inflicting salutary pain" (11), Sedgwick portrays him as capable of a consoling sensitivity. In fact, one of the most surprising revisions this line of analysis reveals is Sedgwick's redemption of the magistrate John Winthrop through friendly affection.

Though less susceptible to Hope's socializing effects than Barnaby Tuttle or Master Cradock, the governor begins, under the insistent pressure Hope's actions exert, to register the problematic disjunction between public and private spheres his doctrinaire beliefs impose. For example, after Hope shows "exemplary humility and deference" in the full disclosure of her recent and highly unorthodox activities on Governor's Island and her fortuitous escape, Winthrop pardons her as "one who seems to have so hopeful a sense of error, . . . while the goodwill beaming in his benevolent face, shewed how much more accordant kindness was with his nature, than the austere reproof which he so often believed the letter of his duty required from him" (269). True, he is responding to the self-abasing behavior of a chastised Hope that he regards as necessary for piety and femininity; thus, her "errors" appear "hopeful." Sedgwick implies, however, that Hope's influence serves to draw forth the kindly "nature" Winthrop manfully represses by his dutiful application of the abstract "letter" of Puritan doctrine.

This releasing of "nature" is one step on the path that leads the stern governor to listen sympathetically to Magawisca's testimony at her trial, over which he presides, to cast doubt on Sir Philip's inflammatory account of Magawisca's actions, and to respond powerfully to the prisoner's reminder of his promise to her mother and eloquent plea not to be returned to the jail's dungeon. As Magawisca kneels before Governor Winthrop, her mantle dramatically thrown back to reveal her "mutilated person," the fascinating emblem of her heroic sacrifice for interracial friendship, an agonized Everell responds impulsively by calling for her "liberty." All the onlookers in the room (except the dour magistrate-judges) are electrified by the affecting spectacle and echo Everell's cry. Even Winthrop vibrates with the collective mood and responds to Magawisca's wielding of the "wand" of feeling: "The Governor rose, waved his hand to command silence, and would have spoken, but his voice failed him; his heart was touched with the general emotion, and he was fain to turn away to hide tears more becoming to the man, than the magistrate" (293).

By the narrative's conclusion, Sedgwick implies that her Winthrop resolves the "strange contrariety of opinion and feelings" besetting "the breasts of a great majority of the audience" which are torn between their limited reason (that counsels suspicion of Indians as aliens and, thus, enemies) and "the voice of nature" (that perceives and sympathizes with Magawisca's likeness and nobility) (294). By the time Hope furtively slips away at nine that evening with Master Cradock to release Magawisca, Winthrop regards her disappearance as "somewhat unseasonable" but assures an anxious Fletcher, "[W]e may trust your wildwood bird; her flights are somewhat devious, but her instincts are safer than I once thought them" (303). Earlier, Winthrop declared himself "impatient to put jesses on this wild bird"—that is, limit her unsupervised flights through leashing and domesticate her through matrimony (155). Now, he expresses confidence not only in the "instincts" with which Hope, like an unfettered bird, will find her way safely home but also in the spontaneous, intuitive, and nonrational sympathies that have all along guided Hope's actions outside the bounds of legalistic Puritan morality.[18]

In his final appearance in the narrative, Winthrop treats the outcome of Hope's "devious" evening flight—achieving the escape of Magawisca—with a "clemency" to which, the text assures us, he was always "disposed." Furthermore, Sedgwick observes that this reenergized disposition is "so beautifully illustrated by one of the last circumstances of his life, when being, as is reported of him, upon his death-bed, Mr. Dudley pressed him to sign an order of banishment of an heterodox person, he refused, saying,—'*I have done too much of that work already*'" (343; her emphasis). Thomas Dudley, father of Anne Bradstreet and deputy governor under Winthrop, was a highly respected though notably inflexible Puritan leader and a particularly harsh prosecutor of Anne Hutchinson during her trial and excom-munication in 1636–37. With this deathbed anecdote, Sedgwick's Winthrop caps his long tenure at the helm of the Massachusetts Bay colony not quite by protecting the heterodox, who at that period in New England history were frequently Quaker women opposing patriarchal Puritan intolerance, but at least by refusing to further contribute to the regime's authoritarian practices.

Disinterest: An Angelic "Modell" of Female Friendship

Sedgwick's fictionalized (perhaps even wishful) account of Winthrop's evolution illustrates a shift in the conception of friendship: from the classical insistence on *philia*'s basis in dispassionate "reason" to a romantic emphasis on "nature" or "instincts." This shift reflects historical trends in culture, politics, and religion that advanced the cultural ideal of equality and mutuality in same-sex relations, "heart-religion" among Christian revivalists, and the superiority of affection over rationality, thereby contributing to the cultural idealization of women's moral and emotional capacity. By the early nineteenth century, women's bonds became, for good or ill, the model for "sentimental" friendship.

It is not surprising, then, that in Cott's historical examination of women's relations in the early nineteenth century, Sedgwick's sentiments constitute an important historical resource. In Cott's account, they illustrate the "sacredness" of women's friendship in comparison to "carnal" heterosexual relationships and also white women's growing consciousness of their moral superiority to men. Cott cites an entry Sedgwick pens in her diary after meeting the internationally re-nowned English actress Fanny Kemble, who toured the East Coast in 1832 and went on to marry a southern planter and publish a journal highly critical of slavery in the South. In that entry, Sedgwick declares with characteristic force: "I do not believe that men can ever feel so pure an enthusiasm for women as we can feel for one another. . . . [O]urs is nearest to the love of angels" (*Bonds* 189).

By "the love of angels," Sedgwick refers to feelings that are not just free from carnality but are also "disinterested"—free from partiality and the desire for personal gain. Her use of the term "disinterest" adapts the distinction made by David Hume, an eighteenth-century Scottish philosopher who viewed friendship as part of what he called "disinterested commerce," which he contrasted with the self-interested commerce of market relations bound by promises and legal contracts (Silver 1480). Disinterest, or what Adam Smith calls "sympathy," is the emotion that founds sociability and underwrites morality, leaving economic relations conveniently free from moral strictures; it is not coincidental that Smith authored both *The Theory of Moral Sentiments* and the bible of laissez-faire capitalism, *The Wealth of Nations*.

As we will see, a romanticized disinterest underlies Sedgwick's understanding of the "véritable amité" that for her is necessary for true love, but it is also the basis for her conception of ethical action, *communitas*, and social and political justice. Like the Scottish philosophers, and Adam Smith in particular, who believed sympathy and society arise from individuals' need for recognition and approbation, Sedgwick champions disinterest as the discipline of resisting self-indulgence through an intense sympathy with the needs and desires of others. Unlike these male philosophers, however, she routes her advancement of disinterest and sympathy through Winthrop's notion of Christian charity but differs from the Puritan approach by placing women as agents (rather than "woman" as figure) in the forefront as models of disinterest. Later in the nineteenth century, though we see hints of it in Sedgwick's handling in *Hope Leslie*, disinterest becomes indistinguishable from a sentimentalized selflessness and abasing self-sacrifice specifically associated with domesticated femininity, the cult of "true womanhood," and required of women.

In its tempering form in *Hope Leslie*, disinterest is the moral virtue in highest narrative esteem and evokes several heightened editorial asides. In one such comment, Sedgwick instructs readers on how to regard Hope's puzzling resignation after she not only forces the man (Everell) she (just realizes she) loves into the arms of her dearest friend (Esther) but also allows him to believe she favors his despicable rival (Gardiner). Hope reasons naively, "After a little while . . . I shall feel as I did when we lived together in Bethel; if all that I love are happy, I must be happy too." The narrator then cautions her readers: "If the cold and selfish laugh to scorn what they think the reasoning of ignorance and inexperience, it is because they have never felt, that to meditate [on] the happiness of others, is to enter upon the ministry, and the joy of celestial spirits. Not one envious or repining thought intruded into the heaven of Hope Leslie's mind. Not one malignant spirit passed the bounds of that paradise, that was filled with pure and tender affections, with projects of goodness, and all their cheerful train" (*HL* 224).

The heightened and didactic language here and in other asides extolling disinterest implies, without a trace of irony, that in her "innocence" of intention, Hope does the work of angels and thus experiences a "heaven on earth" that is difficult for "cold and selfish" people to comprehend.[19] By advancing the value of disinterest, Sedgwick links her narrative not only to the fleeting world of republican and civic virtues where (propertied, wealthy, and usually male) citizens sacrifice personal gain for the common good but also to the emerging cultures of sentimentalism, which commend self-sacrifice against the perceived self-centeredness of Jacksonian democracy, liberalism, and even first-wave feminism. Not merely a "domestic" virtue in Sedgwick's mind, disinterested action allows female characters to act in the public social sphere, where their deeds often have political ramifications.

Bidding to radically expand the category of republican citizenship, Sedgwick casts Magawisca, the allegorical figure of "charity," as the narrative's standard for disinterested action. Sir Philip Gardiner exemplifies disinterest's nadir, and seduction is its horrific consequence. Everell expresses the text's moral revulsion against such actions when he alludes to accusations that his attachment to Hope is mercenary but cannot even utter the phrase "interested motives. . . . [I]t seemed as if the words blistered his tongue" (221). Sedgwick's representation of the difficulty of achieving true disinterest echoes Winthrop's quandary in "A Modell" about the best way to inculcate Christian love so that it becomes reflexive and spontaneous. Making charitable love "instinctive" or "prompt upon all occasions to produce the same effect," he argues, can be accomplished only "by frameing these affections of love in the hearte," by preparing and fashioning the affections through the use of the imagination to feel what others feel (*WP* 288). The perceptible pangs or tears of sympathy produced by literally feeling with another—putting oneself in another's place—in turn produce a "native desire" (also the desire of/for the native) to do good for the other.

In spite of faults and lapses, the text insists that Hope acts truly selflessly, even if she fails to correctly assess her feelings for Everell and his for her. According to the text's logic of affiliation, however, their "true" love can also be "disinterested" because it is based on "true" friendship. Both are willing to sacrifice their untransferable love for what they (mis)perceive to be the predilection of the other—an example of disinterestedness gone awry. At the height of his feelings, Everell "had cherished for Hope a consecrating sentiment—he had invested her with a sacredness which the most refined, the purest, and most elevated love throws around the object of its devotion" (*HL* 178). In this, he seems to anticipate Hester Prynne's insistence that her "adulterous" love with Dimmesdale "had a consecration of its own" beyond theocratic morality or legality (Hawthorne 140). Using the language of friendship, which is so easily mistaken for discourses of romantic love, Everell entertains a "vision of [Hope's] ideal perfection." Anxious when she "permit[s] herself to be obscured by mystery" and linked to the dishonorable Gardiner, his "disjointed thoughts . . . indicated the ardor, the enthusiasm, the disinterestedness of Everell's passion" (*HL* 178–79, 207). While "ardor" and especially "enthusiasm" are terms of heightened, even uncontrollable emotion often associated with unruly religious zeal or romantic and erotic passions, Sedgwick links them here explicitly with "disinterestedness." One could even say that, contrary to the conventional understanding of romance, Sedgwick keys Everell's ardor and enthusiasm to a specifically "American" notion of affect that, thus, provokes and produces his "disinterested" love.

By contrast, Esther's unrequited and unhealthy love for Everell renders her, from her first appearance in the text, "interested." Her passionate and uncontrollable feelings "not mingling with his, they were, like a stream, that being dammed-up, flows back, and spreads desolation, where it should have produced life and beauty" (136). In Sedgwick's fictional world, the wages of passion lay waste to life and devastate nature; this strong image suggests that self-contamination ensues when artificial strictures, like the Puritan letter of the law, impede the natural flow of human feelings. Although Esther "was always characterized by a religious epithet—she was the 'godly,' or the 'gracious maiden,' " "approved by our elders, the pattern of our deacons' wives," her practical piety and hewing to doctrine and patriarchal authority deform a generous nature and prevent instinctive charity (136, 133). She struggles throughout the narrative, like Hope but with less success, to achieve a calm disinterestedness. Her failures suggest the fallibility of the Puritan model of required—or what we might call "deliberative" (rather than instinctive)—generosity offered by Winthrop in his "Modell."

Sedgwick explores the "angelic" nature of female "enthusiasm." This includes Everell and, to a lesser extent, as I have suggested, a revised conception of the character of Winthrop himself, in the broad network of same-sex and often cross-racial affiliations presented in her narrative. The relationship of Hope and Esther, described in their first scene alone together as "two confidential young friends," presents a limited and failed form of such an affiliation (133). Although Sedgwick explicitly distinguishes them from the "modern belles" of her present day, Hope and Esther's relationship conforms stylistically to early-nineteenth-century friendships: they are age-mates from similar backgrounds and class; they share a room, a bed, affectionate kisses, a love object, and confidences. They are finely attuned to each other's emotional states and psychological turmoil. For example, when they are out walking and meet Everell, who has unexpectedly arrived from England, Hope perceives Esther's agitation and later, in the privacy of their shared room (an anachronistic luxury in early-seventeenth-century Boston, even for the governor's residence), encourages her to unburden herself. Hope is deeply moved when Esther confesses her passion, "and taking a generous interest in her happiness, she had, with that ardent feeling with which she pursued every object that interested her, resolved to promote it in the only mode by which it could be attained" (212). Hope's characteristic "ardor," like Everell's, also motivates her generosity and devoted friendship. Only later does she discover that these amicable desires conflict with her own feelings for Everell.

In a parallel scene, after Hope's secret meeting with Magawisca in the Boston cemetery, Esther urges her discomfitted friend, "Unburthen your heart then, to me. . . . [M]ost gladly would I pay back the debt of sympathy I owe you" (179). Esther imagines an economy of friendship balanced by debts and repayments in which "interest" can play a part. Ironically, Hope cannot confide her secret because it does not concern only personal matters of the heart, as does Esther's secret, but involves public matters pertaining to the state (Puritan-Indian relations). Bearing her burden alone, Hope resolves "to act most heroically; to expel every selfish feeling from her heart, and to live for the happiness of others" (213). Though she acts "rashly" in bringing Esther and Everell together, ironically accomplishing the designs of the Puritan patriarchs, the narrator observes that Hope's "feelings were as near to pure generosity as our infirm nature can approach" (215).

Given her role as marriage resister, it is not surprising that Esther is the character who articulates a full-blown discourse of Christian friendship. Although her universally bestowed "disinterested devotion" gets the novel's last word (350), she achieves it at great cost. It remains a devalued form of female affiliation available to elite and middle-class women in antebellum America that Sedgwick seeks to restore to dignity.[20] All of Esther's suppressed emotions come to a head in a key scene in which she vents her anger at Hope for effecting the engagement with Everell that Esther sorely desires but finally realizes she must forgo. Contrary to all the "laws" of friendship, however, Esther refuses to explain to Hope the cause of her anger. In the flashback immediately following their tearful confrontation, we witness Esther refusing Everell's plea for help in rescuing Magawisca. In this scene, the betrothed lovers articulate opposed understandings of "charity" and its ethical/political basis. Realization of their profound differences not only hinders their emotional attachment but also clarifies why this attachment cannot be founded on the friendship requisite, in Sedgwick's view, for disinterested love. Esther's unquestioning adherence to "the letter of the law" generates her failure to act on or even entertain a romantic/democratic sympathy that embraces the "other" as a subject. This failure underlies Esther's avowal of Christian friendship with Hope, a connection that seems inadequate to Sedgwick's impetuous heroine because it is essentially apolitical, founded not in present action but in heavenly promise.

In the flashback scene, Everell plays Hope's role but fails to persuade or convert Esther to their view. Despite her "true" love for Everell, Esther refuses to "waver from the strictest letter of her religious duty, as that duty was interpreted by her conscience," because she finds no "scripture warrant for interfering between the prisoner and the magistrates" (277–78). Strongly vexed by her passive obedience to authority, Everell questions whether all acts "of mercy, or compassion, or justice" require scriptural authority and argues that "there must be warrant, as you call it, for sometimes resisting legitimate authority, or all our friends in England would not be at open war with their king. With such a precedent, I should think the sternest conscience would permit you to obey the generous impulses of nature, rather than to render this slavish obedience to the letter of the law" (278). Both invoke the inviolability of "conscience," but Esther grounds hers in a received interpretation of scripture from male Puritan elders while Everell's, like Hope's supremely independent and unperturbed conscience (180), proceeds directly from the "heart."

Their disagreement gets at the crux of Sedgwick's ethical and political concerns. Linking the Puritan revolution in old England with the "spirit" of "nature" and democratic impulses rather than with the "letter of the law" and authoritarianism, Sedgwick implies that Puritan New England dampens and rigidifies the radical tenor and tolerationist policies of the English Independents. In her stubborn defense, Esther anticipates the argument a beleaguered Governor Winthrop would mount in his "little speech" to the General Court in July 1645 on the eve of his departure from public office that asserts the unquestionable, even sacred "authority of those chosen servants of the Lord" whom the people have elected as magistrates (*HL* 278). In this speech, Winthrop argues that "liberty" is the freedom to submit oneself to a higher power: to God, elected rulers, and husbands. The "true wife," like the believing saint or obedient citizen, he declares, "accounts her subjection her honor and freedom, and would not think her condition safe and free, but in her subjection to her husband's authority" (*Winthrop's Journal*

2:239). What Winthrop doesn't account for is women's double subjection to husband and God.

Abashed by Esther's "scruples" in a matter he felt "to be authorized by the most generous emotions of his heart," Everell perceives "a painful discord between them; that there was, to use the modern German term, no elective affinity" (*HL* 278). "Concord" is Aristotle's term for the political form of *philia*; its negative case signals that the lovers' tiff is also an allegory for the deep political differences in these positions on the ethics of resistance to legitimate authority. Sedgwick alludes to Johann Wolfgang von Goethe's darkly romantic novel of 1809, which represents affinities and passions as "natural" and inexorable as chemical reactions. Through this allusion, Sedgwick hints that Esther and Everell's engagement is "unnatural," while Everell and Hope's connection satisfies some "natural," or more precisely, "sentimental" scheme endorsed by the wishes of their deceased mothers.

Esther widens the abyss between them when she discloses that she has been secretly meeting with Magawisca in her dungeon after hearing Governor Winthrop say that if the prisoner could be persuaded to convert, remain in the English settlement, and "join the catechized Indians," the magistrates might "grant her Christian privileges" and free her (279). In performing what she nominates this "labour of love," Esther echoes the very phrases and exclusionary ideas about Christian community Winthrop promotes in "A Modell of Christian Charitie" (*WP* 292). In that address, he explains that the "Lawe of Grace . . . teacheth us to put a difference betweene Christians and others. Doe good to all especially to the household of faith" he concludes, quoting Galatians 6:10 (284). Sedgwick has Hope counter this narrow view when she cites scripture to mollify Master Cradock, who "scruple[s] if it be lawful for a Christian man to lend this aid to an idolater" and participate in the scheme to release Magawisca; "we are commanded to do good to all," Hope reminds her tutor. In this, she cleverly amends the exhortation in the title of Cotton Mather's influential Puritan tract *Bonifacius* (1710)—not just "doing good" but "doing good *to all*"—and thus argues against making distinctions based on religious or cultural differences (*HL* 311–12).[21]

Esther's break with Everell and her ventriloquism of Winthrop's endorsement of a principle of exclusion contribute to the crisis in her friendship with Hope. She takes refuge in a Christian friendship whose ethnocentrism proves to be a deterrent to ethical action in the present. Unnerved by accusations that she has wronged Esther, Hope begs for details, admonishing, "[H]ave not you yourself, a thousand times, said there should be no disguises with friends; no untold suspicions; no unexplained mysteries" (276). Friendship requires the physical privacy that fosters individual (bourgeois) subjectivity and independent thought and at the same time allows for privileged disclosures and frankness that encourage intersubjective and self-critiquing (mirroring and reflexive) relations. By contrast, in this scene Esther continually "represses" Hope, as if her impetuous friend embodies Esther's own rebellious—what she calls "sinful"—inclinations. When Esther finally gains control of herself, she "knelt down, and drew Hope down beside her, and in a low, but perfectly firm voice, supplicated for grace to resist engrossing passion, and selfish affections. She prayed they might both be assisted from above, so that their mutual forgiveness, and mutual love, might be perfected, and issue in a friendship which should be a foretaste of heaven" (276).

In this prayer, the language of Winthrop's "Modell" and the heady spiritualism of post-Revolutionary Revivalism meet and mingle. The attitude of entreaty (to which Hope must be "drawn down"), the solicitation of heavenly guidance to resist "engrossing passion, and selfish affections" rather than present injustice, and the plea for "mutual forgiveness" as a preview of "perfected love" and paradise all echo Winthrop (via Paul, Augustine, and Aelred of Rievaulx) and anticipate the less doctrinaire Unitarian notion of universal benevolence. In the Christian tradition, earthly friendship requires the presence of a third—God—and is merely precursory, a "foretaste" of the heavenly mutuality to come. The text implies that only divine intervention can bridge such differences in temperament and values as those between Esther and Hope. The allusion to the sacramental nature of friendship echoes Winthrop and other Puritan writers on the character of charity; the implication that women are fit vehicles, perhaps fitter than men, for ennobling, heavenly friendship is Sedgwick's innovation.

Finally, the "gracious," "godly," and male-identified Esther ironically fails to achieve "angelic love." Still, Sedgwick suggests that her "natural" instincts have not been completely deformed by Puritan strictures when Esther offhandedly mentions to Hope, as a token, perhaps, of the promise of their regenerated love, Everell's plan to rescue Magawisca. This hint leads Hope to replace her unbending friend as Everell's accomplice, ethical peer, and eventually fiancée as well.

The Other as Saint and Rebel

If Hope is "angelic" in the narrative's sentimentalized rhetoric, Magawisca is "saintly" (*HL* 312). Both embody a spiritual "love" the narrative contrasts with Esther's slavish obedience to the "letter of the law." Sedgwick explicitly links Hope and Magawisca as disinterested moral agents through recurring allusions to the "instinct" of fledgling birds. In another narrative aside, Sedgwick observes "how difficult the ascent to the heights of disinterestedness; but let not the youthful aspirant be discouraged; the wing is strengthened by use, and the bird that drops in its first flutterings about the parent nest, may yet soar to the sky" (213). While the deliberateness of sacrifice runs counter to the reflexivity of innate behaviors, such as birds' knowledge of flight or the path of seasonal migration, Sedgwick emphasizes the self-transcending, "artless," and thus "natural" origin of these impulses to do good. She does so in order to include the unconverted Magawisca, who initially appears to Everell "to embody nature's best gifts, and her feelings to be the inspiration of heaven" (53). Likewise, "her affection for Everell Fletcher had the tenderness, the confidence, the sensitiveness of woman's love; but it had nothing of the selfishness, the expectation, or the earthliness of that passion" (263).

Years later, Hope instantly recognizes Magawisca when she appears at the Winthrop residence in Boston as "the heroine of Everell's imagination, whom he had taught her to believe, was one of those, who, 'Without arte's bright lampe, by nature's eye, / Keep just promise, and love equitie'" (186). From William Morrell's poem "New England" (1625), these lines (303–4) actually refer to native insistence on honoring "vows" (contracts) without the benefit of literacy (22). Sedgwick's most radical move is to have Magawisca embody this discourse when, "impelled . . . by that inspiration that teaches the bird its unknown path," she miraculously ascends the rock to intercede in her father's execution of Everell at the beginning of the narrative (*HL* 93). This signal act of "instinctive" or disinterested—not deliberative or legal—charity recalls an obscured history of female charity and sets the pattern for all the other interventions in the narrative.

Ironically, for a story highlighting female friendship, this defining act proceeds from a heterosexual bond. In fact, the interracial friendships in *Hope Leslie* unfold as a multilayered, cross-referenced network of sympathetic alliances featuring Magawisca and Hope but begin with the profound affinity that arises between Magawisca and Everell when these "representatives" of different cultures live together and learn about each other. It is not accidental that the form of Magawisca's sacrifice for Everell reprises the story told—and perhaps invented, certainly embellished—by the early English colonist John Smith of his rescue by Powhatan's young daughter Pocahontas in what would become "the first great American romance" (Hulme 138).

The extent of Sedgwick's departure from Cooper's representations of interraciality can be measured by her subversion of this myth and its emphasis on romance. Magawisca uses a figure associated with Indian tribes from the Condolence Councils and Iroquois Covenant diplomacy discussed in chapter 1: "[O]ur hands," she tells Everell, "have taken hold of the chain of friendship," an image of affective egalitarianism that implies agency, intention, and work (*HL* 46). Everell's feelings for Magawisca further associate him with female friendship. Mrs. Fletcher remarks about Magawisca that there is something "in her mien that doth bring to mind the lofty Judith, and the gracious Esther" (*HL* 32). Both of these biblical figures risked their lives to save their people; the comparison emphasizes Magawisca's courage and fierce sense of national pride. Everell counters passionately, "Oh, mother! is she not more like the gentle and tender Ruth?" (33). Seeing with the eyes of affection, Everell imagines Magawisca as Ruth, the biblical emblem of cross-cultural female friendship, whose desire to remain with her mother-in-law, Naomi, results in her willingness to take on the other's cultural identity. By countering his mother's association of Magawisca with heroic and patriotic biblical figures with the figure of Ruth, the loving convert, Everell reveals a wish for Magawisca's conversion to Christianity. It is a desire for which he will castigate Esther when she later acts on it through her attempts to proselytize the Pequot prisoner.

A historical source for Magawisca's character and her heroic intervention further support Everell's self-implication in female friendship. Early in 1781, Elizabeth Freeman, a slave woman belonging to Colonel John Ashley of Sheffield, Massachusetts, came to Theodore Sedgwick, Catharine's father, seeking aid and advice. Apparently, in trying to protect her sister, also a slave of the Ashleys, from Mrs. Ashley, who was threatening her with a shovel, Freeman took a blow on her own arm, an injury from which she never fully recovered. Having heard the Declaration of Independence read, Freeman asked the prominent Berkshire county lawyer, "Won't the law give me my freedom?" (Sedgwick, *Power* 125).[22] Despite the fact that the Ashleys were longtime friends and relatives, Theodore Sedgwick took up the case and won Freeman's freedom, citing the recently established Massachusetts Declaration of Rights and that in Massachusetts, "slavery had never received specific legal sanction" (Welch 14). Acting on Freeman's behalf, Theodore Sedgwick was among the first to legally question the right to own slaves; the case he successfully argued contributed to the abolition of slavery in the state of Massachusetts.[23] In gratitude, Freeman joined the Sedgwick household as a devoted servant and lived with the family until Theodore's second marriage in 1808, thereafter remaining close to the Sedgwicks until her death twenty years later, just after the appearance of *Hope Leslie*. Sedgwick and Freeman are buried next to each other in the pie-shaped Sedgwick family plot in Stockbridge, Massachusetts.

At Freeman's death, Sedgwick composed an epitaph eulogizing her as "the tenderest friend," having "no superior or equal" (*Power* 71). This history allows us to speculate that standing behind Magawisca's sacrifice for Everell and qualifying its heterosexual and imperial connotations are several types of female ties: a sororal bond between slave women and Sedgwick's filial affection for Freeman, who represented an indestructible—we might say instinctive or "native"—desire for freedom.[24]

Reunion and Separation: The Ethical Failure of Friendship

Although Sedgwick responds to and challenges Cooper's masculinist vision in many ingenious ways, the crux of her revision emerges in her account of the secret meeting between Hope and Magawisca in Boston's cemetery. This scene corresponds to the dramatic pledge of loyalty between Hawk-eye and Chingachgook that concludes *The Last of the Mohicans*. Rather than make this scene the narrative's denouement, Sedgwick places it at the center, where it links the early account of Everell's friendship with Magawisca at Bethel with the events seven years later that hinge on the interwoven romance/reunion plots. In this pivotal position, the cemetery scene displaces the horrific violence and cannibalism visited on mothers and children outside Fort William Henry that Cooper situates at the heart of *Mohicans*. A scaled-down version of this atrocity occurs on the threshold of the Fletcher homestead at the beginning of Sedgwick's narrative, where it links native and English males' aggression against mothers and children. The cemetery scene subtly alludes to this, since the graves over which the heroines meet and weep are the resting places of their mothers, both victims of patriarchal cruelty. Offsetting these deaths, however, is not the interracial marriage-under-denial that Cooper reserves for Cora and Uncas but the enduring tie between Faith and Oneco, which more accurately depicts the history of interracial coupling and assimilation of English settlers to native culture like that of the "unredeemed captive," Eunice Williams, a distant relative of Sedgwick's.[25]

Unlike the final scene of Cooper's novel, Sedgwick's encounter does not celebrate a melancholic securing of a fantasy of friendship. Rather, it represents the first phase of Hope's ethical movement, her repositioning through her confrontation of her own privileges and ethnocentrism. Hope sees Magawisca through Everell's idealizations but also brings to this secret encounter a self-serving and naive desire that her younger sister be restored to her unchanged by her encounters with the New World—a restoration to "natural," familial, unproblematized affiliation. Magawisca brings to this meeting her wariness of the English settlers tempered by her earlier experience of Everell's belief in the "natural" equality of all people and her remembrance of his family's kindness to her.

In the first tense moments of their meeting, Hope bristles impatiently at Maga-wisca's poetical manner of speech. Magawisca's revelation of Faith's marriage to Oneco, however, produces a palpable physical revulsion: "'God forbid!' exclaimed Hope, shuddering as if a knife had been plunged in her bosom" (*HL* 188). This biting insult to the nobility of her bloodline angers the proud Maga-wisca, who regains her composure only when Hope invokes the memory of her departed mother, whose grave is nearby. This inadvertently touches an analogously tender "chord" in Magawisca's heart, since her mother also rests in this graveyard, and thus bridges their differences to produce a "harmony" of "sympathy" between them (188). Mollified, Magawisca offers an anxious Hope the assurance that Faith is still "part of the Christian family" through her conversion to Catholicism. Somewhat relieved, Hope displays her political naïveté in urging Magawisca to come openly among the English, who would honor her for the unforgettable sacrifice she made for Everell—offering, in effect, to help reunite Magawisca with Everell in recompense for Magawisca's efforts in making Hope's reunion with Faith possible.

Hope's privileged position allows her *not* to comprehend the complexity and danger of the women's encounter, which Magawisca grasps all too fully. At the mention of Everell's name, Magawisca betrays her "weakness," which proves to be the antithesis of Hope's—her deep regard for a son of her enemy and her ability to (imagine) love across racial and ethnic differences, which Hope at present cannot. When Hope impetuously presses the issue of Everell's inclusion in their plans, thinking "she had touched the right key," Magawisca reveals that she has promised her father and has "repeated the vow here on my mother's grave" not to indulge feelings that could tempt her from her loyalty to her people (190). When Hope persists, Magawisca invokes a hard-won self-discipline that enables her to resist what even she recognizes as Hope's powerfully persuasive charms, which Magawisca conflates with the alluring "call" of a mate: "that no one can look on you and deny you aught; that you can make old men's hearts soft, and mould them at your will; but I have learned to deny even the cravings of my own heart; to pursue my purpose like the bird that keeps her wing stretched to the toilsome flight, though the sweetest note of her mate recalls her to the nest" (190–91).

The image of the bird ignoring its mate's love-call fuses heterosexual desire and homosocial affiliation. In avian terms, "mate" refers to one of a pair of birds matched by opposite genders for the purposes of reproduction. But more generally, the word denotes matching by similarity and equality, as in a "counterpart," "companion," "suitable associate or equal adversary; an equal in status," "friend" (*OED*).[26] With this layered image, Magawisca also discloses the source of her sadness in her unfulfilled spiritual love for her corresponding other, who is Everell; at this point, Hope is his less-than-satisfactory substitute. At the end of this key scene, Hope and Magawisca secure a basic mutual trust, reveal something of themselves in order to find common ground, and conclude a "treaty," but they have not freely chosen each other or acted on the desire to do good for the other's sake alone. Hope recognizes the women's passivity in the process of their bonding when she exclaims, "[M]ysteriously have our destinies been interwoven. Our mothers brought from a far distance to rest together here—their children connected in indissoluble bonds!" (*HL* 192).

The scene of the sisters' reunion on a murky cove of Governor's Island five days later marks the second phase of Hope's epistemic repositioning. On the island, she is literally separated from the Puritan center of Boston and also isolated psychologically, through a series of romantic misunderstandings, from her "friends." Finally beholding her "loved, lost sister" (in the text called Mary, her original name) in "her savage attire, fondly leaning on Oneco's shoulder, her heart died within her; a sickening feeling came over her, an unthought of revolting of nature" (227). Sedgwick closely details Hope's inability to abide the differences, marked externally by clothes and the choice of a "mate," that separate Hope from her biological sister. In this moment of existential crisis, the self confronts the other within the same and confronts difference within the familial and familiar, which produces a reflexive ("unthought") physical sensation of abjection ("sickening"). It is as if the self experiences itself as contaminated merely by the very *idea* of the other within the same and must eject the revolting presence.

These overpowering feelings inhibit the usually impetuous Hope's "first impulse" to embrace her sister; Magawisca must literally bring the sisters' hands together. Frustrated to tears by her inability to speak to Faith, who no longer comprehends English, or to provoke memories of their childhood together or of their deceased mother (a tactic that produced common ground with Magawisca), Hope faces "the melancholy truth" of this loss of communication and a shared past that seems "to open a new and impassable gulf between them." Magawisca gently intercedes, offering to translate, but Hope insults her again, impugning her integrity by asking her to promise to "interpret truly for me" (228). This recalls the moment at the end of *Mohicans* where Hawk-eye takes it upon himself *not* to interpret the native eulogies accurately, thinking their vision of the interracial "mating" of Uncas and Cora in the afterlife would offend Colonel Munro. It is a further indication that Hope cannot yet recognize Magawisca as a "faithful" cultural mediator.

Facing someone "so near to her by nature, so far removed by habit and education" throws Sedgwick's heroine into epistemological chaos (228). In a reading of this scene that counters Fetterley's argument for the text's failure to address the dilemma of difference, Susanne Opfermann contends, "Metaphorically, the sisters who belong to different cultures convey the concept of equality *and* difference," and they do so, ironically, through the articulation of mutually exclusive but equally valid perspectives. Thus, Opfermann argues that Sedgwick's presentation of this interracial encounter expresses a belief that different cultures "may still be of equal value" (42–43). What Opfermann sees as a confrontation of relatively equal cultural positions can also be read as a staging of Hope's attempt to impose her (dominant, English, white) perspective on a younger sister, whose "face, pale and spiritless, was only redeemed from absolute vacancy by an expression of gentleness and modesty" (*HL* 229). In Faith's "vacantness" and in her conventionally self-abasing feminine qualities, Fetterley argues, "Hope confronts the terror of non-identity—that absence of and from the self she hopes to escape through identification with the brother—to which her identification with her sister inevitably leads" (510–11). As Opfermann observes, however, despite Hope's perception of Faith's lack of spirit, the younger sister manages to decisively evade all of Hope's strenuous attempts to bring her back to her English origins.

When Hope, "shuddering and heartsick," tries to make her sister "look more natural to her" by "disguising" the "savage aspect" of her "singular" and "gaudy" native dress first, by removing Faith's mantle of feathers and then by cloaking her with her own silk mantle, Faith "gently" refuses while Oneco exults in this "triumph" (*HL* 228). Hope's ploy reveals that "naturalness" for her does not include cultural differences and that she, like other European colonists, imagines ontological similarity as a function of appearance and dress. Desperate, Hope reverts to bribery, heaping on Faith the jewels from her own hands that have caught the simple girl's attention, a tactic that casts Hope in the stereotypic role of arrogant colonizer and elicits Magawicsa's contempt. Finally, Faith rejects and reverses Hope's version of the history that has brought them to this pass: "What Hope considers her captivity, Faith regards as her liberation" (Opfermann 43). At the last moment, as the danger of detection increases, Hope draws Faith down on the shore, prays brokenheartedly, "and committed her sister to God." Only when Hope releases Faith, implicitly accepting her changed and chosen identity, can Faith respond by returning the embrace and weeping "on her bosom" (*HL* 231).

Although Sedgwick's readers may have come to different conclusions about this interaction, it is fair to say from our current perspective that Sedgwick's titular heroine does not fully accept the "natural equality" of all people Sedgwick herself proclaims in her preface. Nor does Hope ever fully resolve the dilemma represented by her sister-as-Indian/other. Even as Hope bids a final farewell to Magawisca, whose decision to leave the English settlements is surely influenced by the failed comprehension of "friends" like her, Hope asks Magawisca for "some charm, by which I may win my sister's affections" (331). Hope, the ultimate charmer, finds herself stymied by an otherwise passive girl who is simultaneously like her (by nature) and so radically unlike her (by her choice of identity). When Sir Philip Gardiner, leading a band of Puritan soldiers, interrupts the sisters' reunion, capturing and restoring Faith to her Anglo-American family in Boston, Hope experiences her sister's profound and irrevocable differences up close. This intimate contact with someone so familiar and at the same time so different is the final step that prepares Hope to make an authentically "friendly"—that is, disinterested—gesture of interracial affiliation, her risky and dramatic intercession on Magawisca's behalf.

Finally recovered from her frightening experiences on Governor's Island, which result in a life-threatening fever, Hope anticipates her sister's company. But she can only describe the drooping figure she meets in the Winthrops' parlor as "this poor home-sick child," an acknowledgment of her sister's ontological displacement in the Winthrop household. Although now ostensibly "free" from an English point of view, Faith experiences her restoration from a native perspective as captivity and is restless "like an imprisoned bird fluttering against the bars of its cage" (265–66). When their frivolous Aunt Grafton complains that Faith stubbornly insists on covering the English silks she has forced her to wear with "her Indian mantle" (an ironic reversal of Hope's earlier attempt at cultural cloaking) and unaccountably refuses to wear her aunt's "beautiful rainbow necklace," preferring a "string of all colored shells," Hope defends her sister's actions and their deeper significance: "I suppose she has the feeling of the natives, who seem to have an almost superstitious attachment to that oriental costume" (266).

Although Hope's attitude belittles Indian attachment to crucial markers of national identity such as dress, which the English Puritans also possessed and imposed on the peoples they conquered, it firmly rejects Aunt Grafton's uninspected and "tyrannous" notions of English cultural superiority, expressed through the politics of dress (Q. Miller 121). In recognizing that Faith shares these "native feelings," Hope tentatively accepts that Faith "is" native. She grants her sister a measure of self-definition when she accepts that Faith might have "some reason for preferring those shells that we do not know" and observes that the difference between "preferring bright shells to bright stones" is, in reality, almost negligible. Furthermore, perceiving that Faith's necklace has a crucifix attached to it and "dreading lest her sister should be exposed to a new source of persecution, she interposed: 'Let her have her own way at present . . . best leave her to herself.'" Aunt Grafton petulantly yields to Hope's suggestion that they grant Faith Hope's signature, specifically American desire, conceding, "Well—very well, take your own way." In this case, having her own way leads Hope to protect Faith's right to follow her native "way," thereby granting her sister a similar freedom of choice and similar respect for those choices (*HL* 266–67). It is an unobtrusive moment, but as Quentin Miller's study of the narrative's cultural politics of dress demonstrates, it represents "perhaps" the most important turning point in the evolution of Hope's character (134).

Later that day, after Everell's failed attempt to release Magawisca from prison the night before, a chastened Hope appeals to Governor Winthrop to free Magawisca "on her merits, and rights"—that is, on account of her indisputably virtuous actions but also because of her "natural" entitlements as a sentient being (*HL* 273). These natural rights Hope can now credibly champion. Having more of an effect on the governor than she realizes, Hope nevertheless feels checked, and after the inconclusive trial, which returns Magawisca to the dungeon, she joins Everell in engineering the prisoner's escape.

In the final conversation between Magawisca and her white friends, they mutually affirm a three-way friendship now sealed by active risk and sacrifice on all parts. But this fledgling friendship cannot prevent their ultimate separation, the requisite "vanishing" of the Indians prophesied in the poetic epigraph at the opening of Sedgwick's narrative and characteristic of so many contact narratives of the time.[27] At the moment of separation, Magawisca reiterates her undying siblinglike affection for Everell and her realization that it is only possible in an afterlife "where there will be no more gulfs between us, and I may hail thee as my brother" (330). Everell urges her to stay and "enjoy this friendship," an Aristotelian proposition Hope repeats, using the poeticized native idiom that Cooper's characters employ and that she arrogantly dismissed on her first meeting with Magawisca: "[R]eturn and dwell with us—as you would say, Magawisca, we will walk in the same path, the same joys shall shine on us, and, if need be that sorrows come over us, why, we will all sit under their shadow together" (330).

Unmoved, Magawisca repeats the chilling sentiments from the speech she gave at her trial that ended with her echo of the demand of the American revolutionaries for liberty or death. In that speech, she shocked the English onlookers by confirming her enmity with them and appearing, from their perspective, to admit her guilt. But she emphatically lays the blame on the English settlers for initiating the cycles of violence and revenge and metaphorically rejects the interracial handshake the English offered in bad faith: "Can we grasp in friendship the hand raised to strike us?" she demands (292). In language only slightly gentler and with the stark imagery of light and dark used earlier in the text to connect but ultimately distinguish the temperamentally antithetical Hope and Esther, Magawisca rejects Cooper's fantasy of interracial harmony, seeming to confirm at the final moment the settlers' fear of inexorable enmity: "[T]he Indian and the white man can no more mingle, and become one, than day and night" (330).

To mingle and become one would make Magawisca interchangeable with her historical counterpart, Pocahontas. In writing her historical fiction, Sedgwick sought to imagine an outcome different from this romanticized account of Anglo-Indian encounter, which, even in her day, had become the dominant myth of American origins. From her interactions with the colonial magistrates, with Esther Downing, and even with Hope Leslie, Magawisca realizes that "becoming one" would require Indian assimilation, conversion to Christianity (like the kidnapped Pocahontas), which she and her tribe steadfastly resist, and their complete loss of cultural identity. Or, it would involve taking up the fruitless task of "teaching" those in power about the exotic, misconstrued other. Even Everell, in his last, desperate plea to retain Magawisca, tries to disguise the structures of colonial power by begging her to stay and teach the whites how "to be happy . . . without human help or agency" as they stereotypically imagine the Indians to be (333).

Friendship, by contrast, advances a spiritual mingling without dependence, and democracy, by extension, requires like-mindedness and parity among on-tological equals. Both preserve the separation, indeed, the "sovereignty" of the self and the rights of individual citizens. This sovereignty, Sedgwick suggests, should also extend to Indian "nations," even those the United States Supreme Court, in its infamous decision in the 1831 case of *Cherokee Nation v. Georgia*, declared "may, perhaps be denominated domestic dependent nations" ("Cherokee Nation"). The marital happiness Magawisca foresees in her next breath for Everell and Hope, despite their current romantic misunderstanding, will occur because their "souls were mated," their "affections mingled like streams from the same fountain" (*HL* 330). Although Magawisca promotes this monoracial and heteronormative outcome, so many elements in Sedgwick's narrative undermine it. The "oneness" produced by marriage should not be confused with the "one-ness" necessary for friendship or for political community among divergent peoples with a history of intercultural violence.

Grasping desperately at Magawisca's hints about his reconciliation with Hope, Everell reveals that the "lastness" of the scene consigns his Indian friend to symbolic death: "And may not the last words of a friend, be, like the sayings of a death-bed, prophetic?" (331). As in *The Last of the Mohicans*, in Sedgwick's romance, the union of the white hero and heroine necessitates the Indian's political death. The difference is that Sedgwick's white protagonists themselves represent an antiauthoritarian political strain. Furthermore, Magawisca's vanishing represents the only way she and her people, including the Indianized white sister, can escape assimilation and, thus, refuse imperial nostalgia and cultural death.

The mood in this scene is suffused with sadness and loss but not, I would argue, with melancholy, as the final exchange of friendship tokens suggests. Hope offers Magawisca "as a memorial of us both . . . a rich gold chain, with a clasp containing . . . a lock of Everell's hair, taken from his head when he was a boy, at Bethel—it will remind you of your happiest days there," she explains (333). Chains, we know from earlier discussions, are a multivalent, poly-cultural image for friendship, personal and political. Both Magawisca and Everell use the image of a chain to describe their most "ardent" emotional and spiritual connections.

Magawisca, however, refuses Hope's gold chain with its scrap of Everell's boyish hair that would also remind her of her captivity and servitude among the English. She asks, instead, for the small painted miniature of Everell that, since his engagement to Esther, Hope wears hidden in "her bosom." "I know," she tells Hope, "thou wilt freely give me the image when thou hast the living form" (333). Magawisca asks that the women act on their struggling friendship by "freely" giving and agreeing to share their most precious possession—the beloved friend. By asking Hope to give up the "likeness" of Everell she has cherished, Magawisca recognizes Hope's affiliation with him, yet maintains her claim to a prior and equally compelling connection. By this means, Magawisca can retain Everell, not as an internalized, cannibalized, disavowed imago, but as an external, nonincorporative, "heteropathic" marker of affiliation.[28]

As a signifier of nonappropriation, this portrait quotes and reverses the Washington medal Chingachgook wears around his neck at his death in Cooper's *The Pioneers* that signifies, at least outwardly, his conversion to Christianity and his acceptance of white power. By contrast, the image of Everell remains close to Magawisca's heart but separable from her and her political loyalties, an example of what I am calling, after Kaja Silverman's theorization of an ethical relation to the other, friendship-at-a-distance. In an interesting parallel, early in the narrative when Sedgwick offers her readers a "formal" portrait of *her* favorite, the unconventional Hope Leslie, rather than "state characters" and "gallery portraits," her authorial introduction takes the form of a "miniature picture that lies next our heart" (*HL* 121). Both are fictional mirrors by which Sedgwick's readers and Sedgwick herself can measure their moral and spiritual reflections.

The narrative forces us to regard Magawisca's choice to leave as a failure—the demise of the possibility of an American interracial community—for, as the narrator observes, "*all* shrunk from it as from witnessing the last gasp of life" (334; my emphasis). There is no iconic interracial handshake at this conclusion, as in Cooper's tale; rather, Magawisca has to join Hope's and Everell's hands together, as she does for Hope and Faith in the first tense moments of their reunion, thus positioning Everell, finally, in place of the lost sister. In accepting Magawisca's choice and the ultimate failure of friendship to establish a sustainable community, these future Americans recognize the limits of their comprehension—and thus control—of the other. This failure, however, in the words of Judith Butler, signals "the advent of ethical recognition, understood as the recognition of the limits of comprehensibility" of the other, which clears the way for the future possibility of ethical friendship across difference ("For a Careful Reading" 141).

The Persistence of Second Selves

          Friendship: A Celebration of Humanity
is a lavish compilation of photographs that appeared in 2001 as part of the
M.I.L.K. Collection: Moments of Intimacy, Laughter and Kinship. Two other
volumes in the series explore themes of love and family, while this one poses the
related question, "What is a friend?" After a worldwide competition for inclusion
in the volume that director Geoff Blackwell describes as "the photographic event
of our time," he selected 100 photographs from over 40,000 submissions from 162
countries. These, he believes, "speak to all of us with clarity, universality, and—to
use that elusive and neglected word—joy" (17).

    This use of photography replicates Edward Steichen's immensely popular 1955
exhibit, The Family of Man, which appeared at the Museum of Modern Art in
New York City and contained over 500 images from sixty-eight countries. According to Steichen, the project "was conceived as a mirror of the universal
elements and emotions in the everydayness of life—as a mirror of the essential
oneness of mankind throughout the world" (5). The exhibit eventually toured
thirty-seven countries and appeared in inexpensive editions avidly purchased by
middle-class American households. According to Marianne Hirsch, Steichen's
collection established photography as a premier means of communicating the
universality of human experience through the consolidation of a "familial gaze," a

phenomenon sparked by the popularity of family photography throughout Cold War–time America. Hirsch describes this gaze as "the conventions and ideologies of family through which [members] see themselves" and through which they "struggle for control of image, narrative, and memory" (*Familial Gaze* xi). This gaze was the "key" to the enormous appeal of the exhibit and the collection because in "revealing points of intersection between the familial relation, on the one hand, and cross-racial and cross-national interaction, on the other," the photographs could "transform diversity into specular mirroring," thereby celebrating and preserving cultural differences—in this case, Western cultural superiority—within a universalizing frame (*Family Frames* 50).

The M.I.L.K. Collection stages a similar mirroring in relation to the new millennium's defining mode of intimacy, the "family of choice." Although it depicts a wide range of people from many cultures, the collection ultimately confirms friendship's basis in endogamous homogeneity.[1] I was immediately struck by how few photographs depict relationships between friends across cultures, ages, or genders. There are several quirky scenes of people and their pets, a poignant glimpse of a young black nurse and her elderly white charge in an affectionate embrace, and a hopeful sequence of black and white toddlers in sundresses sharing ice cubes on a sweltering summer day in Nashville, Tennessee. The majority of the photographs, however, depict pairs or groups of people who are visually nearly interchangeable. They are often captured (or posed) with their heads inclined toward each other, in a "sharing" posture, as in the arresting photograph of two elderly Thai women, laughing merrily and snugly framed by their traditional headdresses and enormous sprays of drying grasses in baskets carried on their backs (28–29). One could fold this photograph in half at the point where the women's faces meet and produce mirror images, like the conventional "inkblots" of psychologists. Just as the subjects of these images mirror each other, the images themselves, to use Steichen's words, are meant to mirror the viewers, bringing us into that intimate space of twoness that, ironically, expresses our "essential oneness."

The popular Irish writer Maeve Binchy draws a very different conclusion from the photographs in the collection—or brings to her understanding of the images a desire for the renovating effects of friendship so strong as not to be dislodged. In her prologue, Binchy observes about the collection: "It proves, if ever it needed to be proved, that friendship need have nothing to do with coming from the same background and sharing all the same interests. A friendship can grow on the most unlikely ground" (21). This assertion repudiates similarity as the basis of friendship in order to clear the way for an inclusive universalism where external, material differences are no barrier to the growth of intimacy.

In doing so, however, Binchy discounts a tradition that stretches back thousands of years, in which the central, indeed categorical, prerequisite for friendship was not merely liking but likeness. Most of the photographs in the volume, such as the image of the laughing Thai women, give visual support to the necessity—even unquestioned naturalness—of similarity for amicable intimacy. The double-page spread immediately following Binchy's prologue illustrates this point. The black and white photograph shows six Vietnamese boys taking a break from their school lessons in Phan Rang City. They stand shoulder to shoulder against a mud wall, smiling infectiously and looking directly into the camera. After the debacle of the Vietnam War, this engaging image offers at the outset what Binchy identifies more generally as "the healing magic of friendship" (23) in the form of a cross-cultural connection with U.S. consumers of the collection. However, the boys' implicit affiliation with each other seems to rest on their startling visual similarity—of culture, age, height, demeanor—disrupted only by the slightly different shirts they wear and gaps left by lost front teeth (24–25).

Binchy submits the photographs in *Friendship* as proof *against* the powerful ideal of the classical and early modern ages, which restricted friendship to aristocratic men of the ruling class. Thus, even to depict women, children, cross-gender pairs, and people of a variety of cultures as friends is, in itself, an important discursive intervention. But this broad array provides evidence of the persistence, even at the turn of the twenty-first century, of Aristotle's notion of perfect friendship as a mirroring and, to some extent, exclusive dyad.

An advertisement for *Friendship* appearing in *The New Yorker* magazine on August 6, 2001, makes this connection explicit. It depicts the book with its cover displaying a striking close-up by photographer Janice Rubin of six-year-olds Natasha and Mitalee, dancers performing at the 1992 Houston International Festival in Texas. Dressed identically in traditional Rajasthani *lehengas*, heads bent together, the girls smile shyly as they gaze intently into each other's eyes, oblivious to the activity around them. It is a striking image of intimacy, and its placement on the collection's cover suggests that friendship is a powerful cultural image that can connect a wide swath of humanity through the recognition of similar early and formative experiences of mutual regard. The highlighting of pre-adolescent girls, however, reinforces the modern notion that intimacy and affect are the psychological terrain of females and feminization and plays into the recent, politically conservative elevation of minors, even fetuses, as representatives of what Lauren

Berlant identifies as an increasingly problematic and shrinking "intimate public sphere" (4–5).

As if haunted by the past, *The New Yorker* advertisement announces in large print next to the cover image, "True friends are a sure refuge." This phrase comes from Aristotle's most important discussion of friendship in books 8 and 9 of the *Nicomachean Ethics* (*NE* 8:1, 1) and appears in *Friendship* as a punning commentary on a photograph of three youths huddled under a rain-soaked umbrella, waiting for the start of an outdoor rock concert in London (87). The adage expresses a common contemporary notion that "real" friends represent a secure space of authenticity and intimacy to which we can withdraw from a public realm increasingly characterized by threat and instability. But by "true" friends, Aristotle refers to his idea of *agathôn philia*, the friendship of virtuous people, based on rationally conceived affection and the moral and spiritual equality of the friends. This was the highest form of friendship because it was complete or perfected (*teleia*), the ideal against which Aristotle measured all other types of friendships and the basis of personal as well as public life and republican politics.

This study posits the existence and importance of such an ideal of friendship in early American writing and suggests that our future may depend upon its renascence in the twenty-first century. I applaud the globalizing reach of the photographs in *Friendship* and Binchy's hopeful view of friendship even as I critique them. It is hard, if not impossible, to elude the grasp of entrenched discourses and their implications; the best we can do is make them work for our own visions of a democratic future.

If I have succeeded in demonstrating the persistence of the Aristotelian ideal of friendship in early American literature and culture, I have also shown its various ideological deployments and transformations and its contradictory effects—at once inclusive and exclusive, oppressive and empowering. I believe that our national as well as global future lies in reclaiming and, as my title indicates, perfecting friendship as an engine of equality and self-knowledge, especially friendships across differences. In this spirit, I support attempts like those of feminist theorist Chela Sandoval, who advances new discursive "technologies" for global political transformation that promote "equalizing power between socially and psychically differing subjects" (23–24). To transform "consciousness" in this way, Sandoval reaches back to the pre-contact "Mayan code of honor" that recommends a form of address to others practically indistinguishable in its import from Aristotle's key notion that "the friend is another self": "In Lake'ch: I am another yourself" (Argüelles 196). Let this be our blueprint and "model" for meeting each other in the new millennium.

NOTES

Introduction

1. See Cosslett's study of British Victorian fiction by women about women's friendship as well as Auerbach's examination of the theme of community and Todd's study of friendship plots in British and European fiction. More recently, Haggerty traces resistance to "heteronormative values in general," including female friendship in British fiction from the later eighteenth century (2).

2. All references to the *Nicomachean Ethics* books 8 and 9 are from Pakaluk's 1998 translation, abbreviated as *NE*, unless otherwise indicated. I sometimes consult and quote other translations for comparison.

3. For a description of these trends in sociology, see Pahl and O'Connor.

4. For an extended discussion of Schmitt's ideas, see Derrida, *Politics of Friendship*, especially chapters 4, 5, and 6 (75–170).

5. "Elective affinities" is also the name Max Weber gave to a general theory of social change exemplified in his study *The Protestant Ethic and the Spirit of Capitalism* (1930), where the fortuitous interaction of elements from different sociocultural systems—in this case, the "elective affinity" between Puritan ethical norms and emerging capitalist business practices in seventeenth-century England—produced a major transformation he called "the spirit of capitalism." See Swatos 163.

6. In her introduction, Griffin offers an analysis of this friendship and its historical implications as "proof of the importance of sister-friendships in life as well as fiction" for black women (6). See also her commentary throughout *Beloved Sisters*.

7. Critics also negatively associate the homosocial/homosexual with race and with interracial relations. Lawrence began this trend in his 1923 *Studies in Classic American Literature*, which was taken up and expanded by Fiedler in his controversial 1948 essay "Come Back to the Raft Ag'in, Huck Honey!" published in *Partisan Review*, whose contention about the linkage and centrality of "the Negro and the homosexual" in American literature (143) he more fully develops in *Love and Death in the American Novel*. In the 1980s, critics like Martin and Boone argued that representations of male interracial bonding serve to subvert heteronormative and misogynist values. For a critique of their claims and further discussion of this issue, see Wiegman's chapter 5, "Canonical Architecture," in *American Anatomies*. For the most recent linkage of male

interracial homosocial bonding and eroticism, see Erkkila's reading of the friendship in *The Last of the Mohicans* as "the fantasy of blood mixtures—of sex and rank and color—without the threat of generation" (19).

8. Leites makes a similar point but ignores its implications, arguing that "in the realm of marriage . . . the aristocratic idea of friendship among males . . . did not simply give way. . . . [I]t would be better to say that the idea of friendship among males gave way to the love between husband and wife" (393–94). For an extensive discussion of Milton's deliberate misreading of Paul's recommendation that "it is better to marry than to burn," his appropriation of classical friendship doctrine for companionate marriage, and its implications for early modern thought and gender relations, see Luxon.

9. I share this concern with recovering the classical sources of what will become U.S. literature and culture with Shields, who posits the importance of the Aeneas myth and Republican Rome as a counterweight to the Adamic myth and the Judeo-Christian tradition and calls for a revaluation of early American literature and the "cultural blindness" to our classical past more broadly (xxi–xxiv).

10. This history includes the responses of black women to the white suffragists of the mid-nineteenth century (see Giddings) and the responses of women of color to Robin Morgan's *Sisterhood Is Powerful* in 1970 (see B. Smith; Moraga and Anzaldúa). On the issue of separate spheres, see the collection of essays edited by Davidson. For an excellent summary of these issues in feminist criticism and theory, see Wiegman, "What Ails Feminism Criticism? A Second Opinion."

11. See, for example, Samuels's collection *The Culture of Sentiment*, Barnes's *States of Sympathy*, Stern's *The Plight of Feeling*, Burgett's *Sentimental Bodies*, D. Nelson's *National Manhood*, and Stearns and Lewis's collection *An Emotional History of the United States*, among others.

12. I say "theoretical" because scholars have begun to question the assumption labeled by sociologists as "status homophily" in contemporary friendship practice—the unconscious "patterning" of choice by similarities of gender, ethnicity, and social attributes like class position, age, and marital status—as well as the social construction of "similarity" itself (O'Connor 38). They argue that various forms of social patterning limit the exercise of choice that has long been considered an important and defining feature of friendships, both ancient and modern (Allan 47). For a feminist analysis of this, see Ackelsberg (342–43).

13. See, for example, Butler's critique of myths of coherence that are based, in part, on the Freudian chiasmus of desire and identification in "Gender Trouble, Feminist Theory, and Psychoanalytic Discourse" and Fuss's *Identification Papers*.

14. Kierkegaard critiques friendship on the grounds that it is partial, extends only to one, and thus is unjust when compared to the love of neighbor, which he regards as eternal and extending to all (Pakaluk, *Other Selves* 233; see Kierkegaard, *Works of Love*). Reinhard offers a psychoanalytic approach to ethics through the figure of the neighbor as an alternative to the familial "genealogical initiatives" advanced by Freud. The

neighbor, he argues, "instantiates both the barest minimum of political association and the impossibility of the actualization or fulfillment of such a relationship" and evades the complications of family because the "neighbor-hood entails relations of nearness and contiguity that are necessarily arbitrary, accidental, and transient" (165). Coming from a Lévinasian perspective, Reinhard uses the figure of the neighbor to formulate a comparative reading practice that he contrasts with Booth's model of reading as "friendship" based on explicitly Aristotelian ideas and developed in his 1988 study, *The Company We Keep*. I argue that the friend and friendship represent a different relationship to the other from that theorized by Lévinas; it is not one of obligation but choice and thus offers more potential for ethical action and political "actualization."

15. In explaining why psychoanalysis has ignored male hysteria, J. Mitchell points to "a larger omission . . . of the key role played in the construction of the psyche by lateral relations" or "sibling relations" that include nonbiological relations or "peers and partners." "Anthropology," she continues, "has long recognized the significance of these relations (although not in relation to hysteria); psychoanalysis has subsumed them to the vertical child-parent relationship" (x–xi). Said charges: "What one discerns today is religion as the result of exhaustion, consolation, disappointment. Its forms in both the theory and practice of criticism are varieties of unthinkability, undecidability, and paradox together with a remarkable consistency of appeals to magic, divine ordinance or sacred texts" and can be found in "those versions of such actively radical positions as Marxism, feminism, or psychoanalysis that stress the private and hermetic over the public and social" (290–91).

16. Similarly, Traub examines how, in the face of new medical science and the prevailing ideology of companionate marriage, English Renaissance writers drew on the classical discourse they translated as "amity" to create representations of female homoeroticism that at least imagined female independence (8).

17. To give just one example from popular culture, the August 2001 issue of *O: The Oprah Magazine*, a mass culture monthly addressed specifically to a multiracial readership of women, was dedicated to an exploration and celebration of what it calls "cherishment . . . the essence of friendship" (131). The calendar for August, which includes daily reminders and incentives for self-help, cites the iconic Aristotelian adage "A friend is a second self" alongside encomiums on friendship by Emily Dickinson and Eleanor Roosevelt, Ralph Waldo Emerson and Henry David Thoreau, Toni Morrison and Gloria Naylor (34).

18. Taussig, for example, argues for Plato as the source of English romanticism's fixation with "transcendent" (ideal) as opposed to "empiricist" (practical or instrumental) friendship and with the cloying emotion increasingly associated with women's bonds.

19. For a Lacanian reading of Cicero's friendship tropes, see Leach.

20. Shannon compares friendship to twinship and finds the essential difference to be choice: "[W]hile twinship seems to split or divide a preexisting single 'nature,' friendship is understood actively to conjoin preexisting, separate, 'unnaturally' like natures,"

recognizing but exceeding nature to form "a new body, an *institutio polis* of the tiniest, most speculative kind" (*Sovereign Amity* 43).

21. Heckel, who writes the notes to Curtius's *History*, explains that, despite its popularity, "this story was not given by Ptolemy or Aristobulus, and it is probably fictitious" (273). Arrian, another Roman general and historian of Alexander who drew on sources different from Curtius, gives a slightly altered punch line that emphasizes Alexander's magnanimity, another trait this incident was frequently called upon to illustrate, while retaining the emphasis on the men's interchangeability: "But Alexander declared that she had not erred, as Hephaestion, too, was an 'Alexander.'" The editor explains: "This comment puns on the root meaning in Greek of the name Alexander, 'protector of men'" (Romm 55), a play on words that by another means draws attention to the men's likeness.

22. See book 1:13, where Aristotle distinguishes between (and thus associates) the freeman's rule over slaves, the husband's rule over his wife, and the man's rule over children (*Politics* 1144). Hanke describes the famous debate in Valladolid in 1550–51 between the Spanish clerics Las Casas and Sepúlveda over the methods of colonial conversion in which Aristotle's theory of natural slavery played a major role. See also Brading. Pagden explains that "civil slavery" was a legal institution imposed as punishment or because of capture in a "just" war, whose causes were always "accidental," while "natural slavery" described a category of "man" with just enough reason to recognize his inferiority and need to be ruled by superiors. Thus, natural slaves submit willingly to their subordination. The problem remained, however, how to determine who was a natural slave. Aristotle suggests three solutions, all of which contribute in different ways to the association of slavery and racial/ethnic identity: physical determinism, genetic transmission (through mothers), and outsider ("barbarian") status (Pagden 40–48).

23. Several studies find that the demographic characteristics most frequently cited as the cause for inhibiting contemporary friendships are racial differences and socioeconomic status, and if left uninterrogated, the assumption of pervasive endogamy in friendships produces and reproduces itself, privileging a history rooted in inequality and reifying an oppressive class system (McCullough 10, 27).

24. V. Clark argues that non-Western cultures offer "traditions of imagining beyond difference" such as the "marasa consciousness" of Haitian Vodoun in which "the Divine Twins" of Iwa and Legba provide a "spiralist" image that "invites us to imagine beyond the binary" of the Hegelian dialectic of "master/slave, patriarchy/matriarchy, domestic/maroon, rural/urban" (46, 43).

25. My emphasis on friendship's tropes of visual likeness finds support in Wiegman's argument that our "cultural fascination with interracial male bonding narratives" points to "the enduring—and rapidly transforming—problem of vision and modernity, where the incorporation of the subject into visually coded corporeal identities takes center stage as the defining problem of the public sphere. . . . In our seduction into the

visual realm of culture . . . we encounter both the threat and utopic possibility of contemporary social critique" (*American Anatomies* 146).

26. One recent instance will suffice. At the multifaith funeral service held for former president Ronald Reagan on June 11, 2004, at which former senator John Danforth, an Episcopalian priest, officiated, Danforth drew his homily from the Sermon on the Mount, apparently Reagan's favorite biblical theme. According to a CBS news report on the service, Reagan frequently quoted the passage from Matthew 5:14–16, "You are the light of the world, a city set on a hill cannot be hid," to "project his view of America as a beacon of freedom and hope. 'If ever we have known a child of light, it was Ronald Reagan,' Danforth said" ("A Nation Bids Reagan Farewell").

27. I also draw on Penelope Deutscher's illuminating reading of mourning, "cultural cannibalism," and friendship politics in the work of Derrida and Luce Irigaray. According to Deutscher, although these thinkers eventually diverge, they both imply that the successful introjection of the lost other that occurs in normal mourning, understood psychoanalytically, is a form of appropriation and cultural cannibalism, while the failed incorporation of melancholia, labeled "endocryptic identification" by Nicolas Abraham and Maria Torok, leaves the other undigested. Thus, Deutscher concludes, "from the perspective of the ethics of alterity, successful mourning fails. . . . [N]ondigestion is the emblem of greater fidelity to the other, and recognition of the other's difference," and ethics is grounded in the paradox of failure as success (166). She goes on to contrast Derrida's notion of the always already "mourning subject" and "cannibal self" that interiorizes but fails to efface the other with Irigaray's "anticannibal ethics" and suggests, "A stronger politics of friendship might be one prepared to negotiate the inevitable play of projection and friendship, not one concerned to disavow that play" (178).

28. Glenn's space flight was the third of six in the Mercury Project, which lasted from May 1961 to May 1963. Each astronaut chose a name for his spacecraft and appended the number 7 to signify the teamwork of the group (the seventh astronaut, Shorty Powers, did not fly). The other names, in order of flight, are: Alan Shepard, *Freedom* 7; Gus Grissom, *Liberty Bell* 7; Scott Carpenter, *Aurora* 7; Wally Shirra, *Sigma* 7; and Gordon Cooper, *Faith* 7. The names show a revealing progression from "freedom" through "friendship" to "faith."

Chapter One

1. For the ancient context of friendship doctrine, I draw from Easterling's short study, Hyatte (1–42), C. White's chapter 2, and Stern-Gillet's analysis. Konstan's introduction to *Friendship in the Classical World* provides a philological approach. See also *Greco-Roman Perspectives on Friendship* edited by Fitzgerald and the very thorough "Reviving Greco-Roman Friendship: A Bibliographic Review" by Devere.

2. Phaedrus, in Plato's *Symposium*, suggests that Achilles and Patroclus were lovers, even ridiculing Aeschylus for claiming that Achilles was the lover (rather than the

beloved) when he was clearly the more beautiful and younger of the two (179d–180a, 21). Konstan examines other references to this belief in the ancient canon and points out that this "idea was common enough for the Alexandrian commentator Zenodotus to have supposed that a particularly intense expression of Achilles' love for Patroclus had been interpolated by someone who wished to represent their relationship as erotic" (*Friendship* 38). In 1908, Carpenter published *Ioläus: An Anthology of Friendship*, a compilation of examples of male friendships throughout history, which makes a case for the overlooked importance of friendship but also seeks to provide a historical grounding for the prevalence of homosexual relationships. Interestingly, Carpenter mentions only one example of female friendship, that of Lady Eleanor Butler and Sarah Ponsonby, and only because Byron refers to it in a letter Carpenter quotes (171–72). Modern scholars, like Clarke and Boswell, take up the argument again.

3. An exception is Plato. Though often associated with the practice of erotic pederasty, Plato in the *Symposium* has Socrates advocate a higher, spiritual form of love between men as equals that rises above but doesn't exclude sensuality (209b–212b, 46–49). See also Boswell, who argues for the compatibility of friendship and erotic love (76–80).

4. Gonzalez conveniently summarizes the plethora of conflicting readings of this dialogue and offers his own, which also depends upon the dramatic setting to lend it coherence, though he focuses on different elements than I do. He confirms that "the *aporia* is rooted in the very nature of friendship, rather than representing a failure to understand it," and that Plato "fundamentally disagrees" with the view of friendship in Aristotle's *Ethics* (70–71).

5. Though Plato does not explicitly exclude women from this higher form of love, Allen discusses how this particular understanding of friendship implicitly excludes them (89ff.).

6. In this I diverge slightly from Pakaluk's most recent translation of *Nicomachean Ethics* (1998), where his preferred term is "complete"; other translations, such as "perfect," "virtue," "primary," and "ideal" friendship, are in common usage.

7. I take my cue from Schollmeier, who argues that Aristotle's theory of friendship, if not ignored by moral philosophers, puzzles them because they do not read it in terms of his principle of happiness and his "unique conception of a human good—a conception of another self." Read in this light, his "theory appears to be at once altruistic and pluralistic" (2).

8. For a catalog of the ancient sources for these common ideas, see the first two entries in Erasmus's *Adages*, which are "Amicorum communia omnia" (Between friends all is common) and "Amicitia aequalitas. Amicus alter ipse" (Friendship is equality. A friend is another self) (29–50).

9. Stern-Gillet gives a detailed technical discussion of Aristotle's unsystematic ideas on selfhood (37–58). Also helpful is the short essay by Aubenque, who explores the "other self" contention in relationship to God and concludes, "[F]riendship is nothing less than divine intention extended to the human level" (26).

10. Many scholars consider this briefer treatise, whose Latin title means "Great Ethics," to be a "post-Aristotelean epitome" not written by Aristotle but perhaps compiled from the notes of one of his students and expressing the substance of Aristotle's ideas on ethics, "whether as fountain-head or as derivative," contained in his two other ethical treatises, the *Nicomachean Ethics* and the *Eudemian Ethics* (Armstrong 427).

11. Saxonhouse, for example, examines pre-Socratic and Aristotelian thought and finds it wrestling with "a fear that differences bring on chaos and thus demands that the world be put into an orderly pattern." She argues that for these thinkers, the unassimilable elements were "the female, sexuality, and the family" and concludes, "While the others warn us, however, it is only Aristotle who . . . is able to overcome the fear and welcome the diverse," especially in his emphasis on the senses and in his view of the polis, which he sees as composed of people of diverse standing, talents, and rewards (x).

12. Von Leyden examines the physical and metaphysical aspects of Aristotle's definition of equality in order to illuminate his political notion of "proportionate equality," which attempts to reconcile the strict numerical equality advocated by the democrats with the oligarchs' claim of special privilege for wealth or noble birth (4). He does not consider the function of equality in Aristotle's theory of friendship, or friendship as an underpinning for the constitution of political societies.

13. In the *Eudemian Ethics*, Aristotle asserts explicitly: "It is in the household that one finds the first origins and sources of friendship, of constitutional government, and of justice," so that the friendship of comrades, discussed below, is based on fraternal friendship, which is based on a form of self-love learned in the household (qtd. in Pakaluk, "Political Friendship" 208).

14. Pakaluk observes that Aristotle chooses the bond between comrades to illustrate complete friendship because it encompasses the three kinds of "unity"—equality, similarity, and sameness—possible in friendship, unity being the defining "function" or "work" of friendship, and because it "seems to be an extension of self-love," the standard of true friendship ("Political Friendship" 201–2, 208).

15. See A. Mitchell, who argues that New Testament authors, particularly Paul, Luke, and John, adopt the Greco-Roman *topos* of friendship though conspicuously avoid the words *philia* and *philos*. An important consequence of this shift in language and emphasis is a blurring of the distinction between love and friendship, so that later depictions of friendship bonds abandon what Konstan calls the "restrained and chaste code" of classical antiquity for more "extravagant," romanticized demonstrations of amiable affection (*Friendship* 173). Konstan provides a more detailed discussion of the semantic shift (*Friendship* 149–73), which C. White downplays (54). She provides an account of all the scriptural references to *philia/amicitia/agape* and comparisons with classical ideas (45–60, esp. 55). Hyatte provides a survey of the later history (43–86), while G. and S. Clark offer a general discussion of friendship in the Christian tradition.

16. All biblical citations are from the King James Version.

17. C. White examines the classical sources of Augustine's conception of friendship and

his Christian modifications (185–217). Burt summarizes Augustinian friendship, which is best expressed in the marital "unity of heart" and gender hierarchy of Adam and Eve and provides a model for the family as the basic unit of "a society of friends." Augustine said, "Friendship begins with one's spouse and children, and from there moves on to strangers. But considering the fact that we all have the same father (Adam) and the same mother (Eve) who will be a stranger? Every human being is neighbor to every other human being (*Sermon 2999D*, 1; qtd. in Burt 118).

18. Scott, who is an important source for Cooper's forest romances, depicts courtly love co-existing with "manly love" between men of the nobility and the lower classes of forest dwellers. Tennyson famously celebrates chivalry in his *Idylls of the King*, and in his poem *In Memoriam* he laments the premature death of his great friend Arthur Hallam. Ironically, the last two lines of this Ciceronian lament are more often cited in the context of heterosexual love, which suggests how easily these discourses merge: "More than my brothers are to me. . . . / My love shall no further range. . . . / Such friendship as had master'd time. . . . / Tis better to have loved and lost / Than never to have loved at all" (st. xxvii; qtd. in Richards 98, 108). For more on chivalric friendship in literary history, see Hyatte (87–136).

19. Although Cicero and Montaigne both disqualify women from the highest form of friendship, Shannon contends that Renaissance homonormative logic extends to women in the form of "chastity," which offers them limited access to the "masculine" virtues of autonomy, self-disposition, and homosocial amity (*Sovereign Amity* 69). By contrast, Hudson, who historicizes friendship discourses of the period as part of a newly emerging "economy of representation" in humanist rhetoric based on developments in real economic relations, insists on its gendered nature and argues that in becoming "symbolically indispensable to the conception of friendship as gift-exchange," women suffer a diminution in images of positive agency (11).

20. Cicero enumerates the "first law of friendship" and several corollary "principles" (xiii.44; 66). Renaissance writers emulated and expanded upon this idea. Walter Dorke, for example, in 1589 published *A Tipe or Figure of Friendship* that listed twenty laws of "Amitie" (Shannon, *Sovereign Amity* 5). In 1657, Jeremy Taylor subtitled his *A Discourse of the Nature, Offices, and Measures of Friendship* "With Rules of Conducting It."

21. Newfield carefully distinguishes Whitman's "homotopia," an understanding of "mass democracy" in which male "friendship avoids termination in monogamous privacy and opens out to the multitudes" and mass rule, from more mainstream, middle-class notions of male friendship, like Emerson's, which fears the crowd and supports the values of "self-differentiation, accumulation, and boundary defense" (106, 101).

22. Tocqueville observes: "Men living in aristocratic ages . . . often sacrifice themselves for other men. In democratic times, on the contrary, when the duties of each individual to the race are much more clear, devoted service to any one man becomes more rare; the bond of human affection is extended, but it is relaxed" (2:105). The equality of

"otherhood" requires a rejection of local, specific, and embodied characteristics that, as B. Nelson notes insightfully, meshes fatally with "modern imperialism," in which white purveyors of "progress" destroy the cultural specificities of dark "others" (136–37). Feminist theorists have explored ways out of the brother/other binary. See, for example, *Feminism and Community*, edited by Weiss and Friedman.

23. Smith continues, differentiating his view from Aristotle's and Montaigne's, by remarking: "They who would confine friendship to two persons, seem to confound the wise security of friendship with the jealousy and folly of love" (225). Den Uyl and Griswold offer a detailed account of the similarities and differences between Smith's theory of sympathy and Aristotle's.

24. This point illustrates the difference between Smith's socially oriented conception and Aristotle's dyadic pairs: for Aristotle, a single friend or small circle of friends best serves this function, while in Smith's system, it is served much better by "a mere acquaintance" and best of all by "an assembly of strangers" (23).

25. See Crain 15. Barnes also makes this point (22) but emphasizes what Marshall identifies as "an epistemological and aesthetic problem"—that "rather than rescuing us from our isolated position as distinct individuals, sympathy reproduces our isolation by offering us a vision of unity while simultaneously confirming the impossibility of its attainment" (25).

26. For a translation of this document and other documents relating to Spanish treatment of the Indians, including an excerpt from Sepúlveda's *Democrates Alter* (in Spanish, *Democrates segundo*) on "Just War Against the Barbarians," see Gibson (58–60, 113–20).

27. In this reading of Montaigne and Certeau, I am indebted more than my citations indicate to both of Freccero's essays on the subject.

28. Freccero argues that the same cannibalistic process is at work in both Derrida's and Certeau's identification with and incorporation of Montaigne ("Toward" 373).

29. For a fascinating contemporary example of the convergence of friendship, homosociality, and cannibalism, see Schneebaum's narrative of his sojourn in the 1960s with a band of cannibalistic Indians in the jungles of Peru and the touching documentary film, released in 2000 and directed by David and Laurie Gwen Shapiro, recounting his reunion with some of these friends. Traub discusses melancholic identification among lesbians and in queer history (326–54).

30. I offer an extensive discussion of the representational politics of Williams's *Key* in *The Work of Self-Representation* 181–228.

31. In his use of the term "courtesy," Williams echoes Francis Bacon's Essay XIII, "Of Goodness and Goodness of Nature," which asserts: "If a Man be Gracious, and Courteous to Strangers, it shewes, he is a Citizen of the World: And that his Heart is no Island, cut off from other Lands; but a Continent, that joynes to them" (40). For Bacon, true courtesy is epitomized by "*St. Pauls* Perfection"; a willingness to die in order to ensure "the Salvation of his Brethren, it shewes much of a Divine Nature, and a kinde of Conformity with *Christ* himselfe" (41; his emphases).

32. In *The History and Present State of Virginia* (1705), Beverly comments on the marriage of Pocahontas and Rolfe: "Intermarriage had indeed been the method proposed very often by the Indians in the Beginning, urging it as a certain rule that the English were not their friends if they refused it. And I can't but think it would have been happy for that country had they embraced this Proposal" (18–19). Byrd amplifies this sentiment in *The History of the Dividing Line* (c. 1738) (which appears in Byrd's larger *Histories of the Dividing Line Betwixt Virginia and North Carolina*): "The Natives could, by no means, perswade themselves that the English were heartily their Friends, so long as they disdained to intermarry with them. And, in earnest, had the English consulted their own Security and the good of the Colony—Had they intended either to Civilize or Convert these Gentiles they would have brought their Stomachs to embrace this prudent Alliance." He points out the French monarch's monetary reward to settlers, male or female, who intermarried with natives and how this had strengthened their "interest" among the Indians and worked in favor of the Catholic religion to the detriment of English efforts at colonization (3–4).

33. In his entry in this helpful sourcebook edited by Jennings, Fenton describes several other metaphors for the extension and maintenance of treaty relations in circulation at the time, the "chain" being the most famous (21–22). For more on the role of the Covenant Chains, see Jennings, *The Ambiguous Iroquois Empire*, which focuses on Iroquois-English relations; Richter and Merrell's collection, which builds on Jennings's important revisionist work; Dennis, who examines Iroquois-European relations during the seventeenth century; and Fenton's compendious study.

34. The letters of Thomas Jefferson illustrate this shift. In 1802, he addresses Handsome Lake, chief of the Seneca, as "Brother" and talks about the Seneca as "our red brethren . . . brethren of the same land." But in his 1806 letter to Wolf and the People of the Mandan Nation, he addresses them as "My children" and, after assuring them that "[t]he French, the English, the Spaniards" have left America, asserts, "We are now your fathers" (*Writings* 8:187–89, 200–202).

35. Fiering argues that this repudiation led to "the remarkable transformation in attitudes towards feelings that occurred in the seventeenth century" and that the popularity of the Scottish moralists in America "was based on an inner affinity between sentimentalism and Puritan religious thought" (5). He offers the example of Charles Morton (1627–98), a dissenting minister and "America's first professional philosopher," who emigrated from England in 1686 to assume the presidency of Harvard but, because of the charter crisis, became a fellow, teacher, and, in 1697, vice president of the college (207). Although Morton considered friendship an aid in the exercise of virtue, which remained "the primary means of finding happiness," he spent a good deal of energy criticizing Aristotelian ethics, as did other Protestant theologians, for "lacking an adequate treatment of social virtues like benevolence, and . . . giving insufficient attention to the passions" (237). Fiering also points out that in 1520, Martin Luther complained about Aristotle's *Ethics* that "no book is more directly contrary to God's

will and the Christian virtues," and Cotton Mather confided to his diary: "There are some very unwise Things done, about which I must watch for opportunities, to bear public Testimonies. One is, the Employing so much Time upon Ethicks, in our Colledges. A vile Peece of Paganism" (qtd. in Fiering 10).

36. McMahon, who studies heterosexual friendships in the early republican period, finds evidence to suggest that "men and women confronted—perhaps embraced—the tension inherent in achieving emotional and intellectual 'sameness' against cultural prescriptions of gender and sexual 'difference'" (82).

37. This fear is echoed throughout classical thought. Konstan points out that Aulus Gellius, second-century Latin author and grammarian, "observes in his *Attic Nights* that the problem of how far one should go in violating the law for the sake of a friend was a favorite topic in the philosophical schools, and he cites a Greek formulation of the dilemma: 'whether one ought to assist a friend contrary to what is just and to what extent and in what ways.'" Konstan puts this issue in terms of the tension between friendship as a private relation and the interests of the community and state ("Friendship and the State" 3).

38. Mavor describes the events that led up to the "elopement"; the "system" of retirement, self-improvement, and commitment to embody perfect friendship adopted by the "ladies of Llangollen," as they became known; and the myths that grew up around them (194–211). An account in London's *General Evening Post* of 1790 broadcast their story widely, and their cottage became a tourist destination. The prolific English writer Anna Seward (1742–1809), who visited the retreat and admired its occupants, composed a long poem, *Llangollen Vale* (1796), extolling romantic retirement from the world and the virtues of women's friendship.

39. Taussig discusses the role of "enthusiasm" in friendship discourse in England during this period. While some, like Ann Yearsley, believed the Platonic idea of friendship could not be embodied without a "quasi-religious enthusiasm," others like Jane Austen in *Love and Friendship* (1790) satirized the "enthusiastic sensibility" and its propensity for forming rapid friendships, which prove to be empty and hypocritical (55, 61–65).

40. The last and most contemporary essay in Pakaluk's collection *Other Selves*, which he calls "the first serious work by an English-speaking philosopher on that subject since Emerson" (248), was written in 1970 by a woman, Elizabeth Telfer, but makes no mention of gender and uses the male pronoun throughout. The explosion of feminist scholarship produced several works on friendship, including Hunt, Raymond, Lugones and Spelman, and Lugones (in collaboration with Rozezelle), "Sisterhood and Friendship," among others. In her 1992 study of women's friendships, O'Connor finds, "across a variety of disciplines, there is evidence of a lack of attention to friendships between women" (10).

41. A term coined by Derrida in a 1975 critique of Lacan's reading of Poe's *The Purloined Letter*, phallogocentrism has appealed to feminist critics for the way it "brings together

the feminist critique of Patriarchy and the deconstructionist critique of Language" (Wright 316; see Paul Smith's discussion in Wright 316–18).

42. Langer offers a different reading of Aristotle's cryptic phrase, arguing that Montaigne may have consulted a sixteenth-century Latin translation of a faulty Greek edition of Diogenes Laertius's *Lives of Eminent Philosophers*, in which this remark of Aristotle's is reported, and that far from the "melancholy reflection" Montaigne attributes to it, Aristotle was making "a theoretical ethical point"—that given the rarity of true friendship, which he frequently asserted in his *Ethics*, it is impossible to have many friends (15–19).

43. J. Scott provides the classic theoretical statement of this "dilemma," how it played out legally in the divisive 1979 Sears case, and how deconstruction offers an alternative approach in her essay "Deconstructing Equality-versus-Difference." See also Jakobsen. For an extended feminist conversation on this "dilemma," see Nicholson, introduction to *Feminist Contentions*.

44. Young offers an important opposition and implicit critique of Aristotelian friendship when she argues that community-oriented politics presumes "that subjects can understand one another as they understand themselves" (300).

45. Philosophers raise the concern that friendship is a form of "partiality" that leads to "cronyism" and nepotism in the public sphere. See, for example, Pahl and M. Friedman, who outlines the "partiality debates" and their impact on the notion of the "social self."

Chapter Two

1. Dawson argues against the widely held belief that Winthrop first delivered the sermon during the sea crossing but rather delivered it at the point of embarkation in Southampton, England, and considers the implications of its "English context"; see "John Winthrop's Rite of Passage" and " 'Christian Charitie.' " Bremer imagines Winthrop delivering his address at the Church of the Holy Rood in Southampton in March 1630 but concludes that its original delivery is still unconfirmed (*John Winthrop* 173–75). Jackson suggests the "likelihood that Winthrop delivered the sermon many times, even to the same crowd, likely two or three times aboard the *Arbella* as well . . . as a source of renewable inspiration." He argues, "[O]ur insistence on finding the exact moment it was first delivered is a historical retrojection of our own values (both of authenticity and, more subtly, as part of our need to correct and complete originary myths) on a culture that would not, likely, have placed such emphasis on our meaning of 'original.' . . . That Winthrop used the biblical trope of a 'Citty upon a Hill' many times in speeches before this one seems to support my reading here" (personal communication).

2. In this I echo Bremer, who explains that while Perry Miller's influential reading of the early Puritans never claimed they saw themselves as a unique beacon of reform, many

attributed this belief to Miller and named Winthrop's "A Modell" as its key text. This set off a heated debate about New England's shaping role in American national destiny whose major texts Bremer cites and critiques (*John Winthrop* 181, 433).

3. Winthrop, *Winthrop Papers* 291. All subsequent citations, abbreviated as *WP* and given parenthetically, are from this edition.

4. Jalalzai examines a similar tension between hierarchical "corporeal models" and "egalitarian contractual models" of community in Winthrop's address with respect to Puritan attitudes toward racial difference and shows how the latter model invited Indians into the Puritan covenant while the former excluded Indian converts on the basis of their unassimilable "corporeal identities" (265).

5. See, for example, Bremer's comparison of passages from Winthrop's address and from the sermons of John Knewstub (1579), an influential Puritan minister in Suffolk ("Heritage" 536–37). See also his description of the address's wider ministerial context (*John Winthrop* 179–80).

6. For example, in the passage from 1 Corinthians 13 cited in the next paragraph, the King James Bible uses the word "charity," while the Geneva Bible uses the word "love" in the main text and "charity" in the marginal commentary.

7. For a summary of the scholarship on "nomenclature and interpretation of conceptions of friendship" in the Greco-Roman periods, see Devere 153–55.

8. See Pakaluk's most recent translation of *Nicomachean Ethics*, which uses the word "complete" to describe "the friendship of good people alike in virtue" (1156b; 8:3, 4).

9. According to Burt, Augustine addressed this problem by distinguishing the physical inequality of the sexes from the spiritual equality of "souls" reflected in their equality of rights and duties in marriage. However, he did hold that wives (not women in general) were subordinate (by nature or free choice) to husbands (not men in general) because men excelled in "speculative reason" while women excelled in "practical reason," the former being the more important of the two. But since marriage is modeled on the relationship of Christ to the church and itself models the "friendly society," wifely subordination models the necessity for the deference to authority in any orderly organization (Burt 100–111). This reasoning resembles Aristotle's distinction between the sexes in marriage.

10. W. C. McWilliams outlines the Calvinist conception of the "human covenants" as "a progressively narrowing hierarchy" of "stages of alienation" until the final reunion of "fraternity with all men, a true fraternity purged of the dross of imperfection and sin." These are: Original Sin/Individualism; Covenant of Nature/Brotherhood of Blood; Political Covenant/Civic Fraternity; Church Covenant/Brotherhood of visible Christians; Covenant of Grace/Brotherhood of man (123–30). One can only wonder where women fit into this scheme.

11. In 1630, the year of Winthrop's departure, William Ames, the eminent English Puritan divine, took up the task his teacher Alexander Richardson left unfinished at his death and began writing *Technometria*, an attempt to give Peter Ramus's influential logical

method an overall theory, which became known as "technologia." The result, published the year of his death in 1633, determined the early curriculum at Harvard and set the course of higher education in America. In Thesis 77, Ames eschews the radical Puritan rejection of classical (pagan) learning and advocates a Christian humanist "friendship" with the "truth" it contained: "Thus, let us not become the slaves of anyone, but, performing military service under the banner of free truth, let us freely and courageously follow the truth that leads and calls away from the hallucinations of our elders, as they are men who have also been created in the image of Adam. Testing all things, retaining that which is good, let Plato be a friend, let Aristotle be a friend, but even more let truth (*veritas*) be a friend" (*Technometry* 106–7). According to Gibbs's commentary, the final sentence of this thesis, which appeared on the title or subtitle page of every edition of Ames's *Philosophemata* and was used by Ramus and quoted by several New England divines, is based on a passage from book 1 of Aristotle's *Nicomachean Ethics*: "Yet it would perhaps be thought to be better, indeed to be our duty, for the sake of maintaining the truth even to destroy what touches us closely, especially as we are philosophers or lovers of wisdom; for, while both are dear, piety requires us to honour truth above our friends" (*Ethica Nicomachea* 1:6, 939; Ames 163).

12. I am indebted to Stacey Choi, a student in Early American Literature, Spring 2003, for this point.

13. However, corporate language appears as early as 1553, in the founding of the Russia Company, "the first English joint-stock company of importance," whose charter described it as constituted of "one bodie and perpetuall fellowship and communaltie." This language combines the character of "contemporary regulated and livery companies" and the "'fellowship' . . . common in the early gilds" (W. Scott 19). I am indebted to Michelle Burnham for pointing out this connection. Jalalzai cites Canning, who locates debates about the corporate nature of cities and kingdoms in the writing of Roman canonists like Pope Innocent IV in 1250 (Canning 473; qtd. in Jalalzai 271).

14. On the transformations of the metaphorical body, Dawson cites Kantorowicz 194–232, and on the convergence of the body's religious and political meanings, he quotes the summary from Barkan 67–68. Whereas Dawson sees continuity and even "unity" among the three bodies—ecclesiastical, political, and commercial—invoked by Winthrop ("'Christian Charitie'" 125), I agree with Bercovitch that there is a conflict between the spiritual equality, however imperfectly achieved, of the regenerate "body" of the church as conceived by the New England Puritans and the divinely sanctioned social hierarchy, which Winthrop endorses at the opening of his discourse.

15. It would be revealing to follow up the gendered nature of Paine's emotional rhetoric, which Coviello and other critics ignore, and try it against his discourse of equality. For example, Paine rejects the argument that independence will allow one colony to strive "for superiority over another" by declaring, "Where there are no distinctions there can be no superiority; perfect equality affords no temptation." He refers to republican

forms of government, "formed on more natural principles," which he contrasts with monarchies like Britain's (27).

16. All citations from the *Oxford English Dictionary*, abbreviated *OED*, are from the on-line edition, <http://dictionary.oed.com/entrance.dtl>, copyright 2006, and continually updated.

17. For a more extensive exploration of Taylor's deployment of the feminine in relation to the Puritan notion of "redeemed subjectivity," see Schweitzer 79-125.

18. Michaelsen reads this passage as very explicitly referring to a hierarchical "commercial" system in which the mouth represents the rich and the other parts are the poor, and these "parts" are expected to return wealth, duly transformed, to the rich, who, as Winthrop earlier notes, have a natural inclination to "eate upp the poore" (*WP* 283).

19. Dawson rejects Michaelsen's reading of Winthrop's covenant as premodern contract, calling it monologically legal, weak, and "an oversimplification" (" 'Christian Charitie' " 119). Still, he grants the address's "pervasive legal tenor" (121) and covenant's coloration by "its long service in the specialized language of medieval philosophy and its recent place in commercial practice" (120). And he finally understands Winthrop's use of the term as fusing "several registers of binding responsibility" such as obligations among saints, marriage and family ties, the shareholders' corporate bond, the commitment made by the leaders in the Cambridge Agreement of 1629 to emigrate, the Company's leasing of ships, supporters' financial connections, the formal patent from the Crown, the responsibilities of settlement, and the governing structures set up in New England (122). However, Dawson does not specify how and on what levels these various meanings involve participants.

20. See Pateman's *The Sexual Contract*, which argues that the social contract theory of Enlightenment thinkers implies a "sexual contract" related to the marriage contract—the only contract considered acceptable for women to enter (with the blessings of the father)—that kept women as wives subordinated to the authority of men as husbands.

21. Most dissenting English theologians, including William Ames and William Perkins, who were favorites among the New England Puritans, believed "that the mutuality of the covenant did not imply any equality between parties" (Gordis 388). P. Miller, however, views the Puritans' federal "covenant as contract" and deplores "the subversively rationalistic elements in the marrow of Puritan divinity" that bind human and God in "some level of equality" (*Errand* 101-2).

22. I am indebted in this line of argument to Shannon's discussion in " 'A Parfecte Consent': Being and Agreeing to be Double" (*Sovereign Amity* 38-46).

23. For an especially rich, historically grounded study of early modern friendship in England that raises many of the questions about its public and political nature also central to this study, see Bray's groundbreaking work, *The Friend*.

24. In addition to Churchyard's *A sparke of frendship*, Shannon cites other "occasional publications" such as Thomas Breme's *The mirrour of friendship: both how to knowe a perfect friend, and how to choose him* (1584) and a host of translations, emblem books,

and commonplace books that recycled the highlights of Cicero's *De amicitia* for a Tudor readership (*Sovereign Amity* 28).

25. In its emphasis on the emotions, Winthrop's Puritan vision moves away from the ancients' emphasis on rational desire and anticipates later writers like Jonathan Edwards. On the "inner affinity between sentimentalism and Puritan religious thought" and their use of the passions, see Fiering 5.

26. W. C. McWilliams also reads Winthrop's address as an important contribution to what he calls "the idea of fraternity in America," which he sees anchored more in scriptural and religious authority and less in the secular classical writings (133).

27. I draw on Luxon's helpful discussion of this complex biblical crux (131–35). By contrast, Anderson argues that the "shee" of Winthrop's passage is Eve, a personification of the soul, addressing Adam in intensely sexual terms that feminize him and exalt Eve as a version of Mary but also make her Winthrop's "model citizen" (12–13). This curious misreading allows Anderson to claim this moment as an "important modification of the hierarchical tradition" that places heterosexual intimacy at the heart of American notions of community (14). While I agree that Winthrop strategically displaces egalitarian relations with heterosexual ones, I don't see this as a progressive modification of "the hierarchical tradition" but as a reinforcement of it. Furthermore, Anderson's reading ignores the important distinction between prelapsarian and fallen marriage and dismisses what he himself acknowledges as Winthrop's citation of David and Jonathan as "the second of the instructive instances" of a social ideal "more demanding and more rewarding (he [Winthrop] suggests) than marriage" (12). Nevertheless, Anderson argues that the "fluidity of gender" he reads in this passage promotes a Puritan/American communitarian vision that places marriage at its moral center and, correspondingly, elevates women and domesticity "as a privileged sphere of meaning" (2). This not only ignores what Anderson himself acknowledges is Winthrop's preferred social model—male friendship—and links women to an essentialist domesticity but also illustrates the critical and heteronormative myopia concerning the importance, even existence, of friendship as a defining mode of affiliation. Bremer, who sees Winthrop drawing on his close relationship with his wife, Margaret, for this passage, notes the two examples Winthrop gives to express his idea of love, "between husband and wife, and that between David and Jonathan," but does not comment on their differences (*John Winthrop* 177).

28. Dillon cites the Puritan writer Thomas Gataker, whose *A Marriage Praier* (1624) describes the ideal helpmeet's specifically gendered "womans trade" (18–19). See also Shannon, "Likenings," and Hudson.

29. See, for example, Thomas Hooker's *Survey of the Summe of Church Discipline* (1648, 66–67; qtd. in S. Foster 36).

30. For the most recent scholarship on the relation of David and Jonathan, including a detailed examination of their covenant and its political context, see Ackerman, who

uses biblical scholarship as well as recent studies in sexuality and homosexuality to contextualize what she calls "heroic love" rather than friendship.

Chapter Three

1. Pateman argues that the Enlightenment social contract theory implies a "sexual contract" that subordinated women, but she does not explore nonsexual/nonmarriage relationships between men and women and their implications for political agency and citizenship.

2. For a more extensive discussion of this passage as a moment in which "Milton strained to redefine marriage as the friendship Socrates recommended—an erotics beyond the sexual" (140), see Luxon (123–56).

3. Pakaluk gathers the essential readings from the ancient and early modern tradition on friendship in a single volume entitled *Other Selves*. For a broad survey of this tradition up to early Christianity, which claims transhistorical continuity for ideal or perfect friendship, see Konstan, *Friendship in the Classical World*. Rouner's collection updates the growing scholarship on notions of friendship in other cultures and in the modern world based on the classical inheritance.

4. These lines are from "The Maid's Soliloquy," which was first published anonymously but has recently been attributed to a man, Lewis Morris. The earliest known printing was in the *Gentleman's Magazine*, January 17, 1747, 42, and the earliest North American printing was in the *New York Evening Post*, December 21, 1747, 1.

5. The groundbreaking study on this phenomenon is still Smith-Rosenberg, "The Female World of Love and Ritual" in *Disorderly Conduct*, augmented by Cott and by Chambers-Schiller, who argues that during the last decades of the eighteenth century and into the nineteenth century, the percentage of unmarried women continued to rise steadily.

6. "Political coverture" is Jackson's term for a model of civic obligation based on "nuptial coverture," a legal notion defined by Timothy Walker: "Marriage makes the husband and wife one person, and that person is the husband" (*Introduction to American Law* [1855] 232; qtd. in Jackson 293). Northern supporters of the Union promoted the idea of political coverture in the debates of 1860 to underscore the willing and irrevocable self-subjection of citizens to a sovereign government. Jackson's essay gives helpful background from Enlightenment political theory for these debates in which the Northerners sound suspiciously like the politically conservative John Winthrop speaking before the General Court in 1645.

7. Mulford details the printing history of Foster's novel and provides an insightful historical context, including versions of the account that appeared in newspapers and private letters (xlii).

8. Sharon M. Harris, for example, reads *The Coquette* as an overt challenge to "the sexist

bases of the new nation's political ideologies" (3) that attempt "to veil the power of women's communities such as the one that emerges after Eliza's death"; this new community suggests "a potentially different future" (17–18). While I agree with Harris's political reading of the novel, I am less sanguine about the progressive character of the community that survives Eliza.

9. Reading Foster's novel in tandem with her next publication, *The Boarding School*, a "hybrid" genre of "conduct fiction," Pettengill concludes that they reveal female friendship's ideological function as "complex, malleable, and often contradictory," conservatively limiting women to the roles of wives and mothers on the one hand but progressively privileging women's relationships and experiences on the other (189). However, neither Pettengill nor other studies of Foster's female community takes into account the history of friendship as a social/political affiliation or the contested place of women's friendship in that history.

10. All references are to the edition edited by Mulford and will include the letter number in roman numeral followed by the page number in that edition.

11. Helpful background on the emergence of "republicanism" as a paradigm for early modern history can be found in Rodgers. Mulford distinguishes three understandings of republicanism in circulation in Foster's time. One of these forms was popular among the educated elite and drew its sources "from ancient political history and theory," which suggests their familiarity with the classical sources of friendship as well (xiv–xv).

12. Cicero, whose *De amicitia* shaped early modern and republican notions of friendship, viewed sympathy as the first stage in the construction of the highest form of friendship: "Men find themselves thrown together by a feeling of sympathy and goodwill; they learn first of all to govern those passions to which most men are enslaved; then they learn to take delight in decency and justice. Finally, the one learns to stand by the other in his every need, and never under any circumstances to demand of him anything but what is honorable and right. Then they will not only love and cherish each other, but will also know mutual respect" (xxii.82; 81).

13. See Aristotle, *NE* 9:4, 29, and Cicero's *De amicitia*, xxii.80 (80), for the first formulation. The idea of "one soul in two bodies" appears nowhere in Aristotle's writing; Diogenes Laertius quotes it in his testament of Aristotle in *Lives of Eminent Philosophers*: "To the query, 'What is a friend?' his reply was, 'A single soul dwelling in two bodies'" (1:463). Montaigne echoes the essence of this phrase in his essay "On Friendship," and Shakespeare, as we will see, slightly amends it.

14. For a detailed account of the similarities and differences between Adam Smith's theory of sympathy and Aristotle's theory of friendship, see Den Uyl and Griswold.

15. Smith-Rosenberg discusses this opening association in terms of the Declaration of Independence's linking of liberty and the pursuit of happiness as unalienable rights, balanced by "prudence." But she sees Eliza's understanding of "pleasure" as sensual and physical, thus invested with "an equally dangerous emotion—individualism"

("Domesticating 'Virtue'" 170–71). I see Eliza more interested in public agency and social conversation and her individualism balanced by her desire for friendship, even with the despicable Sanford.

16. For a detailed account of the "complex temporal perspective" within which *De amicitia* is dramatically set and the dialogue's Lacanian portrayal of desire, loss, and mirrored subjectivity, see Leach.

17. Later on, Julia Granby uses the language of state sovereignty to describe a "normalizing" of relations after Eliza discovers Sanford's marriage and seems to give up on him, but Julia's blindness to the fact that "commerce" does commence makes her usage of the trope exceedingly ironic. That Eliza is ahead of her time is borne out when several decades later, Elizabeth Cady Stanton would claim that "the individual sovereignty of woman is more sacred than any human tie" (Stanton, Anthony, and Gage 91), an idea she traced through Jefferson and Madison back to Locke but which was a concern of friendship theorists like Aristotle as well.

18. For an analysis of the language of brothers and sisters as a political strategy for women of the period seeking equality with men and inclusion as citizens in the nation, see Fetterley and my critique of her argument in chapter 5.

19. As Stern notes, Locke's sensationalist psychology links fancy to the imagination. Formerly connected with the error of "fantastical" ideas, "fancy" by the end of the century was an aesthetic faculty capable of manipulating experience but not transforming it. Thus, fancy allows Eliza to imagine "what for Locke, would be an 'unreal combination'—the coexistence of romantic liberty and sympathetic connectedness," but does not allow her the means to change her situation (102).

20. Because Stern does not recognize the text's use of "friendship" as different from eighteenth-century notions of "sympathy," she articulates this point as a failure of Eliza's self referentiality: "When Eliza can no longer provide the mirror of compassion *for herself*, once she loses the capacity to see her dissent from the majority's tyranny as a valid desire, her interpellation into the ideology of republican fellow-feeling becomes complete" (75; my emphasis). Placing the blame on the failure of the "sisterly watch" of monitory friends, Pettengill likewise argues that Eliza "breaks the chain" of the female circle of friends when in Letter XLI she "lay[s] aside [her] pen and deliberate[s]"—that is, when she ceases to look to her friends as confidantes, finds her mother inadequate, and turns to Sanford (197).

21. Foster makes two slight changes in Addison's lines. The play has "leagues of pleasure" and "severest virtue" (103).

22. According to the *OED*, in the early seventeenth century, the now rare phrase "carnal confederacy" was still in use.

23. Davidson points out that on receiving Boyer's pompous response to her letter, Eliza writes, "Oh my friend, I am undone." These are the "precise words that in seduction novels typically signal a woman's fall," and soon thereafter Eliza begins the sexual affair with Sanford (introduction xviii).

Chapter Four

1. For one account of this evolution, see Baym, "How Men and Women Wrote Indian Stories," where she argues that "striking traces of women's Indian stories" appear in Cooper's later novels in the Leatherstocking Tales, in which Anglo and native women play more central, less stereotyped roles (84–85).

2. See <http://www.mohicanpress.com/m007010.html> for the film's script. In this version, the success of Nathaniel's quest for Cora and Uncas's failure in his romantic quest for Alice reconfigure the male interracial family into a heterosexual affiliation between whites and presages a monoracial American national destiny built upon the demise and sentimental incorporation of Indians and Indianness. For an account of how Cooper "devoted his early career to reimagining national origins so as to negotiate a reconciliation between New and Old World" that stages the disappearance of the troubling racial other, see Gardner 81–124.

3. Two other readings that take account of the interracial friendship also do not consider its historical or gendered contexts. In Kelly's 1983 deconstructive analysis, he argues that the "brotherhood" between Natty and Chingachgook fuses white and red "gifts" —the corrupt and inapplicable European notions of "friendship" as allegiance and loyalty with the "savage" Indian notion of honor as revenge—to produce a synthesis that is both "derivative and innovative" and, thus, serves as a powerful if paradoxical source for a distinctive American identity. Their special "kinship," however, is only "an intermediate state of cultural development" in what will be a new genealogy of white male power embodied in the synthetic character of Duncan Heyward (49). J. McWilliams elucidates the political implications of the friendship when he argues that the bond between Natty and Chingachgook unifies the five Leatherstocking Tales, "shapes the plot in all the tales except *The Prairie*," and "raises questions as troublingly important in the 1990s as in the 1820s. Why is it that the deepest relationship in the capacious world of the Leatherstocking Tales is an interracial, wholly asexual, and often wordless bond between two males? What status can such a friendship have within either white or red culture? Does the intensity of an interracial friendship depend on its alienation from both races? What does such a male bond imply about the way 'civilized' society privileges a marriage between man and woman, whether they be of one race or of two? And finally, what is the worth of red and white cultures if their most admirable representatives can exist only apart from both of them?" (13). He backs away from these questions and shuts down possible answers, however, when he concludes that the "emotional climax" of the final scene in *Mohicans* "affirms universalist assumptions" by providing "a moment only, a glimpse of an aracial world that lies within present human capacity only at times of severest loss" (65–66). In queer studies, Martin and Boone examine representations of interracial male bonds, especially in Melville and Twain, and conclude that they constitute a "radical democratic"

and "potentially subversive force against a society of male heterosexual domination" (Martin 94, 14). Martin, however, does not consider Cooper's pair, and Boone specifically excludes it on the shaky grounds that Cooper's friendship plots are inextricable from his romance and marriage plots and thus do not constitute truly "male romances." More recently, Erkkila dismisses the interracial friendship in the novel as "the love triangle of Hawk-eye, Uncas, and Chingachgook [that] enables the fantasy of blood mixture" (19).

4. Wiegman offers a critique of the "canonical architecture" supporting male interracial buddy narratives more generally, including Fiedler's analysis of Cooper (*American Anatomies* 149–78). Similarly, Samuels argues that the massacre of women and children and the cannibalism of the Huron express "the extreme form that fear of women and natural reproduction takes in this novel" ("Generation through Violence" 104).

5. See Baym, Karcher, Gould, and Opfermann. It would be revealing to factor into this debate the opinions of native writers such as William Apess; see, for example, Bergland 111–44 and Walker 41–59.

6. All references to this text (*LM*) and other novels by Cooper are from the standard editions published by State University of New York Press at Albany and will be cited parenthetically with an abbreviation of the title.

7. In his discussion of the necessity of friendship for political stability, Aristotle employs an image inverted and used by Cooper in this speech and elsewhere in *Mohicans*: "[W]hen men are at enmity with one another, they would rather not even share the same path" (*Politics* 1295b, 1221).

8. See Cicero, *De amicitia* v.19 (54). Montaigne makes this point in the extreme: "[T]he more they [family relations] are friendships which law and natural obligation impose on us, the less of our choice and free will there is in them. And our free will has no product more properly its own than affection and friendship" (137).

9. See my discussion of friendship and loss in chapter 1. For more on the politics of absence and presence in friendship doctrine, see Derrida, *Politics of Friendship*, and *The Work of Mourning/Jacques Derrida*, edited by Brault and Naas, a collection of elegies that examines how death structures friendship.

10. Heyd observes that in the civil rights movement of the 1960s, interracial handshakes counteracted racist body language and policies. Demonstrators at the March on Washington on August 28, 1963, wore large buttons showing a black and white hand clasped in friendship. Versions of this gesture graced the badges of the activists of the Mississippi Freedom Summer and the NAACP. Jewish artist Ben Shahn depicted a white hand pulling up a black hand under the words, in Hebrew and English, "Thou Shalt Not Stand Idly By" in a 1965 lithograph (120). Interracial protesters often held hands at demonstrations, and Martin Luther King, among other speech makers of the time, famously evoked images of whites and blacks hand in hand. In Richard Wright's novel *Native Son* (1940), a misunderstood interracial handshake triggers the tragic

events that lead to the protagonist's death. Finally, Heyd argues, the clasped hands evolved into the raised fist of the Black Panther Party (118–21).

11. This was Cooper's formula for "traditional republicanism," which he expressed optimistically in *Notions of the Americans* (1828) and as conservative antidote in *The American Democrat* (1838). Watts explains, quoting from the latter text, that "the principle of equality must be understood to address the issue of rights before the law, *not* social condition. Each [*sic*: male] citizen's political and civil rights—suffrage, eligibility to office, equal standing before the law—should remain unquestioned but 'equality of condition is incompatible with civilization, and is found only to exist in those communities that are but slightly removed from the savage state'" (66; Watts's emphasis).

12. See note 7 above for the source of this image in Aristotle's *Politics*.

13. On their first view of Uncas, the "ingenuous Alice gazed at his free air and proud carriage, as she would have looked upon some precious relic of the Grecian chisel, to which life had been imparted, by the intervention of a miracle" (*LM* 53). Later, in Huron captivity, Uncas "possessed much more of the air of some finely moulded statue, than of a man having life and volition" (245), and after a failed attack by Magua, the narrator comments, "Marble could not be colder, or steadier, than the countenance he [Uncas] put upon this sudden and vindictive attack" (251).

14. In the final chase, the narrator observes that "Magua, though daring and much exposed, escaped from every effort against this life, with that sort of fabled protection, that was made to overlook the fortunes of favoured heroes in the legends of ancient poetry" (*LM* 335).

15. When they are up north, Magua enters the neighboring camp of the Delaware under the guise of friendship (*LM* 287), gives out gifts divided according to rank, much like the governmental agents' bestowal of peace medals, and demagogically invokes the principle of racial unity: "The Hurons love their friends the Delawares. . . . Why should they not! they are colored by the same sun, and their just men will hunt in the same grounds after death. The red-skins should be friends, and look with open eyes on the white men" (*LM* 289–90). His theory of friendship stands in stark contrast to Uncas's or Hawk-eye's, which is based upon action and proven loyalty.

16. According to Peck's review of the critical literature, Philbrick's essay was "a key development" in interpretation that made simplistic applications of the "myth and symbol" school impossible (13–14).

17. Similarly, in Erkkila's recent reading of the tropes of crossing in early American culture, Cooper's novel is awash in blood and blood rites, while the interracial friendships he depicts are glancingly mentioned as a "love triangle" that enables a "fantasy of blood mixture" (19).

18. See, for example, Herndl, who examines both Cooper's novel and Mann's film in terms of manipulating spectatorial sympathy.

19. Beard, in his "Historical Introduction" to the novel, points out that though Gamut is "the emblem of human community and sociability, . . . [and] serves constantly in his

grotesque role of buffoon and psalmist to register contrasting attitudes of the other characters," he also "is symptomatic of pervasive incongruities" (xxxii).

Chapter Five

1. Sedgwick follows the seventeenth-century sources and refers to the tribe as the "Pequod," but the modern spelling is "Pequot."

2. For a more detailed account of this debate, see Gould, Baym, Karcher, and Opfermann. Freibert and White cite Barnett's definition of the frontier romance as a tale "containing Indian characters and written between 1790 and 1860" and her list of more than seventy works, eleven by Cooper and the majority by male writers. "Women, however," they counter, "played an important role in the development of the form and authored one-quarter of the examples published before 1828, when the frontier romance had become a clearly recognizable genre" (103). Burnham examines the interdependence of the captivity narrative and the sentimental romance, thereby placing *Hope Leslie* in a line of frontier narratives by women not mentioned by Baym, two of which are Susannah Rowson's *Reuben and Rachel; or Tales of Old Times* (1798) and Harriet Cheney's *A Peep at the Pilgrims in Sixteen Hundred Thirty-Six. A Tale of Olden Times* (1824). In *Hope Leslie*—hereafter abbreviated as *HL* in citations—Sedgwick acknowledges Cheney as "a sister labourer" in the field of historical romance (*HL* 56).

3. For a comparison of Child's text and Sedgwick's, see Karcher; Opfermann does an informative comparison of Cooper, Child, and Sedgwick on gender, interracial relations, and their cultural implications. Singley makes a strong argument for Sedgwick's feminist alternative in her essay on *Hope Leslie*, which she subtitles "Radical Frontier Romance."

4. Weierman explores the extensive interracial relations of the Sedgwicks and their intermarriages, religious missions, and land deals with the Stockbridge Indians, which she characterizes as "a shameful family history of Indian mistreatment—source of the family's wealth and position" and a necessary context for reading *Hope Leslie*. She concludes that although Sedgwick "sought out and embraced" these connections and used her fiction to "honor" Indians, in her autobiographical writing she ultimately "refuses to be interrogated" on the matter (415, 443).

5. Karafilis examines the historical context of *Hope Leslie*'s exploration of "ethical political agency" and argues that in developing what she calls, after political theorist Chantal Mouffe, a "radical democratic individualism," Sedgwick seeks to expose "the artificiality of the polarity" between individualism and communitarianism and thus counter the valorization of "rugged individualism" and the depreciation of communitarianism by many Jacksonian democrats. Emerson looks at the rhetorical shift from "equality" as "equivalence" or sameness in the post-Revolutionary years to a new emphasis on "equity," a concept she claims is "more amenable to the liberalism that characterizes much nineteenth-century thinking" (83).

6. Since the novel's republication in the Rutgers American Women's Writers Series in 1987 brought increased attention, critics have recognized Sedgwick's political challenge to Cooper and the centrality of female affiliation but not their investment in historical discourses of friendship. Fetterley charts how celebrations of Sedgwick's progressive vision of gender relations and racial constructs—"a hagiography directly proportional to the misogyny informing previous treatments" (citing Castiglia ["In Praise"] and Zagarell)—give way to critiques implicating early women writers like Sedgwick "in a variety of nineteenth-century racist, classist, and imperialist projects" (citing Brodhead, Merish, and Thomson) (492). Recent critical consensus refuses this binary of "celebration and critique," stressing instead the text's "equivocal" resolution of "the Indian problem" and the "woman question" (D. Nelson, *Word* 77) or praising, as Fetterley does, its paradoxes and refusal to achieve the coherence that legitimates republican ideology and politics (493). Baym concludes that both male and female authors of "Indian stories" reinforce stereotypes of the "vanishing Indian" and thus support the inevitability of white dominance. Q. Miller, among others, observes that while romance conventions force Hope to marry the white hero, Sedgwick gives the final word to the heroine's puritanical friend, Esther Downing, whose refusal to marry illustrates that institution's irrelevance "to the contentment, the dignity, or the happiness of woman" (*HL* 350). The text's very irresolution on these issues illustrates, in the words of Ford's Foucauldian reading, the existence and circulation of a "plurality of *discourses* which produce power" as well as the "unavailability of a truly liberating discourse" (83, 86; his emphasis).

7. Foregrounding the question of freedom and resistance to lawful authority as "*the* ideological ground for all other issues" in Sedgwick's fiction, Susan K. Harris redefines this more broadly as "Republican Womanhood" (273, 279; her emphasis).

8. Compare Cooper, who in the preface to the first edition of *Mohicans* differentiates virile male readers from "the more imaginative sex" and clergymen, who will mistake his "narrative" for "fiction" and whom he therefore advises *not* to read his book (*LM* 1).

9. Chicana theorist Alarcón calls the feminist strategy of equating white women with white men "the logic of identification" and argues that eliding sexual difference in order to produce theoretical/legal equality between the two excludes women/people of color. This equation, she argues, is the first "often veiled" step in the construction of a feminist "standpoint epistemology," championed by many feminist theorists across the disciplines in the 1980s that proceeds, paradoxically, to assert "oppositional thinking" or "counteridentification" with men in its promotion of a specifically "female identity" that erases differences among and within women in its bid for unanimity (358).

10. See, for example, Zagarell, D. Nelson, and most recently Karafilis.

11. A good deal of postcolonial theory calls for problematizing positionality, especially among hegemonic discourses; see Spivak. Lugones and Spelman contend that repositioning is necessary for the difficult labor of interracial friendship and is a prelude to

anti-racist work. hooks gives a more practical description of "shifting location" and ties it to travel and theorizing (165–78). M. B. Pratt and Frankenberg offer poignant accounts of the struggle and costs of "shifting locations."

12. This epigraph illustrates the rhetorical slipperiness of these ideas because the "lost sister" in this chapter is not Faith, who was reunited with Hope in the previous chapter, but Hope herself, who has been separated again from her sister and besieged by drunken sailors from Chaddock's ship.

13. These two understandings of women's condition—united by shared oppression and suing for equality with men, or united by shared gender power different from and complementary to men's and suing for protective legislation and the maintenance of gender difference—produce divergent and seemingly incompatible political and cultural strategies in the nineteenth century. The latter, often called "women's culture" and later "difference feminism," was epitomized by Catharine Beecher, sister of the famous Harriet, who authored domestic manuals that exhorted women to the proper exercise of female power from within the domestic sphere. The former, labeled "equalist feminism," was embodied by suffragists like Elizabeth Cady Stanton and Susan B. Anthony, who critiqued domesticity as an imposition on women's freedom, wanted equality with men, and were accused of robbing women of their femininity. Feminists throughout the last two centuries have made expeditious use of both of these seemingly exclusive positions, as Sedgwick does. See Cott's "Conclusion: On 'Women's Sphere' and Feminism," in *Bonds* 197–206 and "Feminist Theory." The classic essay "deconstructing" these positions is by J. Scott.

14. For earlier attempts at formulating friendship as a theoretical model for relations across difference, see Lugones and Spelman and also Lugones's "Playfulness," an essay S. Friedman recommends to feminists for its suggestiveness in "looking to move beyond the difference impasse" (76).

15. There is more than a hint of gender-bending in Hope's universal charisma. Sedgwick compares her "classical" beauty to that "with which poetry has invested Hebe." A few pages later, she introduces Rosa, fancifully cross-dressed as Gardiner's page, with a close paraphrase from *Comus* discussed earlier: "[S]mooth as Hebe's was his unrazored lip" (cf. l. 290; *HL* 122, 127). Hebe was the Greek goddess of youth, daughter of Zeus and Hera, and cupbearer to the gods on Mount Olympus until she was married off to Heracles. Ganymede, who replaced Hebe, was a beautiful Trojan boy whom Zeus, disguised as an eagle, snatched up from Mount Ida and brought to heaven, where he became one of Zeus's lovers. Some scholars interpret this liaison as a justification for homosexuality within Greek culture or as a reflection of current social practices. Apollodorus (b. 180 B.C.E.), a Greek writer and author of the collection of essays *On the Gods*, claimed the myth indicated the triumph of patriarchy over matriarchy, while Plato cited it as precedence for pederastic practices (*Encyclopedia Mythica*).

16. The other reference to this pair indirectly alludes to their friendship. It comes in John

Eliot's opening prayer at Magawisca's trial, where he mentions "diverse instances of 'kindness and neighbourlike conduct that had been shown them [the Puritans] by the poor heathen people,'" especially Monoca's "well known and signal mercies" as well as Magawisca's "valiant act" in saving Everell, and hints "at the authorities for the merciful requital of these deeds" in various biblical examples, including "David's generosity to Mephibosheth, the son of Jonathan, the son of Saul, wherein he passed by the evil that Saul had done him, and only remembered the favours of Jonathan" (*HL* 283).

17. Cooper similarly disparaged "equality" in *The American Democrat* (1838), where he distinguishes between equality before the law (a natural right) from equality of social condition, thus justifying the unequal distribution of wealth and privilege and rule by what John Adams called "a natural aristocracy" (see chapter 4, note 11). Emerson explains: "Equality is one element in a larger problematic of the North Atlantic Enlightenment, whose assumptions about a rational universe are so often contradictory." Nature, hailed as the source of inherent equal rights, often achieves order through inequality; thus, "the necessarily uneven or unequal distributions of power and goods [were] thought to be both a sign of nature's judiciousness and the mark of civilized societies" (79).

18. In fact, Hope (and by extension, Magawisca) resolves a thorny problem the real Winthrop considered in his address, how "to drawe men to the workes of mercy" so that it is not merely "an outward exercise," "the fulfilling of the lawe," but "a Habit in a Soule" that makes Christian love reflexive and spontaneous. Realizing that "force of Argument from goodnes or the necessity of the worke" appeals only to the "rationall minde," Winthrop argues that a "sensiblenes and Sympathy of each others Condicions will necessarily infuse into each parte a native desire and endeavour, to strengthen defend preserve and comfort the other" (2:288–89). In other words, Winthrop argues that in order to make charitable love "instinctive," one must be able to feel what others feel and act on that knowledge. This is precisely Hope's and, more surprisingly, Magawisca's "native" desire.

19. All of the major characters strive for disinterestedness, but Hope most often elicits the description of "angelic" from other characters and the narrator despite possessing a disposition called "gay" and "profane," one that even betrays "a little of the spoiled child" to Esther's "precise" scrutiny (*HL* 181). For example, when Jennet, the Fletcher's Indian-hating servant, opines that "Satan, or at least one of his emissaries, had opened the prison door" for the release of Nelema, Digby counters "that an angel had wrought for the innocent old woman" (113). Or, Magawisca, when she realizes that Hope has come to release her from the dungeon, is filled "with emotions of joy, resembling those a saint may feel, when she sees in vision the ministering angels sent to set her free from her earthly prison: 'I will do all thou shalt command me, Hope Leslie; thou art indeed a spirit of light, and love, and beauty'" (312).

20. As I argue in chapter 3, republicanism puts special emphasis on the social and political

importance of marriage. For this reason, Gussman finds that Sedgwick "rarely criticizes or advocates against marriage per se. Rather, by juxtaposing good and bad unions, Sedgwick instructs readers on how to achieve the ideal" (256).

21. Even the obedient Mrs. Fletcher finds scriptural warrant for widening the scope of Christian charity when she makes what will be her final request that her husband send Everell to live for a time with her brother, who is not a Puritan, so that he can spend some years in the homeland. She reasons, "[A]s I remember there was a good Samaritan, and a faithful centurion, I think we are permitted to enlarge the bounds of our charity to those who work righteousness, albeit not of our communion" (*HL* 35).

22. In a journal entry written a month before Freeman's death in 1829, Sedgwick recollects Freeman's bid for liberty: "Her spirit spurned slavery. 'I would have been willing,' she has often said to me in speaking of the period when she was in hopeless servitude, 'I would have been willing if I could have had one minute of freedom—just to say "*I am free*" I would have been willing to die at the end of that minute.' With this feeling ever alive she heard the Declaration of Independence read. 'If all are free and equal,' she said, 'why are we slaves?' and at her instance my father commenced a suit in the Supreme Court the result of which was . . . that the blacks of the Commonwealth were restored to their natural rights—declared free" (*Power* 125–26).

23. This, however, represents only one side of Theodore Sedgwick's personality, which E. H. Foster describes as "authoritarian and arrogant . . . unable to entertain new ideas—unless they had Federalist sanction or that of the Constitution" (28). Although he participated in other legal efforts to free slaves and was a member of the Abolition Society of Pennsylvania, Theodore also spoke in Congress against the abolition of slavery nationally and "was largely responsible for the first Fugitive Slave Law (1791), which he thought was essential for the well-being of the South and hence of the rest of the country as well" (29–30).

24. Kelley argues that Sedgwick divides her representation of Freeman into two distinct portraits: "the beloved Mumbet . . . inscribed in the autobiography and journals . . . as an icon . . . untouched by the disabilities of the racially based institution of slavery that dominated late eighteenth-century America" and "Elizabeth Freeman, the African American who had challenged slavery's legality," celebrated and inscribed with agency by Sedgwick in her sketch "Slavery in New England," published in *Bentley's Miscellany* in 1853 (16–17). Thus, one could argue the iconic, maternal figure of the nurturing woman of color—the "mammy"—lurks behind Sedgwick's portrayal of Magawisca. Castiglia draws out these negative implications, arguing that Hope's relationship to Magawisca rehearses Sedgwick's relationship with Freeman, and in both "the use of the exoticized women of color to represent the wild 'other' of domesticity builds on constructions of Native and African Americans as more 'natural,' less 'civilized' than whites, even while the white heroines criticize such constructions" (*Bound and Determined* 163).

25. I allude to the study of Williams's story by Demos. See also Weierman.

26. Later, when the party of ill-sorted lovers visits Governor's Island and they reminisce about the early days in Bethel, Digby describes the happiness of Everell and Hope but alludes to the prior connection between Everell and Magawisca using the same term. He says to Everell: "It is odd what vagaries come and go in a body's mind; time was, when I viewed you as good as mated with Magawisca" (*HL* 214). In the farewell scene, Magawisca reminds them: "Nelema told me your souls were mated" (330).

27. This two-stanza epigraph, not identified in any edition of the text, comes from a poem entitled "Sachem's Hill" by Eliza Cabot Follen in her *Poems* (1839). A close friend of Sedgwick's and a prolific writer, Follen went on to marry over Sedgwick's strenuous objection and became a prominent abolitionist. Follen's poem not only stages the vanishing of Indians in the vicinity of Boston but also presents them as proleptically Christian, a view Sedgwick would have endorsed.

28. Silverman discusses two forms of adult identification with others, based upon German philosopher Max Scheler's study *The Nature of Sympathy* (1923). "Idiopathic" identification is "incorporative" and "annihilatory" in relation to the other, like Cheng's notion of "racial melancholy." But Scheler posits a "heteropathic" or excorporative identification-at-a-distance, where "the visual imago itself remains stubbornly exterior" to the self. Silverman proposes this "externalizing logic" as "a gift of love" that "is a necessary step in the coming of the subject to an ethical or nonviolent relation to the other" (23, 2–3).

Epilogue

1. There is a large anthropological literature on friendship in different cultures. See, for example, Brain and more recently Bell and Coleman. For a discussion of friendship in different cultures from a philosophical perspective, see part 2 of *The Changing Face of Friendship*, edited by Rouner. For a comparative analysis, see *Friendship East and West*, edited by Leaman.

WORKS CITED

Ackelsberg, Martha A. " 'Sisters' or 'Comrades'? The Politics of Friends and Families."
Families, Politics, and Public Policy: A Feminist Dialogue on Women and the State. Ed.
Irene Diamond. New York: Longman, 1983. 339–56.

Ackerman, Susan. *When Heroes Love: The Ambiguity of Eros in the Stories of Gilgamesh
and David.* New York: Columbia University Press, 2005.

Adams, Abigail. *The Book of Abigail and John: Selected Letters of the Adams Family, 1762–
1784.* Ed. L. H. Butterfield, Marc Friedlaender, and Mary-Jo Kline. Cambridge: Harvard University Press, 1975

Addison, Joseph. *Cato. The Miscellaneous Works of Joseph Addison.* Vol. 2. London: Lewis
A. Lewis, 1830. 43–138.

Aelred of Rievaulx. *Spiritual Friendship.* Trans. Marg Eugenia Laker. Washington, D.C.:
Cistercian Publications Press, 1974.

Aguilar, Grace. *Woman's Friendship; A Story of Domestic Life.* New York: A. Appleton and
Company, 1857.

Alarcón, Norma. "The Theoretical Subject(s) of *This Bridge Called My Back* and Anglo-
American Feminism." *Making Face, Making Soul, Haciendo Caras: Creative and Critical Perspectives by Feminists of Color.* Ed. Gloria Anzaldúa. San Francisco: Aunt Lute
Books, 1990. 356–69.

Allan, Graham. *Friendship: Developing a Sociological Perspective.* Hempstead, N.Y.: Harvester Wheatsheaf, 1989.

Allen, Jeffner. *Lesbian Philosophy: Explorations.* Palo Alto, Calif.: Institute for Lesbian
Studies, 1986.

Ames, William. *Technometry.* 1633. Trans. Lee W. Gibbs. Philadelphia: University of
Pennsylvania Press, 1979.

Anderson, Douglas. *A House Divided: Domesticity and Community in American Literature.* Cambridge: Cambridge University Press, 1990.

Anzaldúa, Gloria. "(Un)natural Bridges, (Un)safe Spaces." *This Bridge We Call Home:
Radical Visions for Transformation.* Ed. Gloria Anzaldúa and AnaLouise Keating. New
York: Routledge, 2002. 1–5.

Argüelles, José. *The Mayan Factor: Path beyond Technology.* Santa Fe: Bear and Company, 1996.

Aristotle. *Ethica Nicomachea. The Basic Works of Aristotle.* Ed. Richard McKeon. New
York: Random House, 1941. 935–1126.

——. *Magna Moralia*. Trans. G. Cyril Armstrong. Loeb Classical Library. Cambridge: Harvard University Press, 1990. Vol. 23 of *Aristotle in Twenty-three Volumes*. 1926–90. 426–685.

——. *Nichomachean Ethics*. Trans. T. Irwin. Indianapolis: Hackett, 1985.

——. *Nicomachean Ethics, Books VIII and IX*. Trans. Michael Pakaluk. Oxford: Clarendon Press, 1998.

——. *Politics. The Basic Works of Aristotle*. Ed. Richard McKeon. New York: Random House, 1941. 1114–1316.

Armstrong, G. Cyril. Introduction. *Magna Moralia*. Trans. G. Cyril Armstrong. Loeb Classical Library. Cambridge: Harvard University Press, 1990. Vol. 23 of *Aristotle in Twenty-three Volumes*. 1926–90. 426–45.

Aubenque, Pierre. "On Friendship in Aristotle." *Friendship*. Spec. issue of *South Atlantic Quarterly* 97.1 (Winter 1998): 23–28.

Auerbach, Nina. *Communities of Women: An Idea in Fiction*. Cambridge: Harvard University Press, 1978.

Bacon, Francis. *The Essays or Counsels, Civill and Morall*. 1601. Ed. Michael Kiernan. Cambridge: Harvard University Press, 1985.

Barkan, Leonard. *Nature's Work of Art: The Human Body as Image of the World*. New Haven, Conn.: Yale University Press, 1975.

Barnes, Elizabeth. *States of Sympathy: Seduction and Democracy in the American Novel*. New York: Columbia University Press, 1997.

Barnett, Louise K. *The Ignoble Savage: American Literary Racism, 1790–1890*. Westport, Conn.: Greenwood Press, 1975.

Bartolovich, Crystal. "Consumerism, or the Cultural Logic of Late Cannibalism." *Cannibalism and the Colonial World*. Ed. Francis Barker, Peter Hulme, and Margaret Iverson. New York: Cambridge University Press, 1998. 204–37.

Baym, Nina. "How Men and Women Wrote Indian Stories." *New Essays on* The Last of the Mohicans. Ed. H. Daniel Peck. Cambridge: Cambridge University Press, 1992. 67–86.

Beard, James Franklin. "Historical Introduction." *The Last of the Mohicans; A Narrative of 1757*. By James Fenimore Cooper. Albany: State University of New York Press, 1983. xv–xlviii.

Bell, Sandra, and Simon Coleman, eds. *The Anthropology of Friendship*. New York: Berg, 1999.

Bercovitch, Sacvan. "Puritan Origins Revisited: The 'City upon a Hill' as a Model of Tradition and Innovation." *Early America Reexplored: New Readings*. Ed. Klaus H. Schmidt and Fritz Fleischman. New York: Peter Lang, 2000. 31–48.

Bergland, Renée. *The National Uncanny: Indian Ghosts and American Subjects*. Hanover, N.H.: University Press of New England, 1999.

Berlant, Lauren. *The Queen of America Goes to Washington City: Essays on Sex and Citizenship*. Durham, N.C.: Duke University Press, 1997.

Beverly, Robert. *The History and Present State of Virginia*. 1705. Ed. Louis B. Wright. Chapel Hill: University of North Carolina Press, 1947.

Binchy, Maeve. Prologue. *Friendship: A Celebration of Humanity*. New York: William Morrow, 2001. 19–23.

Blanchot, Maurice. *Friendship*. Trans. Elizabeth Rottenberg. Stanford, Calif.: Stanford University Press, 1997.

Bloch, Ruth. "The Gendered Meanings of Virtue in Revolutionary America." *Signs* 3 (Summer 1987): 37–58.

Boone, Joseph Allen. *Tradition Counter Tradition: Love and the Form of Fiction*. Chicago: University of Chicago Press, 1987.

Booth, Wayne C. *The Company We Keep: An Ethics of Fiction*. Berkeley: University of California Press, 1988.

Boswell, John. *Same-Sex Unions in Premodern Europe*. New York: Villiard Books, 1994.

Bradford, William. *Of Plymouth Plantation, 1620–1647*. Ed. Samuel Eliot Morison. New York: Alfred A. Knopf, 1952.

Brading, D. A. *The First America: The Spanish Monarch, Creole Patriots, and the Liberal State, 1492–1867*. Cambridge: Cambridge University Press, 1991.

Brain, Robert. *Friends and Lovers*. London: Hart-Davis, MacGibbon, 1976.

Brault, Pascale-Anne, and Michael Naas, eds. *The Work of Mourning / Jacques Derrida*. Chicago: University of Chicago Press, 2001.

Bray, Alan. *The Friend*. Chicago: University of Chicago Press, 2003.

Bremer, Francis J. "The Heritage of John Winthrop: Religion along the Stour Valley, 1548–1630." *New England Quarterly* 70.4 (December 1997): 515–47.

———. *John Winthrop: America's Forgotten Founding Father*. Oxford: Oxford University Press, 2003.

Brodhead, Richard. *Cultures of Letters*. Chicago: University of Chicago Press, 1993.

Brown, Gillian. *The Consent of the Governed: The Lockean Legacy in Early American Culture*. Cambridge: Harvard University Press, 2001.

Burgett, Bruce. *Sentimental Bodies: Sex, Gender and Citizenship in the Early Republic*. Princeton, N.J.: Princeton University Press, 1998.

Burnham, Michelle. *Captivity and Sentiment: Cultural Exchange in American Literature, 1682–1861*. Hanover, N.H.: University Press of New England, 1997.

Burt, Donald X. *Friendship and Society: An Introduction to Augustine's Practical Philosophy*. Grand Rapids, Mich.: William B. Eerdmans, 1999.

Burton, Robert. *The Anatomy of Melancholy*. 1621. New York: Vintage Books, 1977.

Butler, Judith. *Bodies That Matter: On the Discursive Limits of "Sex."* New York: Routledge, 1993.

———. "For a Careful Reading." *Feminist Contentions: A Philosophical Exchange*. By Seyla Benhabib, Judith Butler, Drucilla Cornell, and Nancy Fraser. New York: Routledge, 1995. 127–44.

——. "Gender Trouble, Feminist Theory, and Psychoanalytic Discourse." *Feminism/Post-modernism*. Ed. Linda J. Nicholson. New York: Routledge, 1990. 324–40.

——. "Melancholy Gender/Refused Identification." *Constructing Masculinity*. Ed. Maurice Berger, Brian Wallis, and Simon Waston. New York: Routledge, 1995. 21–36.

——. *The Psychic Life of Power: Theories in Subjection*. Stanford, Calif.: Stanford University Press, 1997.

Byrd, William. *Histories of the Dividing Line Betwixt Virginia and North Carolina*. 1841. Raleigh: North Carolina Historical Commission, 1929.

Cabeza de Vaca, Alvar Nuñez. *The Narrative of Cabeza de Vaca*. 1542. Ed. Rolena Adorno and Patrick Charles Pautz. Lincoln: University of Nebraska Press, 1999.

Calloway, Colin G. *New Worlds for All: Indians, Europeans, and the Remaking of Early America*. Baltimore: Johns Hopkins University Press, 1997.

Canning, J. P. "Law, Sovereignty, and Corporation Theory, 1300–1450." *The Cambridge History of Medieval Political Thought c. 350–1450*. Ed. J. H. Burns. Cambridge: Cambridge University Press, 1998. 454–519.

Carpenter, Edward. *Ioläus: An Anthology of Friendship*. 1908. New York: Mitchell Kennerley, 1917. <http://www.fordham.edu/halsall/pwh/iolaus.html>.

Castiglia, Christopher. *Bound and Determined: Captivity, Culture-Crossing, and White Womanhood from Mary Rowlandson to Patty Hearst*. Chicago: University of Chicago Press, 1996.

——. "In Praise of Extra-vagrant Women: *Hope Leslie* and the Captivity Romance." *Legacy* 6 (Fall 1989): 3–16.

Certeau, Michel de. *Heterologies: Discourse on the Other*. Trans. Brian Massumi. Minneapolis: University of Minnesota Press, 1986.

——. *The Writing of History*. Trans. Tom Conley. New York: Columbia University Press, 1988.

Chambers-Schiller, Lee Virginia. *Liberty, a Better Husband: Single Women in America: The Generations of 1780–1840*. New Haven, Conn.: Yale University Press, 1984.

Chapman, Mary, and Glenn Hendler, eds. *Sentimental Men: Masculinity and the Politics of Affect in American Culture*. Berkeley: University of California Press, 1999.

Cheng, Anne Anlin. *The Melancholy of Race*. New York: Oxford University Press, 2001.

"Cherokee Nation v. Georgia." <http://www.cviog.uga.edu/Projects/gainfo/cherovga.htm>. December 19, 2005.

Chesnutt, Charles. *The Journals of Charles W. Chesnutt*. Ed. Richard Brodhead. Durham, N.C.: Duke University Press, 1993.

Cicero. *On Old Age and On Friendship*. Trans. Frank O. Copley. Ann Arbor: University of Michigan Press, 1967.

Clark, Gillian, and Stephen R. L. Clark. "Friendship in the Christian Tradition." *The Dialectics of Friendship*. Ed. Roy Porter and Sylvana Tomaselli. New York: Routledge, 1989. 26–44.

Clark, Vèvè A. "Developing Diaspora Literacy and *Marasa* Consciousness." *Comparative*

American Identities: Race, Sex, and Nationality in the Modern Text. Ed. Hortense J. Spillers. New York: Routledge, 1991. 40–61.

Clarke, W. M. "Achilles and Patroclus in Love." *Hermes* 106 (1978): 381–96.

Code, Lorraine. *What Can She Know? Feminist Theory and the Construction of Knowledge.* Ithaca, N.Y.: Cornell University Press, 1991.

Colacurcio, Michael. " 'The Woman's Own Choice': Sex, Metaphor, and the Puritan 'Sources' of *The Scarlet Letter*." *New Essays on* The Scarlet Letter. Ed. Michael Colacurcio. Cambridge: Cambridge University Press, 1985. 101–35.

Cooper, D. Jason. *Mithras: Mysteries and Initiation Rediscovered.* York Beach, Maine: Samuel Weiser, 1996.

Cooper, James Fenimore. *The Deerslayer, or The First War-Path.* 1841. Albany: State University of New York Press, 1987.

———. *The Last of the Mohicans; A Narrative of 1757.* 1826. Albany: State University of New York Press, 1983.

———. *The Pathfinder, or the Inland Sea.* 1840. Albany: State University of New York Press, 1981.

———. *The Pioneers, or the Sources of the Susquehanna; A Descriptive Tale.* 1823. Albany: State University of New York Press, 1980.

Cornell, Drucilla. "What Is Ethical Feminism?" *Feminist Contentions: A Philosophical Exchange.* By Seyla Benhabib, Judith Butler, Drucilla Cornell, and Nancy Fraser. New York: Routledge, 1995. 75–106.

Cosslett, Tess. *Woman to Woman: Female Friendship in Victorian Fiction.* Atlantic Highlands, N.J.: Humanities Press, 1988.

Cott, Nancy. *The Bonds of Womanhood: "Women's Sphere" in New England, 1780–1835.* New Haven, Conn.: Yale University Press, 1977.

———. "Feminist Theory, Feminist Movements: The Past before Us." *What Is Feminism: A Re-examination.* Ed. Juliet Mitchell and Ann Oakley. New York: Pantheon, 1986. 49–62.

Coviello, Peter. "Agonizing Affection: Affect and Nation in Early America." *Early American Literature* 37.3 (2002): 439–68.

Crain, Caleb. *American Sympathy: Men, Friendship, and Literature in the New Nation.* New Haven, Conn.: Yale University Press, 2001.

Curtius Rufus, Quintus. *The History of Alexander.* Trans. John Yardley with notes by Waldemar Heckel. Harmondsworth, U.K.: Penguin Books, 1984.

Dallmayr, Fred. "Derrida and Friendship." *The Challenge to Friendship in Modernity.* Ed. Preston King and Heather Devere. Portland: Frank Cass, 2000. 105–30.

Davidson, Cathy. Introduction. *The Coquette.* By Hannah Webster Foster. Ed. Cathy Davidson. New York: Oxford University Press, 1986.

———. Preface. *No More Separate Spheres!* Spec. issue of *American Literature* 70 (1998): 443–64.

Dawson, Hugh J. " 'Christian Charitie' as Colonial Discourse: Rereading Winthrop's Sermon in Its English Context." *Early American Literature* 33 (1998): 117–49.

——. "John Winthrop's Rite of Passage: The Origins of the 'Christian Charitie' Discourse." *Early American Literature* 26 (1991): 219–31.

Dekker, George, and John P. McWilliams, eds. *Fenimore Cooper: The Critical Heritage*. London: Routledge and Kegan Paul, 1973.

Delbanco, Andrew. *The Puritan Ordeal*. Cambridge: Harvard University Press, 1989.

Demos, John. *The Unredeemed Captive: A Family Story from Early America*. New York: Knopf, 1994.

Dennis, Matthew. *Cultivating a Landscape of Peace: Iroquois-European Encounters in Seventeenth-Century America*. Ithaca, N.Y.: Cornell University Press, 1993.

Den Uyl, Douglas J., and Charles L. Griswold Jr. "Adam Smith on Friendship and Love." *Review of Metaphysics* 49 (March 1996): 609–37.

Derrida, Jacques. " 'Eating Well,' or the Calculation of the Subject: An Interview with Jacques Derrida." *Who Comes after the Subject?* Ed. Eduardo Cadava, Peter Connor, and Jean-Luc Nancy. New York: Routledge, 1991. 96–119.

——. *Mémoires: For Paul de Man*. Trans. Cecile Lindsay, Jonathan Culler, Eduardo Cadava, and Peggy Kamuf. Ed. Avital Ronell and Eduardo Cadava. New York: Columbia University Press, 1989.

——. "The Politics of Friendship." *Journal of Philosophy* 85 (November 1988): 632–44.

——. "Politics of Friendship." Trans. Gabriel Motzkin and Michael Syrotinski, with Thomas Keenan. *American Imago* 50.3 (1993): 353–91.

——. *Politics of Friendship*. Trans. George Collins. London: Verso, 1997.

Deutscher, Penelope. "Mourning the Other, Cultural Cannibalism, and the Politics of Friendship (Jacques Derrida and Luce Irigaray)." *differences: A Journal of Feminist Cultural Studies* 10 (1998): 159–84.

Devere, Heather. "Reviving Greco-Roman Friendship: A Bibliographic Review." *The Challenge to Friendship in Modernity*. Ed. Preston King and Heather Devere. Portland: Frank Cass, 2000. 149–87.

Dietz, Mary. "Citizenship with a Feminist Face: The Problem with Maternal Thinking." *Political Theory* 13 (February 1985): 19–38.

Dillon, Elizabeth Maddock. *The Gender of Freedom: Fictions of Liberalism and the Literary Public Sphere*. Stanford, Calif.: Stanford University Press, 2004.

Donne, John. *John Donne: The Complete English Poems*. Ed. A. J. Smith. London: Penguin Books, 1986.

Easterling, Pat. "Friendship and the Greeks." *The Dialectics of Friendship*. Ed. Roy Porter and Sylvana Tomaselli. New York: Routledge, 1989. 11–25.

Ellison, Julie. *Cato's Tears and the Making of Anglo-American Emotion*. Chicago: University of Chicago Press, 1999.

——. *Delicate Subjects: Romanticism, Gender, and the Ethics of Understanding*. Ithaca, N.Y.: Cornell University Press, 1990.

Elyot, Thomas. *The Boke Named The Governour*. 1531. Ed. Foster Watson. New York: Everyman Press, 1907.

Emerson, Amanda. "From Equivalence to Equity: The Management of an Ancient American Myth." *differences: A Journal of Feminist Cultural Studies* 14 (2005): 78–105.

Encyclopedia Mythica. <http://www.pantheon.org/mythica>.

Erasmus. *Adages.* Trans. Margaret Mann Phillips. Toronto: University of Toronto Press, 1982. Vol. 31 of *The Collected Works of Erasmus.* 86 vols. 1974–93.

———. *Apophthegmes.* Trans. Nicholas Udall. London: Richard Grafton, 1542. December 5, 2005. *Early English Books Online.* <http://gateway.proquest.com/openurl?ctx—ver=Z39.88-2003&res—id=xri:eebo&rft—id=xri:eebo:image:5790>.

Erkkila, Betsy. *Mixed Bloods and Other Crosses: Rethinking American Literature from the Revolution to the Culture Wars.* Philadelphia: University of Pennsylvania Press, 2005.

Euripides. *Orestes.* Trans. E. P. Coleridge. *The Perseus Digital Library.* <http://www.perseus.tufts.edu>.

The Federalist Papers. Ed. Clinton Rossiter. New York: New American Library, 1961.

Felix, Marcus Minucius. *The Octavius of Marcus Minucius Felix.* Trans. G. W. Clarke. New York: Newman Press, 1974.

Fenton, William N. *The Great Law and the Longhouse: A Political History of the Iroquois Confederacy.* Norman: University of Oklahoma Press, 1998.

Fetterley, Judith. " 'My Sister! My Sister!': The Rhetoric of Catharine Sedgwick's *Hope Leslie.*" *No More Separate Spheres!* Spec. issue of *American Literature* 70 (1998): 491–516.

Fiedler, Leslie. "Come Back to the Raft Ag'in, Huck Honey!" *The Collected Essays of Leslie Fiedler.* Vol. 1. New York: Stein and Day, 1971. 142–51.

———. *Love and Death in the American Novel.* New York: Anchor Books, 1966.

Fiering, Norman. *Moral Philosophy at Seventeenth-Century Harvard: A Discipline in Transition.* Chapel Hill: University of North Carolina Press, 1981.

Fitzgerald, John T., ed. *Greco-Roman Perspectives on Friendship.* Atlanta: Scholars Press, 1997.

Fliegelman, Jay. *Prodigals and Pilgrims: The American Revolution against Patriarchal Authority, 1750–1800.* Cambridge: Cambridge University Press, 1982.

Ford, Douglas. "Inscribing the 'Impartial Observer' in Sedgwick's *Hope Leslie.*" *Legacy* 14 (1997): 81–97.

Foster, Edward Halsey. *Catharine Maria Sedgwick.* New York: Twayne, 1973.

Foster, Hannah Webster. *The Coquette.* The Power of Sympathy *and* The Coquette. Ed. Carla Mulford. New York: Penguin, 1996.

Foster, Stephen. *Their Solitary Way: The Puritan Social Ethic in the First Century of Settlement in New England.* New Haven, Conn.: Yale University Press, 1971.

Foucault, Michel. "Friendship as a Way of Life." *Ethics: Subjectivity and Truth.* Ed. Paul Rabinow. Trans. Robert Hurley and others. New York: New Press, 1997. Vol. 1 of *Essential Works of Foucault, 1954–1984.* 3 vols. 1997. 135–40.

———. *The Order of Things: An Archaeology of the Human Sciences.* 1971. New York: Vintage Books, 1994.

Frankenburg, Ruth. "When We Are Capable of Stopping, We Begin to See: Being White, Seeing Whiteness." *Names We Call Home: Autobiography on Racial Identity*. Ed. Becky Thompsom and Sangeeta Tyagi. New York: Routledge, 1996. 3–17.

Freccero, Carla. "Cannibalism, Homophobia, Women: Montaigne's 'Des cannibales' and 'De l'amitié.' " *Women, "Race," and Writing in the Early Modern Period*. Ed. Margo Hendricks and Patricia Parker. New York: Routledge, 1994. 73–83.

——. "Toward a Psychoanalytics of Historiography: Michel de Certeau's Early Modern Encounters." *South Atlantic Quarterly* 100.2 (Spring 2001): 365–79.

Freibert, Lucy M., and Barbara A. White, eds. *Hidden Hands: An Anthology of American Women Writers, 1790–1870*. New Brunswick, N.J.: Rutgers University Press, 1985.

Freud, Sigmund. *The Ego and the Id*. 1923. New York: Norton, 1962. Vol. 19 of *Standard Edition*. 24 vols. 1953–74.

Friedman, Marilyn. *What Are Friends For? Feminist Perspectives on Personal Relationships and Moral Theory*. Ithaca, N.Y.: Cornell University Press, 1993.

Friedman, Susan Stanford. *Mappings: Feminism and the Cultural Geography of Encounter*. Princeton, N.J.: Princeton University Press, 1998.

Friendship: A Celebration of Humanity. New York: William Morrow, 2001.

Fuss, Diana. *Identification Papers*. New York: Routledge, 1995.

Gardner, Jared. *Master Plots: Race and the Founding of an American Literature, 1787–1845*. Baltimore: Johns Hopkins University Press, 1998.

Geneva Bible, The Annotated New Testament 1602 Edition. Ed. Gerald T. Sheppard. New York: Pilgrim Press, 1989.

Gibson, Charles, ed. *The Spanish Tradition in America*. Columbia: University of South Carolina Press, 1968.

Giddings, Paula. *When and Where I Enter: The Impact of Black Women on Race and Sex in America*. New York: Bantam Books, 1984.

Gonzalez, Francisco J. "Plato's *Lysis*: An Enactment of Philosophical Kinship." *Ancient Philosophy* 15.1 (1995): 69–90.

Gordis, Lisa. "The Experience of Covenant Theology in George Herbert's *The Temple*." *Journal of Religion* 76.3 (1996): 383–401.

Gould, Philip. *Covenant and Republic: Historical Romance and the Politics of Puritanism*. New York: Cambridge University Press, 1996.

Griffin, Farah Jasmine, ed. *Beloved Sisters and Loving Friends: Letters from Rebecca Primus of Royal Oak, Maryland, and Addie Brown of Hartford, Connecticut, 1854–1868*. New York: Ballantine, 1999.

Gussman, Deborah. " 'Equal to Either Fortune': Sedgwick's *Married or Single?* and Feminism." *Catharine Maria Sedgwick: Critical Perspectives*. Ed. Lucinda Damon-Back and Victoria Clements. Boston: Northeastern University Press, 2003. 252–67.

Haan, Richard L. "Covenant and Consensus: Iroquois and English, 1676–1760." *Beyond the Covenant Chain: The Iroquois and Their Neighbors in Indian North America, 1600–*

1800. Ed. Daniel K. Richter and James H. Merrell. Syracuse, N.Y.: Syracuse University Press, 1987. 41–57.

Haggerty, George E. *Unnatural Affections: Women and Fiction in the Later Eighteenth Century*. Bloomington: Indiana University Press, 1998.

Hanke, Lewis. *Aristotle and the American Indians: A Study in Race Prejudice in the Modern World*. London: Hollis and Carter, 1959.

Harris, Sharon M. "Hannah Webster Foster's *The Coquette*: Critiquing Franklin's America." *Redefining the Political Novel: American Women Writers, 1797–1901*. Ed. Sharon M. Harris. Knoxville: University of Tennessee Press, 1995. 1–22.

Harris, Susan K. "The Limits of Authority: Catharine Maria Sedgwick and the Politics of Resistance." *Catharine Maria Sedgwick: Critical Perspectives*. Ed. Lucinda Damon-Back and Victoria Clements. Boston: Northeastern University Press, 2003. 272–85.

Hawthorne, Nathaniel. *The Scarlet Letter*. 1850. New York: Norton, 1962.

Heckewelder, John. *An Account of the History, Manners, and Customs of the Indian Nations, Who Once Inhabited Pennsylvania and the Neighbouring States*. Vol. 1. Philadelphia: Abraham Small, 1819.

Heller, Agnes. "The Beauty of Friendship." *Friendship*. Spec. issue of *South Atlantic Quarterly* 97.1 (Winter 1998): 5–22.

Hemphill, C. Dallett. "Class, Gender, and the Regulation of Emotional Expression in Revolutionary-Era Conduct Literature." *An Emotional History of the United States*. Ed. Peter Stearns and Jan Lewis. New York: New York University Press, 1998. 33–51.

Hendler, Glenn. *Public Sentiments: Structures of Feeling in Nineteenth-Century American Literature*. Chapel Hill: University of North Carolina Press, 2001.

Herndl, Diane Price. "Style and the Sentimental Gaze in *The Last of the Mohicans*." *Narrative* 9.3 (October 2001): 259–82.

Heyd, Milly. *Mutual Reflections: Jews and Blacks in American Art*. New Brunswick, N.J.: Rutgers University Press, 1999.

Hirsch, Marianne. *Family Frames: Photography, Narrative, and Postmemory*. Cambridge: Harvard University Press: 1997.

——. "Introduction: Familial Looking." *The Familial Gaze*. Ed. Marianne Hirsch. Hanover, N.H.: University Press of New England, 1999. xi–xxv.

Hirshman, Linda Redlick. "The Book of 'A.'" *Feminist Interpretations of Aristotle*. Ed. Cynthia A. Freeland. University Park: Pennsylvania State University Press, 1998. 201–47.

Hock, Ronald F. "An Extraordinary Friend in Chariton's *Callirhoe*: The Importance of Friendship in the Greek Romances." *Greco-Roman Perspectives on Friendship*. Ed. John T. Fitzgerald. Atlanta: Scholars Press, 1997. 145–62.

Holy Bible, King James Version. Cleveland: World Publishing Company, n.d.

Homer. *The Iliad*. Trans. Robert Fagles. New York: Viking, 1990.

——. *The Odyssey*. Trans. Robert Fagles. New York: Viking, 1996.

hooks, bell. *Black Looks: Race and Representation*. Boston: South End Press, 1992.

Hudson, Lorna. *The Usurer's Daughter: Male Friendship and Fictions of Women in Sixteenth-Century England*. New York: Routledge, 1994.

Hulme, Peter. *Colonial Encounters: Europe and the Native Caribbean, 1492–1797*. London: Methuen, 1986.

Hunt, Mary. *Fierce Tenderness: A Feminist Theology of Friendship*. New York: Crossroad, 1991.

Hyatte, Reginald. *The Arts of Friendship: The Idealization of Friendship in Medieval and Early Renaissance Literature*. Leiden: E. J. Brill, 1994.

Iamblichus. *On the Pythagorean Way of Life: Text, Translation, and Notes*. Ed. John Dillon and Jackson Hershbell. Atlanta: Scholars Press, 1991.

Innes, Stephen. *Creating the Commonwealth: The Economic Culture of Puritan New England*. New York: W. W. Norton, 1995.

Irigaray, Luce. *Etre Deux*. Paris: Grasset, 1997.

——. *I Love to You: Sketch for a Felicity within History*. Trans. Alison Martin. New York: Routledge, 1996.

Jackson, Gregory. " 'A Dowry of Suffering': Consent, Contract, and Political Coverture in John W. De Forest's Reconstruction Romance." *American Literary History* 15.2 (Summer 2003): 276–310.

Jakobsen, Janet R. *Working Alliances and the Politics of Difference: Diversity and Feminist Ethics*. Bloomington: University of Indiana Press, 1998.

Jalalzai, Zubeda. "Race and the Puritan Body Politic." *MELUS* 29 (Fall/Winter 2004): 259–72.

Jefferson, Thomas. *Jefferson's Literary Commonplace Book*. Ed. Douglas L. Wilson. *The Papers of Thomas Jefferson*, 2nd series. Princeton, N.J.: Princeton University Press, 1989.

——. *The Writings of Thomas Jefferson: Being His Autobiography, Correspondence, Reports, Messages, Addresses and Other Writings, Official and Private*. 9 vols. Ed. H. A. Washington. New York: H. W. Derby, 1861.

Jennings, Francis. *The Ambiguous Iroquois Empire: The Covenant Chain Confederation of Indian Tribes with English Colonies from Its Beginning to the Lancaster Treaty of 1744*. New York: W. W. Norton, 1984.

Jennings, Francis, ed., with William N. Fenton, Mary A. Druke, and David R. Miller. *The History and Culture of Iroquois Diplomacy: An Interdisciplinary Guide to the Treaties of the Six Nations and Their League*. Syracuse, N.Y.: Syracuse University Press, 1985.

Johnson, Edward. *Johnson's Wonder-Working Providence: 1628–1651*. Ed. J. Franklin Jameson. New York: Charles Scribner's Sons, 1910.

Joplin, Patricia Klindienst. "The *Voice of the Shuttle* Is Ours." *Stanford Literature Review* 1 (Spring 1984): 25–53.

Kantorowicz, Ernst. *The King's Two Bodies: A Study in Mediaeval Political Theology*. Princeton, N.J.: Princeton University Press, 1967.

Karafilis, Maria. "Catharine Maria Sedgwick's *Hope Leslie*: The Crisis between Ethical Political Action and U.S. Literary Nationalism in the New Republic." *American Transcendental Quarterly* 12 (1998): 327–44.

Karcher, Caroline. Introduction. *Hobomock and Other Writings on Indians*. By Lydia Maria Child. New Brunswick, N.J.: Rutgers University Press, 1986. ix–xxxviii.

Kelley, Mary, ed. Introduction. *The Power of Her Sympathy: The Autobiography and Journal of Catharine Maria Sedgwick*. Boston: Massachusetts Historical Society, 1993. 3–41.

Kelly, William P. *Plotting America's Past: Fenimore Cooper and the Leatherstocking Tales*. Carbondale: Southern Illinois University Press, 1983.

Kerber, Linda. *Women of the Republic: Intellect and Ideology in Revolutionary America*. Chapel Hill: University of North Carolina Press, 1980.

Kierkegaard, Søren. *Works of Love*. Trans. Howard Hong and Edna Hong. Princeton, N.J.: Princeton University Press, 1995.

Kolodny, Annette. *The Lay of the Land: Metaphor as Experience and History in American Life and Letters*. Chapel Hill: University of North Carolina Press, 1975.

Konstan, David. "Friendship and the State." *Hyperboreus* 1.2 (1994/95): 1–10.

———. *Friendship in the Classical World*. Cambridge: Cambridge University Press, 1997.

———. *Sexual Symmetry: Love in the Ancient Novel and Related Genres*. Princeton, N.J.: Princeton University Press, 1994.

Lacan, Jacques. *Écrits: A Selection*. Trans. Alan Sheridan. New York: W. W. Norton, 1977.

The Lady's Magazine and Musical Repository (New York). November 1801. 245–47.

Laertius, Diogenes. *Lives of Eminent Philosophers*. Trans. R. D. Hicks. 2 vols. Loeb Classical Editions. Cambridge: Harvard University Press, 1979–80.

Lang, Amy Schrager. *Prophetic Woman: Anne Hutchinson and the Problem of Dissent in the Literature of New England*. Berkeley: University of California Press, 1987.

Langer, Ullrich. *Perfect Friendship: Studies in Literature and Moral Philosophy from Boccaccio to Corneille*. Geneva: Librairie Droz, 1994.

Lauter, Paul, et al., eds. *Heath Anthology of American Literature*. 2 vols. Boston: Houghton Mifflin, 2002.

Lawrence, D. H. *Studies in Classic American Literature*. 1923. New York: Viking Press, 1961.

Leach, Eleanor Winsor. "Absence and Desire in Cicero's *De Amicitia*." *Classical World* 87.2 (1993): 3–20.

Leaman, Oliver, ed. *Friendship East and West: Philosophical Perspectives*. Richmond, Surrey: Curzon Press, 1996.

Leites, Edmund. "The Duty to Desire: Love, Friendship, and Sexuality in Some Puritan Theories of Marriage." *Journal of Social History* 15.3 (1982): 383–408.

Lewis, Jan. "The Republican Wife: Virtue and Seduction in the Early Republic." *William and Mary Quarterly* 44.4 (October 1987): 689–721.

———. " 'Those Scenes for Which Alone My Heart Was Made': Affection and Politics in the

Age of Jefferson and Hamilton." *An Emotional History of the United States*. Ed. Peter Stearns and Jan Lewis. New York: New York University Press, 1998. 52–65.

Lewis, R. W. B. *The American Adam: Innocence, Tragedy, and Tradition in the Nineteenth Century*. Chicago: University of Chicago Press, 1955.

Looby, Christopher. *Voicing America: Language, Literary Form, and the Origins of the United States*. Chicago: University of Chicago Press, 1996.

Lugones, María. "Playfulness, 'World'-travel, and Loving Perception." *Making Face, Making Soul, Haciendo Caras: Creative and Critical Perspectives by Feminists of Color*. Ed. Gloria Anzaldúa. San Francisco: Aunt Lute Books, 1990. 390–402.

Lugones, María, in collaboration with Pat Alake Rosezelle. "Sisterhood and Friendship as Feminist Models." *The Knowledge Explosion: Generations of Feminist Scholarship*. Ed. Cheris Kramarae and Dale Spender. New York: Teachers College Press, 1992. 406–12.

Lugones, María, and Elizabeth V. Spelman. "Have We Got a Theory for You! Feminist Theory, Cultural Imperialism, and the Demand for 'The Woman's Voice.'" *Women and Values: Readings in Recent Feminist Philosophy*. Ed. Marilyn Pearsall. Belmont, Calif.: Wadsworth, 1986. 19–31.

Luxon, Thomas. *Single Imperfection: Milton, Marriage and Friendship*. Pittsburgh: Duquesne University Press, 2005.

MacIntosh, Peggy. "White Privilege and Male Privilege: A Personal Account of Coming to See Correspondences through Work in Women's Studies." *Race, Class, and Gender: An Anthology*. Ed. Margaret L. Andersen and Patricia Hill Collins. Belmont, Calif.: Wadsworth, 2001. 95–105.

Madison, James. *The Papers of James Madison*. 17 vols. Ed. Robert A. Rutland et al. Chicago: University of Chicago Press, 1977.

Mann, Michael, dir. *The Last of the Mohicans*. Twentieth Century Fox. 1992. <http://www.mohicanpress.com/mo07010.html>.

Marshall, David. *The Surprising Effects of Sympathy: Marivaux, Diderot, Rousseau, and Mary Shelley*. Chicago: University of Chicago Press, 1988.

Martin, Robert K. *Hero, Captain, and Stranger: Male Friendship, Social Critique, and Literary Form in the Sea Novels of Herman Melville*. Chapel Hill: University of North Carolina Press, 1986.

Mavor, Elizabeth. *The Ladies of Llangollen: A Study in Romantic Friendship*. London: Michael Joseph, 1971.

McClintock, Anne. *Imperial Leather: Race, Gender, and Sexuality in the Colonial Context*. New York: Routledge, 1995.

McCullough, Mary. *Black and White Women as Friends: Building Cross-Race Friendships*. Cresskill, N.J.: Hampton Press, 1998.

McMahon, Lucia. "While Our Souls Together Blend: Narrating a Romantic Readership in the Early Republic." *An Emotional History of the United States*. Ed. Peter Stearns and Jan Lewis. New York: New York University Press, 1998. 66–90.

McWilliams, John. The Last of the Mohicans: *Civil Savagery and Savage Civility*. New York: Twayne, 1995.

McWilliams, Wilson Carey. *The Idea of Fraternity in America*. Berkeley: University of California Press, 1973.

Meilaender, Gilbert. *Friendship: A Study in Theological Ethics*. Notre Dame: University of Notre Dame Press, 1981.

Merish, Lori. " 'The Hand of Refined Taste' in the Frontier Landscape: Caroline Kirkland's *A New Home, Who'll Follow?* and the Feminization of American Consumerism." *American Quarterly* 45 (1993): 485–523.

Michaelsen, Scott. "John Winthrop's 'Modell' Covenant and the Company Way." *Early American Literature* 27.2 (1992): 85–100.

Miller, Perry. *Errand into the Wilderness*. Cambridge: Belknap Press, 1956.

———. *Nature's Nation*. Cambridge: Harvard University Press, 1967.

———. *The New England Mind: The Seventeenth Century*. New York: Macmillan, 1939.

Miller, Quentin. " 'A Tyrannically Democratic Force': The Symbolic and Cultural Function of Clothing in Catharine Maria Sedgwick's *Hope Leslie*." *Legacy* 19.2 (2002): 121–36.

Milton, John. *The Doctrine and Discipline of Divorce*. London, 1644. *Milton Reading Room*. November 24, 2005. <http://www.dartmouth.edu/~milton/reading_room/links/index.shtml>.

———. "A Mask Presented at Ludlow Castle, 1634." *Milton Reading Room*. December 10, 2005. <http://www.dartmouth.edu/~milton/reading_room/links/index.shtml>.

———. *Paradise Lost*. *Milton Reading Room*. December 15, 2005. <http://www.dartmouth.edu/~milton/reading_room/links/index.shtml>.

Minow, Martha. *Making All the Difference: Inclusion, Exclusion, and American Law*. Ithaca, N.Y.: Cornell University Press, 1990.

Mitchell, Alan C. " 'Greet The Friends by Name': New Testament Evidence for the Greco-Roman *Topos* on Friendship." *Greco-Roman Perspectives on Friendship*. Ed. John T. Fitzgerald. Atlanta: Scholars Press, 1997. 225–62.

Mitchell, Juliet. *Mad Men and Medusas: Reclaiming Hysteria*. New York: Basic Books, 2000.

Montaigne, Michel de. "Of Friendship." *The Complete Essays of Montaigne*. Trans. Donald M. Frame. Stanford: Stanford University Press, 1958. 135–44.

Moore, Lisa L. *Dangerous Intimacies: Towards a Sapphic History of the British Novel*. Durham, N.C.: Duke University Press, 1997.

Moraga, Cherríe, and Gloria Anzaldúa, eds. *This Bridge Called My Back: Writings by Radical Women of Color*. New York: Kitchen Table, 1983.

Morgan, Edmund S. "John Winthrop's 'Modell of Christian Charity' in a Wider Context." *Huntington Library Quarterly* 50.2 (Spring 1987): 145–51.

———. *The Puritan Dilemma: The Story of John Winthrop*. Boston: Little, Brown, 1958.

Morrell, William. *New England; or, A Briefe Enarration of the Ayre, Earth, Water, Fish and Fowles of that Country, with a Description of the Natures, Orders, Habits, and Religion of the Natives; in Latine and English Verse*. London, 1625.

Moulton, Gary E., ed. *The Journals of the Lewis and Clark Expedition*. 13 vols. Lincoln: University of Nebraska Press, 1983–2001.

Mulford, Carla. Introduction. *The Power of Sympathy and The Coquette*. New York: Penguin, 1996. ix–li.

"A Nation Bids Reagan Farewell." June 11, 2004. <http://www.cbsnews.com/stories/2004/06/05/national/main621238.shtml>. November 26, 2005.

Nelson, Benjamin. *The Idea of Usury: From Tribal Brotherhood to Universal Otherhood*. 2nd ed. Chicago: University of Chicago Press, 1969.

Nelson, Dana. *National Manhood: Capitalist Citizenship and the Imagined Fraternity of White Men*. Durham, N.C.: Duke University Press, 1998.

——. *The Word in Black and White: Reading "Race" in American Literature, 1638–1867*. New York: Oxford University Press, 1992.

Newfield, Christopher. *The Emerson Effect: Individualism and Submission in America*. Chicago: University of Chicago Press, 1996.

Nicholson, Linda. Introduction. *Feminist Contentions: A Philosophical Exchange*. By Seyla Benhabib, Judith Butler, Drucilla Cornell, and Nancy Fraser. New York: Routledge, 1995. 1–16.

Norton, Anne. *Reflections on Political Identity*. Baltimore: Johns Hopkins University Press, 1988.

Nussbaum, Martha. *The Fragility of Goodness: Luck and Ethics in Greek Tragedy and Philosophy*. Cambridge: Cambridge University Press, 1986.

O: The Oprah Magazine. August 8, 2001.

O'Connor, Pat. *Friendships between Women: A Critical Review*. New York: Guilford Press, 1992.

Opfermann, Susanne. "Lydia Maria Child, James Fenimore Cooper, and Catharine Maria Sedgwick: A Dialogue on Race, Culture, and Gender." *Soft Canons: American Women and Masculine Tradition*. Ed. Karen Kilcup. Iowa City: University of Iowa Press, 1999. 27–47.

Pagden, Anthony. *The Fall of Natural Man: The American Indian and the Origins of Comparative Ethnography*. Cambridge: Cambridge University Press, 1982.

Pahl, Ray. *On Friendship*. Cambridge, Eng.: Polity Press, 2000.

Paine, Thomas. "Common Sense." *The Complete Writings of Thomas Paine*. Ed. Philip S. Foner. New York: Citadel Press, 1945. 3–46.

Pakaluk, Michael. "Political Friendship." *The Changing Face of Friendship*. Ed. Leroy S. Rouner. Notre Dame: University of Notre Dame Press, 1994. 197–213.

——, ed. *Other Selves: Philosophers on Friendship*. Indianapolis: Hackett, 1991.

Parker, Arthur C. *The Life of Ely S. Parker, Last Grand Sachem of the Iroquois and General Grant's Military Secretary*. Buffalo, N.Y.: Buffalo Historical Society, 1919.

Pateman, Carole. *The Sexual Contract*. Stanford, Calif.: Stanford University Press, 1988.

Peck, H. Daniel. Introduction. *New Essays on* The Last of the Mohicans. Ed. H. Daniel Peck. Cambridge: Cambridge University Press, 1992. 1–23.

Pettengill, Claire C. "Sisterhood in a Separate Sphere: Female Friendship in Hannah Webster Foster's *The Coquette* and *The Boarding School*." *Early American Literature* 27 (1992): 185–203.

Philbrick, Thomas. "*The Last of the Mohicans* and the Sounds of Discord." *American Literature* 43 (March 1971): 25–41.

Plato. *Lysis. Other Selves: Philosophers on Friendship*. Ed. Michael Pakaluk. Indianapolis: Hackett, 1991. 1–27.

——. *The Symposium and The Phadras: Plato's Erotic Dialogues*. Trans. William S. Cobb. Albany: State University of New York Press, 1993.

Pratt, Mary Louise. *Imperial Eyes: Travel Writing and Transculturalism*. London: Routledge, 1992.

Pratt, Minnie Bruce. "Identity: Skin Blood Heart." *Yours in Struggle: Three Feminist Perspectives on Anti-Semitism and Racism*. Brooklyn: Long Haul Press, 1984. 11–87.

Price, A. W. *Love and Friendship in Plato and Aristotle*. Oxford: Clarendon Press, 1989.

Prucha, Francis Paul. *Indian Peace Medals in American History*. Madison: State Historical Society of Wisconsin, 1971.

——. *Peace and Friendship: Indian Peace Medals from the Schermer Collection National Portrait Gallery*. Washington, D.C.: Smithsonian Institution, 2001.

Pudaloff, Ross. "Cooper's Genres and American Problems." *English Literary History* 50 (Winter 1983): 711–27.

Rans, Geoffrey. *Cooper's Leather-Stocking Novels: A Secular Reading*. Chapel Hill: University of North Carolina Press, 1991.

Raymond, Janice. *A Passion for Friends: Toward a Philosophy of Female Affection*. Boston: Beacon Press, 1986.

Reinhard, Kenneth. "Freud, My Neighbor." *American Imago* 54.2 (1997): 165–95.

Richards, Jeffrey. "'Passing the Love of Women': Manly Love and Victorian Society." *Manliness and Morality: Middle-Class Masculinity in Britain and America, 1800–1940*. Ed. J. A. Mangan and James Walvin. New York: St. Martin's Press, 1987. 92–122.

Richter, Daniel K., and James H. Merrell, eds. *Beyond the Covenant Chain: The Iroquois and Their Neighbors in Indian North America, 1600–1800*. Syracuse, N.Y.: Syracuse University Press, 1987.

Ricoeur, Paul. *Oneself as Another*. Trans. Kathleen Blamey. Chicago: University of Chicago Press, 1992.

Roach, Joseph. *Cities of the Dead: Circum-Atlantic Performance*. New York: Columbia University Press, 1996.

Robinson, Forrest G. "Uncertain Borders: Race, Sex, and Civilization in *The Last of the Mohicans*." *Arizona Quarterly* 41.1 (Spring 1991): 1–28.

Rodgers, Daniel T. "Republicanism: The Career of a Concept." *Journal of American History* 79 (June 1992): 11–38.

Rollins, Hyder Edward, ed. *Tottel's Miscellany (1557–1587)*. Cambridge: Harvard University Press, 1965.

Romero, Lora. *Home Fronts: Domesticity and Its Critics in the Antebellum United States*. Durham, N.C.: Duke University Press, 1997.

Romm, James, ed. *Alexander the Great: Selections from Arrian, Diodorus, Plutarch, and Quintus Curtius*. Trans. Pamela Mensch and James Romm. Indianapolis: Hackett, 2005.

Ronda, James. "The Objects of Our Journey." *Lewis and Clark: Across the Divide*. By Carolyn Gilman. Washington, D.C.: Smithsonian Books, 2003. 15–49.

Rosaldo, Renato. *Culture and Truth: The Remaking of Social Analysis*. Boston: Beacon Press, 1989.

Rose, Suzanna. Foreword. *Friendships between Women: A Critical Review*. By Pat O'Connor. New York: Guilford Press, 1992. ix–x.

Rothleder, Dianne. *The Work of Friendship: Rorty, His Critics, and the Project of Solidarity*. Albany: State University of New York Press, 1999.

Rouner, Leroy S., ed. *The Changing Face of Friendship*. Notre Dame: University of Notre Dame Press, 1994.

Said, Edward. *The World, the Text, and the Critic*. Cambridge: Harvard University Press, 1983.

Samuels, Shirley. "Generation through Violence: Cooper and the Making of Americans." *New Essays on* The Last of the Mohicans. Ed. H. Daniel Peck. Cambridge: Cambridge University Press, 1992. 87–114.

——, ed. *The Culture of Sentiment: Race, Gender, and Sentimentality in Nineteenth-Century America*. New York: Oxford University Press, 1992.

Sandoval, Chela. "AferBridge: Technologies of Crossing." *This Bridge We Call Home: Radical Visions for Transformation*. Ed. Gloria Anzaldúa and AnaLouise Keating. New York: Routledge, 2002. 21–26.

Saxonhouse, Arlene. *Fear of Diversity: The Birth of Political Science in Ancient Greek Thought*. Chicago: University of Chicago Press, 1992.

Schmitt, Carl. *The Concept of the Political*. Trans. George Schwab. New Brunswick, N.J.: Rutgers University Press, 1976.

Schneebaum, Tobias. *Keep the River on Your Right*. London: Cape, 1970.

Schollmeier, Paul. *Other Selves: Aristotle on Personal and Political Friendship*. Albany: State University of New York Press, 1994.

Schweitzer, Ivy. *The Work of Self-Representation: Lyric Poetry in Colonial New England*. Chapel Hill: University of North Carolina Press, 1991.

Scott, Joan. "Deconstructing Equality-versus-Difference: Or, the Uses of Poststructuralist Theory for Feminism." *Conflicts in Feminism*. Ed. Marianne Hirsch and Evelyn Fox Keller. New York: Routledge, 1990. 135–48.

Scott, William Robert. *The Constitution and Finance of English, Scottish and Irish Joint-Stock Companies to 1720*. Vol. 1. Cambridge: Cambridge University Press, 1912.

Sedgwick, Catharine Maria. *Hope Leslie; or, Early Times in the Massachusetts*. 1827. Ed. Mary Kelley. New Brunswick, N.J.: Rutgers University Press, 1987.

——. *The Power of Her Sympathy: The Autobiography and Journal of Catharine Maria Sedgwick*. Ed. Mary Kelley. Boston: Massachusetts Historical Society, 1993.

Sedgwick, Eve Kosofsky. *Between Men: English Literature and Male Homosocial Desire*. New York: Columbia University Press, 1985.

Seneca. "On Philosophy and Friendship." *Ad Lucilium Epistulae Morales*. 3 vols. Trans. Richard M. Gummere. Loeb Classical Library, vol. 1. New York: G. P. Putnam's Sons, 1917. 42–57.

Shakespeare, William. *A Midsummer Night's Dream*. *The Riverside Shakespeare*. Boston: Houghton Mifflin, 1997. 251–83.

Shannon, Laurie. "Likenings: Rhetorical Husbandries and Portia's 'True Conceit' of Friendship." *Renaissance Drama* 31 (2002): 3–26.

——. *Sovereign Amity: Figures of Friendship in Shakespearean Contexts*. Chicago: University of Chicago Press, 2002.

Shapiro, David, and Laurie Gwen Shapiro, dirs. *Keep the River on Your Right*. Videorecording. New Video Group, 2000.

Shields, John C. *The American Aeneas: Classical Origins of the American Self*. Knoxville: University of Tennessee Press, 2001.

Shuffleton, Frank. "Mrs. Foster's Coquette and the Decline of the Brotherly Watch." *Studies in Eighteenth Century Culture* 16 (1986): 211–24.

Silver, Alan. "Friendship in Commercial Society: Eighteenth-Century Social Theory and Modern Sociology." *American Journal of Sociology* 95.6 (May 1990): 1474–1504.

Silverman, Kaja. *The Threshold of the Visual World*. New York: Routledge, 1996.

Singley, Carol. "Catharine Maria Sedgwick's *Hope Leslie*: Radical Frontier Romance." *Desert, Garden, Margin, Range: Literature on the American Frontier*. Ed. Eric Heyne. New York: Twayne, 1992. 110 aa.

Slotkin, Richard. Introduction. *The Last of the Mohicans*. By James Fenimore Cooper. New York: Viking Penguin, 1986. ix–xxviii.

——. *Regeneration through Violence: The Mythology of the American Frontier, 1600–1860*. Norman: University of Oklahoma Press, 1972.

Smith, Adam. *The Theory of Moral Sentiments*. Ed. D. D. Raphael and A. L. Macfie. New York: Oxford University Press, 1976.

Smith, Barbara, ed. *Homegirls: A Black Feminist Anthology*. New York: Kitchen Table, 1983.

Smith, John. *The Complete Works of Captain John Smith, 1580–1631*. 3 vols. Ed. Philip L. Barbour. Chapel Hill: University of North Carolina Press, 1986.

Smith-Rosenberg, Carroll. *Disorderly Conduct: Visions of Gender in Victorian America*. New York: Oxford University Press, 1985. 53–76.

——. "Domesticating 'Virtue': Coquettes and Revolutionaries in Young America." *Literature and the Body: Essays on Populations and Persons*. Ed. Elaine Scarry. Baltimore: Johns Hopkins University Press, 1988. 160–84.

Spelman, Elizabeth. *Inessential Woman: Problems of Exclusions in Feminist Thought*. Boston: Beacon Press, 1988.

Spivak, Gayatri. *The Post-colonial Critic: Interviews, Strategies, Dialogues.* New York: Routledge, 1990.

Stanton, Elizabeth Cady, Susan B. Anthony, and Matilda Joslyn Gage, eds. *History of Woman Suffrage.* Vol. 3. Rochester, N.Y.: Charles Mann, 1886. 6 vols. 1876–85.

Stauffer, John. *Imagining Equality: American Interracial Friendship in History and Myth.* New Haven, Conn.: Yale University Press, forthcoming.

Stearns, Peter, and Jan Lewis, eds. *An Emotional History of the United States.* New York: New York University Press, 1998.

Steichen, Edward. *The Family of Man.* New York: Museum of Modern Art, 1955.

Stern, Julia. *The Plight of Feeling: Sympathy and Dissent in the Early American Novel.* Chicago: University of Chicago Press, 1997.

Stern-Gillet, Suzanne. *Aristotle's Philosophy of Friendship.* Albany: State University of New York Press, 1995.

Stone, Lawrence. *The Family, Sex and Marriage in England, 1500–1800.* New York: Harper and Row, 1979.

Swatos, William H., Jr. *Encyclopedia of Religion and Society.* Walnut Creek, Calif.: Alta-Mira Press, 1998.

Taussig, Gurion. *Coleridge and the Idea of Friendship, 1789–1804.* Newark: University of Delaware Press, 2002.

Taylor, Edward. *The Poems of Edward Taylor.* Ed. Donald S. Stanford. New Haven, Conn.: Yale University Press, 1960.

Teeven, Kevin M. *A History of the Anglo-American Common Law of Contract.* New York: Greenwood Press, 1990.

Thomson, Rosemarie Garland. "Benevolent Maternalism and Physically Disabled Figures: Dilemmas of Female Embodiment in Stowe, Davis, and Phelps." *American Literature* 68 (1996): 555–86.

Tocqueville, Alexis de. *Democracy in America.* 2 vols. New York: Vintage Books, 1945.

Todd, Janet. *Women's Friendship in Literature.* New York: Columbia University Press, 1980.

Todorov, Tzvetan. *The Conquest of America: The Question of the Other.* Trans. Richard Howard. New York: Harper and Row, 1984.

Traub, Valerie. *The Renaissance of Lesbianism in Early Modern England.* Cambridge: Cambridge University Press, 2002.

Valeri, Mark. "Puritans in the Marketplace." *The World of John Winthrop: Essays on England and New England, 1588–1649.* Ed. Francis J. Bremer and Lynn A. Botelho. Boston: Massachusetts Historical Society, forthcoming. 1–81.

Vermaseren, M. J. *Mithras, the Secret God.* Trans. Therese and Vincent Megaw. New York: Barnes and Noble, 1963.

von Leyden, W. *Aristotle on Equality and Justice.* New York: St. Martin's Press, 1985.

Wahl, Elizabeth Susan. *Invisible Relations: Representations of Female Intimacy in the Age of Enlightenment.* Stanford, Calif.: Stanford University Press, 1999.

Walker, Cheryl. *Indian Nation: Native American Literature and Nineteenth-Century Nationalism*. Durham, N.C.: Duke University Press, 1997.

Ward, Julia K. "Aristotle on *Philia*: The Beginning of a Feminist Ideal of Friendship?" *Feminism and Ancient Philosophy*. Ed. Julia K. Ward. New York: Routledge, 1996. 155–71.

Warner, Michael. *The Letters of the Republic: Publication and the Public Sphere in Eighteenth-Century America*. Cambridge: Harvard University Press, 1990.

Watts, Steven. " 'Through a Glass Eye, Darkly': James Fenimore Cooper as Social Critic." *Journal of the Early Republic* 13 (Spring 1993): 55–74.

Weierman, Karen Woods. "Reading and Writing *Hope Leslie*: Catharine Maria Sedgwick's Indian 'Connections.' " *New England Quarterly* 75 (2002): 415–43.

Weiss, Penny A., and Marilyn Friedman, eds. *Feminism and Community*. Philadelphia: Temple University Press, 1995.

Welch, Richard E., Jr. "Mumbet and Judge Sedgwick: A Footnote to the Early History of Massachusetts Justice." *Boston Bar Journal* 8 (January 1964): 12–19.

Weller, Barry. "The Rhetoric of Friendship in Montaigne's *Essais*." *New Literary History* 8–9 (1978–79): 503–32.

White, Carolinne. *Christian Friendship in the Fourth Century*. Cambridge: Cambridge University Press, 1992.

White, John. *John White's Planters Plea 1630*. Facsimile. Rockport, Mass.: The Sandy Bay Historical Museum, 1930.

White, Richard. "The Fictions of Patriarchy: Indians and Whites in the Early Republic." *Native Americans and the Early Republic*. Ed. Frederick E. Hoxie, Ronald Hoffman, and Peter J. Albert. Charlottesville: University Press of Virginia, 1999. 62–84.

Whitman, Walt. "Democratic Vistas." *Prose Works*. 2 vols. Ed. Floyd Stovall. New York: New York University Press, 1964.

———. *Whitman: Complete Poetry and Collected Prose*. New York: The Library of America, 1982.

Wiegman, Robyn. *American Anatomies: Theorizing Race and Gender*. Durham, N.C.: Duke University Press, 1995.

———. "What Ails Feminist Criticism? A Second Opinion." *Critical Inquiry* 5 (Winter 1999): 362–79.

Williams, Roger. *Complete Writings*. 7 vols. New York: Russell and Russell, 1963.

———. *A Key into the Language of America*. 1643. Ed. John J. Teunissen and Evelyn J. Hinz. Detroit: Wayne State University Press, 1973.

Winterer, Caroline. *The Culture of Classicism: Ancient Greece and Rome in American Intellectual Life, 1780–1910*. Baltimore: Johns Hopkins University Press, 2002.

Winthrop, John. *Winthrop Papers*. Vol. 2. Boston: Massachusetts Historical Society, 1931.

———. *Winthrop's Journal: "History of New England," 1630–1649*. 2 vols. Ed. James Kendall Hosmer. New York: Charles Scribner's Sons, 1908.

Woolf, Virginia. *A Room of One's Own*. New York: Harcourt, Brace, Jovanovich, 1957.

Wright, Elizabeth, ed. *Feminism and Psychoanalysis: A Critical Dictionary*. Oxford: Blackwell, 1992.

Young, Iris Marion. "The Ideal of Community and the Politics of Difference." *Feminism/Postmodernism*. Ed. Linda J. Nicholson. New York: Routledge, 1990. 300–323.

Zagarell, Sandra. "Expanding 'America': Lydia Sigourney's *Sketch of Connecticut*, Catharine Sedgwick's *Hope Leslie*." *Tulsa Studies in Women's Literature* 6 (Fall 1987): 225–45.

INDEX

Civil War: American, 4, 18; English, 167

Clark, George Rogers, 18, 19

Clark, Gillian and Stephen R. L., 217 (n. 15)

Clarke, W. M., 216 (n. 2)

Class, 3–5, 15–16, 28, 75, 110, 146, 149, 156, 214 (n. 23); and friendship, 168, 191, 212 (n. 12); and gender, 3, 4; and race, 8, 41, 67, 69, 133–34, 156

Classicism, 64, 178

Clytemnestra, 33

Code, Lorraine, 70–71

Colacurcio, Michael, 93–96, 100

Columbus, Christopher, 53

Commerce, 32, 52, 61, 84–86, 92, 95, 99–100, 188; "familiar," 22, 73–75, 81–82, 87–88

Common sense, 36; Scottish Common Sense philosophy, 13, 28

Commonwealth, 82, 88; Christian, 44, 74–76, 78–80, 97–98, 100, 177; Commonwealth of Massachusetts, 237 (n. 22)

Community, 10–14, 22, 26–27, 30, 69–70, 71, 82, 93, 107, 123, 166, 170, 193, 203, 205; Winthrop's models of, 75, 97, 178, 183

Companionate marriage, 75, 96, 124, 183, 212 (n. 8)

Concord, 24, 34, 39, 53, 69, 146–47, 153–55, 158, 193

Condolence Councils, 61, 139, 195

Conduct books, 2, 65, 113, 228 (n. 9)

Conquistadors, 54–56

Conscience, 25, 166–67, 173, 177, 192; corporate, 81; social, 53

Consent, 47–48, 87–90, 114, 152, 184; in friendship, 49, 50, 91, 140; political, 96, 144. *See also* Contracts

Contracts, 55, 80, 195; and covenant, 89, 225 (nn. 19, 21); and friendship, 48, 75, 103, 181; language of, 22, 90, 104; legal, 47, 74, 81, 88, 188; marriage as contract,

23, 96, 106; sexual, 225 (n. 20), 227 (n. 1); social, 89; and women, 89, 166. *See also* Consent; Covenant; Handshake

Cooper, James Fenimore, 8, 19, 24–25, 42, 63, 83, 133–68, 179, 195–97, 202–5; and interraciality, 24, 135–41, 143–45, 166–67, 202–3, 231 (n. 4); and male romance, 133–34, 141, 237 (n. 3); and republicanism, 83, 140, 144, 232 (n. 11), 236 (n. 17); and Sedgwick, 24, 63, 137, 166–68, 179, 195–97, 202; and sympathy, 144, 153–54; women in works of, 230 (n. 1)

—Works: *The American Democrat*, 232 (n. 11), 236 (n. 17); *The Deerslayer*, 136, 142, 160–63; *The Last of the Mohicans*, 24–25, 42, 135–67, 179, 197, 199, 204; *Notions of the Americans*, 232 (n. 11); *The Pathfinder*, 142; *The Pioneers*, 19, 159, 166, 204

Cooper, Susan, 153

Cooperation, 19, 35, 56

Cornell, Drucilla, 25, 165

Cott, Nancy, 5, 175, 187, 227 (n. 5), 235 (n. 13)

Courtesy, 60, 113, 146–48, 184, 219 (n. 31)

Covenant, 61–62, 79–80, 88–96, 98, 139, 195, 223 (n. 10), 227 (n. 30); and contract, 88–89; Covenant Chains, 61–62, 139, 220 (n. 33); marriage as, 96–98; Winthrop's notion of, 89, 223 (n. 4), 225 (nn. 19, 21). *See also* Contracts

Coverture, 106; political, 107, 227 (n. 6)

Coviello, Peter, 73–74, 86, 116, 224 (n. 15)

Crain, Caleb, 8, 219 (n. 25)

Cronyism, 222 (n. 45)

Curtius Rufus, Quintus, 14–15, 214 (n. 21)

Dallmayr, Fred, 11, 68

Damon and Phintias (Pythias), 32, 41, 50–51

Handshake, 18, 63, 143, 152, 157, 203; "good faith," 47, 90, 96; interracial, 138–40, 205, 231 (n. 10). *See also* Consent; Contracts

Hanke, Lewis, 214 (n. 22)

Happiness, 35, 42, 52, 111, 117, 123, 124, 130, 149, 188, 191, 203, 216 (n. 7), 220 (n. 35), 228 (n. 15), 234 (n. 6), 238 (n. 26)

Harmony, 3, 146–47, 153–54, 198; interracial, 203; universal, 31

Harris, Sharon M., 227 (n. 8)

Harris, Susan K., 234 (n. 7)

Hawthorne, Nathaniel, 23, 25, 93, 100, 190; *The Scarlet Letter*, 100

Heckewelder, John, 63, 138

Hector, 41

Heller, Agnes, 36

Hephaestion, 14–15, 30, 33, 214 (n. 21)

Herndl, Diane Price, 232 (n. 18)

Heteronormativity, 6, 22, 65, 75, 105, 110, 130, 143, 173, 203, 211 (nn. 1, 7)

Heyd, Milly, 231 (n. 10)

Heyward, Duncan, 42, 141, 149, 230 (n. 3)

Hippothales, 33–34

Hirshman, Linda Redlick, 70

Homer, 45, 65, 173; *Iliad*, 29–30, 41; *Odyssey*, 29–30

Homoeroticism, 6, 30, 213 (n. 16)

Homonormativity, 16, 46, 50, 75, 105, 110, 128, 218 (n. 19)

Homosexuality, 6, 68, 211 (n. 7), 216 (n. 2), 227 (n. 30), 235 (n. 15)

Homosociality, 6, 15, 22, 30, 43, 65, 93, 211 (n. 7), 218 (n. 19), 219 (n. 29); in Cooper's novels, 134, 141–44, 158; in Foster's *The Coquette*, 101, 111, 115, 117, 124, 127–28, 130; male, 97–98, 123, 128, 173; as normativity, 9–12, 24, 28, 45–47, 105–7; in Sedgwick's *Hope Leslie*, 166, 175, 198

Honor, 33, 45, 47, 51, 52, 60, 79, 124, 128, 147–51, 230 (n. 3), 233 (n. 4); civic, 13; masculine codes of, 144, 162, 171, 185, 192, 198, 210

Hooker, Thomas: *Survey of the Summe of Church Discipline*, 226 (n. 29)

Hudson, Lorna, 218 (n. 19)

Huguenots, 57

Hume, David, 51, 188

Hunt, Mary, 221 (n. 40)

Hyatte, Reginald, 215 (n. 1), 217 (n. 15), 218 (n. 18)

Hysteria, male, 213 (n. 15)

Iamblichus, 31–32, 41–42; *De vita pythagorica*, 31

Identification, 5, 11, 43, 50, 52, 54, 58, 59, 87, 129, 130, 134, 160, 169, 175, 200, 212 (n. 13), 219 (nn. 28, 29), 234 (n. 9); endocryptic, 215 (n. 27); heteropathic, 204, 238 (n. 28)

Identity, 16, 17, 28, 46–47, 54, 56, 149, 154, 169, 196, 200–201, 203; American, 25, 116, 134, 163, 166, 230 (n. 3); female, 234 (n. 9); feminist, 12; gender, 11, 16, 47, 129; Indian, 152; masculine, 106; national, 23–24, 67, 137, 160, 201; racial, 16, 28, 158, 214 (n. 22)

Imagination, 26, 52, 71, 86, 115, 141, 143, 146, 159, 171, 178, 189, 195, 229 (n. 19); American political, 23; of friendship, 28; paternal, 166

Imperialism, 24, 135, 157; modern, 219 (n. 22)

Incorporation, 58, 88–89, 129, 159, 163, 214 (n. 25), 215 (n. 27), 219 (n. 28), 230 (n. 2); of the other, 11

Indians, American, 25; in Cooper's fiction, 139–63; in English New World writing, 59–61; in film, 230 (n. 2); in French New World writing, 57–58; and frontier romance, 233 (n. 2); "Indian stories," 137; and peace medals, 17–22; in Puritan covenant, 223 (n. 4); in Sedgwick's fiction, 165–205, 233 (n. 4), 234 (n. 6); in Spanish New World writing, 53–57, 219 (n. 26); vanishing, 144, 160, 238 (n. 27); views of friendship, 61–64, 138, 145, 220 (n. 32)

Individualism, 83, 108, 127, 223 (n. 10), 228 (n. 15), 229 (n. 15), 233 (n. 5); American, 136; democratic, 54; heroic, 7; hyperindividualism, 71; liberal, 10, 25, 170

Inequality, 7, 30, 36, 37, 41, 53, 64, 75, 84, 89, 96, 100, 114, 117, 122, 141, 214 (n. 23), 223 (n. 9), 236 (n. 17)

Interchangeability, 15, 16, 24, 27–30, 32, 41–42, 48, 50–51, 52, 70, 85, 91, 98, 99, 110, 214 (n. 21). *See also* Doubling

Interraciality, 6, 195

Intersubjectivity, 10, 12, 13, 44, 50, 71, 111, 194

Intimacy, 4, 5, 14, 43–45, 60, 109, 122, 125, 135, 207, 208, 209, 210; civic, 131; heterosexual, 226 (n. 27); interracial, 24, 134; "odd civic intimacy," 73, 116

Irigaray, Luce, 215 (n. 27)

Jalalzai, Zubeda, 223 (n. 4)
James I (king of England and Scotland), 76
James II (king of England) (James VII of Scotland), 150
Jefferson, Thomas, 64, 73–74, 108, 113, 220 (n. 34), 229 (n. 17); and peace medals, 18–19
Jennings, Francis, 60–62, 220 (n. 33)
Jesuit Relations, 61–62
Jesus, 44, 55, 79, 84–88, 90, 92, 95, 97, 100, 134, 184, 219 (n. 31), 223 (n. 9); friendship with, 78
Johnson, Edward, 97

Justice, 11, 37, 55, 84, 95, 148, 166–67, 170, 174, 188, 192, 194; distributive or proportionate, 38, 88; and friendship, 9, 34, 38, 64, 67, 173, 176, 217 (n. 13), 228 (n. 12)

Kant, Immanuel, 11, 67
Karafilis, Maria, 233 (n. 5), 234 (n. 10)
Karcher, Caroline, 231 (n. 5), 233 (nn. 2, 3)
Kelley, Mary, 237 (n. 24)
Kelly, William, 150, 230 (n. 3)
Kemble, Fanny, 187
Kerber, Linda, 169
Kierkegaard, Soren: *Works of Love*, 212 (n. 14)
King, Charles Bird, 19
King, Martin Luther, 231 (n. 10)
Kinship, 40, 43–44, 50, 63, 75, 77, 96, 98–99, 110, 139–40, 146, 168, 175, 176, 207, 230 (n. 3)
Knewstub, John, 76, 223 (n. 5)
Konstan, David, 30–32, 39, 77, 221 (n. 37); *Friendship in the Classical World*, 66, 77, 106, 215 (n. 1), 216 (n. 2), 217 (n. 15), 227 (n. 3); *Sexual Symmetry*, 39

La Boétie, Étienne de, 40, 58, 116, 145. *See also* Montaigne, Michel de
Lacan, Jacques, 213 (n. 20), 221 (n. 41), 229 (n. 16); and mirror stage, 14; and neighbor, 11
Lady's Magazine and Musical Repository, 2, 65, 67
Laelius, Gaius, 36, 39, 42, 77, 79, 94, 116
Laertius, Diogenes: *Lives of Eminent Philosophers*, 222 (n. 42)
Langer, Ullrich, 45, 222 (n. 42)
Latin, 54, 65–66, 78, 81, 94, 117, 150, 173, 178; instruction in, 10, 13, 46, 110
Law, 9, 29, 51, 74, 81, 84, 92, 93, 99, 190–92, 196, 231 (n. 8), 232 (n. 11), 234

(n. 7), 236 (nn. 17, 18); common, 89;
Deuteronomic, 51; Fugitive Slave Law,
237 (n. 23); Hebraic, 92; letter of, 190–
94; love based in, 100–104; natural, 64,
78, 106

Lawrence, D. H.: *Studies in Classic American Literature*, 7, 136, 211 (n. 7)

Leach, Eleanor, 40, 214 (n. 19), 229 (n. 16)

Leites, Edmund, 212 (n. 8)

Lesbianism, 219 (n. 29)

Lewis, Jan, 113, 212 (n. 11)

Lewis, Meriwether, 18, 19, 22

Lewis, R. W. B., 7

Liberalism, 108–9, 170, 189

Liberality, 87, 93, 151

Liberté, egalité, fraternité, 10

Liberty, 4, 7–8, 17, 23, 50, 112, 174, 182,
186, 228 (n. 15), 229 (n. 19), 237 (n. 22);
Christian, 90, 96, 173, 177, 192; or
death, 180, 202; female, 107–8, 130;
Liberty Bell, 7, 215 (n. 28); and marriage, 104, 106

Likeness, 1, 95, 99, 110, 138, 186; attraction
of, 94; and contracts, 89; and equality in
friendship, 16, 35, 77, 144; in friendship,
28, 37, 94, 105; and interchangeability,
16, 48–50, 52, 85, 214 (n. 25); in Renaissance thought, 9, 46. *See also* Sameness;
Similarity; Similitude

Literacy, 2, 195

Locke, John, 229 (nn. 17, 19)

Looby, Christopher, 157

López Palacios Rubios, Juan, 54

Love, 4, 17, 112, 114, 207; Christian, 74,
76–78, 84–88, 92–94, 116, 145, 177–78,
183, 189, 193–94, 223 (n. 6), 236 (n. 18);
courtly, 46, 218 (n. 18); of enemies, 43;
female world of, 6–7, 108, 127–30; of
friend, 14, 29, 33, 35–36, 90–92, 97, 113,
125–26, 175, 228 (n. 12), 238 (n. 28);
heterosexual, 6, 18, 23, 36, 95–96, 105,

110, 118, 124–25, 179–81; interracial,
139, 166, 198; and law, 93, 100; of liberty, 174, 182; manly, 1, 10, 30, 33, 50,
66, 97–98, 147, 216 (n. 2); of mother for
child, 38, 71; of neighbor, 56, 77, 92,
162, 212 (n. 14); self-love, 14, 84, 92–93,
217 (nn. 13, 14); spiritual, 22, 46, 84, 94–
95, 187–88, 199, 216 (nn. 3, 5); universal, 44, 77; versus friendship, 2, 10, 46–
47, 103, 121, 141–43, 176, 181, 213 (n. 8),
217 (n. 15), 226 (n. 27), 227 (n. 30)

Lugones, María, 175, 221 (n. 40), 234
(n. 11), 235 (n. 14)

Lust, 6, 104

Luther, Martin, 51, 220–21 (n. 35)

Luxon, Thomas, 47, 212 (n. 8), 226 (n. 27)

Madison, James, 229 (n. 17)

Mann, Michael, 196

Marriage, 29, 38, 88, 106, 115, 223 (n. 9),
226 (n. 27), 237 (n. 20); of Adam and
Eve, 75, 105; arranged, 51, 111; companionate, 75, 96, 124, 183–84, 212 (n. 8),
213 (n. 16); competition with friendship,
5, 10, 24, 32, 43, 110, 138, 161–63, 179–
80, 203; consensual, 104–6, 149; entombing friendship, 23, 103, 122–31,
148; federalist, 106, 119, 133, 184; and
friendship, 6, 7, 9, 34, 65, 92, 94–101,
137–45, 212 (n. 8), 227 (n. 2); hierarchical, 22–23, 111, 121; interracial, 60, 166,
169, 197–98, 220 (n. 32); male, 136, 160;
marriage contract, 225 (n. 20); marriage
resister, 181, 191; mystical, 87, 136; in
Renaissance thought, 46–47

Marshall, David, 219 (n. 25)

Marx, Karl, 10–11

Marxism, 213 (n. 15)

Masculinity, 64, 106–7, 120, 131, 148–53;
and freedom, 122; and friendship, 10, 13,
24, 30, 40, 65–66, 90–91, 105–6, 123,

Neighbor, 46, 56, 77, 82, 92, 99, 162, 182;
and Kenneth Reinhard, 213 (n. 14); and
Kierkegaard, 212–13 (n. 14); and Lacan,
11; as oneself, 93
Nelson, Benjamin, 51, 219 (n. 22)
Nelson, Dana, 234 (n. 10); *National Man-hood*, 106, 111, 212 (n. 11); *The World in Black and White*, 234 (n. 6)
Neoplatonism, 32
Newfield, Christopher, 218 (n. 21)
New tribalism, 12
New World, 17, 54–55, 57, 74, 88–89, 166,
177, 183, 197
Nietzsche, Friedrich, 69
Nobility, 33, 148, 154, 161, 167, 184, 198;
and friendship, 14, 42, 60, 145–47
Norton, Anne: *Reflections on Political Identity*, 27
Nuñez Cabeza de Vaca, Alvar, 54
Nussbaum, Martha, 70

O: The Oprah Magazine, 213 (n. 17)
Odyssey, 29–30
Oedipal model, 11
Old World, 17, 149–50, 183
Oneness, 95, 126, 203, 207, 208
Opfermann, Susanne, 200, 231 (n. 5), 233
(nn. 2, 3)
Orestes, 33, 42, 45, 51
Other, 1–2, 17, 27, 35–38, 42, 48, 59,
69–71, 113, 130, 142, 165, 180, 199, 238
(n. 28); address to, 210; appropriation
of, 11, 25, 163; demonic, 128; desire of,
33, 188; ethical relation to, 204–5, 215
(n. 27); feeling with, 171, 189, 192;
loving, 93–95, 177, 182; racial, 54–58,
63, 134–35, 145, 159, 194–97, 201–3,
230 (n. 2); other-self logics of friend-ship, 74; semiotics of, 24; unruly, 23;
wish to be, 11. *See also* Derrida,
Jacques

Otherhood, 51–53, 219 (n. 22)
Ovando, Juan de, 56–57

Pacuvius, Marcus, 42
Pagden, Anthony, 214 (n. 22)
Pahl, Ray, 12, 211 (n. 3), 222 (n. 45)
Paine, Thomas, 73, 86, 224 (n. 15); "Com-mon Sense," 75
Pakaluk, Michael: *Nicomachean Ethics*,
books 8 and 9, 211 (n. 2), 216 (n. 6), 223
(n. 8); *Other Selves*, 33–34, 44, 212
(n. 14), 221 (n. 40), 227 (n. 3); "Political
Friendship," 217 (n. 13)
Parker, Ely S., 19
Passion, 3–4, 23, 39, 94, 95, 154; for
friends, 14, 33, 145; friendship as, 117; as
irrational, 9, 16, 31, 53, 64, 66, 77, 98–
99, 111, 176, 190, 194, 228 (n. 12); psy-chology of, 64, 220 (n. 35), 226 (n. 25);
romantic, 123, 142, 191
Pateman, Carole, 227 (n. 1); *The Sexual Contract*, 225 (n. 20)
Patroclus, 30, 41, 45, 65, 215–16 (n. 2)
Paul (apostle), 77, 84–85, 95, 100, 105,
177–78, 194
Peace medals, 17–19, 232 (n. 15)
Peck, H. Daniel, 232 (n. 16)
Pederasty, 14, 30–34, 216 (n. 3), 235 (n. 15);
erastes and *eromenos*, 31, 33. *See also*
Plato
Penelope, 30
Perkins, William, 225 (n. 21)
Petrarch, Francesco, 13
Pettengill, Claire, 107, 115, 127, 228 (n. 9),
229 (n. 20)
Phallogocentrism, 59, 67–68, 221 (n. 41);
carno-phallogocentrism, 59–67
Philanthropia, 32, 43
Philbrick, Thomas, 153–55, 157, 232
(n. 16)
Philia, 12–13, 28–34, 38, 43, 64, 68, 76–

78, 85, 92, 95, 98–99, 104, 110, 113, 178, 180, 187, 193, 210; Chrysostom's use of, 77. *See also* Aristotle; Friendship

Philoi, philos, 28–39, 76, 86, 106, 169, 178

Philosophy, 3, 9–13, 34, 39, 45, 55, 92, 94, 110, 138–39, 182; modern secular, 11; Scottish Common Sense, 13, 28

Philotes, 28, 31–32, 76, 169

Plato, 9, 28, 67, 82, 91, 182, 213 (n. 18), 216 (n. 3), 224 (n. 11); *Lysis,* 14, 33–34; *Republic,* 117; *Symposium,* 36, 181, 215 (n. 2), 216 (n. 3); on women, 39

Pleasure, 38, 52, 71, 85–86, 118, 120, 122–24, 127–28, 163, 172, 228 (n. 15); divine, 155; from friendship, 31, 35, 71, 99, 111–12

Plymouth Plantation, 82–83

Pocahontas, 25, 61, 195, 203

Poe, Edgar Allan, 8, 221 (n. 41)

Polis, 3, 9, 16, 29, 173, 182

Politics, 1, 4–5, 68, 222 (n. 44); of affiliation, 25, 27, 116, 215 (n. 27); American, 22, 81; of consent, 144; cultural, 201–2; democratic, 3, 10, 28, 69, 113, 117–18; gender, 137; identity, 12; of mirroring, 12–17; racial, 24, 134; republican, 167, 182, 210, 234 (n. 6)

Popular culture, 163; friendship-themed TV shows, 12

Pratt, Minnie Bruce, 235 (n. 11)

Pre-Socratics, 13, 31, 43

Primus, Rebecca, 1, 4–5, 16

Protestantism, 51, 57, 59, 61, 64, 74–76, 89–90, 96, 124, 175, 184; Dutch, 61–62; and marriage, 96

Prucha, Francis Paul, 18, 19

Prynne, Hester, 23, 25, 100, 190

Public social sphere, 23, 107, 109, 121, 189

Pudaloff, Ross, 140

Puritanism, 22–23, 74, 80–81, 86–87, 90, 101, 104, 174, 191–94, 199, 201, 211

(n. 5), 220 (n. 35), 222 (n. 2), 223 (nn. 4, 11), 224 (n. 14), 225 (nn. 17, 21); and liberality, 93–98; in *The Scarlet Letter,* 100; and Sedgwick, 166–71; and Winthrop, 76, 83–84, 89, 100, 116, 155, 177–78, 181–86, 187–88, 226 (nn. 25, 27)

Puritans, 22, 23, 25, 60, 64, 74, 76, 78–104, 116–17, 155, 170–201. *See also* Puritanism

Pylades, 33, 42, 45, 51

Pythagoras, 31–32, 36, 39, 46, 116, 133; emblematic stories of, 41; notion of *philia,* 32–34

Queer theorists/activists, 11, 12, 219 (n. 29), 230 (n. 3)

Race, 3, 8, 16, 59, 67, 133, 138, 140, 153, 158–59, 168, 170, 211 (n. 7), 214 (n. 23), 223 (n. 4), 230 (n. 3), 232 (n. 15), 234 (n. 6); racism, 171, 175. *See also* Friendship: interracial; Interraciality

Raleigh, Sir Walter, 51

Ramus, Peter, 223 (n. 11)

Rationality, 23, 70, 91, 225 (n. 21); in commerce, 81–83; and friendship, 16, 35, 54–55, 64–65, 103–4, 110, 118–19, 126, 144, 175, 186–87, 210; rational desire, 6, 9, 43, 91, 226 (n. 25); rational discourse, 109

Raymond, Janice, 70, 221 (n. 40)

Reagan, Ronald, 215 (n. 26)

Reciprocity, 29, 37, 43, 67–70, 86, 95

Reflection, 27, 41, 92–93, 105, 119, 181, 204

Reinhard, Kenneth, 213 (n. 14)

Renaissance, 139, 179; and friendship, 9, 15, 22, 24–25, 46–51, 64, 66, 74, 85, 90–92, 110, 126, 181, 213 (n. 16), 218 (nn. 19, 20); and similitude, 43, 46, 48, 147

Republic: Greek, 9, 98, 118; Roman, 8–9,

13, 39, 77, 98, 116; U.S., 2, 7, 23, 66, 75, 108, 113, 120, 140, 165
Republicanism, 8, 22, 39, 64, 83, 109–10, 116, 140, 165–67, 173; civic, 22, 109
Requerimiento, 54–56
Respect, 2, 16, 69, 77, 80, 82, 107, 133, 153, 187, 202; and distinction, 19; and friendship, 143, 228 (n. 12); for others, 11, 59
Revolution: American, 23, 63, 180, 202; English Puritan, 167, 192; French, 10
Richardson, Alexander, 223 (n. 11)
Richter, Daniel K., 220 (n. 33)
Ricoeur, Paul, 27, 70; *Oneself as Another*, 27, 70
Rights, 27, 38, 53, 55–56, 63, 70–71, 89, 107–8, 111, 166, 170, 174, 196, 202–3; natural, 17, 69, 89, 174, 202
Ritual, 7, 18, 29, 57, 61, 107–8, 110, 171; ritual objects, 18
Robinson, Forrest G., 141
Rochefoucauld, François La, 181
Rodgers, Daniel T., 228 (n. 11)
Romance, 2; of Amadis de Gaule, 45; in American culture, 5, 135, 165; chivalric, 42, 46; in friendship, 42, 46, 168; frontier, 24, 63, 134, 137, 166, 169, 218 (n. 18), 233 (nn. 2, 3); Greek, 39; heterosexual, 5–7, 46; historical, 140, 165; of *Hope Leslie*, 25, 137, 190, 204, 233 (n. 2), 234 (n. 6); of John Smith and Pocahontas, 195; in *The Last of the Mohicans*, 135, 137–38, 140, 197, 204, 231 (n. 3); male, 133–34, 231 (n. 3); in *The Pioneers*, 166
Romanticism, 10, 25, 64
Rome, 98, 139, 144
Ronda, James, 18–19, 22
Rouner, Leroy S., 227 (n. 3), 238 (n. 1)
Rowson, Susannah: *Reuben and Rachel; or Tales of Old Times*, 233 (n. 2)
Ruth, 98–99, 196

Sacrifice, 22, 42, 86, 95, 108, 121, 127, 136, 147, 171, 178, 186, 188–89, 195, 197–98, 202
Sagoyewatha (Red Jacket), 19. *See also* Peace medals
Said, Edward, 213 (n. 15)
Sameness, 1, 5, 15, 28, 37, 47, 54, 68–70, 77, 140, 169. *See also* Equality; Interchangeability; Likeness; Similitude
Samuel, Shirley, 159–60, 212 (n. 11)
Sappho, 30
Saxonhouse, Arlene, 217 (n. 11)
Saul (king of Israel), 97–98, 236 (n. 16)
Scaevola, Q. Mucius, 39
Scheler, Max: *The Nature of Sympathy*, 238 (n. 28)
Schmitt, Carl, 4, 211 (n. 4)
Schneebaum, Tobias, 219 (n. 29)
Schollmeier, Paul, 216 (n. 7)
Scott, Joan, 222 (n. 43), 235 (n. 13)
Scott, Sir Walter, 46, 51
Scott, William Robert, 224 (n. 13)
Sedgwick, Catharine, 233 (nn. 1–3); and classicism, 178–82; and Cooper, 166–68; critical reception, 234 (n. 6); and disinterest, 187–94; and Elizabeth Freeman, 237 (nn. 22, 24); and ethical failure of friendship, 197–205; and failure of brothers, 169–76; and feminism, 235 (n. 13); and gender-bending, 235 (n. 15); *Hope Leslie*, 24–25, 63, 137, 165–204; and Indians, 233 (n. 4); and Lydia Maria Child, 165–66, 233 (n. 3); and Magawisca, 194–97; and marriage, 237 (n. 21); and Milton's *Comus*, 171–75; and politics, 234 (n. 5); revision of canonical friendship, 168, 176–82; revision of Winthrop's model, 182–87, 192–94
Seneca, 19, 36, 40
Sensibility, 7, 9, 53, 63, 77, 103, 107–8, 110, 118, 175

Sentimentalism, 7–8, 28, 107, 189, 212 (n. 11), 226 (n. 25); and Puritan religious thought, 220 (n. 35), 226 (n. 25)

Sepúlveda, Ginés de, 54–56, 214 (n. 22), 219 (n. 26)

Seward, Anna: *Llangollen Vale*, 221 (n. 38)

Sexuality, 6, 13, 16, 28, 67–68, 133, 136

Shakespeare, William, 3, 110, 144, 228 (n. 13); *The Merchant of Venice*, 51; *A Midsummer Night's Dream*, 125

Shannon, Laurie: *Sovereign Amity*, 9, 13, 15, 46–48, 74, 85, 90–91, 110, 128, 144, 173–74, 218 (n. 19)

Shields, John C., 212 (n. 9)

Silver, Alan, 51, 52

Silverman, Kaja, 238 (n. 28)

Similarity, 11, 54; and difference, 27–28; and equality, 36–37, 47, 99, 123, 139, 141, 144, 176, 198; in friendship, 14, 28, 44, 47, 75, 91, 93, 208–9, 212 (n. 12), 217 (n. 14); physical, 14, 30; and sympathy, 154. *See also* Interchangeability; Likeness; Similitude

Similitude, 1, 4–5, 15, 26, 28; Aristotle's notion of, 68, 142; in Renaissance thought, 43, 46–51, 74, 147; and utopian parity, 15, 74, 104. *See also* Likeness; Sameness; Similarity

Sin, 43–45, 73, 78, 81, 83

Sisigambis, 14

Sister-friendship, 211

Sisterhood, 7, 168–69, 174–76

Six Nations of the Iroquois, 19, 62–63

Slavery, 16–17, 24, 34, 53–55, 63, 111, 135, 187, 196; civil, 214 (n. 22); natural, 16–17, 24, 53–55, 160

Slotkin, Richard: *Regeneration Through Violence*, 7, 136, 143, 153–54, 167

Smith, Adam: *The Theory of Moral Sentiments*, 3, 8, 52, 64, 108, 113, 117, 154,

188, 228 (n. 14). *See also* Benevolence; Sympathy

Smith, Barbara, 219 (n. 23)

Smith, John, 60, 82, 195

Smith, Paul, 222 (n. 41)

Smith-Rosenberg, Caroll, 5, 7–8, 108

Sociability, 28, 34–35, 52, 71, 103, 110, 113–15, 122, 128, 154, 157, 176, 188

Social disintegration, 82

Socrates, 14, 32–34

Sollors, Werner: *Neither Black nor White yet Both*, 6

Song of Roland, 45

Song of Solomon, 87

Soul, 6, 15, 32–33, 40, 54, 75, 77, 85, 87, 90–91, 94–95, 97–100, 105, 110, 126, 129, 159, 179, 181, 185, 203, 223 (n. 9), 228 (n. 13), 236 (n. 18), 238 (n. 26)

Sovereignty, 18, 25, 47, 121, 140, 144, 162, 173, 203

Spelman, Elizabeth, 39, 234 (n. 11), 235 (n. 14)

Spenser, Edmund, 60

Spirituality, Christian, 22, 116; and females, 99, 167–68, 176, 181; and friendship, 5–6, 9–16, 99, 117, 126, 167, 203, 210; in *Hope Leslie*, 167–68, 172–73, 176–77, 181, 185, 194, 199, 203–4; in *The Last of the Mohicans*, 135, 138–40, 160–63, 167

Spivak, Gayatri, 234 (n. 11)

Standing surety, 51

Stanton, Elizabeth Cady, 229 (n. 17), 235 (n. 13)

Stearns, Peter, 212 (n. 11)

Stern, Julia: *The Plight of Feeling*, 107, 114, 212 (n. 11), 229 (n. 19)

Stern-Gillet, Suzanne, 29–30, 35, 41, 216 (n. 9)

Stoicism, 8, 36, 39, 121, 139, 156; Ciceronian model of, 28; and Major Sanford, 111, 117, 172

Stone, Lawrence, 52, 96

Stranger, 11, 29, 51, 90, 107, 114, 124, 131, 143, 219 (n. 24)

Substitution, 38, 41–42, 51, 126. *See also* Interchangeability

Symbiosis, 30, 41

Symmetry, 9, 36, 39, 67, 69

Sympathy, 2–3, 8–9, 134, 144, 153–55, 169–70, 174, 185, 188–89, 191–92, 212 (n. 11), 219 (n. 25), 238 (n. 28); in Adam Smith, 188, 219 (n. 23), 228 (n. 14); in *The Coquette*, 108–9, 121, 229 (n. 20); democratic, 192; equality through, 85–86; in friendship, 9, 13, 53, 110; Greco-Roman notion of, 32, 43, 113, 228 (n. 12); in *Hope Leslie*, 174, 185–88, 191, 198; neoclassical notions of, 67; and republican ideology, 108; and Scottish Common Sense philosophers, 13, 28, 64; spectatorial, 155, 232 (n. 18); Winthrop's call to, 86, 95, 188, 236 (n. 18)

Taussig, Gurion, 213 (n. 18), 221 (n. 39)

Taylor, Charles, 27

Taylor, Edward, 86–87, 94, 221 (n. 39), 225 (n. 17)

Taylor, Jeremy: *A Discourse of the Nature, Offices, and Measures of Friendship*, 218 (n. 20)

Technologia, 224 (n. 11)

Telfer, Elizabeth, 221 (n. 40)

Tennyson, Alfred Lord, 46; *Idylls of the King*, 218 (n. 18); *In Memoriam*, 218 (n. 18)

Theory, 8, 15–16, 52–54, 70–71, 81, 89, 105, 166, 176–77, 188, 213 (n. 15); feminist, 25, 68, 210, 212 (nn. 10, 13), 219 (n. 22), 222 (n. 43), 235 (n. 13); of friendship, 13, 27, 85, 181, 228 (n. 14); postcolonial, 234 (n. 11); poststructuralist,

12; queer, 11–12, 219 (n. 29), 230 (n. 3); of social change, 211 (n. 5); of social contract, 227 (n. 1), 235 (n. 20)

Thoreau, Henry David, 213 (n. 17)

Timocracy, 37

Titus and Gysippus, 50, 91

Tocqueville, Alexis de, 11, 51

Todd, Janet, 107, 211 (n. 1)

Todorov, Tzvetan: *The Conquest of America*, 17, 53–57, 151, 159

Tottel's Miscellany, 15, 85

Transvestite, 174

Traub, Valerie, 213 (n. 16), 219 (n. 29)

Tribalism, 12, 180

Troy, 29, 41

Twain, Mark, 8, 230 (n. 3)

Twins, twinning, 14, 50, 110, 213–14 (n. 20). *See also* Doubling; Mirror

Udall, Nicolas, 15, 92

United States, 17–19, 22, 26, 50, 73, 81, 85, 134, 203; and Indian relations, 17

Universalization, 51

Utopia, 11, 15, 69, 74, 93, 109, 144, 178

Valeri, Mark, 81–82

Violence, 7, 16, 22, 24, 40, 55, 57, 117, 135, 143, 147–48, 153–54, 157, 167, 171, 197, 202–3

Virtue, 2, 38–40, 67, 109, 117, 120, 122–24, 128, 144, 168, 174, 177–78, 184–85, 216 (n. 6), 220 (n. 35), 229 (n. 21); American political, 174; Christian, 43–45, 77, 94, 177, 221 (n. 35); civic, 117, 167, 173, 189; in *The Coquette*, 109–10, 117, 120, 122, 124, 128, 161, 229 (n. 15); and ethics, 70; female, 172, 174, 184; and friendship, 3, 14, 31–36, 47, 52, 77, 92, 110, 221 (n. 38), 223 (n. 8); in *Hope Leslie*, 167–68, 171–72, 174, 184–85, 188–89; masculine, 66, 128, 173, 218 (n. 19)